Clean Architecture

Building Scalable and Maintainable Software

Clean Architecture
Building Scalable and Maintainable Software

Vinu V Das

Tabor Press

ISBN 978-1-997541-33-2

Table of Contents

Chapter 1. The Purpose of Clean Architecture

In the fast-evolving landscape of software development, gaining mastery over architectural discipline is no longer optional—it is essential. Modern codebases grow in both size and complexity, exposed to changing business requirements, shifting frameworks, and diverse deployment environments. This chapter lays the groundwork for understanding why a deliberate, principled approach to structuring your system pays dividends in stability, adaptability, and team productivity. We will explore how unchecked technical debt accumulates, the historical currents that have shaped today's architectural thinking, and the fundamental philosophies that distinguish merely organized code from truly resilient design. You'll also be guided through early indicators that signal the need for a cleaner foundation, and practical first steps to begin evolving your code toward an architecture that endures.

1.1 Articulating the Need for Architectural Discipline

Before diving into specific symptoms, it's essential to appreciate how ungoverned growth undermines even the most talented teams. Software systems naturally accumulate complexity as features—and bug fixes—are piled atop one another. Without a guiding architectural discipline, the codebase will tend to become entangled, with modules depending on one another in unclear ways. Over time, developers spend more effort untangling hidden dependencies than delivering new customer value. This drift toward accidental complexity obscures the core business rules, making them hard to identify and verify. New team members often flounder, unable to locate the right modules or understand data flows without extensive onboarding. Build and test pipelines decelerate under the weight of monolithic suites and environment mismatches. What once took minutes to validate now requires hours of regression testing. Release cycles become unpredictable and fraught with integration challenges. As technical debt compounds, customer-facing defects slip through, eroding trust. Team morale dips under the burden of repetitive firefighting. Establishing architectural guardrails is the antidote to this entropy—providing clarity, resilience, and predictability.

1.1.1 The escalating cost of entropy in modern codebases

Entropy in software mirrors the physical concept: systems left unchecked will naturally disorder. As feature branches proliferate, small inconsistencies—naming conventions, error-handling patterns, configuration keys—begin to diverge. Each deviation increases cognitive load: developers must remember which module uses which convention. Over time, micro-decisions aggregate into macro-problems—common services are duplicated, leading to subtle data inconsistencies. For example, two teams may each implement their own version of a "UserValidator," resulting in conflicting validation logic in production. These duplicated fragments become maintenance hotspots; a change in policy requires edits in multiple places. Without architectural discipline, there is no single source of truth for core business rules. Continuous integration times balloon as test suites grow to cover divergences and guard against regressions. The longer a codebase evolves without refactoring, the higher the risk that a simple change introduces unintended side effects. Fixing a bug in one subsystem often triggers failures elsewhere, spawning urgent bug-fix branches and further entropy. Eventually, velocity grinds to a halt, and the system becomes a fragile artifact rather than a living product. Recognizing and countering entropy early is critical to sustaining healthy development velocity.

1.1.2 Symptoms of architectural decay (tight coupling, brittle tests, deployment gridlock)

Architectural decay often reveals itself in frustratingly tangible ways. Tight coupling between modules is one of the earliest red flags: low-level utility classes import high-level business logic, inverting the intended dependency flow. This makes isolated testing nearly impossible—the test for one component drags in a cascade of dependencies. As a result, teams resort to end-to-end tests, which are slower to execute and harder to interpret. Over time, these brittle tests fail intermittently due to minor changes in unrelated modules, leading developers to ignore or disable them. Deployment gridlock follows: feature branches cannot merge until extensive manual smoke tests confirm stability. Even minor UI tweaks require multiple service restarts, database schema checks, and environment tweaks. Worse yet, hotfixes become so risky that they demand full regression cycles and cross-team coordination. In extreme cases, teams bifurcate into "stability" and "innovation" silos, hampering collaboration. Monitoring and observability breaks down too—an error thrown in one layer propagates ambiguously through five others, making root-cause analysis arduous. Without clear architectural boundaries, responsibility blurs, and no single team owns end-to-end outcomes. These symptoms, if left unaddressed, lead to sprints consumed by integration and firefighting rather than forward momentum.

1.1.3 Stakeholders hurt by technical debt (developers, product, operations, customers)

Technical debt exacts a toll on every stakeholder group, not just the engineering team. Developers feel the pain first: their daily work involves navigating convoluted code paths, patching fragile tests, and wrestling with opaque error messages. This constant friction leads to burnout and high turnover, which in turn raises hiring and onboarding costs. Product managers suffer shifting timelines as estimates balloon to account for hidden complexity. Release roadmaps slip, and planned features are deferred to "cleanup sprints," eroding stakeholder confidence. Operations grapple with unstable deployments, spending nights investigating environment drift and manual rollback procedures. This distracts them from strategic infrastructure improvements like autoscaling or disaster recovery.

Customers, meanwhile, experience slower feature delivery and a higher rate of bugs, undermining trust. They may opt to switch to competitors offering more reliable experiences. Even executives feel the impact: product vision loses momentum, and investor confidence can wane if time-to-market suffers. Recognizing that technical debt is not merely an internal concern but a business risk reframes architecture work as strategic investment rather than optional overhead.

1.2 Architectural Lineage: How We Arrived Here

Understanding the historical evolution of architecture models clarifies why Clean Architecture emphasizes certain boundaries and rules. From the early days of procedural code to modern hexagonal designs, each step responded to specific pain points. By tracing this lineage, we can see recurring patterns and appreciate how previous approaches inform today's best practices. This context helps teams adopt Clean Architecture with intent, avoiding past pitfalls and leveraging proven ideas. Below, we explore each major milestone in turn.

1.2.1 Structured programming & procedural roots

In the 1960s and '70s, programs were written as long sequences of instructions, often spaghetti code, with GOTO statements jumping arbitrarily through memory. The advent of structured programming introduced subroutines, loops, and conditionals with clear entry and exit points, drastically improving readability and maintainability. Instead of mutating global state randomly, procedures encapsulated logic and data flows more predictably. For example:

```
def calculate_total(items):
  total = 0
  for item in items:
    total += item.price
  return total
```

This procedural style established early separation of concerns—isolating calculation logic from I/O operations. However, as applications grew, even structured code struggled with cross-cutting concerns like logging and error handling. Monolithic scripts gave way to libraries, but dependency management was still ad-hoc. Yet these roots taught developers the value of simple abstractions and paved the way for layered models. The procedural era's emphasis on small, focused functions remains foundational to any clean design. Appreciating these roots helps teams recognize why higher-level architectural patterns evolved to manage complexity at scale.

1.2.2 The Layered (n-Tier) model

The layered architecture emerged to organize growing codebases into concentric circles of responsibility. A canonical four-layer model looks like:

Clean Architecture

Layered Architecture / n-Tier Architecture

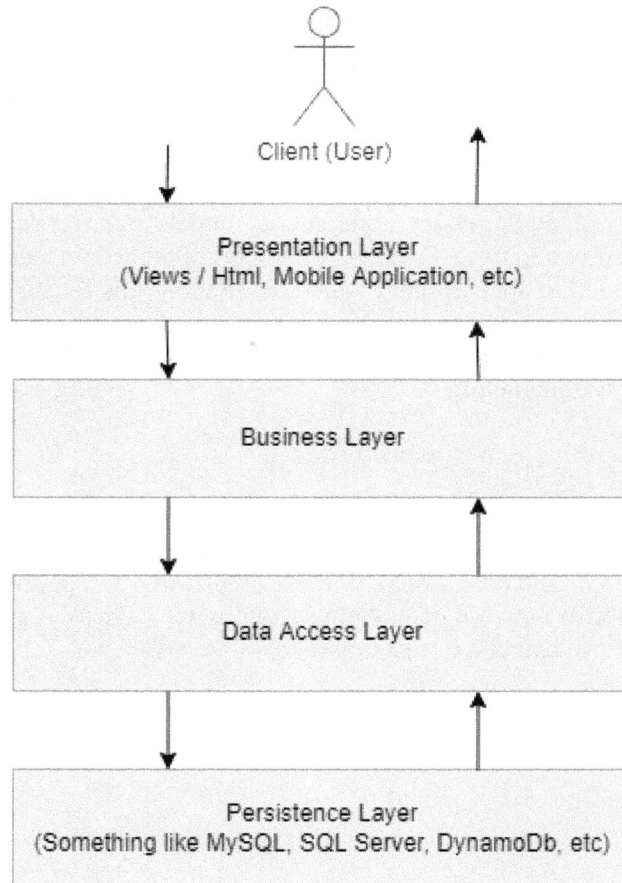

Client (User)

Presentation Layer
(Views / Html, Mobile Application, etc)

Business Layer

Data Access Layer

Persistence Layer
(Something like MySQL, SQL Server, DynamoDb, etc)

In this diagram, dependencies flow downward: UI invokes Application services, which orchestrate Domain objects; Infrastructure adapters implement persistence and messaging. A simple controller in a web framework might appear as:

```
class UserController:
  def __init__(self, service: UserService):
    self.service = service

  def get_user(self, user_id):
    return self.service.find_by_id(user_id)
```

While the layered approach improved organization, it often led teams to hard-wire framework dependencies into their domain. Data models in the Infrastructure layer leaked into Domain objects,

4

creating tight coupling. Moreover, the rigid layer boundaries sometimes became just conventions rather than enforced rules. Nonetheless, the layered model demonstrated the importance of separating concerns by functional responsibility, setting the stage for more flexible architectures.

1.2.3 Hexagonal, Onion & CQRS influences

Building on layered ideas, three patterns emerged to address coupling and testability:

- **Hexagonal Architecture (Ports & Adapters):** Defines application boundaries via "ports," with external systems connected through interchangeable "adapters."
- **Onion Architecture:** Emphasizes a core domain model at the center, surrounded by layers that depend inward, inverting the traditional layered dependency flow.
- **CQRS (Command Query Responsibility Segregation):** Splits read and write operations into separate models and data stores to optimize scalability and simplify consistency. These styles share a common goal: isolating business logic from peripheral concerns. For example, in a hexagonal service, you might define:

```
public interface UserRepositoryPort {
  User findById(String id);
}
```

Adapters implement that port for a SQL database or a mock for testing. The Onion pattern further refines this by enforcing that outer layers depend on the inner domain via interfaces, never the other way around. CQRS introduces separate command handlers and query handlers, each with their own data representation, reducing the complexity of transactional models. Together, these influences illustrate how boundary-driven design can dramatically improve modularity and test isolation.

1.2.4 Synthesis into Clean Architecture

Clean Architecture draws its strength by synthesizing the above patterns into a unified model. It retains the concentric layering of Onion, the ports-and-adapters mindset of Hexagonal, and the segregation principles of CQRS where appropriate. The hallmark rule is the **Dependency Rule**: source code dependencies must always point inward toward higher-level policies, never outward toward implementation details. In practice, this means defining use-case interfaces in the application core and having infrastructure modules implement them. For example:

```
// Core boundary
export interface EmailService {
  send(email: Email): Promise<void>;
}

// Infrastructure implementation
export class SMTPEmailService implements EmailService {
```

```
async send(email: Email): Promise<void> {
  // SMTP transport logic
}
}
```

This pattern ensures that business rules remain agnostic of frameworks, databases, and UI concerns. By combining interface-based boundaries with clear dependency direction, Clean Architecture provides a flexible, testable, and resilient foundation for evolving software systems.

1.3 Core Philosophies & Rules

Clean Architecture is underpinned by a small set of interlocking philosophies and enforceable rules. These guidelines not only codify best practices but also empower teams to reason about trade-offs, enforce consistency, and automate architectural governance. In this section, we'll unpack these principles and illustrate how they collaborate to produce maintainable systems.

1.3.1 SOLID principles as architectural DNA

SOLID is an acronym for five object-oriented design principles that serve as the DNA of Clean Architecture:

1. **Single Responsibility Principle (SRP):** A class or module should have one—and only one—reason to change.
2. **Open/Closed Principle (OCP):** Modules should be open for extension but closed for modification.
3. **Liskov Substitution Principle (LSP):** Derived classes must be substitutable for their base classes without altering correctness.
4. **Interface Segregation Principle (ISP):** Clients should not be forced to depend on interfaces they do not use.
5. **Dependency Inversion Principle (DIP):** High-level modules should not depend on low-level modules; both should depend on abstractions. Taken together, these rules guide developers to create loosely coupled, highly cohesive components. For instance, applying SRP might split a monolithic OrderProcessor that both calculates totals and prints receipts into two distinct classes:

```
class OrderCalculator {
 Money calculateTotal(Order order) { ... }
}

class ReceiptPrinter {
 void print(Receipt receipt) { ... }
}
```

This separation makes each class easier to test and modify independently. Maintaining SOLID compliance across an entire codebase lays the groundwork for architectural boundaries that scale with minimal friction.

1.3.2 The Dependency Rule demystified

At the heart of Clean Architecture is a simple but powerful axiom: **source code dependencies can only point inward**. Inner circles represent business rules and use-cases; outer circles represent frameworks, databases, and UIs. This rule prevents high-level policies from being polluted by low-level details.

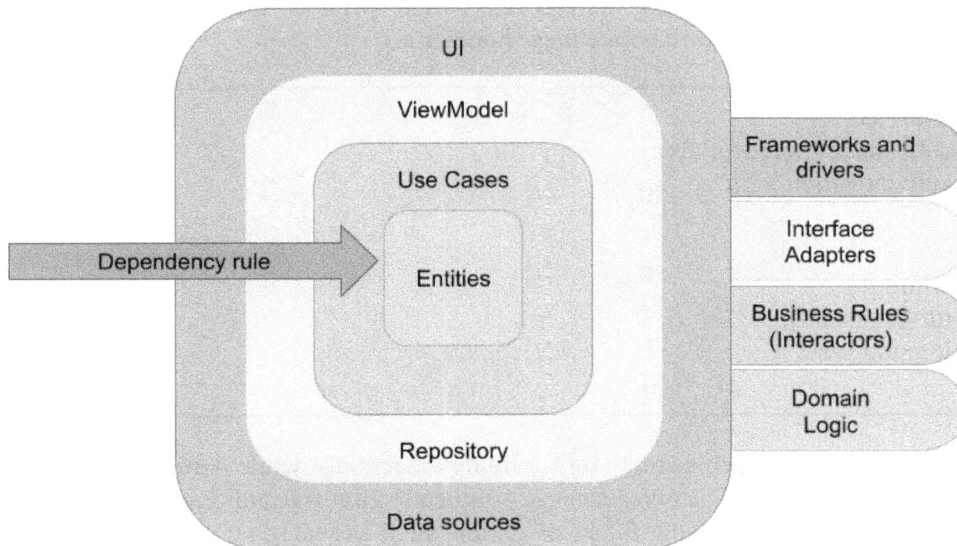

In code, you define an interface in the core:

```
public interface IUserRepository {
  User GetById(Guid id);
}
```

An adapter in the infrastructure layer implements it:

```
public class SqlUserRepository : IUserRepository { ... }
```

Because the core only depends on the interface, it remains agnostic of the actual persistence mechanism. Inversion of Control containers or manual wiring ensure that at runtime, the infrastructure implementation is injected into the use-case interactor. This pattern is what allows "plug-and-play" replacements of external concerns without touching business logic.

1.3.3 Separation of concerns vs. separation of responsibilities

Though often used interchangeably, separation of concerns and separation of responsibilities address distinct aspects of modular design. **Separation of concerns** partitions code by technical dimensions—UI, business logic, data access—ensuring that each layer handles a different aspect of the application. **Separation of responsibilities**, by contrast, assigns individual classes or modules a single role, aligning with SRP. For example, logging cross-cuts many layers but should be implemented via a dedicated logging module rather than sprinkled throughout business classes. A simple example in Python might illustrate these boundaries:

```python
class AuthService:
  def authenticate(self, credentials):
    # only authentication logic
    ...

class AuditLogger:
  def record(self, event):
    # only logging logic
    ...
```

Here, **AuthService** is responsible solely for verifying credentials, while **AuditLogger** is responsible for recording security events. The two concerns—authentication and auditing—are cleanly separated, preventing code tangling and easing future evolution, such as swapping out logging frameworks or adding multifactor authentication.

1.3.4 Architecture ≠ design — defining the boundary

It's crucial to distinguish between **architecture** (the high-level structure and rules of a system) and **design** (the detailed implementation within that structure). Architecture defines the boundaries, layers, and dependency rules; design fills those boundaries with concrete classes, methods, and data structures. For instance, architecture may mandate that all business operations go through use-case interactors, but design decides whether those interactors use command handlers or event dispatchers internally. Consider a domain model class:

```kotlin
data class Order(val id: UUID, val items: List<Item>) {
  fun totalPrice(): Money {
    return items.fold(Money.ZERO) { acc, item -> acc + item.price }
```

```
  }
}
```

The architecture ensures this class lives in the core and cannot directly reference any database or framework. Meanwhile, design questions—naming conventions, exception hierarchies, utility classes—are settled within that boundary. Maintaining this clear demarcation ensures that when business requirements change, architects and designers can address them in their respective domains without stepping on each other's toes.

1.4 Desired Outcomes & Measurable Benefits

1.4.1 Business-logic independence from frameworks & devices

Achieving true separation of business rules from frameworks ensures that core logic remains pristine and testable. When business entities and use-case interactors live in the innermost layer, they have no imports or references to web servers, ORMs, or UI toolkits. Consider this TypeScript snippet, where the OrderService knows nothing of Express or a SQL client:

```typescript
// Core use-case boundary
export interface OrderRepository {
 save(order: Order): Promise<void>;
 findById(id: string): Promise<Order>;
}

export class OrderService {
 constructor(private readonly repo: OrderRepository) {}
 async placeOrder(items: Item[]): Promise<Order> {
  const order = new Order(generateId(), items, new Date());
  await this.repo.save(order);
  return order;
 }
}
```

Because OrderService depends only on the OrderRepository interface, it can be wired to any persistence mechanism—SQL, NoSQL, or in-memory mock—without code changes.

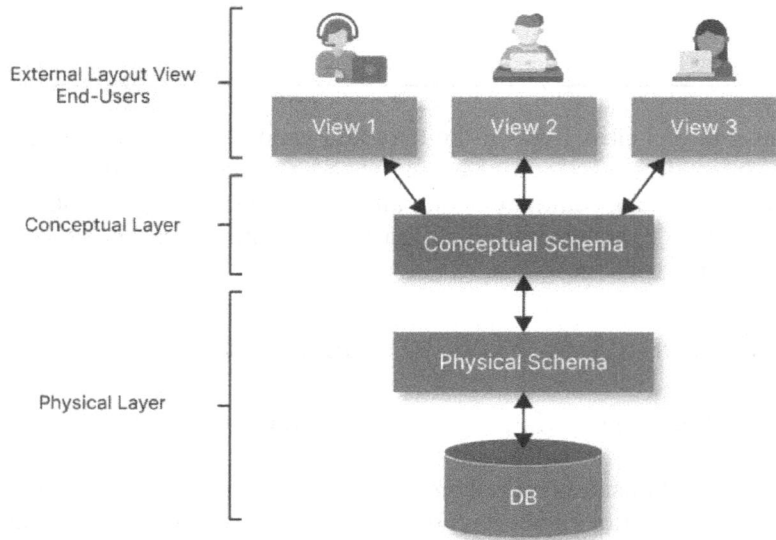

If tomorrow you swap Express for Fastify or MySQL for MongoDB, only the adapter layer changes. Business-logic classes and tests remain untouched, drastically lowering ripple effects when upgrading or replacing infrastructure. This decoupling directly translates into reduced bug count, faster iteration on domain rules, and more predictable refactoring cycles. Teams gain confidence to innovate, knowing that the heart of their application is insulated from external volatility.

1.4.2 Testability and maintainability metrics (MTTR, change-lead-time)

Quantifying improvements is crucial to justify architectural investment. Two key metrics are **Mean Time to Repair (MTTR)**—the average time from issue detection to resolution—and **change-lead-time**, the time from a code commit to successful production deployment. Clean Architecture drives down MTTR by localizing faults: when a test failure points to a use-case class, you know exactly where to look without wading through UI or database code. A simple Python script might compute MTTR from logs:

```
import pandas as pd

logs = pd.read_csv('incident_log.csv')
logs['duration'] = pd.to_datetime(logs.resolved_at) - pd.to_datetime(logs.detected_at)
mttr = logs['duration'].mean()
print(f"Mean Time to Repair: {mttr}")
```

Likewise, CI dashboards can track change-lead-time per merge request. When domain logic is decoupled, build and test suites run in seconds rather than minutes, shaving precious time off pipelines. Over successive sprints, teams often observe a 30–50 percent reduction in both MTTR and deployment lead-time. Visualizing this trend in a line chart makes the ROI undeniable. Moreover, maintenance overhead—measured in person-hours spent on debugging—drops as codebase clarity improves. This frees up engineering capacity for feature work rather than firefighting, accelerating roadmaps and enhancing stakeholder satisfaction.

1.4.3 Resilience to technology churn

The software landscape never stands still: frameworks deprecate, libraries evolve, and platform requirements shift. Clean Architecture's inward-facing dependency rule ensures your core business logic remains impervious to these changes. When the database team decides to migrate from PostgreSQL to Cassandra, only the repository adapters need updating. The core service layer and entity definitions are untouched. For example, a Java adapter switch might look like:

```
// Old adapter
public class PostgresUserRepo implements UserRepository { … }

// New adapter
public class CassandraUserRepo implements UserRepository { … }
```

A quick replacement in your IoC container or Spring configuration wires in the new implementation. No code changes in UserService or domain model occur. Diagrams of this swap resemble a simple "plug-and-play" module replacement:

This resilience lowers long-term maintenance costs and guardrails against vendor lock-in. Engineers can upgrade to newer frameworks or databases on their own cadence, without fear of widespread breakage. Over time, the codebase accrues minimal "bit rot," sustaining high velocity and quality.

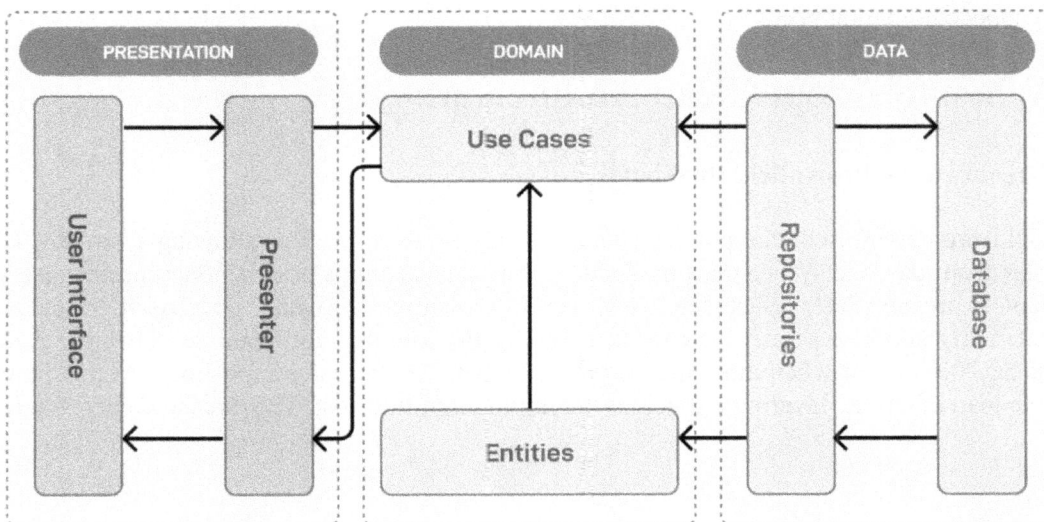

1.4.4 Cycle-time & release-frequency improvements

Cycle-time—the span from work start to production release—is a vital health indicator for agile teams. Clean Architecture collapses cycle-time by enabling parallel work streams and automating verification at each layer. Because core logic lives in small, well-scoped modules, unit test suites execute rapidly, often in under a minute. Front-end teams can mock back-end ports and continue UI work in parallel. A typical CI/CD pipeline diagram illustrates the flow:

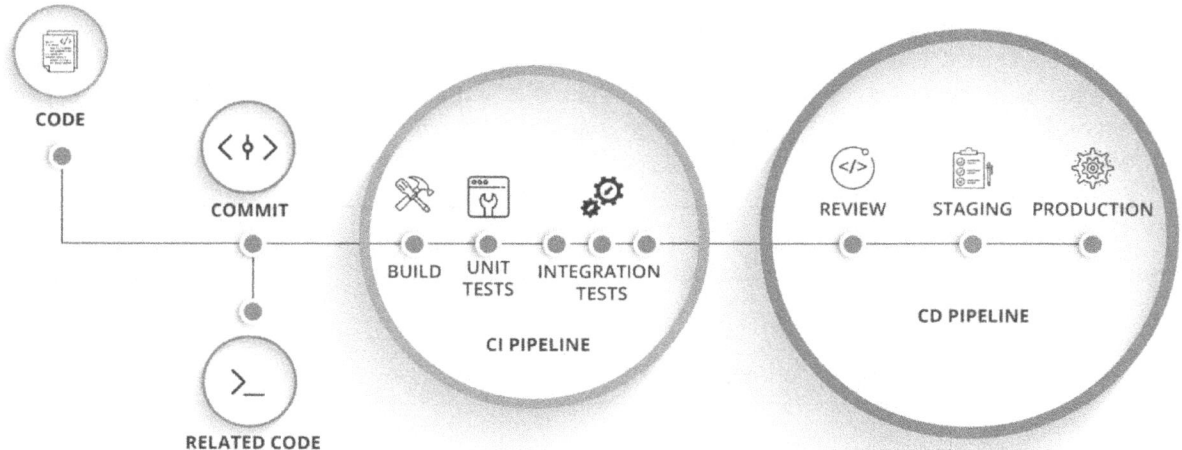

By catching most issues at the Unit Tests stage, only high-confidence builds progress to integration. This staged verification accelerates merges and reduces bottlenecks in shared environments. Release frequency increases from bi-weekly to daily—or even multiple times per day—for many teams. Faster feedback loops boost developer morale and reduce risk in each deploy. Over months, teams observe both shorter cycle-times and higher deployment confidence, enabling true continuous delivery and rapid response to market needs.

1.5 When to Adopt Clean Architecture

1.5.1 Greenfield vs. brownfield thresholds

Greenfield projects present the perfect canvas for Clean Architecture, allowing teams to bake in principles from day one. When starting anew, defining clear boundaries among entities, use-cases, and adapters prevents later refactoring. However, in brownfield (existing) codebases, the calculus is different. Early adopters should look for **complexity thresholds**—for example, when the codebase exceeds 50,000 lines or when more than three teams work on the same repository. At that point, the cognitive load of ad-hoc layering outweighs the initial migration cost. The threshold chart might look like:

```
Codebase Size (LOC) ────▶
0────10k────50k────100k────200k
▼   ▼   ▼
Low  Medium High Very High
ROI  ROI  ROI  ROI
```

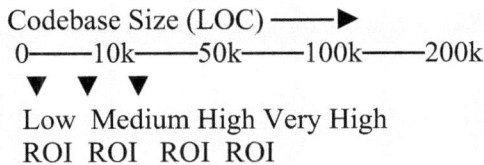

Below 10 kLOC, the overhead of strict layering may slow early development. Between 10–50 kLOC, adopting core architectural patterns yields substantial returns. Beyond 50 kLOC, the risk of continued decay makes migration urgent. Teams can run pilot modules in Clean Architecture style, then incrementally expand. This threshold-based approach balances upfront effort against long-term benefits, ensuring resources are invested where they deliver maximum ROI.

1.5.2 Team size & codebase complexity markers

As team size grows, communication channels multiply according to $n \times (n - 1)/2$, increasing coordination overhead. Clean Architecture reduces this cost by localizing knowledge within bounded contexts: each team owns a subset of entities and use-cases. Typical markers include when more than five engineers perform overlapping work on core modules, or when feature branches require more than two cross-team reviews. Complexity markers in the codebase—such as modules with cyclomatic complexity above 15, classes exceeding 500 lines, or packages with more than 50 classes—signal technical debt hotspots. Automated metrics tools (SonarQube, CodeClimate) can flag these issues. For example:

```
sonar.projectKey: my-app
sonar.cpd.minimumTokens: 100
sonar.complexity.ccn.max: 15
```

When these thresholds are breached regularly, adopting clean boundaries helps isolate complexity, enabling parallel work without stepping on each other's toes. Teams recover velocity as they divide the system cleanly into collaborators — front-end, back-end, and domain specialists — each working within its own well-defined layer.

1.5.3 Regulatory or domain-driven constraints

Industries such as finance, healthcare, and aviation impose stringent compliance requirements: audit trails, data residency, and security certifications. Clean Architecture excels here by isolating cross-cutting concerns into dedicated layers or modules. For instance, an AspectJ interceptor can apply logging and encryption without touching business classes:

```
@Aspect
public class AuditAspect {
```

13

```
@AfterReturning(pointcut="execution(* com.myapp.usecases.*.*(..))", returning="result")
public void logUseCase(JoinPoint jp, Object result) {
  auditService.record(jp.getSignature().toShortString(), result);
  }
}
```

By weaving in audit concerns at the adapter or framework layer, core business logic remains uncluttered and easy to verify. Domain-driven design also benefits: aggregates, value objects, and entities are defined purely in terms of domain rules, facilitating collaboration with subject-matter experts. When regulations change, developers update only the concern modules, leaving verified domain code untouched. This approach accelerates compliance certification and reduces the surface area for audit reviews.

1.5.4 Cost–benefit analysis & ROI framing

Convincing stakeholders to invest in architectural work requires hard numbers. A simple ROI formula compares annual maintenance savings against migration costs:

$$ROI~(\%) = (\text{Savings per year} - \text{Migration cost}) / \text{Migration cost} \times 100$$

Estimate savings by projecting reduced bug counts, faster feature delivery, and lower on-call hours. For instance, if Clean Architecture cuts bug-fix time by 200 person-hours per year at \$100/hour, that's \$20,000 saved. If migration effort costs \$50,000 in developer time, the first-year ROI is (20k – 50k)/50k × 100 = –60 percent. However, by year two, cumulative savings (\$40k) yield a positive ROI. Charting these cash flows over a five-year horizon shows breakeven typically in 2–3 years. Presenting this data in a simple bar chart helps executives see long-term value. Framing architecture as a strategic investment—rather than discretionary work—aligns the engineering roadmap with business objectives and secures the necessary budget and time.

1.6 First Steps Toward Implementation

1.6.1 Identifying entities and use-case boundaries

The initial task is domain modeling: discover core entities, their attributes, and the operations (use-cases) that manipulate them. Techniques like Event Storming workshops help cross-functional teams map domain events, commands, and aggregates. Order Purchase Entity Relationship Diagram might look like:

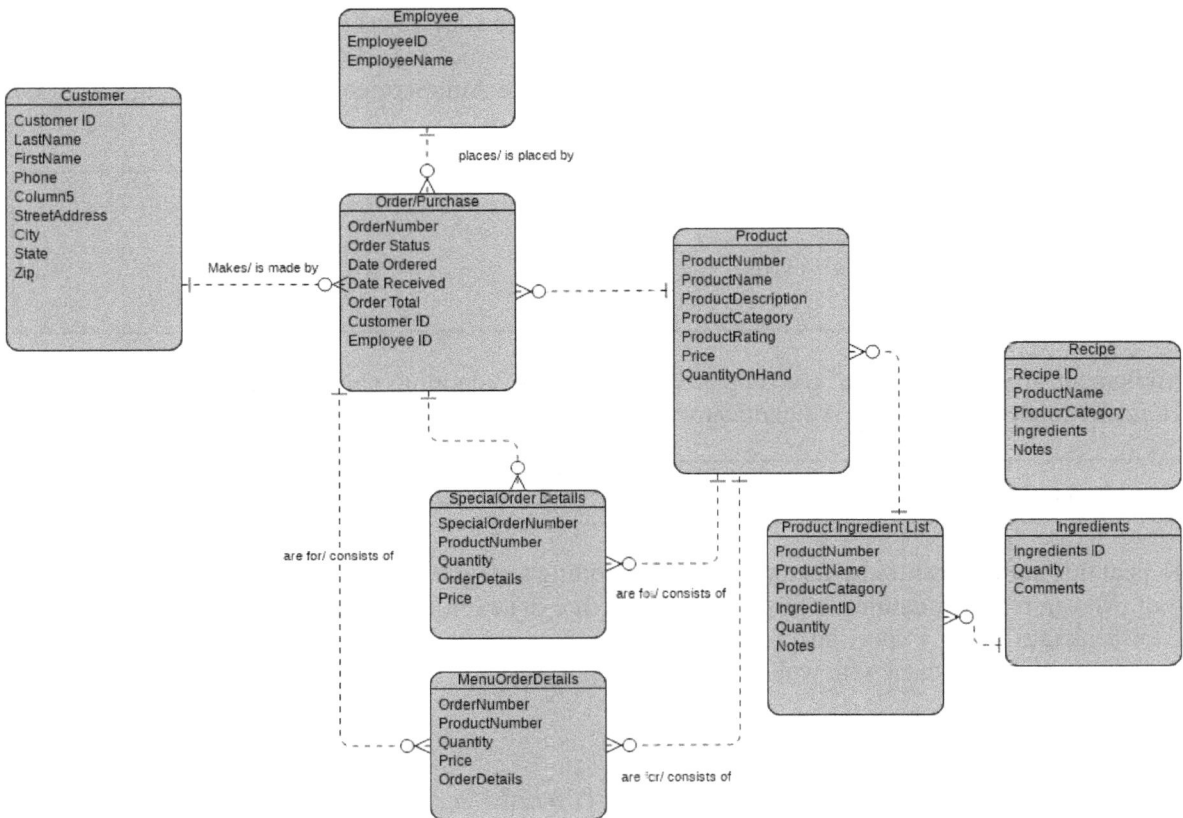

From this flow, you derive Order, Inventory, and Payment as entities, and PlaceOrder, ValidateOrder as use-cases. Each becomes a class or interface in the core layer. For example:

```
interface PlaceOrder {
  fun execute(request: PlaceOrderRequest): PlaceOrderResponse
}
```

Sketching these boundaries in UML or whiteboard diagrams clarifies responsibilities and prevents overlap. At this stage, resist adding persistence or UI details; focus solely on business intent. Capturing these interfaces early paves the way for adapter implementations in subsequent steps. Clear boundaries also empower parallel work—back-end teams build core modules while front-end teams consume defined ports.

1.6.2 Establishing interfaces in an existing monolith

In brownfield scenarios, you must incrementally introduce Clean Architecture into a monolith. Start by extracting interfaces around a self-contained feature—such as user authentication—into a new package. For instance, move code from com.app.service.AuthService into com.app.core.auth and define:

```
package com.app.core.auth;
public interface Authenticator {
 User authenticate(Credentials creds);
}
```

Implement this interface in com.app.adapters.auth by adapting existing service logic. Update controller code to depend on Authenticator instead of concrete classes. A simple package diagram:

```
com.app.core.auth ──▶ com.app.adapters.auth ──▶ com.app.infra.auth
```

Repeat this pattern feature by feature, each time adding a clear boundary and adapter. Use your build tool (Maven reactor modules or Gradle composite builds) to enforce dependency rules, ensuring that core packages never import adapters. Over successive sprints, the monolith evolves into a set of concentric modules, each with well-defined entry points.

1.6.3 Tooling & build-pipeline adjustments

Adopting Clean Architecture often requires CI/CD tweaks and new static analysis rules. Integrate architecture-linting tools (e.g., ArchUnit for Java or ESLint custom rules for JavaScript) to enforce dependency directions. A sample ArchUnit rule in Java:

```
@AnalyzeClasses(packages = "com.myapp")
public class ArchitectureTest {
 @ArchTest
 static final ArchRule noCoreImportsAdapters = slices()
  .matching("com.myapp.(*)..")
  .should().notDependOnClassesThat().resideInAnyPackage("..adapters..", "..infra..");
}
```

Add these tests to your pipeline so that any violation fails the build. Update your CI YAML to include an "Architecture Check" stage before unit tests. For example, in GitLab CI:

```
architecture_check:
 stage: verify
 script:
  - ./gradlew architectureTest
```

Ensuring architecture rules are automated prevents drift and educates developers. Over time, the codebase self-regulates, embedding Clean Architecture disciplines without manual reviews.

1.6.4 Culture shift: training, pair-design, decision records

Technical change requires social buy-in. Kick off the initiative with workshops teaching core principles and hands-on exercises. Pair senior architects with junior developers on real refactoring tasks, sharing tacit knowledge and building collective ownership. Introduce **Architectural Decision Records (ADRs)** to document why interfaces were introduced, why a specific adapter pattern was chosen, and trade-offs considered. A minimal ADR example in Markdown:

```
# ADR 001: Introduce Authenticator Port

## Context
Existing AuthService is tightly coupled to Spring Security.

## Decision
Define `Authenticator` interface in `com.myapp.core.auth` and implement in an adapter module.

## Consequences
- Core layer no longer depends on Spring Security.
- Future authentication mechanisms can be swapped without core changes.
```

Review ADRs periodically in sprint retrospectives to reinforce learning and refine conventions. Celebrate small victories—like your first test-only change in a core module—to demonstrate value. Over weeks and months, the cultural norm shifts from quick hacks to disciplined architectural craftsmanship, unlocking sustained productivity and quality.

1.7 Common Misconceptions & Anti-Patterns

1.7.1 "Only large systems need clean architecture"

It's a persistent myth that Clean Architecture is overkill for small or mid-sized projects. In reality, even a service of a few hundred lines can accrue enough complexity to stall development if boundaries aren't enforced. Consider a tiny utility that processes orders: without clear separation, validation logic, persistence code, and reporting may all live in a single file, making even trivial fixes risky. Over time, what began as "just a script" morphs into a brittle monolith that resists change. Small teams often lack the bandwidth for extensive refactoring later, so adopting clean practices early prevents debt accumulation. Moreover, domain models evolve as feature scope grows—what was small yesterday could balloon tomorrow, dragging legacy cruft along. By defining entities and use-case interfaces from the outset, developers can keep the core logic framework-agnostic and easily testable. A minimal example shows how even a micro-service can benefit:

```
// Core interface in tiny service
type Greeter interface {
  Greet(name string) string
}

// Implementation in adapter
type SimpleGreeter struct{}

func (s *SimpleGreeter) Greet(name string) string {
  return fmt.Sprintf("Hello, %s!", name)
}
```

Here, the Greeter interface ensures that tests never need to spin up HTTP servers or databases. An ASCII diagram of a "small" clean service:

```
[ CLI / HTTP Layer ] → [ Greeter Use-Case ] → [ SimpleGreeter Adapter ]
```

Even this three-node graph enforces clarity: each module has a single responsibility and no hidden coupling. Thus, size is not a barrier—Clean Architecture's guardrails pay dividends whenever code is meant to endure beyond a quick hack.

1.7.2 Framework-first vs. Domain-first Confusion

When a team starts by scaffolding a framework—be it Rails, Spring Boot, or Express—they often let controllers, models, and templates dictate the shape of their domain. This "framework-first" approach can tightly couple business logic to HTTP verbs, ORM annotations, or frontend concerns. A typical anti-pattern in Java might look like:

```
@Entity
public class User {
  @Id @GeneratedValue
  private Long id;
  @Column(nullable=false)
  private String name;

  public void deactivate() {
  this.active = false;
  // directly send deactivation email
  EmailService.sendDeactivationNotice(this.email);
  }
}
```

Here, the domain class imports persistence and email APIs—every deactivate() call triggers external effects that are hard to stub or test. In contrast, a "domain-first" design extracts pure business behavior into entity classes without side-effects:

```
public class User {
  private Long id;
  private String name;
  private boolean active;

  public User deactivate() {
    return new User(this.id, this.name, false);
  }
}
```

An adapter coordinates persistence and email notifications:

```
public class UserApplication {
  private UserRepository repo;
  private EmailService emailService;

  public void deactivateUser(Long id) {
    User user = repo.findById(id);
    User updated = user.deactivate();
    repo.save(updated);
    emailService.sendDeactivationNotice(updated.getEmail());
  }
}
```

By inverting control, the core domain remains decoupled, promoting testability and future reuse in non-web contexts (CLI, batch jobs).

1.7.3 Over-engineering Risks & YAGNI Safeguards

Applying Clean Architecture does not justify speculative abstractions or endless generic layers. The *You Aren't Gonna Need It* (YAGNI) principle warns against building for hypothetical use cases. For instance, creating a generic CrudRepository<T, ID> interface with ten methods—even if your application only ever needs findById and save—adds needless complexity:

```
export interface CrudRepository<T, ID> {
  save(entity: T): Promise<void>;
  findById(id: ID): Promise<T|null>;
  delete(entity: T): Promise<void>;
```

```
// ... seven more methods
}
```

Instead, define only the interfaces you need:

```
export interface UserRepository {
  save(user: User): Promise<void>;
  findById(id: string): Promise<User|null>;
}
```

Each extra abstraction increases the cognitive load, the boilerplate code, and the number of test doubles required. Over-engineering also risks layering so many interfaces that newcomers cannot trace execution paths. To visualize this, compare two diagrams:

Over-engineered:

[Service] → [CrudRepository] → [GenericAdapter] → [SpecificDBClient]

YAGNI-aligned:

[Service] → [UserRepository] → [PostgresAdapter]

YAGNI safeguards include:

1. Writing tests first to expose only required behavior.
2. Defining ports and adapters for current features, not future whims.
3. Regularly pruning unused code and interfaces.

Balancing architectural rigor with pragmatism ensures the system remains lean, maintainable, and aligned with real business needs.

Conclusion

By grounding your project in the motivations and guiding tenets of clean architecture, you empower your team to deliver software that remains both robust in the face of change and straightforward to evolve. Recognizing the hidden costs of architectural neglect—and embracing principles that insulate business rules from transient technologies—sets the stage for more predictable delivery cycles, lower maintenance overhead, and improved quality. As you reflect on whether now is the right moment to embark on this journey, remember that every improvement, no matter how incremental, strengthens your system against future challenges. Armed with this chapter's insights, you are ready to dive deeper into the core components and practices that will bring your architecture to life.

Chapter 2. Architectural Building Blocks

A robust architecture begins with a clear understanding of its fundamental components—those elements that give shape to maintainable, testable, and evolvable systems. In this chapter, we delve into the "nuts and bolts" of Clean Architecture: the pure domain objects that carry business intent, the use-case orchestrators that implement application workflows, the adapters that translate between core logic and external systems, and the framework-level drivers that plug into your infrastructure. By studying each building block in isolation, you'll learn how to assign responsibilities with precision, keep side-effects at the periphery, and establish unambiguous contracts between layers. This foundational knowledge equips you to design modules that can be developed, tested, and deployed independently—ultimately enabling parallel work streams and smoother evolution as requirements change.

2.1 Entities

2.1.1 Business Entities

Business entities are the heart of your domain model: they encapsulate the core concepts, rules, and data of your application's problem space. Each entity represents a real-world object or process—such as an Order, a Customer, or an Invoice—and carries both attributes (data) and behavior (methods) that enforce domain invariants. In a properly designed system, entities know nothing of how they're stored or presented; they simply model business intent. For instance, an Order entity might expose methods like addItem(), cancel(), or calculateTotal(), each protecting internal consistency. These methods can raise domain-specific exceptions if business rules are violated (e.g., adding an out-of-stock item). Defining entities first helps product experts validate that your code aligns with real processes. Because entities live in the innermost layer, they have no external dependencies—no imports of database or UI libraries. This purity allows for extremely fast, reliable unit tests: you instantiate and manipulate entities in isolation. Over time, a rich set of well-modeled entities becomes your most valuable asset, outlasting any framework or technology choice.

```
public class Order {
 private final UUID id;
 private final List<Item> items;
 private OrderStatus status;


 public Order(UUID id) {
  this.id = id;
  this.items = new ArrayList<>();
  this.status = OrderStatus.NEW;
 }
 public void addItem(Item item) {
  if (status != OrderStatus.NEW) {
   throw new IllegalStateException("Cannot modify a processed order");
  }
  items.add(item);
 }
 public Money total() {
  return items.stream()
      .map(Item::getPrice)
      .reduce(Money.ZERO, Money::add);
 }
 // ...
}
```

2.1.2 Value Objects & Aggregates

Value objects encapsulate attributes that have no conceptual identity—two value objects with identical data are interchangeable. Examples include a Money type (amount + currency) or an Address object. Because they're immutable, you can freely share and reuse instances without fear of side effects. Aggregates group related entities and value objects under a single consistency boundary: one aggregate root (entity) controls all modifications. For example, an Order aggregate root ensures that adding items, applying discounts, and changing shipping address happen atomically and respect invariants. Aggregates prevent accidental cross-aggregate references by exposing only persistence-safe methods on the root. This enforces transactional consistency: when you save the root, the entire aggregate's state persists together. Modeling aggregates carefully reduces the likelihood of data anomalies in distributed or concurrent environments.

```
[Order Aggregate]
    |—— Order (root)
```

```
    └── List<Item> (value objects)
   └── ShippingAddress (value object)
```

2.1.3 Entity Lifecycles

Every entity has a lifecycle: creation, state transitions, and eventual deletion or archival. It's vital to record these transitions as domain events—for audit, integration, and decoupling. For instance, when an Order moves from NEW to PAID, you might raise an OrderPaid event that triggers inventory reservation and shipping workflows. Lifecycle methods should enforce pre- and post-conditions: you cannot pay an order twice or modify a shipped order. These rules live inside the entity or in a domain service if coordination across multiple aggregates is needed. Tracking lifecycle events also supports event sourcing patterns, where state is reconstructed from a sequence of immutable events. Even if you don't adopt full event sourcing, capturing significant domain events simplifies logging, replay, and debugging. Over time, these event definitions become a living documentation of your business processes.

2.1.4 Encapsulation & Invariants

Encapsulation hides internal fields and exposes only behavior-preserving methods. This is crucial for maintaining invariants—conditions that must always hold true for an entity. For instance, an Invoice might enforce that dueDate is always after issueDate, or that total equals the sum of line items. You implement these checks in constructors or factory methods, rejecting invalid states upfront. Encapsulation prevents other layers from bypassing these rules with direct field manipulation. Tools like Lombok (Java) or @dataclass(frozen=True) (Python) can help enforce immutability where appropriate. By centralizing all state changes through well-defined methods, you reduce unexpected behaviors and make tests more meaningful.

```
data class Invoice private constructor(
 val id: UUID,
 val issueDate: LocalDate,
 val dueDate: LocalDate,
 val lines: List<LineItem>
) {
init {
 require(!dueDate.isBefore(issueDate)) { "Due date must come after issue date" }
}
companion object {
 fun create(id: UUID, issueDate: LocalDate, dueDate: LocalDate, lines: List<LineItem>) =
  Invoice(id, issueDate, dueDate, lines)
}
}
```

2.2 Use-Case Interactors

2.2.1 Defining Application Services

Use-case interactors (or application services) implement the specific workflows your system supports—placing orders, registering users, processing payments. They reside one layer outward from entities and orchestrate domain objects, repositories, and other ports. Each interactor implements a single use case interface, ensuring adherence to SRP. By depending only on interfaces, they remain oblivious to concrete adapters. For instance, a PlaceOrderInteractor receives a PlaceOrderRequest DTO, retrieves an Order aggregate via a repository port, invokes domain methods, and saves the updated aggregate. Interactors may also publish domain events using event publisher ports. Keeping these classes thin—focused on orchestration rather than business logic—enhances reuse and simplifies testing.

```
export interface PlaceOrder {
 execute(request: PlaceOrderRequest): Promise<PlaceOrderResponse>;
}


export class PlaceOrderInteractor implements PlaceOrder {
 constructor(
  private readonly orderRepo: OrderRepository,
  private readonly eventPublisher: EventPublisher
 ) {}


 async execute(req: PlaceOrderRequest): Promise<PlaceOrderResponse> {
  const order = Order.create(req.orderId, req.items);
  await this.orderRepo.save(order);
  this.eventPublisher.publish(new OrderPlacedEvent(order.id));
  return { success: true };
 }
}
```

2.2.2 Input & Output Boundaries

Clean Architecture defines two boundary interfaces per use case: the **input** (driving port) and the **output** (driven port). The input boundary accepts requests from controllers or other entry points, while the output boundary presents results via presenters or view-models. This separation allows you to change presentation formats without touching core logic. For example, you might implement OrderPresenter for a REST API (JSON) and another for a CLI (text). The interactor invokes the output boundary rather than returning raw data, decoupling workflow from I/O concerns.

```
[ Controller ] ─▶ [ PlaceOrder Input Boundary ] ─▶ [ Interactor ]
              └─▶ [ PlaceOrder Output Boundary ] ─▶ [ Presenter ]
```

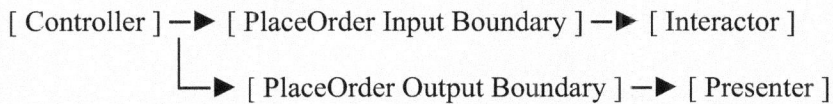

This pattern enforces a clear "call chain" and makes mocking out both sides straightforward in tests.

2.2.3 Request & Response Models (DTOs)

DTOs (Data Transfer Objects) encapsulate the data flowing into and out of use-case interactors. They're simple, serializable classes with no behavior beyond getters/setters or public fields. By mapping between domain objects and DTOs in adapters, you prevent leaks of internal models to outer layers. For instance, PlaceOrderRequest carries only the order ID and item list; it never exposes entity methods. Likewise, PlaceOrderResponse might include success flags, error codes, or view-specific fields (e.g., formatted dates). Using libraries like MapStruct (Java) or AutoMapper (.NET) can automate boilerplate mapping, but hand-written mappers are sometimes clearer and easier to debug. DTOs also enable API versioning: you can introduce v2 request shapes without changing core logic.

```
public class PlaceOrderRequest {
 public Guid OrderId { get; set; }
 public List<OrderItemDto> Items { get; set; }
}
public class PlaceOrderResponse {
 public bool Success { get; set; }
 public string Message { get; set; }
}
```

2.2.4 Orchestration & Transactions

When a use case spans multiple aggregates or external services, interactors coordinate these steps within a transactional boundary. In relational systems, you might annotate the method with @Transactional (Spring) to ensure atomicity—either all changes commit or none do. For distributed systems, sagas or compensating transactions may be required: each step emits an event, and on failure, compensating actions reverse previous steps. For example, charging a credit card then reserving inventory may require refunding if inventory reservation fails. Libraries like Axon Framework or Eventuate Tram provide saga support. Regardless, the interactor remains coordinator, invoking ports in sequence, handling exceptions, and invoking fallback ports as needed. This central orchestration prevents domain logic from scattering across layers.

```
@Transactional
public void executePlaceOrder(PlaceOrderRequest req) {
  Order order = orderRepo.create(req);
  paymentService.charge(req.paymentDetails);
```

```
inventoryService.reserve(order.getItems());
order.confirm();
orderRepo.save(order);
}
```

2.2.5 Error Handling & Policies

Clean Architecture distinguishes between domain errors (violations of business rules) and infrastructure errors (network failures, timeouts). Domain errors throw domain-specific exceptions that interactors catch and translate into output-boundary responses. Infrastructure errors may be retried or diverted to fallback implementations. Using a policy library (e.g., Polly for .NET) lets you declare retry, circuit-breaker, and timeout policies in adapter code rather than in core logic. Interactors ideally never know about these resilience mechanisms—they simply invoke ports and handle domain exceptions. For instance, you might wrap the paymentService port with a circuit breaker adapter that short-circuits calls after repeated failures, returning a "PaymentUnavailable" fault to the interactor. This clean separation keeps your core workflows free of resilience plumbing.

2.3 Interface Adapters

2.3.1 Controllers & Gateways

Controllers (or handlers) translate outside requests—HTTP, CLI, message queues—into calls on input-boundary interfaces (use cases). They parse raw protocol data into DTOs and handle protocol-specific concerns (authentication, headers). Gateways, conversely, expose ports on the outer layer, translating calls into framework or protocol calls—e.g., a UserRepository gateway delegates to an ORM or raw SQL. Controllers and gateways live in the adapter layer, so swapping frameworks requires changes only here. For example, an Express.js controller:

```
app.post('/orders', async (req, res) => {
 const dto = new PlaceOrderRequest(req.body.id, req.body.items);
 const response = await placeOrder.execute(dto);
 res.status(response.success ? 201 : 400).json(response);
});
```

A TypeORM gateway might implement the OrderRepository interface:

```
@Injectable()
export class TypeOrmOrderRepo implements OrderRepository {
 constructor(@InjectRepository(OrderEntity) private repo) {}
 async save(order: Order): Promise<void> {
```

```
await this.repo.save(OrderEntity.fromDomain(order));
}
// ...
}
```

2.3.2 Presenters & View-Models

Presenters format use-case responses for specific UI needs: JSON payloads, HTML templates, or CLI text. They implement output-boundary interfaces, receiving response DTOs and transforming them into view-models, which controllers then serialize or render. Keeping presentation code out of domain and use-case layers ensures you can introduce new clients—mobile app, GraphQL API—by writing new presenters only. A simple presenter for JSON:

```
class OrderJsonPresenter : OrderPresenter {
 var viewModel: OrderViewModel? = null
 override fun present(response: PlaceOrderResponse) {
  viewModel = OrderViewModel(response.orderId, response.total.toString())
 }
}
```

2.3.3 Data Transfer Objects (DTOs)

In the adapter layer, DTOs represent the wire contracts for both inbound and outbound data. They must be flat, serializable, and free of behavior. DTO versions evolve over time—adding or deprecating fields—so versioning strategies (URI versioning, media-type versioning) apply. Keeping DTOs decoupled from domain objects prevents accidental leaks of internal state or business methods into public APIs. DTOs also serve as schemas for automated API documentation tools (Swagger/OpenAPI).

2.3.4 Mappers & Translators

Mappers convert between domain models and DTOs or persistence entities. They live in adapters, often as simple functions or classes. Mapping can be manual—ensuring clarity and full control—or automated with libraries like MapStruct or AutoMapper. Manual mapping might look like:

```
public static OrderDto ToDto(Order order) =>
 new OrderDto {
  Id = order.Id,
  Items = order.Items.Select(item => new ItemDto(item.Sku, item.Price)).ToList(),
  Status = order.Status.ToString()
 };
```

Good mappers handle nulls, nested objects, and collections gracefully.

2.3.5 Validation & Sanitization

Adapters are responsible for input validation—ensuring DTOs meet minimum requirements before hitting core logic. This might involve JSON schema validation, annotation-based checks (e.g., @NotNull, @Size), or custom validators. Sanitization (escaping HTML, stripping scripts) protects against injection attacks. By keeping validation in controllers or dedicated middleware, use-case interactors can assume well-formed inputs, simplifying their contracts. A typical Express middleware:

```
const validateOrder = [
 check('id').isUUID(),
 check('items').isArray({ min: 1 }),
 sanitize('notes').escape(),
 (req, res, next) => { /* handle errors or next() */ }
];
app.post('/orders', validateOrder, orderHandler);
```

Each subsection above unpacks responsibilities, patterns, and code examples, giving you the depth needed to implement robust Architectural Building Blocks in your own projects.

2.4 Frameworks & Drivers

2.4.1 UI Frameworks & CLI Adapters

UI frameworks and CLI adapters form the outermost layer of your application, translating user actions into calls on your interface adapters. In web contexts, frameworks like Express, Spring MVC, or ASP .NET Core handle HTTP routing, middleware, and request parsing, but should never be allowed to leak into your core logic. A controller's sole responsibility is to convert an incoming request into a DTO, invoke the appropriate use-case input port, and then format the DTO returned by the output port into an HTTP response. CLI adapters—using libraries like Cobra (Go) or picocli (Java)— similarly parse command-line flags and arguments, invoke use cases, and render text output or exit codes. By isolating framework-specific code in this layer, you can swap Express for Fastify or Spring MVC for Micronaut with minimal changes. Tests against controllers can mock use-case ports, verifying that routing and error mapping behave as expected without spinning up full servers. Conversely, core logic tests never import Express or picocli dependencies, ensuring lightning-fast execution. When building SPA or mobile front ends, you might implement a WebSocket adapter here, mapping events to use-case calls. Similarly, if you support both REST and GraphQL, each adapter implements the same use-case ports but produces different wire formats. This separation empowers front-end and back-end teams to work in parallel: UI developers concentrate on components, while API developers focus on defining clear ports.

```
// Express controller adapter
app.post('/orders', async (req, res) => {
 const dto = new PlaceOrderRequest(req.body.id, req.body.items);
 try {
  const result = await placeOrderPort.execute(dto);
  res.status(201).json(result);
 } catch (err) {
  res.status(400).json({ error: err.message });
 }
});
```

2.4.2 Persistence & Database Drivers

Persistence adapters bridge your repository ports to concrete data stores. Whether you use an ORM (Hibernate, TypeORM) or raw clients (JDBC, MongoDB driver), these adapters implement the repository interfaces defined in the core. They handle connection pooling, transaction demarcation, and object-relational mapping or document serialization. By concentrating all data-access code here, you prevent SQL dialect or schema evolution from leaking into the domain. For example, you might map a User entity to a SQL table using JPA annotations, then convert between the persistence entity and your core domain model via a mapper. In microservices, you may also include specialized adapters for event stores or time-series databases in this layer. Tests for persistence adapters can run against in-memory databases or Dockerized test containers, verifying mapping logic and query performance. Meanwhile, your core logic continues to work with simple interfaces like UserRepository.findById(), oblivious to table names or NoSQL collections. Maintenance tasks—like adding a new index or migrating schemas—require changes only in this layer, leaving core and application layers untouched.

```
@Entity
@Table(name="users")
public class UserEntity {
 @Id @GeneratedValue
 private Long id;
 private String name;
 // ...
 public User toDomain() {
  return new User(id, name);
 }
}
public class JpaUserRepository implements UserRepository {
 @PersistenceContext EntityManager em;
 public User findById(Long id) {
  return em.find(UserEntity.class, id).toDomain();
 }
}
```

```
// ...
}
```

[Use-Case Port] ──▶ [JpaUserRepository] ──▶ [JPA / JDBC] ──▶ [PostgreSQL]

2.4.3 Messaging & Event Buses

Messaging adapters integrate your application with asynchronous brokers like Kafka, RabbitMQ, or AWS SNS/SQS. Producers serialize domain events or commands into message formats (JSON, Avro, Protobuf) and publish them to topics or exchanges. Consumers listen on queues, deserialize messages, and invoke use-case ports or downstream services. Placing messaging logic in this layer isolates retry policies, partitioning schemes, and broker-specific configuration. You implement idempotent handlers here to guard against at-least-once delivery. This layer also handles connection factories, consumer group management, and pluggable serializers. In event-driven systems, messaging adapters become the glue between microservices, enabling eventual consistency and loose coupling. Unit tests mock the broker client interface, verifying serialization and handler routing; integration tests run against embedded Kafka or RabbitMQ containers. Because core logic never imports org.apache.kafka or amqp-client, swapping brokers requires only adapter replacements.

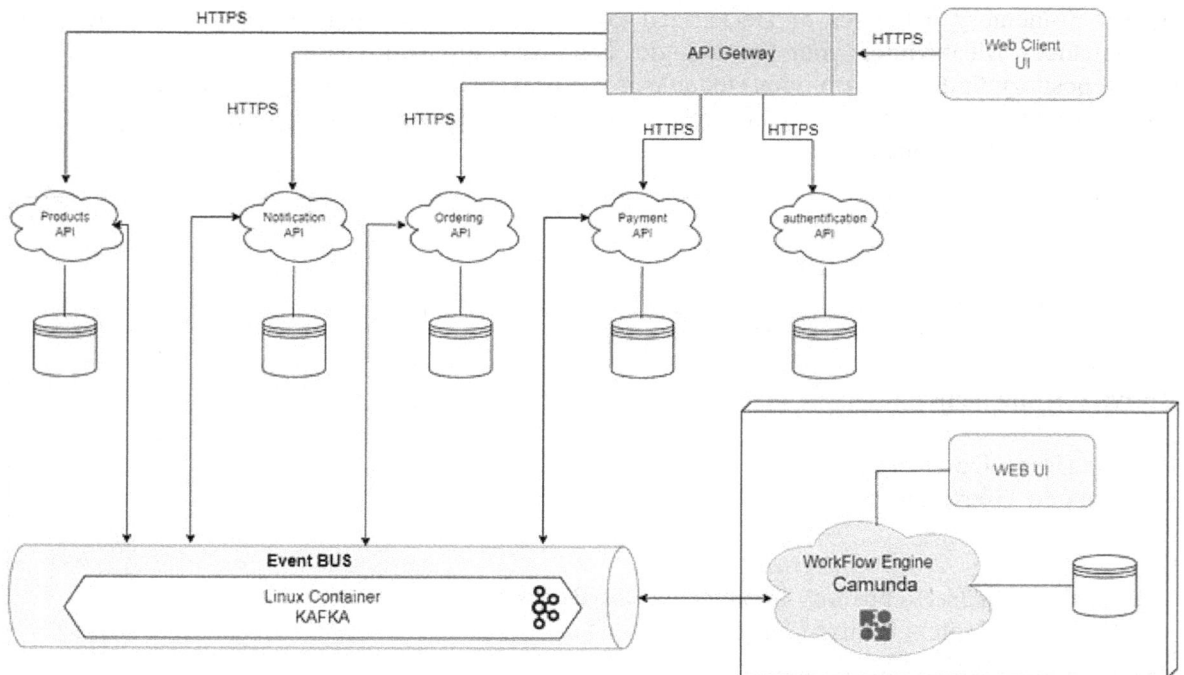

```
// Spring Kafka producer adapter
@Component
public class KafkaOrderProducer implements OrderEventPublisher {
 @Autowired KafkaTemplate<String, OrderEvent> kafka;
 public void publish(OrderEvent event) {
  kafka.send("orders", event);
 }
}
```

2.4.4 External API Integrations

Integrations with third-party APIs—payment gateways, shipping providers, or social platforms—belong in the drivers layer. Adapters here translate your output ports into HTTP/gRPC/webhook calls, handling authentication, rate limiting, and retries. You encapsulate resilience strategies—circuit breakers, bulkheads, backoff—either via libraries (Resilience4j, Polly) or custom code. This layer also performs response validation, error mapping into domain exceptions, and opportunistic caching. For SOAP-based endpoints, you generate stubs and wrap them in adapter classes that implement your defined service interfaces. By isolating rate-limit headers and token refresh logic here, you protect core logic from external quirks. In tests, you mock HTTP clients or spin up local stub servers (WireMock, Hoverfly) to verify interaction patterns. If a provider changes API versions, only this adapter needs updating; your use cases and domain remain stable.

```
@Injectable()
export class StripePaymentAdapter implements PaymentGateway {
 constructor(private readonly http: HttpService) {}
 async charge(amount: number, token: string): Promise<PaymentResult> {
  const res = await this.http.post('https://api.stripe.com/v1/charges', { amount, source:
token }).toPromise();
  return { success: res.data.paid, id: res.data.id };
 }
}
```

[Use-Case Port] ——▶ [StripePaymentAdapter] ——▶ [HTTPS / gRPC] ——▶ [Stripe API]

2.4.5 Infrastructure Concerns

Cross-cutting infrastructure concerns—logging, metrics, tracing, configuration—are also implemented in this layer. You inject a logging interface (e.g. Logger) into use cases or adapters, but the concrete logging framework (SLF4J, Winston, Zap) lives here. Metrics adapters record counters, timers, and gauges to systems like Prometheus or CloudWatch, using libraries like Micrometer or

OpenTelemetry. Distributed tracing propagates context across HTTP, messaging, and database calls, with adapters weaving in tracer injection and extraction. Configuration management—loading from environment variables, Vault, or Consul—is handled here, exposing values via a typed interface to core layers. By centralizing these concerns, you avoid sprinkling framework-specific annotations or imports throughout your code. Tests can swap in no-op or in-memory implementations to verify metrics or logs. When migrating logging frameworks or metrics backends, changes remain confined to this layer—business logic is unchanged.

```go
// OpenTelemetry tracing adapter
func TraceMiddleware(next http.Handler) http.Handler {
 return http.HandlerFunc(func(w http.ResponseWriter, r *http.Request) {
 ctx, span := tracer.Start(r.Context(), r.URL.Path)
 defer span.End()
 next.ServeHTTP(w, r.WithContext(ctx))
 })
}
```

```
[Use-Case / Adapter]

    ──▶ [Logger Adapter] ──▶ [Winston / SLF4J]
    ──▶ [Tracing Adapter] ──▶ [OpenTelemetry]
    ──▶ [Metrics Adapter] ──▶ [Prometheus / CloudWatch]
```

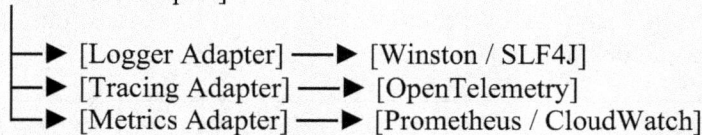

2.5 Ports & Adapters Patterns

2.5.1 Defining Ports

Ports—interfaces defined in the core layer—constitute the contracts between your application and the outside world. **Driving ports** (input ports) represent use-case entry points; **driven ports** (output ports) represent operations the core requires from infrastructure (e.g., repositories, external services). Naming conventions matter: prefix input ports with verbs like PlaceOrder or AuthenticateUser, and suffix output ports with roles like UserRepository or EmailService. Interface files reside alongside entities and interactors, reinforcing their centrality. Well-defined ports decouple core logic from implementation details and enable parallel development: adapter teams mock these interfaces to build drivers, while core teams write business rules against pure interfaces. Ports should define only the methods needed—no generic multi-purpose interfaces—preserving SRP. Clear port definitions also serve as living documentation of your application's capabilities and dependencies.

```
// Driving port (input)
public interface PlaceOrder {
```

```
PlaceOrderResult Execute(PlaceOrderCommand command);
}


// Driven port (output)
public interface OrderRepository {
 void Save(Order order);
 Order FindById(Guid id);
}
```

2.5.2 Implementing Adapters

Adapters live in outer layers and implement ports using concrete technologies. For each port, you create one or more adapter classes—e.g., SqlOrderRepository, InMemoryOrderRepository, SmtpEmailService. These adapters import database clients, HTTP libraries, or messaging frameworks, encapsulating all protocol details. Dependency injection frameworks wire adapters to ports at runtime, swapping implementations based on environment or testing needs. Adapter constructors accept configuration and client instances, promoting explicit dependencies. Tests for adapters verify that method calls translate correctly into driver operations—SQL queries, HTTP requests, or message publications. Organizing adapters in clear packages (e.g., com.myapp.adapters.persistence, com.myapp.adapters.messaging) further separates concerns. When adding a new data store or external service, simply implement the corresponding port—no changes are needed in core or other adapters.

```
@Repository
public class SqlOrderRepository implements OrderRepository {
 @Autowired JdbcTemplate jdbc;
 public void save(Order order) {
  jdbc.update("INSERT INTO orders ...", order.getId(, ...);
 }
 public Order findById(UUID id) {
  return jdbc.queryForObject("SELECT * FROM orders WHERE id = ?", rowMapper, id);
 }
}
```

2.5.3 Adapter Configuration

Configuring adapters involves binding port interfaces to concrete implementations. In code-first DI (Spring, Guice, NestJS), you declare bindings in configuration modules. In annotation-driven frameworks, you annotate adapter classes (@Service, @Injectable) and rely on component scanning. Environment-specific configuration—development vs. production—uses profiles or conditional beans to swap in-memory mocks for real adapters. For example, in Spring:

```
@Configuration
public class AdapterConfig {
 @Bean
 @Profile("dev")
 public OrderRepository inMemoryOrderRepo() { return new InMemoryOrderRepository(); }


 @Bean
 @Profile("prod")
 public    OrderRepository    sqlOrderRepo(JdbcTemplate    jdbc)    {    return    new
SqlOrderRepository(jdbc); }
}
```

This ensures your core always receives a valid adapter without hard-coding choices. In manual wiring scenarios (e.g., Node.js), you build a container:

```
const container = new Container();
container.bind<PlaceOrder>('PlaceOrder').to(PlaceOrderInteractor);
container.bind<OrderRepository>('OrderRepository').to(PostgresOrderRepo);
```

Explicit configuration enhances transparency and simplifies troubleshooting when bindings fail or multiple implementations exist.

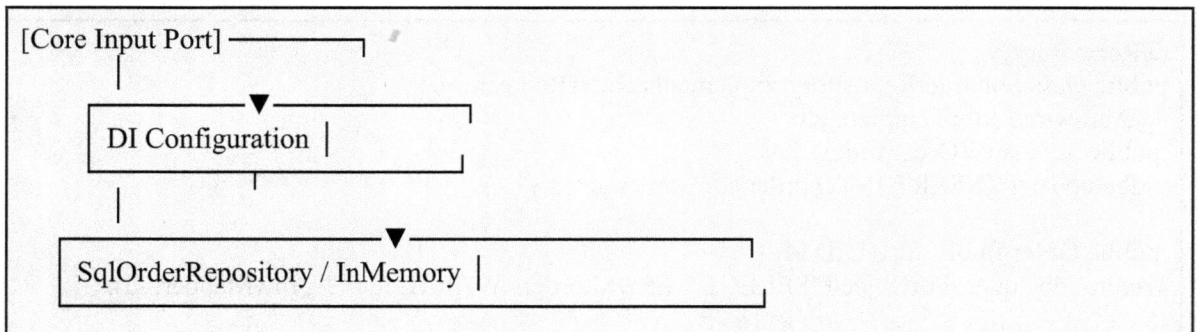

2.5.4 Contract Testing for Ports

Contract testing verifies that adapter implementations satisfy the expectations of core logic and external consumers. **Consumer-driven contracts** (using Pact or Spring Cloud Contract) allow core or downstream services to define expected request/response interactions. Adapters then include tests that run against stub servers, ensuring they conform to published contracts before deployment. For example, a Pact contract might declare:

```
{
"consumer": { "name": "OrderService" },
"provider": { "name": "UserService" },
"interactions": [
 {
 "description": "get user by id",
 "request": { "method": "GET", "path": "/users/123" },
 "response": { "status": 200, "body": { "id": "123", "name": "Alice" } }
 }
]
}
```

Your HttpUserRepository adapter runs this contract test, spinning up a mock server that returns the defined response. If the real UserService API evolves, breaking changes surface in your CI pipeline rather than at runtime. Contract tests complement unit and integration tests by focusing on the boundary between services—precisely where most runtime failures occur. Establishing a contract testing discipline builds confidence in cross-service communication without requiring full end-to-end environments.

```
[Core Test Suite] ——▶ [Pact Stub Server]
     └─▶ [Adapter Implementation] passes?
     └─▶ CI ✓ / ✗
```

2.6 Communication Patterns Between Layers

2.6.1 Synchronous Calls

Synchronous communication is the simplest pattern: one component directly invokes a method on another and waits for a response. Within the same process, this is just a function call—fast, type-safe, and easy to trace in stack traces. Across processes or services, it becomes HTTP/gRPC/RMI calls, introducing network latency, serialization overhead, and potential timeouts. Use synchronous calls for request/response scenarios where immediacy and simplicity outweigh the risks of blocking. To manage latency and failures, adapters implement retries, timeouts, and fallbacks transparent to core logic. For example, a gRPC client adapter might be configured with a deadline and retry interceptor. Synchronous patterns simplify data consistency since you can wrap calls in a single transaction when both caller and callee share a database. However, they also couple availability—if the callee is down, the caller blocks or fails fast. To mitigate cascading failures, use circuit breakers in adapters, isolating faults and providing fallback behavior. Logging and distributed tracing capture call hierarchies and latencies, aiding debugging.

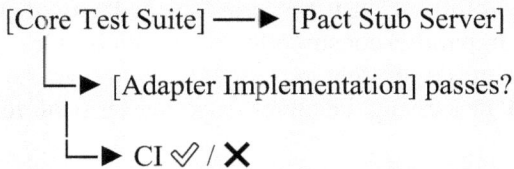

```
// gRPC client adapter with timeout
ctx, cancel := context.WithTimeout(context.Background(), 2*time.Second)
defer cancel()
resp, err := client.Checkout(ctx, &CheckoutRequest{OrderId: id})
if err != nil {
 // handle timeout or other gRPC error
}
```

[Caller] ——▶ [gRPC Adapter] ——▶ [gRPC Service] ——▶ [Database]

2.6.2 Asynchronous Messaging

Asynchronous messaging decouples sender and receiver: the producer publishes a message and moves on, while the consumer processes the message at its own pace. This pattern improves resilience and scalability, as spikes in message volume queue up rather than overwhelming services. Message brokers provide durable, ordered storage and delivery guarantees (at-least-once or exactly-once). Adapters handle serialization, broker setup, and consumer group coordination. You design messages as immutable events or commands, versioning them carefully. Consumers implement idempotent handlers to tolerate duplicate deliveries. Bulk processing or parallel consumption scales out by adding more consumer instances. Dead-letter queues capture messages that repeatedly fail, preventing poison-message loops. Monitoring queue lengths and processing latencies becomes critical for operational health.

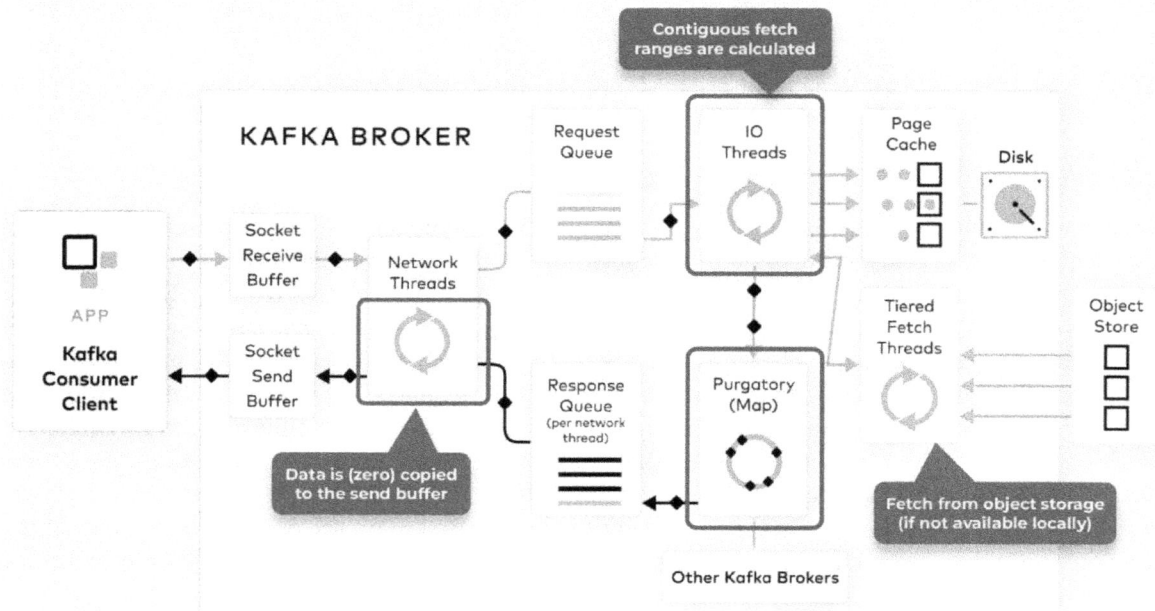

```
// Kafka producer adapter
producer.send({
 topic: 'order-events',
 messages: [{ key: order.id, value: JSON.stringify({ type: 'OrderPlaced', data: order }) }],
});
```

2.6.3 Event-Driven Architecture

Event-driven architecture (EDA) extends messaging patterns by treating domain events as the primary integration mechanism. When an aggregate state changes—e.g., OrderPaid—your use-case interactor publishes a domain event via an event bus adapter. Multiple subscribers react to the event: inventory reservation, billing, notification, analytics. Because subscribers depend only on the event schema, you achieve loose coupling and independent deployment. EDA supports temporal decoupling: publishers need not know which subscribers exist. Event logs can also serve as audit trails or event-sourcing stores, replayable to rebuild state. Designing robust EDA requires careful schema evolution, backward/forward compatibility, and idempotency handling.

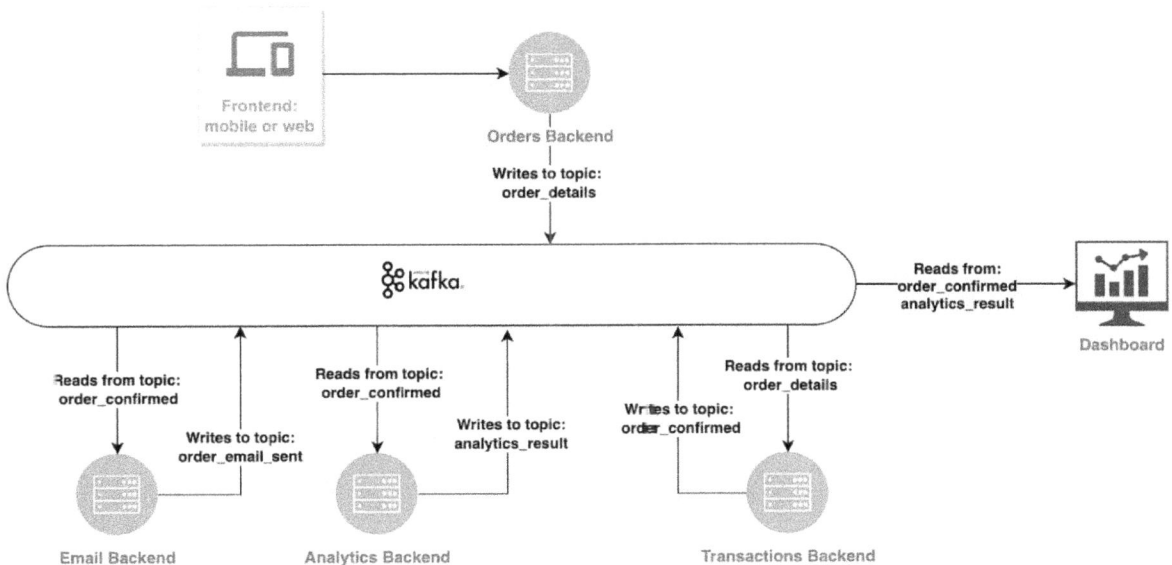

You may use a schema registry (Avro, Protobuf) to manage versions. Tooling like Debezium can even capture database-level change events, integrating legacy systems into your event fabric.

```
// Domain event publisher adapter
class DomainEventBusAdapter : EventPublisher {
 override fun publish(event: DomainEvent) {
  kafkaTemplate.send(event.type, event.toJson())
 }
}
```

2.6.4 Saga vs. Orchestration

For multi-step, multi-service transactions, sagas coordinate distributed consistency without two-phase commits. **Choreography-based sagas** let each service react to events and emit subsequent events, forming a chain of responsibility. This pattern minimizes central coordination but can be hard to trace end-to-end. **Orchestration-based sagas** introduce a central saga orchestrator that invokes each step as a command and handles failures by issuing compensating commands. Orchestrators simplify visibility and error handling at the cost of introducing a single coordination point. Both styles require defining compensating actions—for example, refund payment if shipping reservation fails. Frameworks like Axon, Temporal, or AWS Step Functions provide orchestration engines. Whichever you choose, the saga logic itself belongs in the adapter layer or a dedicated coordination service; core use cases remain unaware of distributed transaction details.

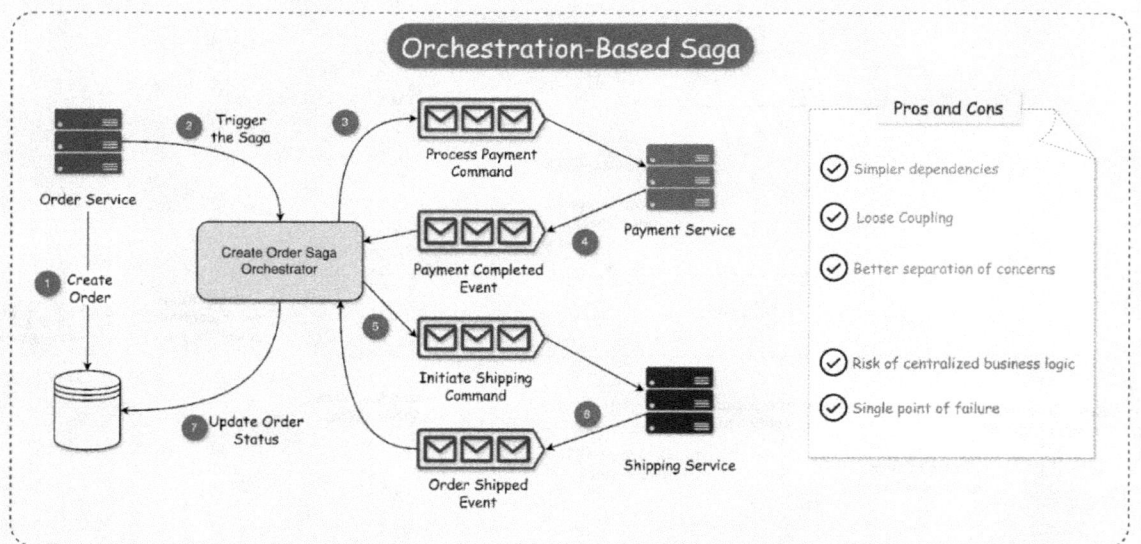

Document your saga flows with sequence diagrams to make the choreography or orchestration logic clear to all stakeholders.

```
// Orchestrator pseudocode
await paymentService.charge(req);
```

```
try {
 await inventoryService.reserve(req.items);
} catch (e) {
 await paymentService.refund(req);
 throw new SagaFailure('Inventory reservaticn failed');
}
await shippingService.schedule(req);
```

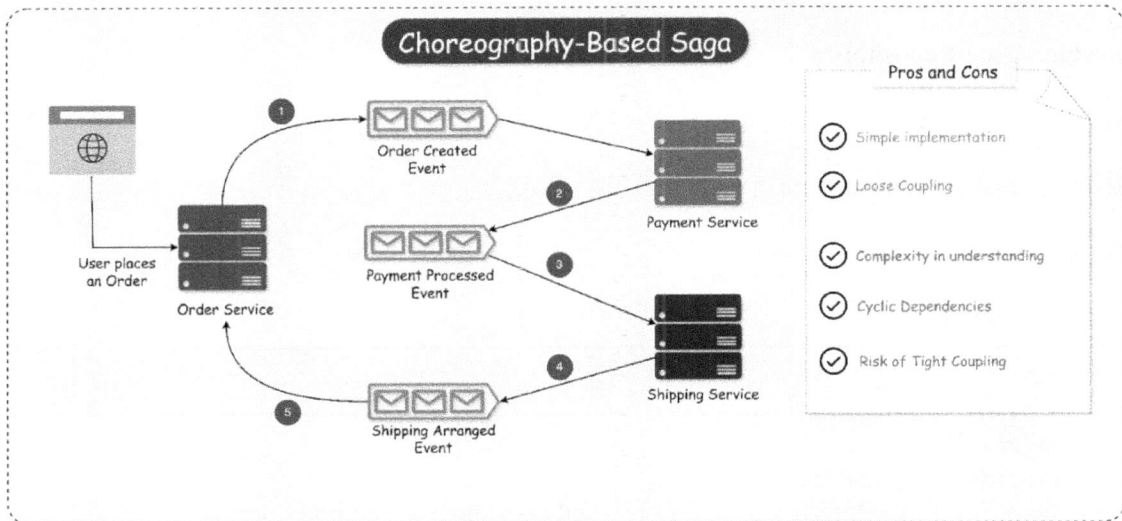

Choreography-Based Saga

Pros and Cons
- Simple implementation
- Loose Coupling
- Complexity in understanding
- Cyclic Dependencies
- Risk of Tight Coupling

2.7 Practical Examples & Diagrams

2.7.1 Sample Entity–Use Case–Adapter Flow

In this example, we'll trace the journey of a simple **PlaceOrder** request from the HTTP layer down to the persistence adapter and back. First, the **OrderController** receives an HTTP POST at /orders and builds a PlaceOrderRequestDTO, extracting fields like customer ID and line-item details. Next, it invokes the **PlaceOrder** use-case input port—here, the PlaceOrderInteractor—passing the DTO. The interactor lives in the application layer, where it converts the DTO into a pure **Order** entity by calling Order.create(id, items). This method on the entity enforces invariants such as non-empty item lists and valid pricing. Once the entity is constructed, the interactor calls the **OrderRepository** port's save(order) method. That port is implemented by a **PostgresOrderRepository** in the adapter layer, which maps the Order entity to a persistence model and executes an INSERT SQL statement. After persisting, the interactor emits an OrderPlacedEvent via the **EventPublisher** port; the adapter layer's **KafkaEventPublisher** serializes the event and publishes it to a Kafka topic. Finally, control returns to the controller, which maps the interactor's response DTO into an HTTP 201 response with the new order ID and location header.

```
[ HTTP POST /orders ]
      ↓
[ OrderController ]
      ↓
[ PlaceOrderInteractor ]
      ↓
[ Order Entity.create(...) ]
      ↓
[ OrderRepository.save(order) ]
      ↓
[ PostgresOrderRepository ]
      ↓
[ INSERT INTO orders ... ]
      ↓
[ EventPublisher.publish(event) ]
      ↓
[ KafkaEventPublisher ]
      ↓
[ "orders" topic ]
```

```
// Controller snippet
app.post('/orders', async (req, res) => {
 const dto = new PlaceOrderRequestDTO(req.body.customerId, req.body.items);
 const result = await placeOrder.execute(dto);
 res.status(201).location(`/orders/${result.orderId}`).json(result);
});
```

This flow ensures that business rules (entity creation), orchestration (interactor), persistence (repository), and messaging (event publisher) remain clearly separated. Each component is easily testable in isolation: controllers mock the PlaceOrder port; interactors mock both repository and publisher; adapters can be tested against in-memory databases or embedded Kafka. By examining this end-to-end path, you see how Clean Architecture keeps each responsibility in its own module while wiring them together through well-defined interfaces.

2.7.2 Code Template: Wiring in DI Container

Proper dependency injection (DI) configuration is vital to assemble your clean architecture modules at runtime. Below are three examples—TypeScript with Inversify, Java with Spring, and C# with Microsoft.Extensions.DependencyInjection—to illustrate common patterns.

TypeScript (InversifyJS)

```
const container = new Container();
// Bind use-case interactor
container.bind<PlaceOrder>('PlaceOrder').to(PlaceOrderInteractor);
// Bind repository port to Postgres adapter
container.bind<OrderRepository>('OrderRepository').to(PostgresOrderRepository);
// Bind event publisher port to Kafka adapter
container.bind<EventPublisher>('EventPublisher').to(KafkaEventPublisher);
// Resolve controller factory
const placeOrder = container.get<PlaceOrder>('PlaceOrder');
```

Java (Spring Framework)

```java
@Configuration
public class ApplicationConfig {
 @Bean
 public PlaceOrder placeOrder(OrderRepository repo, EventPublisher publisher) {
  return new PlaceOrderInteractor(repo, publisher);
 }


 @Bean
 @Profile("prod")
 public OrderRepository postgresOrderRepo(JdbcTemplate jdbc) {
  return new PostgresOrderRepository(jdbc);
 }


 @Bean
 @Profile("dev")
 public OrderRepository inMemoryOrderRepo() {
  return new InMemoryOrderRepository();
 }


 @Bean
 public EventPublisher kafkaPublisher(KafkaTemplate<String, Event> kafka) {
  return new KafkaEventPublisher(kafka);
 }
}
```

C# (.NET Core)

```
public void ConfigureServices(IServiceCollection services) {
  services.AddTransient<PlaceOrder, PlaceOrderInteractor>();
  services.AddScoped<OrderRepository, SqlOrderRepository>();
  services.AddSingleton<EventPublisher, KafkaEventPublisher>();
}
```

A high-level diagram of the DI wiring looks like this:

```
[ DI Container ]
   ├── PlaceOrderInteractor ←— OrderRepository (Postgres / InMemory)
   └── PlaceOrderInteractor ←— EventPublisher (Kafka)
```

Each binding declares exactly which implementation satisfies which port, making the system easy to reconfigure per environment. Unit tests can substitute test doubles by re-binding the ports to mocks or fakes, ensuring consistent behavior without external dependencies.

2.7.3 Layer-Dependency Diagram

Clean Architecture's concentric circles enforce a strict dependency rule: outer layers depend on inner layers, but not vice versa. Below is an ASCII diagram showing these layers and representative modules:

Key points illustrated by this diagram:

1. **Entities** form the nucleus and never import anything from the outer circles.
2. **Interactors** depend only on entity interfaces and output-port interfaces.
3. **Adapters** implement ports defined by inner layers, translating to frameworks.
4. **Drivers** (frameworks, databases, messaging) are the most volatile and sit at the periphery.

This scheme prevents accidental coupling: a domain entity cannot import JDBC classes, and a controller cannot call entity methods directly without going through a use case. Enforcing these rules via static analysis (e.g., ArchUnit, ESLint custom rules) makes architectural drift near impossible.

A more detailed view with packages:

```
com.myapp.entities    ←— (no outgoing deps)
com.myapp.usecases    →— com.myapp.entities
com.myapp.adapters    →— com.myapp.usecases
com.myapp.frameworks  →— com.myapp.adapters
```

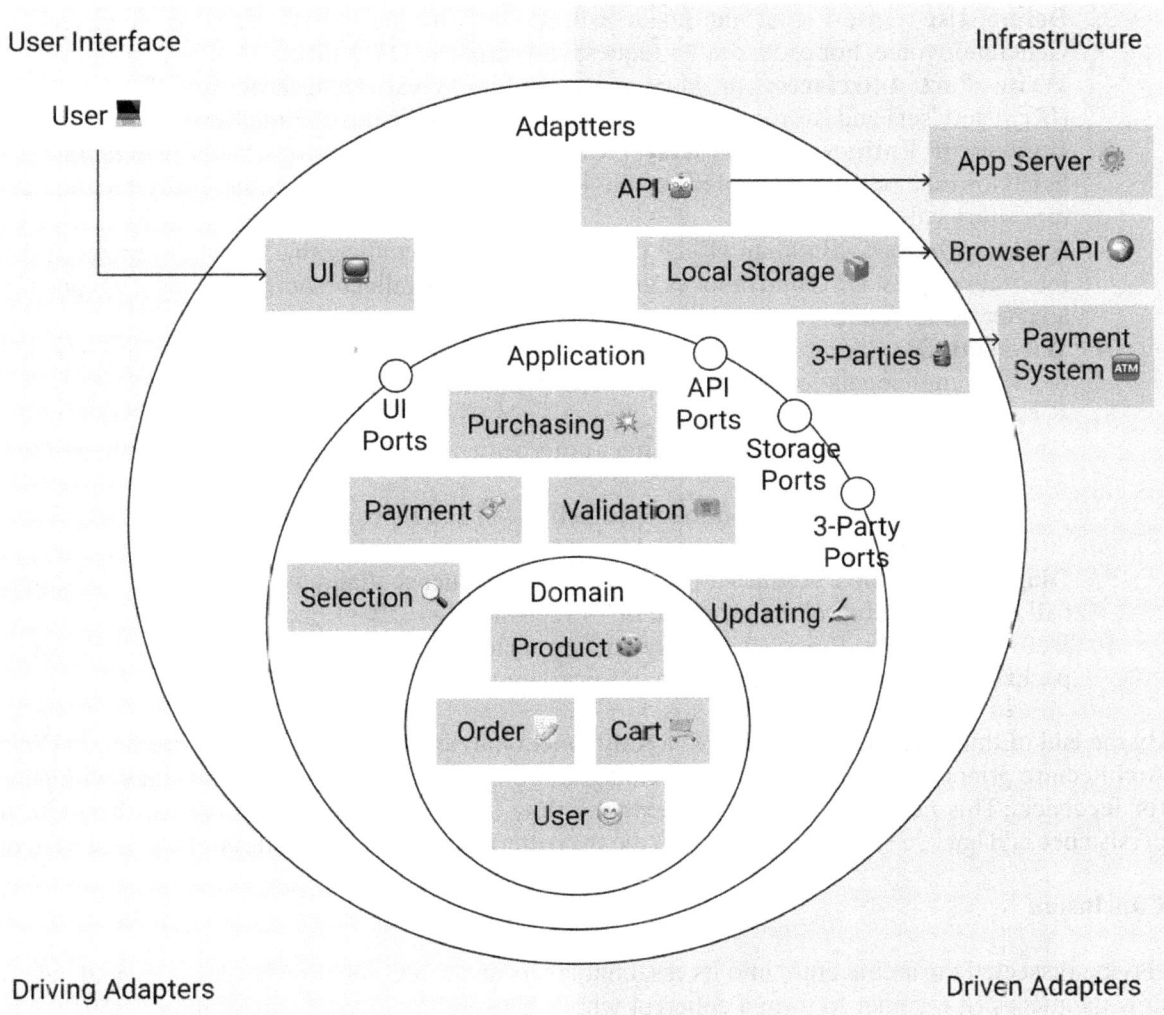

User Interface

Infrastructure

Driving Adapters

Driven Adapters

Integrating CI checks on layer dependencies ensures every pull request upholds this architecture, keeping the dependency graph simple and maintainable as the codebase grows.

2.7.4 Hands-On Exercise

To internalize these building blocks, complete the following step-by-step exercise. It simulates turning a simple feature into a clean-architected module.

1. **Choose a Feature:** Select a small, self-contained feature in your codebase (e.g., "Register User" or "Create Invoice").
2. **Draw the Domain Model:** On paper or whiteboard, sketch the core entities involved, their attributes, and behaviors. Identify invariants (e.g., "email must be unique," "invoice total ≥ 0").

3. **Define Use Cases:** List the main workflows (driving ports) such as RegisterUser, GenerateInvoice. For each, draft a request and response DTO shape.

4. **Write Port Interfaces:** In your core module, create interfaces for the use cases (IRegisterUser) and for required infrastructure (UserRepository, EmailService).

5. **Implement Entities & Interactors:** Code the entities with constructor validations and behavior methods. Then implement the interactor classes, coordinating entity creation and repository calls.

6. **Create Adapters:** Build an HTTP controller (or CLI handler) that translates protocol data into your request DTO and invokes the interactor. In a parallel branch, implement a repository adapter using your preferred ORM or raw SQL.

7. **Wire with DI:** Configure your DI container to bind ports to adapters—start with in-memory or mock implementations, then swap to real persistence and email adapters.

8. **Write Automated Tests:**
   o **Unit tests** for entities (invariant enforcement) and interactors (happy path and error cases).
   o **Adapter tests** for controllers (mock ports) and repositories (in-memory DB).
   o **Contract tests** for external API adapters if applicable.

9. **Diagram the Flow:** Produce an ASCII or UML sequence diagram capturing the end-to-end call chain from controller → interactor → repository → DB → back.

10. **Reflect & Iterate:** Review your code for any accidental dependencies crossing layers. Adjust packages or import statements to re-enforce boundaries.

By the end of this exercise, you will have a fully functional, testable feature built according to Clean Architecture principles. You'll also have the diagrams and test results as artifacts to share with peers for feedback. This hands-on practice cements the flow from HTTP request to domain behavior to persistence and back, ensuring you can replicate the pattern for other features throughout your system.

Conclusion

Having dissected the architecture into its essential layers and roles, you now possess a mental map of how the pieces fit together to form a coherent whole. The entities at your core remain untouched by framework concerns; the interactor layer orchestrates workflows with expressive interfaces; adapters handle the messy details of I/O, and drivers plug into real-world technologies without contaminating business rules. Equipped with these building blocks, you're ready to explore the patterns and practices that govern their composition—discover how ports and adapters weave through your code, how dependency rules enforce clean separations, and how communication flows between layers. In the next chapter, we'll bring these elements to life by examining dependency management and inversion of control, showing you how to wire your modules into a living, breathing application that scales with confidence.

Chapter 3. Managing Dependencies & Inversion of Control

In any nontrivial codebase, how modules depend on one another can make or break maintainability and testability. This chapter tackles the art of controlling those relationships: defining clear rules about who calls whom, in which direction dependencies may flow, and how implementations are wired together at runtime. You'll see why pushing all decisions about concrete classes to the edges of the system protects your core business logic from churn in frameworks and libraries. We'll explore principles that invert traditional coupling—letting high-level policies drive low-level details—and demonstrate patterns that turn dependency chaos into predictable, verifiable wiring. Whether you choose a lightweight, hand-rolled factory or a full-featured IoC container, you'll learn strategies to keep your modules loosely connected, your tests fast and reliable, and your deployment configurations clear and declarative.

3.1 The Dependency Rule in Practice

3.1.1 Understanding the Dependency Rule

The Dependency Rule mandates that **all source-code dependencies must point inward**, from outer layers toward the core, never the other way around. This simple axiom preserves the integrity of your domain model by preventing high-level business logic from becoming entangled with low-level technical details. When inner layers remain ignorant of frameworks, databases, and UI concerns, they become inherently more stable and easier to test. Outer layers, in turn, can evolve freely—swapping HTTP libraries, database engines, or messaging systems—without forcing changes into the nucleus of your application. Violations of this rule often manifest as domain classes importing persistence or UI packages, or as adapters reaching directly into core entity implementations. Such breaches create a brittle coupling that makes refactoring perilous and bug fixes risky. To enforce the rule, teams commonly employ static-analysis tools—like ArchUnit for Java or custom ESLint rules for JavaScript—that flag forbidden dependencies at build time. Complementing automated checks, code-review guidelines reinforce the inward-only flow: reviewers look for any import or include that crosses outward. Over successive sprints, developers internalize this directional constraint, naturally partitioning code into concentric circles. Ultimately, the Dependency Rule provides a robust guardrail: it keeps business policies at the center, cleanly insulated from the ever-shifting landscape of external frameworks.

```
// In the core layer (no framework imports)
public interface UserRepository {
  User findById(UUID id);
}


// In an adapter layer (allowed inward dependency)
public class SqlUserRepository implements UserRepository {
  private final JdbcTemplate jdbc;
  public User findById(UUID id) {
    // JDBC logic here
  }
}
```

Problems
- Layers are highly coupled and dependent each other
- Code Organization hard to maintain
- Locking of frameworks hard to change

Solutions
- Clean Architecture
- The Dependecy Rule

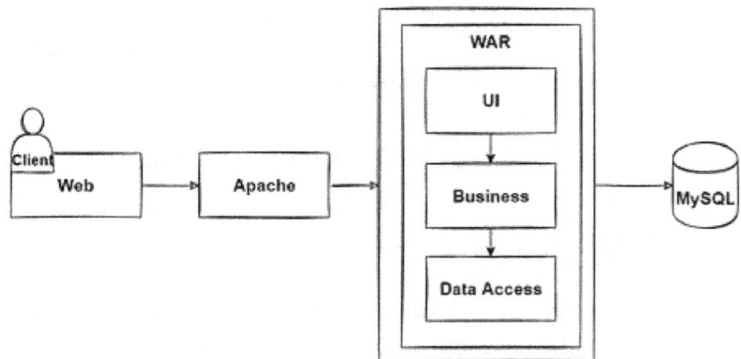

3.1.2 Dependency Flow in Concentric Layers

Clean Architecture arranges code in **concentric circles**, with each ring representing a layer of responsibility. The innermost circle houses **Entities**, which encapsulate pure business rules.

Surrounding that are **Use-Case Interactors**, orchestrating workflows and application logic. Next come **Interface Adapters**, translating between inner constructs and external formats. The outermost ring contains **Frameworks & Drivers**, where actual libraries and protocols live. Dependencies must flow only from outer circles inward—never the reverse. If an adapter attempts to import an entity, that's acceptable; if an entity attempts to import an adapter, it breaks the rule.

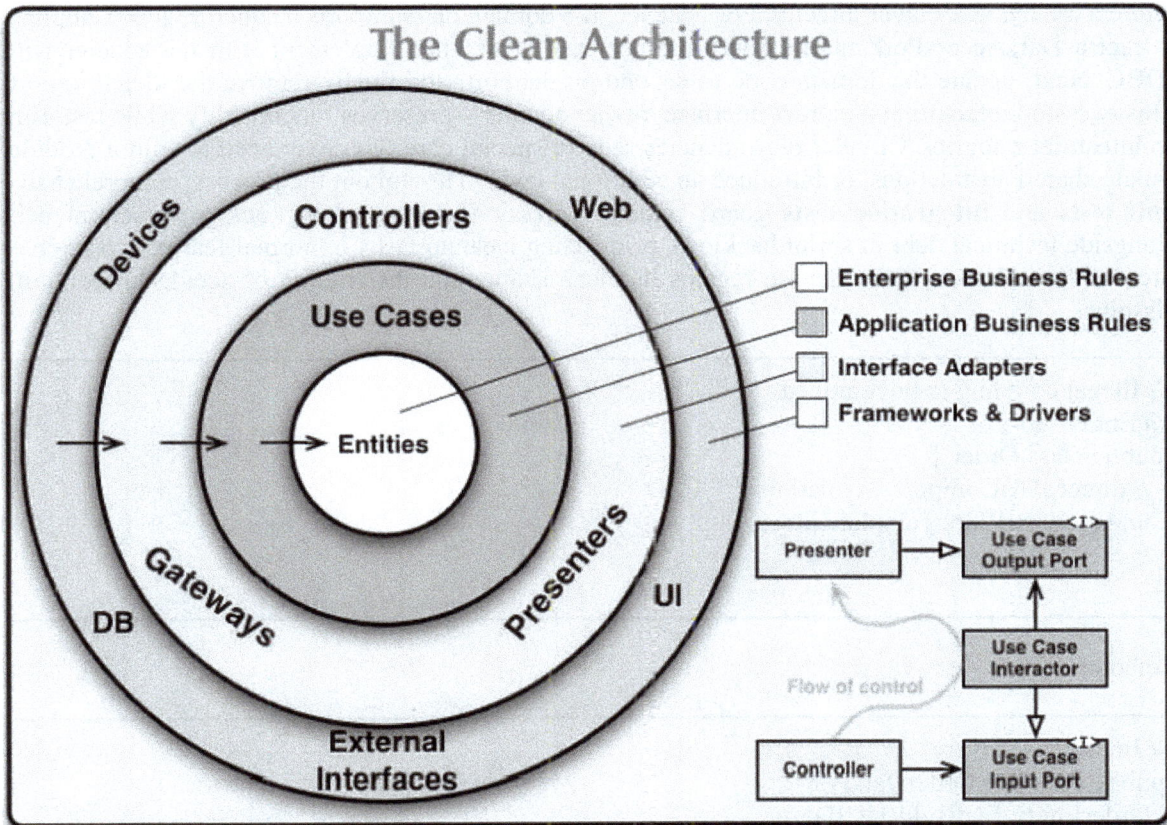

https://blog.cleancoder.com/uncle-bob/2012/08/13/the-clean-architecture.html

To maintain this flow, code organization must mirror the diagram: packages or modules align with layers, and import rules enforce the arrows. Modern build tools can fail the build if a module in one layer illegally imports from another. Over time, the clear layering fosters mental models of where code belongs, speeding both development and onboarding. It also enables independent workstreams: front-end engineers focus on adapters, while domain experts refine entities without stepping on each other's toes.

3.1.3 Identifying & Repairing Violations

47

Even with strict layering, violations inevitably creep in—especially during rapid feature work or spikes of technical debt. The first step in remediation is **identification**. Tools like **ArchUnit** (Java), **Structure101**, or custom **ESLint** rules can scan the codebase and list disallowed dependencies. For example, an ArchUnit test might assert that no class in com.myapp.entities depends on com.myapp.adapters. Once violations are flagged, teams need a **repair strategy**. A common pattern is to introduce a new **port interface** in the inner layer and have the outer layer adapt to it, instead of referencing the inner layer directly. For instance, if a domain class imports a concrete JdbcTemplate, extract a DataAccessPort interface into the use-case layer, then implement it in the adapter with JDBC. Next, update the domain code to depend on the port, and finally remove the illegal import. This two-step refactoring—extract interface, rewire adapter—preserves functionality while restoring architectural integrity. Circular dependencies require special care: you may need to split a module, isolate shared abstractions, or introduce an additional layer. Throughout the process, comprehensive **unit tests** and **integration tests** guard against regression. Teams often track architectural debt alongside technical debt in sprint backlogs, prioritizing cleanup tasks in normal feature work. Over successive iterations, the codebase regains its clean shape, and the friction of accidental coupling dissolves.

```java
// Illegal coupling to be removed
@Entity
public class Order {
  // direct JDBC import—violation!
  @Autowired JdbcTemplate jdbc;
  // ...
}
```

Refactor into:

```java
// In use-case layer
public interface OrderDataPort {
  OrderEntity findById(UUID id);
}



// In adapter layer
public class JdbcOrderDataAdapter implements OrderDataPort {
  @Autowired JdbcTemplate jdbc;
  // implement methods
}
```

3.1.4 Visualizing Dependencies with Graph Tools

Understanding complex dependency graphs by reading import statements alone can be daunting. **Graph visualization tools** like **Graphviz** or commercial products such as **Deptective** provide a high-level overview of module relationships. You can generate a **DOT** file that encodes nodes (packages or modules) and edges (dependencies) and render it into a navigable diagram. For example:

```
digraph CleanArch {
 rankdir=LR;
 Entities -> UseCases;
 UseCases -> Adapters;
 Adapters -> Drivers;
 // Any arrow from Entities to Adapters would show up as a red violation
}
```

Rendering this produces a clear left-to-right flow of dependencies. Teams often color-code nodes: red for violation hotspots, green for compliant modules, yellow for areas under refactoring. Interactive viewers let you click on a node to highlight all its inbound and outbound edges, quickly locating unexpected couplings. In large codebases, **clustered graphs** group related submodules, reducing visual clutter. Beyond static diagrams, some tools can track **dependency churn over time**, showing how architectural health improves or degrades as code evolves. By scheduling regular graph snapshots—say, weekly—teams maintain a visual pulse on architectural drift. Incorporating these diagrams into documentation ensures that new team members quickly grasp the intended layering, accelerating onboarding and reducing accidental rule violations.

3.2 Dependency Inversion Principle (DIP)

3.2.1 High-Level Policies vs. Low-Level Details

The **Dependency Inversion Principle (DIP)** complements the Dependency Rule by specifying that **high-level modules should not depend on low-level modules; both should depend on abstractions**. In practice, this means you define **policy interfaces**—representing business intentions—in the core, and have concrete implementations reside at the periphery. For example, instead of hard-coding email-sending logic inside a use-case, you declare an IEmailSender interface in the application layer:

```
public interface IEmailSender {
 void Send(EmailMessage msg);
}
```

Then, in an outer layer, you implement it:

```
public class SmtpEmailSender : IEmailSender {
 public void Send(EmailMessage msg) {
 // SMTP protocol details
```

```
  }
 }
```

This design ensures that your business workflows remain detached from transport mechanics. It also allows **parallel development**: one team can work on new business rules against the interface, while another builds and optimizes the SMTP adapter. When requirements change—say, migrating to a transactional email API—the swap is confined to the adapter. DIP thus fosters **modularity**, **testability**, and **evolvability** by inverting who depends on whom. High-level modules express what needs to happen, low-level modules express how it happens, and abstractions connect them in a technology-agnostic contract.

3.2.2 Abstraction through Interfaces & Contracts

Building effective abstractions requires designing **minimal, intention-revealing interfaces** that capture exactly the operations needed by core logic. Overly broad or generic interfaces become **leaky abstractions**, forcing core code to handle irrelevant methods or types. For instance, rather than a catch-all IDataAccess with ten CRUD methods, split it into focused contracts like IReadRepository<T> and IWriteRepository<T>. A well-designed interface in Java might look like:

```java
public interface PaymentGateway {
  PaymentResult charge(String accountId, Money amount);
}
```

Notice how the interface uses **domain types** (Money) rather than database or HTTP types. This keeps the contract pure and expressive. Interface versioning is also crucial: when you need to add a new method, consider extending the interface or creating a new version (PaymentGatewayV2) to preserve backward compatibility. Document each interface with precise semantics—idempotency guarantees, error codes, performance expectations—so that implementers know exactly what behavior to provide. Coupling your interfaces with **consumer-driven contract tests** further solidifies these contracts, catching mismatches early in CI pipelines.

3.2.3 DIP Benefits: Testability & Modularity

Adhering to DIP yields immediate benefits in **testing** and **modularity**. Because core modules depend only on interfaces, you can inject **test doubles**—mocks or fakes—for every external dependency, enabling **pure unit tests** with zero external I/O. A simple JUnit example:

```java
@Test
void placeOrder_sendsConfirmation() {
 var mockRepo = mock(OrderRepository.class);
 var mockEmail = mock(IEmailSender.class);
 var service = new PlaceOrderInteractor(mockRepo, mockEmail);
```

```
service.placeOrder(orderData);


verify(mockRepo).save(any(Order.class));
verify(mockEmail).send(any(EmailMessage.class));
}
```

Here, the interactor's behavior is verified in isolation, with no real database or SMTP calls. Modularity improves because each component can be developed, versioned, and deployed independently. Teams work on distinct modules—entities, use cases, adapters—without stepping on each other's dependencies. Over time, you measure coupling by counting interface-to-implementation mappings: a lower ratio signifies a more modular design. Refactoring also becomes safer: you can swap in optimized or experimental adapters behind the same interface without breaking core logic.

3.2.4 Common DIP Anti-Patterns

Even seasoned teams fall prey to DIP anti-patterns that undermine its benefits. One such pitfall is creating **overly generic interfaces**—for example, a IRepository<T> with methods you never use. This bloats the contract, forces mocks to implement unused methods, and masks the true intentions of the abstraction. Another is **leaking implementation types** in method signatures: returning a SqlDataReader from a repository interface ties core logic to ADO.NET, defeating the purpose of the abstraction. Instead, wrap results in domain types or DTOs before they cross the boundary. A third anti-pattern is **bidirectional coupling**, where core code depends on an interface, but the interface also references core-level types inappropriately, creating subtle circularities. The remedy is to extract shared abstractions into a separate package or module that neither layer treats as core. By recognizing and refactoring these anti-patterns—splitting interfaces, isolating true domain types, and reorganizing modules—you restore the clarity and resilience that DIP promises.

3.3 Inversion of Control Techniques

3.3.1 Constructor Injection

Constructor injection is the most straightforward IoC technique: you declare dependencies as parameters in a class's constructor, and a DI container (or manual code) provides the concrete implementations. This approach makes dependencies explicit and ensures that a class cannot be instantiated without its required collaborators, promoting **immutability** and **clear ownership**. For example, in TypeScript with Inversify:

```
@injectable()
class OrderService {
```

```
constructor(
 @inject("OrderRepository") private readonly repo: OrderRepository,
 @inject("IEmailSender") private readonly emailSender: IEmailSender
) {}
}
```

Here, OrderService cannot exist without both an OrderRepository and an IEmailSender. This explicitness aids readability and prevents hidden dependencies. In tests, you simply pass mock implementations to the constructor:

```
const mockRepo = { save: jest.fn() };
const mockEmail = { send: jest.fn() };
const service = new OrderService(mockRepo, mockEmail);
```

No container is needed in unit tests, keeping them lightweight and fast. Constructor injection also aligns with **SOLID** principles, as the dependency graph becomes visible in class signatures, and classes remain closed for modification but open for extension.

3.3.2 Setter / Property Injection

Setter (or property) injection allows optional dependencies to be provided after object construction, useful for breaking circular dependencies or configuring optional behaviors. In C#, you might see:

```
public class ReportGenerator {
[Inject]
public ILogger Logger { private get; set; }


public void Generate(ReportData data) {
 Logger?.Log("Generating report");
 // generation logic...
}
}
```

Here, Logger is not mandatory for the object's core behavior; if it's not set, the code guards against null. This pattern can mitigate circular references when two services depend on each other, but it also introduces **mutable state** and **hidden dependencies**—users of the class cannot tell from the constructor that a dependency is required for full functionality. To minimize risk, document setter-injected properties clearly and use null checks or defaults. Setter injection is best reserved for truly optional collaborators or plugin scenarios where dependencies emerge dynamically.

3.3.3 Interface Injection

Interface injection is a less common IoC style where a dependency injector calls a special method on the target object, passing in the required collaborator. The class implements an injector interface:

```
public class AuditLogger implements Loggable {
  private LoggerBackend backend;


  @Override
  public void setLoggerBackend(LoggerBackend backend) {
    this.backend = backend;
  }
  public void log(String msg) {
    backend.write(msg);
  }
}
```

Here, AuditLogger doesn't receive its LoggerBackend via constructor or setter, but through the setLoggerBackend method defined by the Loggable interface. This approach can be useful in plugin architectures where components are discovered and wired at runtime. However, it obscures dependencies behind interface contracts and is rarely used in mainstream DI frameworks. Where supported, it can decouple injection mechanics from class design but should be applied judiciously to avoid hidden coupling.

3.3.4 Ambient Context Pattern

The **Ambient Context** pattern provides a globally accessible context object—often a static or thread-local holder—that resolves dependencies on demand. For example, a static ServiceLocator.Current property might return a configured container:

```
public static class ServiceLocator {
  public static IServiceProvider Current { get; set; }
}


// usage
var repo = ServiceLocator.Current.GetService<IOrderRepository>();
```

While convenient, ambient contexts introduce **hidden dependencies** and make code harder to test, because any component can reach out to the global context instead of having dependencies injected explicitly. They also risk tight coupling to the context implementation. Use this pattern sparingly—typically for legacy integration or when migrating a brownfield application where refactoring all constructors at once is impractical. Whenever possible, prefer explicit injection to maintain clarity and testability.

3.3.5 Service Locator Pattern

The **Service Locator** pattern centralizes dependency resolution in a registry or locator object. Code that needs a service asks the locator:

```
$repo = ServiceLocator::getInstance()->get('OrderRepository');
$repo->save($order);
```

This approach hides the wiring details from consuming classes, giving them a simple static call to fetch dependencies. However, it suffers from the same drawbacks as the Ambient Context pattern— hidden dependencies, difficulty in unit testing, and the temptation to overuse the locator for convenience. Modern best practices view the service locator as an **anti-pattern**, favoring constructor injection or factories. If you must use a service locator—for example, in legacy code where refactoring is incremental—limit its scope, encapsulate calls behind well-named factory methods, and gradually migrate to explicit injection.

Each of these subsections unpacks the nuances of managing dependencies and applying inversion of control, combining theoretical foundations with practical code examples and diagrams to guide you in building and maintaining a clean, loosely coupled architecture.

3.4 Dependency Injection Containers & Frameworks

3.4.1 Overview of Popular DI Frameworks

Dependency Injection (DI) containers simplify wiring by automatically resolving and instantiating classes based on configured bindings. Spring (Java) is arguably the most mature, using annotations like @Component and @Autowired to scan and inject beans. Guice (Java) offers a lightweight, code-first API where you define modules in Java rather than XML, promoting type safety. Dagger (Java/Kotlin) generates DI code at compile time, avoiding reflection and improving startup performance—ideal for Android. In the Node.js world, InversifyJS uses TypeScript decorators and a fluent API to bind interfaces to classes. .NET's Microsoft.Extensions.DependencyInjection provides a simple, convention-free container built into ASP .NET Core, with extension points for scopes and factories. Each framework balances features—like AOP support, circular dependency detection, and module loading—against startup cost and complexity. For example, Spring's reflection-heavy scanning can add seconds to cold-start time, whereas Dagger's compile-time code gen yields near-zero overhead at runtime. Guice sits in the middle, trading a small reflection cost for a concise API. InversifyJS leverages TypeScript's metadata capabilities, making container setup intuitive for JavaScript developers. Choosing the right container often depends on your team's familiarity, performance constraints, and ecosystem integration. To compare:

Framework	Language	Config Style	Reflection	Compile-time	AOP Support	Startup Impact
Spring	Java	Annotations/XML	High	No	Yes	Medium–High
Guice	Java	Code Modules	Medium	No	Limited	Medium
Dagger	Java/Kotlin	Code/Annotations	None	Yes	No	Low
InversifyJS	TypeScript	Decorators/Code	Medium	No	No	Medium
.NET DI	C#/F#	Code-first	Low	No	Limited	Low

Understanding these trade-offs helps you select a container that aligns with your performance, maintainability, and team skill requirements.

3.4.2 Configuration Styles

DI frameworks typically support multiple configuration styles: **annotation-driven**, **XML/JSON**, and **code-first** (fluent APIs). Annotation-driven configuration embeds metadata directly in classes. For instance, Spring's @Component and @Inject annotations require minimal external configuration and reduce boilerplate. However, they couple your code to the DI framework's annotations, complicating reuse outside a DI context. XML or JSON configuration externalizes wiring into separate files—Spring XML or .NET XML configuration—keeping classes free of framework annotations. This style is verbose but enables reconfiguration without recompilation, useful for multi-environment setups. Modern teams often favor code-first configuration, where modules or service registration calls live in a language-native API. Guice's AbstractModule and .NET's IServiceCollection use fluent methods like bind() or AddTransient() to configure dependencies. Code-first strikes a balance: classes remain framework-agnostic, wiring is type-safe and refactor-friendly, and configuration is centralized. Example in Spring (annotation):

```
@Component
public class OrderService {
 private final OrderRepository repo;
 @Autowired
 public OrderService(OrderRepository repo) { this.repo = repo; }
```

```
}
```

Code-first in .NET:

```
services.AddScoped<IOrderRepository, SqlOrderRepository>();
services.AddTransient<OrderService>();
```

XML in Spring:

```
<bean id="orderService" class="com.myapp.OrderService">
 <constructor-arg ref="orderRepository" />
</bean>
```

Choosing a style depends on organizational standards, the need for externalizing configuration, and the desire to minimize framework annotations in domain code.

3.4.3 Lifecycle Scopes

DI containers offer **lifecycle scopes** that govern how many instances of a service are created and how long they live. Common scopes include **Transient** (a new instance per request/resolution),

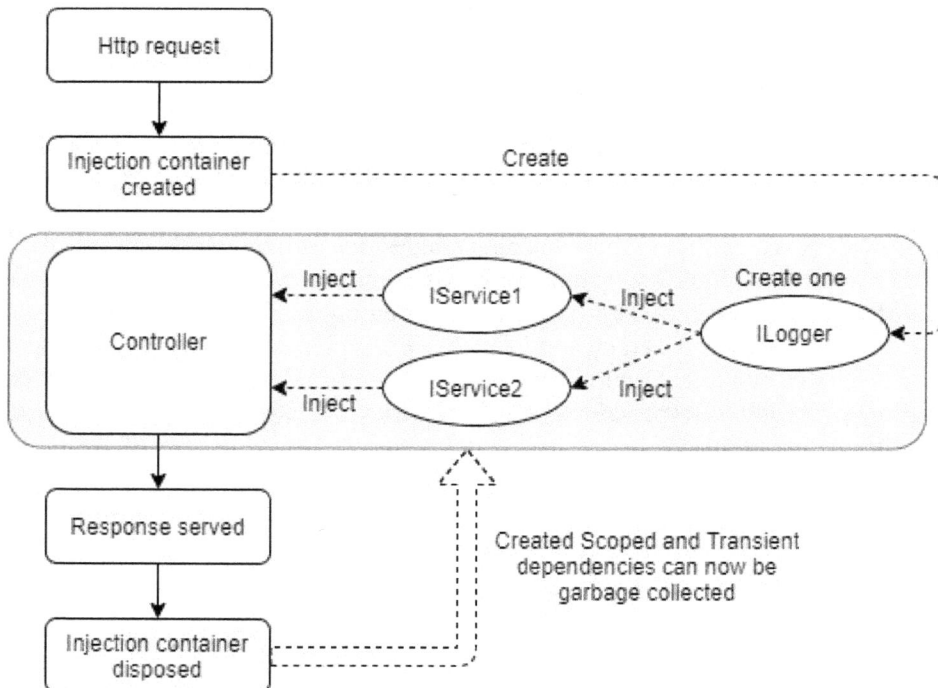

Singleton (one instance for the application lifetime), and **Scoped** (one instance per logical operation, such as an HTTP request). In Spring, @Scope("prototype") yields transient behavior, while the default singleton provides one bean per container. ASP .NET Core's AddTransient(), AddScoped(), and AddSingleton() mirror this pattern. Choosing the right scope is critical: singletons minimize memory and initialization overhead but must be thread-safe. Transients avoid shared state but can increase garbage collection pressure. Scoped lifetimes strike a balance for per-request state, such as database contexts in web applications. Lifecycle scopes also impact disposal: disposable resources tied to scoped instances must be properly released at the end of the scope. For example, an Entity Framework DbContext registered as scoped ensures it shares a transaction per HTTP request and is disposed automatically after the response. A diagram of scopes:

Understanding scopes prevents subtle bugs like shared state corruption in singletons or resource leaks in transients.

3.4.4 Modular Configuration & Composition

Large applications benefit from **modular DI configuration**, where each feature or bounded context manages its own set of bindings. In Guice, you create separate AbstractModule subclasses—for orders, customers, and payments—and then compose them at startup:

```
Injector injector = Guice.createInjector(
 new OrdersModule(),
 new CustomersModule(),
 new PaymentsModule()
);
```

In .NET, you can define extension methods for IServiceCollection:

```
services.AddOrdersModule()
   .AddCustomersModule()
   .AddPaymentsModule();
```

This modular approach improves maintainability by grouping related bindings and reducing coupling between features. It also enables **dynamic module loading** in plugin architectures: you can discover and load feature assemblies at runtime, scanning for modules via reflection or a manifest file. OSGi in Java or Webpack's code-splitting in JavaScript follow similar principles, allowing lazy loading of components.

Modular configuration also supports **environment-specific bindings** by conditionally loading modules based on profiles or command-line flags. For example, a DevDatabaseModule may bind repositories to in-memory implementations, while ProdDatabaseModule binds to real databases. This flexibility enhances testability and simplifies deployment pipelines.

3.4.5 Performance Considerations

While DI containers boost productivity, they can incur performance costs, especially at application startup. Reflection-based containers (Spring, Guice) scan classpaths and analyze metadata, adding milliseconds or seconds to initialization time. Dagger and compile-time containers pre-generate factories to eliminate runtime reflection, yielding near-native performance. To optimize, measure container startup time using benchmarks and consider eager vs. lazy initialization. Eager singletons preload dependencies at startup, making first requests faster but delaying application readiness. Lazy singletons instantiate on demand, distributing initialization cost over time. Containers may support caching resolved dependencies—ensuring that repeated resolutions of the same type reuse instances—but at the expense of increased memory usage. Some frameworks allow you to disable circular dependency checks in production to reduce overhead. In high-throughput services, you can bypass the container at runtime by using factory methods or service locators for performance-critical paths. Always profile both cold and warm starts in representative environments. Diagram of DI performance trade-offs:

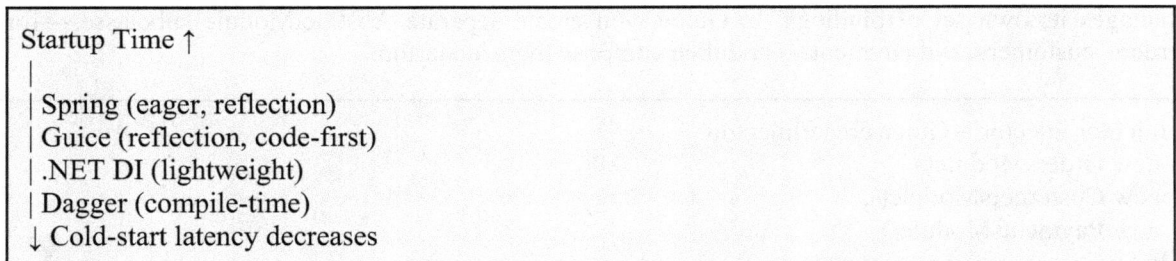

```
Startup Time ↑
|
| Spring (eager, reflection)
| Guice (reflection, code-first)
| .NET DI (lightweight)
| Dagger (compile-time)
↓ Cold-start latency decreases
```

Balancing developer ergonomics and runtime efficiency ensures your DI strategy supports both rapid iteration and production performance.

3.5 Manual Dependency Management

3.5.1 The Composition Root

The **Composition Root** is the single place in your application where you wire up the entire object graph. According to best practices, it should be located in the entry point of your program—main() method, web application initializer, or command-line bootstrapper. By centralizing all bindings, you avoid scattered new calls throughout your code, making dependency changes simple and predictable. A typical Java main() might look like:

```
public class App {
 public static void main(String[] args) {
  Injector injector = Guice.createInjector(
   new ApplicationModule(),
   new InfrastructureModule()
  );
  Application app = injector.getInstance(Application.class);
  app.run();
 }
}
```

Here, the App class assembles all modules and then retrieves the top-level Application object, which already has all its dependencies injected. The Composition Root ensures that core modules never depend on DI code—only the root knows about Guice or Spring. In ASP .NET Core, Program.cs plays this role, calling CreateHostBuilder() to configure services before building and running the host. A clear Composition Root simplifies brownfield refactoring: you incrementally extract wiring from ad-hoc initializers into a structured root without touching business code. Diagrammatically:

```
[Composition Root]
    ├── Binds Use-Cases
    ├── Binds Repositories
    ├── Binds Adapters
    └── Starts Application
```

Maintaining a well-defined Composition Root enhances clarity, debugging, and onboarding.

3.5.2 Factory & Builder Patterns

When a full DI container is overkill—or in environments without one—the **Factory** and **Builder** patterns provide manual wiring with explicit code. A Factory encapsulates complex creation logic:

```
def create_order_service():
 repo = PostgresOrderRepository(db_connection())
 email = SmtpEmailSender(smtp_config())
 return OrderService(repo, email)
```

Here, create_order_service() centralizes instantiation details, so callers simply call the factory rather than using new everywhere. The Builder pattern steps through construction in phases, ideal for objects with many optional parameters:

```
OrderService service = new OrderServiceBuilder()
  .withRepository(new SqlOrderRepo())
  .withEmailSender(new SmtpSender())
  .enableLogging()
  .build();
```

Builders improve readability and prevent combinatorial constructor explosion. Factories and Builders both keep wiring code separate from business logic, preserving SRP. They also support conditional configurations: a factory can inspect environment variables and choose between real and mock implementations. Although manual, this approach offers the same benefits of DI—loose coupling and testability—without container overhead. When projects outgrow simple factories, you can migrate factory logic into a DI container by registering factory methods as providers.

3.5.3 Service Locators vs. Factories

The **Service Locator** pattern uses a global registry to resolve dependencies at runtime, whereas factories explicitly construct objects. With a service locator:

```
$service = ServiceLocator::get('OrderService');
$service->placeOrder($dto);
```

While concise, it hides dependencies behind static calls, making testing harder because you must configure the locator for each test. Factories, by contrast, expose dependencies in function signatures and return constructed instances, improving transparency. For example:

```
$factory = new OrderServiceFactory($orderRepoLocator, $emailSenderLocator);
$service = $factory->create();
```

Here, the factory's constructor clearly documents which locators it uses. Service locators also tend to accumulate global state and can become a dumping ground for miscellaneous services. Refactoring away from service locators involves introducing factories or constructor injection, gradually removing ServiceLocator::get() calls. Diagram:

```
[Caller] ——▶ ServiceLocator ——▶ [OrderRepo]
[Caller] ——▶ Factory        ——▶ [OrderRepo]
```

Factories keep wiring code explicit and constrained to a few classes, whereas service locators can spread hidden dependencies throughout your codebase.

3.5.4 Gradual Adoption in Legacy Codebases

Brownfield applications often start with tightly coupled code littered with new operators. To introduce IoC gradually, begin by identifying a small, self-contained feature—such as notification sending—and extract its wiring into a **mini composition root**. Create factory methods or small modules to construct the feature's objects, and update callers to use the factory instead of direct new calls. Introduce interfaces for key dependencies, refactor concrete classes to depend on these interfaces, and implement adapters that satisfy them. Over successive sprints, expand this pattern to adjacent features, eventually converging on a unified Composition Root. During this transition, maintain backward compatibility by leaving legacy code paths intact, while gradually directing new development through the emerging IoC infrastructure. Leverage **branch-by-abstraction**: introduce an abstraction layer before migrating implementation, ensuring the system remains stable. Document each step and involve multiple team members to spread knowledge. Diagram of incremental migration:

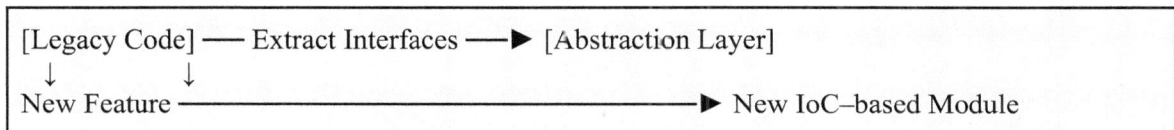

```
[Legacy Code] —— Extract Interfaces ——▶ [Abstraction Layer]
      ↓              ↓
New Feature ————————————————————————————▶ New IoC–based Module
```

This incremental approach balances the urgency of feature delivery with the strategic goal of cleaner architecture, reducing risk and fostering team confidence in the migration.

3.6 Testing with Inversion of Control

3.6.1 Unit Testing with Mocked Dependencies

```
@Test
void placeOrder_savesAndEmails() {
 OrderRepository mockRepo = mock(OrderRepository.class);
 IEmailSender mockEmail = mock(IEmailSender.class);
 PlaceOrderInteractor interactor = new PlaceOrderInteractor(mockRepo, mockEmail);


 PlaceOrderRequest req = new PlaceOrderRequest(...);
 PlaceOrderResponse resp = interactor.execute(req);


 verify(mockRepo).save(any(Order.class));
 verify(mockEmail).send(any(EmailMessage.class));
 assertTrue(resp.isSuccess());
}
```

Unit tests verify individual classes in isolation by **mocking** their dependencies, a practice made straightforward by IoC. For a PlaceOrderInteractor, you mock its OrderRepository and IEmailSender ports.

This test runs in milliseconds because no real database or SMTP server is involved. Mocking frameworks like Mockito (Java), Sinon (JavaScript), or unittest.mock (Python) let you specify return values, throw exceptions, and verify interactions. Tests focus on behavior: did the interactor call the right methods under various conditions? You can simulate exceptional cases—repository failures, email errors—and assert that the interactor handles them gracefully. By keeping mocks local to tests, you avoid polluting production code with test-only logic. Rapid feedback from unit tests enables true Test-Driven Development (TDD), driving clean API design and explicit dependency contracts.

3.6.2 Fake Implementations for Integration Tests

While unit tests validate logic in isolation, **integration tests** verify modules working together. Instead of real dependencies, you use **fake** implementations that mimic behavior without external side effects. For data persistence, an in-memory database such as H2 (Java), SQLite in memory mode (Python), or a mocked repository that stores data in a simple collection suffices:

```
public class InMemoryOrderRepository : IOrderRepository {
 private readonly List<Order> orders = new();
 public void Save(Order order) => orders.Add(order);
 public Order FindById(Guid id) => orders.Single(o => o.Id == id);
}
```

Similarly, you can use a **fake email sender** that records sent messages in a list rather than sending real emails. Integration tests then wire the real interactor with these fakes via the composition root:

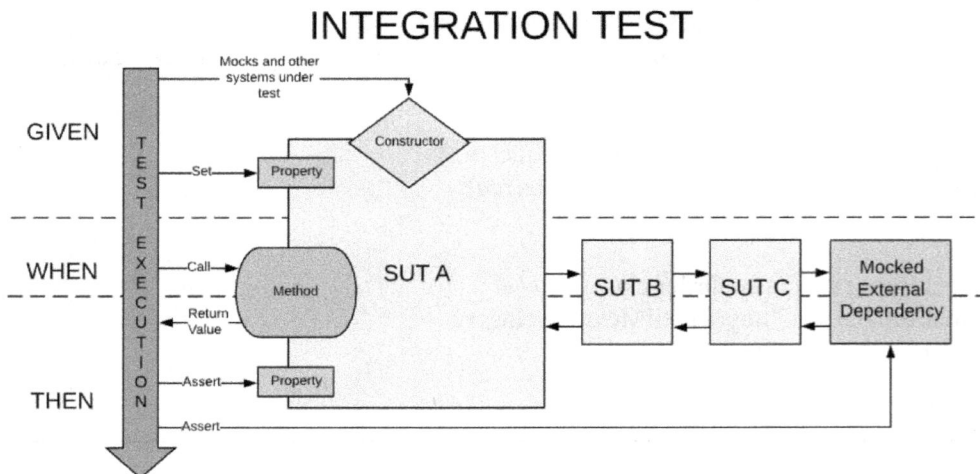

INTEGRATION TEST

```
services.AddScoped<IOrderRepository, InMemoryOrderRepository>();
services.AddSingleton<IEmailSender, FakeEmailSender>();
```

This environment simulates the entire stack—interactors, adapters—but remains fast and repeatable. Integration tests catch wiring mistakes (missing bindings, incorrect configurations) that unit tests cannot. They also verify data mapping and transaction behavior in a lightweight setup. Fakes should replicate production semantics—like primary key generation or error conditions—to make tests meaningful without fragility.

3.6.3 Isolation vs. Integration Testing Strategies

A healthy test suite follows the **testing pyramid**: many fast, isolated unit tests at the base; fewer integration tests in the middle; and very few end-to-end (E2E) tests at the top. Unit tests cover individual classes and boundary conditions. Integration tests exercise multiple components—perhaps a controller, interactor, and repository—using fakes or in-memory stores. End-to-end tests launch the full application stack, including real databases and external services, simulating user workflows. Maintaining a clear separation prevents slow tests from hindering developer feedback loops. Automated CI pipelines often run unit and integration tests on every commit, reserving E2E tests for nightly builds or release stages. Diagram of the pyramid

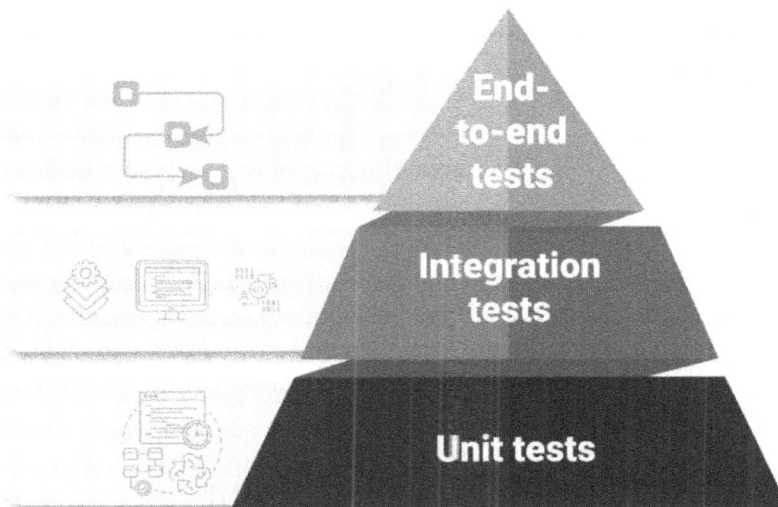

Aligning your IoC strategy with this pyramid means configuring DI containers to support all three layers—explicit bindings for tests, fakes for integration, and real adapters for E2E—so that each test type runs in a context tailored to its purpose.

3.6.4 Configuring DI Containers in Tests

Tests often need to **override or extend** DI container configurations to inject mocks or fakes. In Spring, the @TestConfiguration annotation defines test-specific beans:

```
@TestConfiguration
static class TestConfig {
 @Bean public OrderRepository inMemoryRepo() { return new InMemoryOrderRepository(); }
 @Bean public IEmailSender fakeEmailSender() { return new FakeEmailSender(); }
}
```

With @Import(TestConfig), the test context replaces production beans. In ASP .NET Core, you use a custom WebApplicationFactory to modify the IServiceCollection:

```
public class TestFactory : WebApplicationFactory<Startup> {
 protected override void ConfigureWebHost(IWebHostBuilder builder) {
 builder.ConfigureServices(services => {
  services.RemoveAll<IOrderRepository>();
  services.AddScoped<IOrderRepository, InMemoryOrderRepository>();
 });
 }
}
```

For Guice, you create a **test injector** with test modules:

```
Injector    testInjector    =    Guice.createInjector(new    TestOrdersModule(),    new
InfrastructureModule());
```

Override only the modules you need, leaving the rest unchanged. Keeping test and production containers in parallel structure ensures consistent behavior across environments. Automated tests can spin up containers programmatically, run tests, and tear down resources—all without leaving residues like open connections or background threads. Clear test container configurations reduce flakiness and improve confidence in your DI setup.

3.7 Plugin Architectures & Modularization

3.7.1 Defining Extension Points

Defining clear extension points begins with identifying the exact places in your core logic where variability is anticipated. You declare a **plugin interface**—for example, PaymentMethodPlugin—in your use-case layer, specifying precisely the methods a plugin must implement. Each method in that interface should be minimal and intention-revealing, such as authorize(amount): AuthorizationResult and capture(transactionId): CaptureResult. By keeping the interface narrow, you limit the surface area plugins can affect, reducing the risk of breaking core invariants. It's advisable to document expected behaviors—timeouts, exception semantics, idempotency—in the interface's Javadoc or README so implementers understand the contract. You might annotate the interface with metadata—using Java's @SPI or a custom annotation—to mark it as an extension point. Downstream, a **PluginManager** or **ServiceLoader** will discover implementations at runtime. This manager lives in the adapter layer, decoupling loading logic from both core and plugin code. You can also group related extension points—such as shipping, taxation, and notifications—into separate packages or modules, making the architecture more composable. Over time, adding a new payment provider then becomes as simple as implementing the PaymentMethodPlugin interface, packaging the JAR (or NPM module), and dropping it into your plugins directory. By designing extension points thoughtfully, you ensure that plugins remain true to business intent and don't inadvertently import or depend on forbidden layers.

```
// In core use-case layer
@SPI
public interface PaymentMethodPlugin {
 AuthorizationResult authorize(PaymentRequest request);
 CaptureResult capture(String transactionId, BigDecimal amount);
}
```

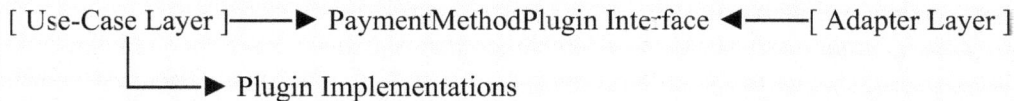

```
[ Use-Case Layer ]———▶ PaymentMethodPlugin Interface ◄———[ Adapter Layer ]
              └——————▶ Plugin Implementations
```

3.7.2 Runtime Module Loading

Once extension points are defined, you need a mechanism to load plugin modules dynamically. In Java, the **ServiceLoader** API reads implementations declared in META-INF/services:

```
ServiceLoader<PaymentMethodPlugin>                loader            =
ServiceLoader.load(PaymentMethodPlugin.class);
for (PaymentMethodPlugin plugin : loader) {
 pluginRegistry.register(plugin);
}
```

In OSGi, you install bundles at runtime and query the OSGi registry for services. In Node.js, you can scan a plugins/ directory for .js files and require() them:

```
fs.readdirSync('./plugins').forEach(file => {
```

```
const plugin = require(`./plugins/${file}`);
container.bind('PaymentMethodPlugin').toConstantValue(plugin);
});
```

Loading modules at runtime introduces ordering and lifecycle concerns: you must define an initialization sequence so that plugins register their routes, database migrations, or event handlers before the application starts accepting requests. You may also need to sandbox plugins to prevent them from calling forbidden APIs—using a custom ClassLoader in Java or VM contexts in Node.js. Configuration files (YAML or JSON) can declare which plugins to enable, their settings, and load order. A robust **PluginManager** handles failures: if one plugin fails to load, the manager logs the error, skips that plugin, and continues initializing the rest, preventing a single broken plugin from taking down the entire system. Monitoring the plugin load process—emitting events like pluginLoaded and pluginLoadFailed—helps in debugging runtime issues.

3.7.3 Ensuring Safe Extensions via Interfaces

Allowing external code to plug into your system demands safeguards to maintain architectural integrity. The primary defense is the **interface boundary**: plugins only see the methods and data types declared in the extension-point interface, not the inner workings of your core or other adapters. You should avoid passing rich domain entities directly—use **DTOs** with only the necessary data. For additional safety, consider **package sealing** (Java's module system) to prevent plugins from accessing internal packages. In Node.js, you can use the vm module to create sandboxes limiting global scope. Runtime checks—such as validating the plugin's manifest version or signature—help ensure only trusted code executes. Contract tests verify plugin behavior against expected interface semantics: for each PaymentMethodPlugin, you run a suite that feeds valid and invalid PaymentRequest objects, asserting correct exception handling and result transformations. You might also implement a **whitelist** of allowed dependencies: each plugin's package.json or MANIFEST.MF lists which modules it may import, and a loader enforces this. Document extension-point invariants clearly, and provide reference implementations to guide plugin authors. By combining interface isolation, sandboxing, and contract testing, you maintain control over plugin interactions without stifling extensibility.

```
// In PluginManager, enforce interface-only access
for (PaymentMethodPlugin plugin : discovered) {
 if (!plugin.getClass().getModule().isExported("com.myapp.plugins")) {
  throw new SecurityException("Plugin not in allowed packages");
 }
 pluginRegistry.register(plugin);
}
```

```
[ PluginCode.js ] sandboxed via vm.createContext({ PaymentAPI })
```

3.7.4 Versioning & Compatibility of Plugins

Managing multiple plugin versions requires a clear **semantic versioning** strategy for both the host application's API and plugin contracts. You label each extension-point interface with a version annotation—e.g., @APIVersion("1.2.0")—and require plugins to declare a plugin-api-version in their manifest. At load time, the **PluginManager** compares the host's supported version range (e.g., ^1.0.0) against each plugin's declared compatibility. If a plugin targets an unsupported major version, the manager rejects it gracefully, logging a clear error. For minor or patch version mismatches, the manager may allow the plugin but emit a deprecation warning, encouraging authors to upgrade. When the host application introduces breaking changes to extension points, you increment the major version and maintain side-by-side support for older plugin APIs via adapters or shims. For example:

```
@APIVersion("2.0.0")
public interface PaymentMethodPluginV2 extends PaymentMethodPluginV1 {
 RefundResult refund(String transactionId, BigDecimal amount);
}
```

A **version negotiation** step in the loader selects the best matching interface—if a plugin implements only V1, it's wrapped with a V1toV2Adapter that throws UnsupportedOperationException for new methods. Visualizing compatibility:

```
Host API v1.x.x ——▶ supports v1.x.x plugins
Host API v2.x.x ——▶ supports v1.x.x (via shim) and v2.x.x plugins
```

By formalizing versioning rules and runtime checks, you prevent silent failures and ensure that plugin authors can plan upgrades in lockstep with your core releases.

3.8 Practical Example: Wiring a Web Application

3.8.1 Composition Root Example Code

Below is a complete **composition root** for a Node.js Express application using InversifyJS as the DI container. This bootstrap code wires controllers, use-cases, and adapters in one place:

```
// composition-root.ts
import 'reflect-metadata';
import express from 'express';
import { Container } from 'inversify';
import { OrderController } from './adapters/OrderController';
import { PlaceOrderInteractor } from './usecases/PlaceOrderInteractor';
import { OrderRepository } from './usecases/ports/OrderRepository';
```

```
import { PostgresOrderRepository } from './adapters/PostgresOrderRepository';
import { PaymentMethodPlugin } from './usecases/ports/PaymentMethodPlugin';
import { StripePlugin } from './plugins/StripePlugin';


const container = new Container();
// Bind use-case interactors
container.bind(PlaceOrderInteractor).toSelf();
// Bind repository port to adapter
container.bind<OrderRepository>('OrderRepository').to(PostgresOrderRepository);
// Bind plugin implementations
container.bind<PaymentMethodPlugin>('PaymentMethodPlugin').to(StripePlugin);
// Bind controllers
container.bind(OrderController).toSelf();


const app = express();
app.use(express.json());
// Resolve controller and register routes
const orderController = container.get(OrderController);
app.post('/orders', orderController.placeOrder);


export { app, container };
```

This single file imports only DI and framework code; neither controllers nor interactors import container logic. The container knows about every module and resolves the full object graph at startup.

```
[ composition-root.ts ]
  ↓
[ DI Container ]
  ↓
[ Controllers ← Interactors ← Adapters ← Plugins ]
```

3.8.2 DI Container Configuration

Container configuration often differs between **development**, **testing**, and **production**. You can externalize bindings into separate modules and load them conditionally based on NODE_ENV or a command-line flag:

```
// config/di-dev.ts
import { Container } from 'inversify';
```

```
import { InMemoryOrderRepository } from '../adapters/InMemoryOrderRepository';
const container = new Container();
container.bind<OrderRepository>('OrderRepository').to(InMemoryOrderRepository);
// other dev-specific bindings...
export default container;
```

```
// config/di-prod.ts
import { Container } from 'inversify';
import { PostgresOrderRepository } from '../adapters/PostgresOrderRepository';
const container = new Container();
container.bind<OrderRepository>('OrderRepository').to(PostgresOrderRepository);
// other prod bindings...
export default container;
```

Then in your bootstrap:

```
import devContainer from './config/di-dev';
import prodContainer from './config/di-prod';
const container = process.env.NODE_ENV === 'production' ? prodContainer : devContainer;
// merge common bindings, then use container as before
```

In Java Spring, the equivalent uses @Profile("dev") and @Profile("prod") on @Configuration classes. In .NET, you can read ASPNETCORE_ENVIRONMENT to decide which IServiceCollection extension methods to call. Centralizing environment-specific bindings makes your application flexible and testable without runtime branching in the business code.

3.8.3 Swapping Implementations On-the-Fly

Sometimes you need to switch implementations without restarting the application—useful for feature flags or A/B testing. You can achieve this by introducing a **proxy adapter** that reads a configuration store on each method invocation:

```
@Injectable()
export class DynamicOrderRepository implements OrderRepository {
 private currentImpl: OrderRepository;
 constructor(
  @inject('SqlOrderRepository') private sqlRepo: OrderRepository,
  @inject('InMemoryOrderRepository') private memRepo: OrderRepository,
  @inject('ConfigService') private config: ConfigService
 ) {}
```

```
private resolve(): OrderRepository {
 return this.config.get('useInMemory') ? this.memRepo : this.sqlRepo;
}
async save(order: Order): Promise<void> {
 return this.resolve().save(order);
}
// similarly for other methods...
}
```

A clients' configuration change—flipping useInMemory—immediately routes subsequent calls to the alternative implementation. You can extend this to swap payment gateways or caching strategies at runtime. For stronger encapsulation, consider using a **Strategy pattern** with a registry of implementations keyed by name, and selecting the strategy based on configuration.

```
[ Service Call ] ──▶ [ Dynamic Proxy ] ──▶ [ Impl A or Impl B ]
```

This technique adds a small performance overhead for the proxy check but provides powerful runtime flexibility for maintenance, canary releases, and operational experiments without redeploying code.

3.8.4 Verifying Dependencies with Static Analysis

To enforce architectural constraints automatically, integrate static analysis into your CI pipeline. For Java projects, **ArchUnit** lets you write tests that fail the build if modules violate rules:

```
@AnalyzeClasses(packages = "com.myapp")
public class DependencyRulesTest {
 @ArchTest
 static final ArchRule noAdaptersInCore = classes()
  .that().resideInAPackage("..core..")
  .should().dependOnClassesThat().resideInAnyPackage("..adapters..");
}
```

In JavaScript/TypeScript, ESLint with the **eslint-plugin-boundaries** plugin can restrict imports by layer:

```
"rules": {
 "boundaries/element-types": [2,
  { "default": "disallow", "rules": [
   { "from": "core", "allow": ["core"] },
   { "from": "adapters", "allow": ["core", "adapters"] }
  ]}
```

```
  ]
  }
```

Running these checks on every pull request catches accidental layer crossings before code merges. For large teams, you can enforce rules centrally in a shared configuration repository. Visual dashboards generated from Graphviz DOT files highlight hotspots and track resolution over time. By combining code-level tests with graphical monitoring, you maintain confidence that your dependency and IoC strategies remain intact as the system evolves.

Conclusion

By mastering dependency management and inversion of control, you gain the leverage to evolve your system with confidence. The guidelines in this chapter show you how to enforce architectural boundaries, inject mock implementations for rapid feedback, and centralize wiring logic so that swapping frameworks or databases becomes a matter of configuration rather than code surgery. When your high-level use cases depend only on abstractions, adding new features, performing refactors, or onboarding new team members transforms from a daunting chore into a streamlined process. With these patterns firmly in place, you'll be ready to focus on delivering business value—secure in the knowledge that the structure of your application can gracefully accommodate whatever the future holds.

Chapter 4. Component Cohesion & Coupling

High cohesion and low coupling lie at the heart of any resilient software system. Cohesion measures how closely related the responsibilities of a single component are, while coupling quantifies the interdependencies between distinct modules. When each component focuses on a single, well-defined purpose, it becomes easier to understand, test, and evolve. Conversely, minimizing unnecessary connections between modules reduces the ripple effects of change, allowing teams to work in parallel without fear of collateral damage. In this chapter, we explore how to quantify these qualities, apply packaging strategies that reinforce them, and leverage refactoring patterns and automated tooling to keep your architecture clean as it scales. Real-world examples and anti-patterns illustrate common pitfalls—such as the "God Class" or shotgun surgery—so you can recognize and correct them early, preserving both developer productivity and code health over time.

4.1 Cohesion Metrics

4.1.1 Single Responsibility & Functional Cohesion

Single Responsibility Principle (SRP) asserts that a module or class should have exactly one reason to change. In practice, this means every method and data member in a class ought to contribute toward a single, well-defined responsibility. For example, consider an OrderProcessor class that both validates orders, calculates totals, and renders invoices. This violates SRP because changes to business rules, tax calculations, or presentation each force edits to the same class. In contrast, a functionally cohesive design extracts each concern into its own module: an OrderValidator, a TotalCalculator, and an InvoiceRenderer. Each of those classes focuses on one task, so a change to invoicing logic never touches validation code.

High functional cohesion reduces the scope of a developer's mental model: to understand or modify a class, they need only think about one concept. Cohesive components are also easier to test—unit tests target a narrow behavior, yielding faster, more reliable feedback. Moreover, cohesive modules encourage reuse: a TotalCalculator used in both an interactive UI and a batch job remains identical, since it has no knowledge of its consumer.

Measuring functional cohesion can be as simple as inspecting method names and fields: if each method operates primarily on the same set of private fields, cohesion is likely high. Tools like SonarQube compute LCOM (Lack of Cohesion of Methods) to flag classes where method pairs share few common attributes. But beyond metrics, code reviews and architectural design sessions should ask: "Does this class do exactly one thing, and do all its operations relate to that single thing?"

When you spot low SRP compliance—classes doing too much—plan refactoring to split responsibilities. Maintain public interfaces so that callers see minimal disruption. Over time, libraries of highly cohesive modules become the bedrock of your system, each with clear ownership and predictable behavior.

4.1.2 Coincidental, Logical & Temporal Cohesion

Not all cohesion is equal. **Coincidental cohesion** is the weakest form, occurring when unrelated functions are grouped arbitrarily. Imagine a utility class SystemUtils containing methods for date formatting, file I/O, and network calls; changes in any of those areas require edits to the same file. This umbrella approach undermines both discoverability and maintainability.

Logical cohesion groups functions by logical category, but they may perform different behaviors based on parameters. For instance, a NotificationService class that sends email, SMS, and push notifications in separate methods exhibits logical cohesion—the category is "notifications," but each method uses completely different protocols and dependencies. While better than coincidental, it still violates SRP because each protocol has unique error-handling, configuration, and testing needs.

Temporal cohesion arises when methods are executed at the same time—such as startup—yet have unrelated tasks. A StartupTasks class that initializes logging, migrates databases, and warms caches demonstrates temporal cohesion: these tasks share only their execution timing, not their logic. While grouping by initialization order makes deployment simple, coupling these operations together means that a failure in cache warming could delay logging setup, introducing interdependencies that are hard to debug.

The goal is **functional cohesion**, where all grouped behaviors contribute to a single well-defined function. Use refactoring patterns like **Extract Class** to move logically distinct concerns into separate modules. For temporal tasks, consider a scheduler or pipeline pattern where each task registers itself rather than hardcoding all startup actions into one class. This lets you adjust execution order, add retries for cache warming, or swap migration strategies independently.

By understanding these cohesion types, you can diagnose structural smells: scan for classes with mixed responsibilities, methods that share no state, or initialization code bundled too tightly. Improving cohesion reduces bug surface area, accelerates feature delivery, and clarifies system intent.

4.1.3 Measuring Cohesion: LCOM Variants

The **Lack of Cohesion in Methods (LCOM)** metric quantifies how methods in a class relate to its fields. LCOM1 compares the number of method-pairs that do not share a field against those that do; high LCOM1 values indicate low cohesion. More advanced variants—LCOM2, LCOM4—use graph-based approaches: build a method graph where nodes are methods and edges connect methods that use the same field; then count connected components. A single connected component implies high cohesion; multiple components signal separated concerns requiring refactoring.

For example, a class with five methods where two groups of methods share disjoint sets of fields yields two components—an LCOM4 of 2. This suggests the class should be split into two or more classes. Tools like SonarQube, CodeClimate, and IntelliJ's metrics plugin compute LCOM and highlight classes exceeding configurable thresholds. Typical best practices aim for LCOM4 = 1; anything above 2 often warrants scrutiny.

However, metrics are guides, not absolutes. Utility classes with only static methods may register poor cohesion despite appropriate design. Therefore, combine metric analysis with code reviews: flag high-LCOM classes for human inspection, then decide if refactoring aligns with project priorities. Over time, track LCOM trends across your codebase: a rising average cohesion score may indicate growing technical debt, whereas a falling score signals healthy refactoring habits.

Using metrics in CI/CD builds—failing only on large regressions—keeps teams aware of architectural health without blocking every commit. Periodic cohesion audits, combined with automated metrics, ensure that your system remains modular and maintainable as it scales.

4.1.4 Improving Cohesion via Refactoring

Refactoring to improve cohesion usually starts with the **Extract Class** or **Extract Module** techniques. Identify clusters of methods and fields that collaborate, then extract them into a new class with a focused name. For example, an OrderProcessor with validation, calculation, and persistence logic can be split into OrderValidator, OrderCalculator, and OrderRepository classes. Each extracted class gets its own file, dependencies, and tests, enforcing SRP and functional cohesion.

When methods share utility code—such as date handling or logging—move those into helper classes or services. Avoid creating catch-all "Helper" classes; instead, group utilities by domain relevance: DateFormatter, AuditLogger, etc. After extraction, update callers to use the new classes. Modern IDEs support automated refactorings that update import statements and method calls reliably.

In more complex scenarios—where cohesion issues span multiple packages—you may need to **Introduce Interface** abstractions to decouple modules before extraction. For instance, if a low-cohesion class directly references both domain entities and UI components, define port interfaces in the domain layer and implement adapters in the UI layer. Then extract domain logic into pure classes while the UI-specific code migrates to adapter packages.

Continuous integration tests guard against semantic regressions during refactoring. Write or update unit tests for each new class to validate behavior. Use test coverage reports to ensure no critical paths are untested after code moves. Over successive refactoring sprints, the codebase's cohesion improves, leading to clearer module boundaries, easier onboarding, and faster feature delivery.

4.1.5 Case Study: Refactoring a Low-Cohesion Module

Imagine a legacy class UserAccountService that handles user registration, authentication, profile updates, password resets, and audit logging. This god-class mixes UI-level flows with business validations and persistence calls. Its LCOM metrics are high: multiple disconnected clusters of methods. Every bug fix—whether a new password policy or an audit-logging tweak—requires navigating a 1,200-line file.

Step 1: Identify Responsibility Clusters Using metrics and IDE usage searches, the team spots four clusters: registration/auth, profile management, password resets, and logging.

Step 2: Extract Domain Logic They create UserAuthenticator, ProfileManager, and PasswordResetManager classes in the domain package, moving corresponding methods and associated data fields. Each class receives focused unit tests verifying only its behavior.

Step 3: Introduce Audit Logger Adapter Audit-logging calls are extracted into an AuditLogger interface in the domain, with implementations—DatabaseAuditLogger and FileAuditLogger—in the adapters layer.

Step 4: Refactor Controller Layer The original controller now depends on focused services:

```
public class UserController {
  private final UserAuthenticator auth;
  private final ProfileManager profile;
  private final PasswordResetManager reset;
  // constructor injection...
  // actions delegate to single-responsibility classes
}
```

Step 5: Verify with Metrics Post-refactoring, SonarQube reports each new class with LCOM4=1. The average class size drops from 400 to 100 lines. Build-time cohesion score rises by 30%.

4.2 Coupling Metrics

4.2.1 Types of Coupling

Coupling describes the degree to which one module depends on another. **Content coupling** (worst) occurs when one module modifies the internal data or code of another—such as calling private methods or manipulating internal data structures directly. This creates a brittle relationship: any internal change breaks the dependent module. **Common coupling** arises when modules share global variables or singletons—updates to globals can have unpredictable ripple effects. **Control coupling** happens when one module passes control flags to another (e.g., process(data, retry=true)), forcing the callee's logic to branch based on upstream decisions. This intertwines flow control and logic across boundaries.

Stamp coupling (also known as data-structure coupling) occurs when modules share composite data structures but use only parts of them. For example, passing a full UserProfile object to a payment module that needs only the user's billing address couples more than necessary. Developers should prefer **data coupling**, where only needed data elements are passed—e.g., passing billingAddress separately. Data coupling is the loose coupling ideal: each module relies solely on explicit data parameters, without hidden dependencies on context or internals.

Strive to eliminate content and common coupling entirely. Replace global state with explicit dependencies (e.g., inject a Configuration service). Refactor control coupling into specialized methods or classes that encapsulate branching logic behind clear intent-revealing interfaces. Audit your codebase with static analysis to flag imports of internal packages, global usage, or direct manipulation of other modules' internals. Over time, reducing coupling increases robustness and parallelizability of the code.

4.2.2 Afferent & Efferent Coupling

Martin's metrics **Afferent Coupling (Ca)** and **Efferent Coupling (Ce)** quantify the number of incoming and outgoing dependencies of a module, respectively. Afferent coupling (Ca) measures how many other modules depend on a given module—high Ca indicates responsibility and potential centrality, but also fragility if that module changes. Efferent coupling (Ce) measures how many modules a given module depends on—high Ce suggests volatility, since many external changes can affect it.

Combine Ca and Ce into the **Instability metric** $I = Ce / (Ca + Ce)$, a value in [0,1]. I near 0 implies stability—many depend on this module but it depends on few—ideal for core libraries or domain entities. I near 1 implies instability—module depends on many but no one depends on it—common for UI adapters or prototypes. Aim to locate critical modules within the balanced region: not too rigid to impede maintenance, yet not so unstable that they break frequently.

Visualizing instability on a scatter plot—with abstractness (proportion of interfaces vs. implementations) on the Y-axis and instability on the X-axis—reveals the "Zone of Uselessness" (high abstractness, high stability) and the "Zone of Pain" (low abstractness, high instability). The ideal "Main Sequence" runs diagonally between the zones, indicating modules that balance abstraction and stability.

Compute Ca and Ce using dependency analysis tools—Structure101, NDepend, or custom scripts parsing import graphs. Generate periodic reports to spot modules drifting into unstable or useless areas, then plan refactoring: increase abstraction for unstable modules or reduce unnecessary dependencies.

4.2.3 Ripple Effect & Change Propagation

High coupling amplifies the **ripple effect**: a small change in one module forces updates in many dependent modules. For example, changing a shared utility function signature can cascade through dozens of callers. The worse the coupling, the farther the ripple travels, increasing risk and hampering agility.

Visualizing call or import graphs helps locate coupling hotspots. Using Graphviz's DOT format, you can generate graphs where node size reflects Ce and node color reflects Ca. A single large red node suggests a central module with many incoming dependencies—ideal for reinforcing stability but also a high-risk change point.

```
digraph Coupling {
 rankdir=LR;
 node [shape=box];
 Core [label="Core (Ca=20, Ce=2)", style=filled, fillcolor=lightcoral];
 API [label="API (Ca=10, Ce=5)", style=filled, fillcolor=lightblue];
 Core -> API;
 // ...
}
```

Analyzing these graphs over time reveals how coupling changes as the codebase evolves. A sudden spike in Ce for a module indicates new dependencies—investigate whether they're necessary or symptoms of architectural drift.

Mitigating ripple effect involves decoupling strategies: introduce stable interfaces, apply the **Facade pattern** to isolate legacy or third-party code behind a thin layer, and refactor scattered coupling points into cohesive modules. Each reduction in coupling shrinks the blast radius of future changes, making the system more resilient.

4.2.4 Reducing Coupling: Dependency Inversion & Facades

Applying **Dependency Inversion** turns coupling to concrete modules into coupling to abstractions. For instance, instead of OrderService depending directly on PaymentGatewayImpl, it depends on an interface IPaymentGateway. This inversion allows you to swap or mock payment implementations without touching OrderService.

The **Facade pattern** further reduces coupling by providing a unified interface to a set of interfaces in a subsystem. Wrap a complex reporting engine API—multiple classes, methods, and configuration—in a single ReportFacade.reportMonthlySales() method. Callers no longer know about the underlying classes, reducing their Ce.

```
// Facade
public class ReportingFacade {
 private final SalesRepository repo;
 private final ChartGenerator chartGen;
 public ReportingFacade(SalesRepository repo, ChartGenerator chartGen) { … }
 public Report generateMonthlySalesReport(YearMonth month) { … }
}
```

Behind the scenes, the facade coordinates multiple modules, but clients see only one dependency. This decouples client code from changes in the reporting subsystem. Over time, you can refine facades to cover new use cases or collapse related subsystems, further minimizing coupling points across your codebase.

4.2.5 Coupling at Multiple Levels

Coupling manifests at **class level** (importing other classes), **package level** (namespaces/modules depending on one another), and **service level** (microservices or processes communicating via network). Each level requires distinct strategies:

- **Class-level:** Use interfaces, apply DIP, and leverage refactorings like Extract Interface.
- **Package-level:** Enforce package boundaries via build tools or lint rules, group related classes cohesively, and avoid cross-package utilities.
- **Service-level:** Version APIs, use API Gateways or BFFs (Backend for Frontend) to minimize direct client-service coupling, and employ asynchronous messaging to decouple services in time.

For service-level coupling, define clear, backward-compatible contracts (OpenAPI schemas, message formats) and use consumer-driven contract testing. Diagramming multi-level coupling highlights critical paths:

Synchronous vs. async communication across microservices

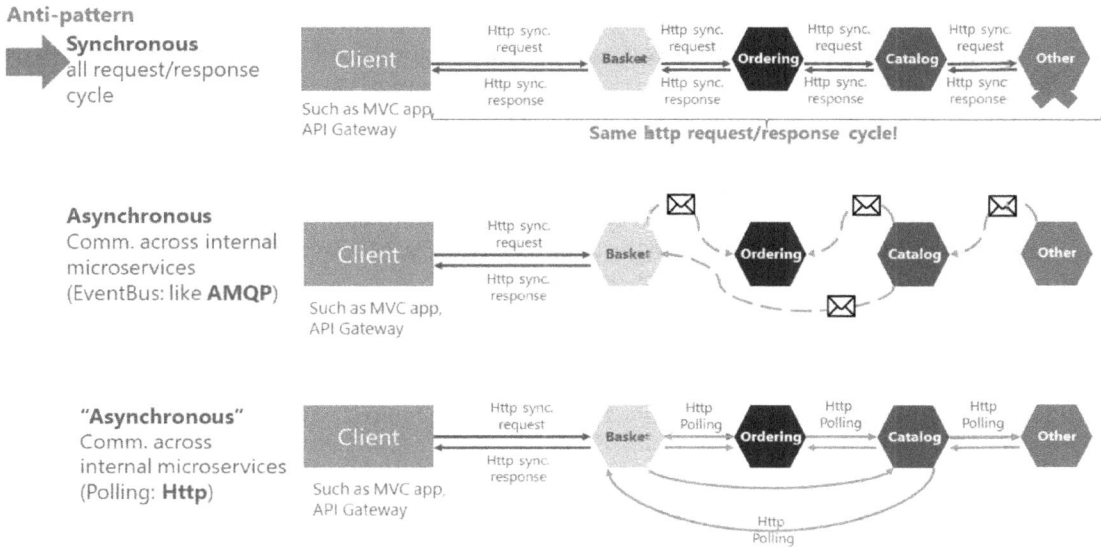

This shows both synchronous and asynchronous coupling. Monitoring service-level coupling via dependency mapping tools and runtime traces ensures that your distributed system remains loosely connected and resilient to failures.

4.3 Packaging Strategies

4.3.1 Layer-Based Packaging

Layer-based packaging organizes code by technical concerns—UI, application services, domain, infrastructure. Each package or folder corresponds to one layer, mirroring Clean Architecture's concentric circles. This clear separation helps developers know where to place new code: UI components go under com.app.ui, use cases under com.app.application, domain entities under com.app.domain, and adapters under com.app.infrastructure.

Advantages include predictability—new team members easily locate code—and enforced layering via import rules. However, it can hinder feature isolation: a feature may require touching multiple packages, scattering changes across layers and increasing coordination overhead.

To implement, configure your build tool (Maven, Gradle, or tsconfig paths) so that each package is a separate module with explicit dependencies only to the layer below. Use static-analysis rules to forbid illegal cross-layer imports. Over time, layer-based packaging simplifies cross-cutting concern management—like security and logging—because adapters can wrap those concerns at layer boundaries.

4.3.2 Feature-Based Packaging

Feature-based (vertical slice) packaging groups all code related to one feature—orders, customers, payments—into its own package or module. Under com.app.orders, you include controllers, use-case interactors, entities, and adapters specific to orders. This collocation boosts developer productivity by focusing changes in one directory, reduces cross-team coordination, and facilitates microservices extraction by turning each feature package into a deployable unit.

However, feature-based packaging can lead to duplication of shared utilities across features. To mitigate, extract truly cross-cutting utilities (logging, common DTOs) into a shared com.app.commons module. For shared domain concepts (e.g., a Money value object), consider a separate domain-common library consumed by each feature.

Feature packaging aligns with team ownership: teams own specific feature slices end to end, from UI to database. It also dovetails with DDD's bounded contexts, reinforcing domain-driven modularity. When extracting microservices, simply promote a feature package into its own codebase with minimal reorganization.

4.3.3 Vertical Slices vs. Horizontal Layers

Both packaging strategies have trade-offs. **Horizontal layering** centralizes common logic but scatters feature code across layers; **vertical slicing** bundles feature logic but can fragment cross-cutting concerns. A **hybrid approach** combines them: core domain entities live in com.app.domain, shared utilities in com.app.commons, while features reside in com.app.features.orders, com.app.features.customers, etc. Each feature module depends on domain and commons but not on other features.

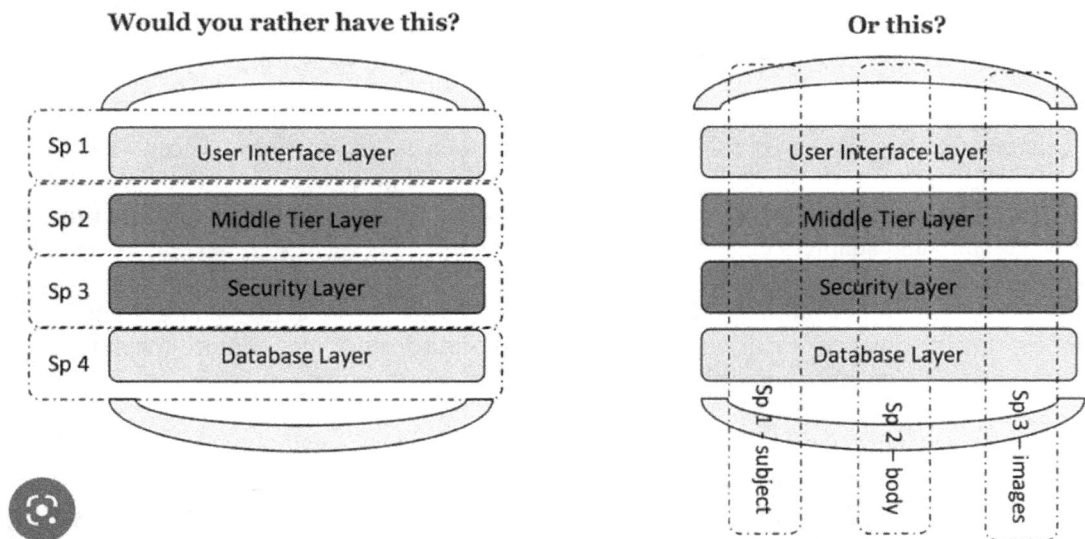

Would you rather have this?   Or this?

This hybrid model preserves the clarity of shared domain concepts while granting teams autonomy over feature lifecycles. It also simplifies dependency management: feature modules declare explicit dependencies on domain and commons. Build tools can enforce acyclic feature dependencies, preventing accidental coupling between features.

4.3.4 Micro-Modules & Component Reuse

Building reusable micro-modules—self-contained libraries with clear public APIs—promotes code sharing across projects. For instance, a payment-core library encapsulates payment domain entities and interfaces, publishable to an internal artifact repository. Downstream services or applications consume payment-core to implement adapters or UIs.

To design micro-modules effectively, limit their public surface: export only interfaces and stable domain types, keep implementation classes package-private. Use semantic versioning to signal breaking changes. Automate module publication via CI/CD pipelines that build, test, and push to Nexus or Artifactory.

Micro-modules accelerate new project setup—developers add dependencies and immediately gain vetted domain logic. They also foster consistency: a common audit-logger module means all teams follow the same conventions. Monitor module usage and health, deprecate old versions gradually, and maintain clear migration guides.

4.3.5 Diagramming Package Boundaries

Visualizing package boundaries and dependencies with UML package diagrams clarifies architecture for stakeholders.

Arrows point from adapters to ports, and from use cases to entities. Tools like PlantUML can render these diagrams from text:

```
package "com.app.orders" {
 class OrderController
 class PlaceOrderInteractor
 interface OrderRepository
}
package "com.app.infrastructure.orders" {
 class SqlOrderRepository
}
OrderController --> PlaceOrderInteractor
PlaceOrderInteractor --> OrderRepository
SqlOrderRepository --> OrderRepository
```

A simple UML snippet might show:

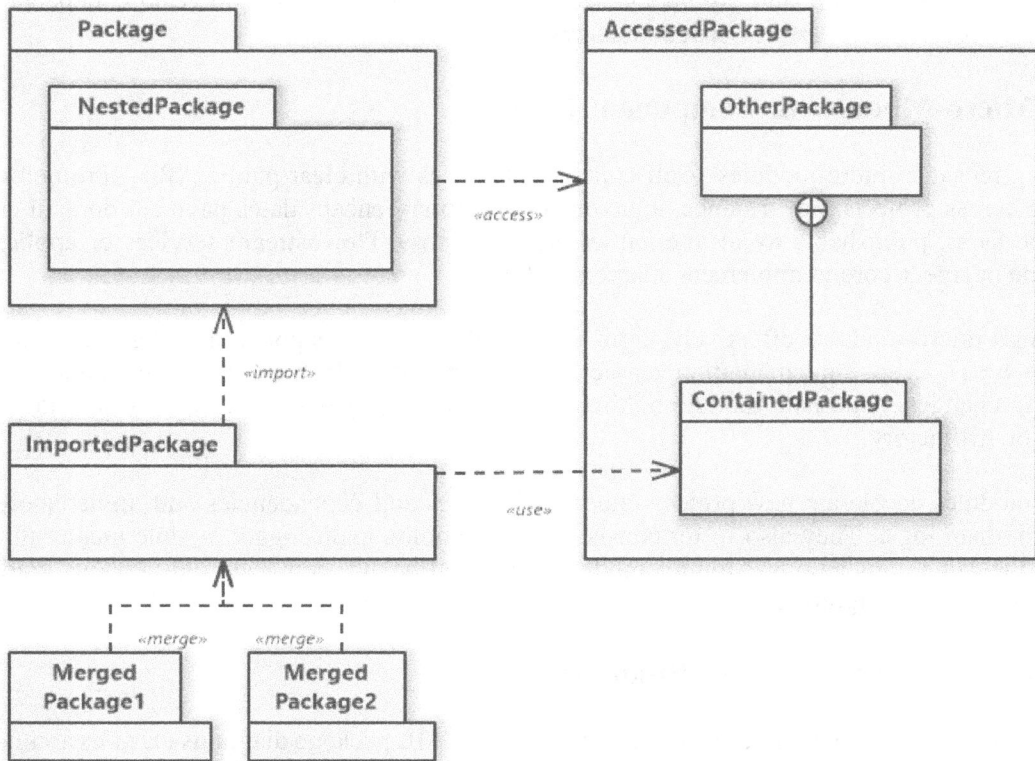

Embedding such diagrams in design docs ensures architects and developers share a common mental model. When packages shift or new modules appear, update diagrams to maintain accuracy. Visual documentation complements code, speeding onboarding and guiding refactoring decisions.

4.4 Balancing Cohesion & Coupling

4.4.1 The Principle of High Cohesion, Low Coupling

High cohesion and low coupling are complementary goals that together produce modules which are both focused and loosely connected. High cohesion means every element—methods and fields—within a component supports a single responsibility or closely related set of behaviors. Low coupling ensures each module depends on as few other modules as possible, and only through well-defined abstractions. When cohesion is high, developers can understand a component's behavior by reading only that component, rather than scanning across many modules. When coupling is low, changes to one module produce minimal ripple effects, reducing the blast radius of defects. Pursuing these principles leads to code that is easier to test: cohesive modules yield narrow, fast unit tests, while loosely coupled modules allow for mocking or stubbing across clear interfaces.

Consider an EmailService that was originally responsible for both sending messages and formatting HTML templates. Splitting this into two modules—TemplateRenderer and MailSender—raises cohesion and decouples presentation from transport. Each class now has one reason to change: business may update template logic without touching SMTP code, or swap to an API-based sender without rewriting templates.

The Netflix Simian Army architecture illustrates this: chaos experiments (cohesive service) run on isolated test modules, not across all services simultaneously (low coupling). This reduces unintended side effects when faults are injected.

A simple dependency diagram shows this separation:

[Controller] ⟶ [TemplateRenderer] ⟶ [MailSender] ⟶ [SMTP / API]

Here, each arrow represents a dependency on an interface, not a concrete class.

In practice, achieving perfect cohesion and zero coupling is unrealistic; trade-offs exist. For example, merging two small cohesive modules may reduce coupling but slightly decrease cohesion if their responsibilities overlap. Always measure the net benefit: does the slight drop in cohesion reduce the mental overhead of tracking two modules?

Cohesion and coupling often pull in opposite directions—maximizing one can sometimes worsen the other. The art lies in finding the balance point where modules remain understandable (cohesive) yet loosely connected enough to evolve independently (coupling minimized).

Modern IDEs can highlight coupling via import graphs, and metrics tools flag cohesion holes. Incorporating these checks into code reviews keeps teams mindful of structural health. Over time, scaffolding new features on a foundation of cohesive, loosely coupled modules becomes straightforward, accelerating delivery without accruing technical debt.

4.4.2 Measuring Trade-Offs

Quantifying cohesion and coupling trade-offs requires composite metrics that capture both dimensions. Robert C. Martin's **Abstractness vs. Instability** graph plots modules according to **Abstractness (A)**—the ratio of abstract artifacts (interfaces, abstract classes) to total artifacts—and **Instability (I)**—the ratio of outgoing dependencies to total dependencies (incoming + outgoing). Modules should ideally lie on the "Main Sequence" diagonal from (A=0, I=1) to (A=1, I=0).

A module with high instability (I close to 1) and low abstractness (A close to 0) resides in the **Zone of Pain**: it depends on many modules while providing no abstraction, making it brittle. Conversely, a module with high abstraction and high stability (I near 0) sits in the **Zone of Uselessness**: it provides many interfaces but few clients, potentially indicating over-engineering.

You can compute A and I with a script that parses your build graph. For Java with Maven, for example:

```
mvn dependency:tree -DoutputType=dot -DoutputFile=deps.dot
# then a Python script to count nodes, edges, and abstract types
```

Or use Structure101's built-in analysis. Visualize the resulting points in a scatter plot:

```
digraph Metrics {
  node [shape=circle];
  Core [pos="0.2,0.9!"];
  Api [pos="0.8,0.2!"];
  Legacy [pos="0.9,0.9!", color=red];
}
```

Plotting these regularly—quarterly or per release—reveals drifting modules that require intervention.

Beyond A/I, use **Cyclomatic Complexity vs. Coupling** charts: plot classes by complexity (number of decision points) against Ce (efferent coupling). Classes in the top-right quadrant (high complexity and high coupling) are prime refactoring candidates.

Balancing these metrics involves setting thresholds: e.g., enforce that no module has I > 0.8 and LCOM4 > 2. When thresholds are breached, triage the module—decide if you should increase abstraction (add interfaces) or reduce dependencies (apply DIP and extract facades). Automating these checks in CI ensures teams receive immediate feedback, preventing metric regressions from accumulating.

4.4.3 Refactoring Strategies for Balance

Refactoring for cohesion and coupling balance often begins with identifying **hotspots**—modules or classes flagged by metrics as overly coupled or poorly cohesive. Once identified, apply patterns such as **Extract Class**, **Extract Interface**, **Facade**, and **Service Layer**.

1. **Extract Class:** When a class has low cohesion (methods that share few fields), group related methods and fields into a new class. For example, split a UserAccountManager into UserAuthenticator and UserProfileManager. Update callers to depend on the narrower classes.
2. **Extract Interface:** Introduce an interface to decouple high-level modules from low-level details. For instance, define INotificationSender and implement it with EmailSender and SmsSender, reducing coupling between use-cases and concrete notifiers.
3. **Facade:** Wrap a complex subsystem behind a simple API. A ReportingFacade might coordinate SalesRepository, ChartGenerator, and PdfRenderer, shielding clients from internal coupling.

4. **Dependency Injection:** Switch direct instantiation (new ConcreteClass()) to constructor injection of interfaces, enabling decoupling and easier mocking.
5. **Modularization:** Move cohesive groups of classes into separate modules or packages with controlled public APIs, reducing inter-module coupling.

A code example showing Extract Interface and DI:

```
// Before: direct coupling
public class OrderService {
 private readonly SqlOrderRepository repo = new SqlOrderRepository();
 // ...
}


// After: DIP and Extract Interface
public interface IOrderRepository { Order GetById(int id); }
public class SqlOrderRepository : IOrderRepository { /* ... */ }
public class OrderService {
 private readonly IOrderRepository repo;
 public OrderService(IOrderRepository repo) { this.repo = repo; }
}
```

Begin refactoring incrementally—one hotspot at a time—and rely on tests to catch regressions. Use semantic versioning when moving classes across modules to inform downstream consumers of breaking changes. Continuous communication with the team prevents duplicated effort and ensures consensus on new module boundaries.

4.4.4 Organizational & Team Alignment

Conway's Law states that system architecture mirrors the organization's communication structure. If your teams are siloed by technical layers—UI team, API team, DB team—you'll naturally adopt a layered packaging strategy, potentially hindering feature delivery. Conversely, feature-oriented teams encourage vertical slicing of code, boosting cohesion within feature modules and reducing inter-team coupling.

Align team boundaries to feature modules or bounded contexts: for an e-commerce platform, a "Checkout Team" might own the entire checkout component (UI, use-cases, persistence), increasing ownership and reducing cross-team dependencies. A "Catalog Team" similarly controls product discovery.

Use a **team-module matrix** to visualize who owns which modules, ensuring clear accountability. Each team controls its code end-to-end, minimizing coupling to other teams. Regular cross-team syncs or guilds manage shared concerns—logging, security—and maintain consistency.

Govern architectural decisions through lightweight **architecture review boards**: before refactoring a shared module, teams discuss impact. Pair-programming across teams fosters knowledge transfer and prevents knowledge silos. Organizational alignment thus becomes a force multiplier for balancing cohesion and coupling, enabling faster, more autonomous team delivery.

4.4.5 Long-Term Maintenance Considerations

Achieving high cohesion and low coupling is not a one-time task—it requires ongoing diligence. As the codebase evolves, new dependencies may creep in, old abstractions become obsolete, and modules drift toward anti-patterns. To guard against this, establish **governance practices**:

- **Architectural reviews:** Allocate time each sprint to review proposed changes for their impact on coupling and cohesion.
- **Coding standards:** Document rules on module boundaries, naming conventions for interfaces, and patterns for dependency management.
- **Automated monitoring:** Integrate metrics collection (LCOM, coupling, complexity) into dashboards. Alert when metrics exceed thresholds.

For example, run a nightly job that executes a Python script to parse SonarQube's API and produce a CSV of modules with LCOM4 > 2 or Instability > 0.8. Developers review the list weekly to plan refactoring.

```
import requests, csv
response                    =                    requests.get('http://sonar/api/measures/component',
params={'metricKeys':'lcom4,instability'})
data = response.json()
with open('architectural_health.csv','w') as f:
  writer = csv.writer(f)
  for comp in data['components']:
    writer.writerow([comp['key'], comp['measures'][0]['value'], comp['measures'][1]['value']])
```

Maintain a **debt register** that logs architectural debt items (low cohesion, high coupling hotspots), prioritizing them alongside functional user stories. Celebrate debt repayments—tracking improvements in metrics over time—to reinforce the value of architecture work. Finally, integrate architecture health into performance reviews and KPIs, making it part of the team's definition of done. By institutionalizing these maintenance processes, cohesion and coupling remain balanced long after initial refactoring efforts.

4.5 Tools & Automation for Metrics

4.5.1 Static-Analysis Tools

Static-analysis tools scan code without executing it, flagging structural issues related to cohesion and coupling. **SonarQube** provides built-in metrics such as LCOM, cyclomatic complexity, and coupling between object classes (CBO). By configuring quality gates—e.g., LCOM4 $\leq$ 2 and CBO $\leq$ 10—you can automatically fail builds that introduce architectural regressions. A sample sonar-project.properties:

```
sonar.projectKey=my-app
sonar.sources=src
sonar.java.coveragePlugin=jacoco
sonar.couplingBetweenObjects.max=10
sonar.lcom4.max=2
```

Structure101 offers visualizations and rule enforcement for package dependencies, enabling you to define forbidden cycles or layers. It can auto-generate dependency graphs and highlight hotspots.

For JavaScript/TypeScript, **ESLint** with plugins like eslint-plugin-boundaries or import/no-cycle enforces import rules. Example .eslintrc.js snippet:

```
module.exports = {
 plugins: ['boundaries'],
 rules: {
  'boundaries/element-types': ['error',
   { default: 'disallow',
    rules: [{ from: 'domain', allow: ['domain'] }] }]
 }
};
```

Integrate these tools into local pre-commit hooks (Husky for JS, pre-commit for Python) to provide immediate feedback within developers' IDEs, preventing architecture violations before pushes.

4.5.2 IDE Plugins & Live Feedback

Real-time feedback accelerates adherence to cohesion and coupling rules. IntelliJ IDEA's **Structural Search & Replace** can detect anti-patterns like God Classes or forbidden imports on the fly. The **SonarLint** plugin connects to SonarQube, surfacing the same quality issues in the IDE that the CI would later flag.

Visual Studio Code users can install **ESLint** and **SonarLint** extensions to highlight problematic imports or high-complexity functions as they code. A sample settings.json:

```
{
 "eslint.enable": true,
 "sonarlint.connectedMode.project": "my-app",
 "files.exclude": { "**/node_modules": true }
}
```

Live diagrams plugins—such as **Dependency Cruiser** in VSCode—generate mini-dependency graphs of the current file's imports. Hovering over edges reveals coupling degrees, helping developers refactor before committing.

By making architecture rules part of the everyday coding experience, you reduce review friction and foster collective ownership of module quality. Developers internalize architectural constraints, writing code that aligns with cohesion and coupling goals from the first line.

4.5.3 CI/CD Integration

Embedding metric checks into CI/CD pipelines ensures that architecture regressions block merges and deployments. In a GitHub Actions workflow:

```
jobs:
 build:
  runs-on: ubuntu-latest
  steps:
  - uses: actions/checkout@v2
  - name: Run ESLint
   run: npm run lint
  - name: Run SonarQube Scan
   uses: sonarsource/sonarcloud-github-action@master
   with:
    projectKey: my-org_my-app
  - name: Fail on Quality Gate
   run: |
    status=$(curl            -s            -u            $SONAR_TOKEN:
https://sonarcloud.io/api/qualitygates/project_status?projectKey=my-org_my-app \
     | jq -r .projectStatus.status)
    if [ "$status" != "OK" ]; then exit 1; fi
```

Jenkins pipelines can invoke **Gradle's check** task, which runs ArchUnit tests and fails on forbidden dependencies:

```
stage('Architecture Check') {
 steps {
  sh './gradlew archUnitTest'
 }
}
```

Include a separate **architecture** stage before unit and integration tests to catch violations early. Provide developers with clear error messages pointing to specific rules and file locations, facilitating quick fixes. Over time, the CI becomes a trusted gatekeeper, maintaining the architectural integrity of the codebase.

4.5.4 Visualization Dashboards

Interactive dashboards help teams monitor cohesion and coupling trends. Use **Graphviz** to generate daily dependency graphs:

```
./gradlew dependenciesGraph -Poutput=deps.dot
dot -Tpng deps.dot -o deps.png
```

Publish deps.png to a Confluence page or internal web portal. Tools like **Deptrac** (PHP) or **NDepend** (.NET) offer web dashboards with clickable nodes and historic trend charts.

For custom solutions, ingest metrics into **Grafana** via Prometheus exporters. Write a small Prometheus exporter in Python:

```python
from prometheus_client import Gauge, start_http_server
g = Gauge('module_instability', 'Instability metric per module', ['module'])
# read JSON from analysis tool and set g.labels(module).set(value)
start_http_server(8000)
```

Teams then view instability and cohesion metrics on Grafana graphs, set alerts when thresholds cross, and slice by feature or team. Visualization not only informs architects but also motivates developers—seeing improvements in real time reinforces best practices and fosters healthy competition among teams to maintain module quality.

4.6 Case Studies & Anti-Patterns

4.6.1 The God Class Anti-Pattern

A **God Class** centralizes too many responsibilities—validation, business logic, persistence, presentation—into one sprawling class, often exceeding thousands of lines. Symptoms include massive constructor parameter lists, dozens of fields, extremely high cyclomatic complexity, and poor cohesion metrics (LCOM4 $\gg$ 1). God Classes arise when teams prioritize speed over structure, tacking new features onto a familiar class rather than creating focused modules. These classes are single points of failure: a bug in one method can have unforeseen side effects in unrelated behaviors.

```
public class UserManager {
 private JdbcTemplate jdbc;
 private EmailService email;
 private PdfGenerator pdf;
 // ... dozens more fields


 public void register(UserDto dto) { /* validation, persistence, email, logging... */ }
 public void deactivate(int id) { /* more logic... */ }
 public void generateReport(int id) { /* PDF, DB joins, formatting... */ }
 // 50+ methods
}
```

Refactoring begins with **Extract Class**: group related methods—registration, deactivation, reporting—into UserRegistrationService, UserDeactivationService, and UserReportGenerator. Introduce interfaces for each new class, update callers, and remove methods from the God Class. Repeat until the God Class vanishes into cohesive components. Diagram before/after:

```
[ UserManager ] (God Class)
 ├── register()
 ├── deactivate()
 ├── generateReport()
 └── ...
```

becomes

```
[ UserRegistrationService ]
[ UserDeactivationService ]
[ UserReportGenerator ]
```

This modularization reduces complexity, clarifies ownership, and improves testability.

4.6.2 Shotgun Surgery

Shotgun Surgery occurs when a single change—say, renaming a field—requires edits scattered across many classes and modules. It signals high coupling and poor cohesion: related logic lives in multiple places instead of a single, cohesive component. For example, adding a new property user.timezone might force updates to JSON serializers, database mappers, validation logic, UI forms, email templates, and logging statements. Detect shotgun surgery by tracking the file-change count for bug fixes: if more than five files change for a minor feature, investigate coupling. Combat it with **Feature Envy** refactoring: move methods closer to the data they operate on, or create an **Accessor** class encapsulating the shared logic. For the timezone example, introduce a UserContext class that holds all user metadata, and refactor dependent code to query UserContext.getTimezone() instead of spreading timezone handling across modules.

```
// Before: direct field usage in many places
const tz = user.timezone;


// After: encapsulate
class UserContext {
 constructor(private user: User) {}
 getTimezone(): string { return this.user.timezone; }
}
// callers use
const tz = new UserContext(user).getTimezone();
```

This consolidation localizes changes: adding a new locale property affects only UserContext, not every caller. Over time, this reduces dev cycles and limits risk.

4.6.3 Circular Dependencies

Circular dependencies between modules or classes violate acyclic dependency principles and often lead to runtime errors or complex initialization order issues. In JavaScript, you might see moduleA requiring moduleB, which in turn requires moduleA, resulting in an undefined export. In Java, circular package dependencies obscure build order and hamper reuse.

Detect cycles with dependency-analysis tools (e.g., Madge for JS, ArchUnit for Java). Once identified, break cycles by introducing **interfaces** or **event-driven decoupling**. For example, if OrderService depends on EmailService, which in turn depends on OrderService to fetch order details, extract an OrderQueryPort interface implemented by OrderService in a separate core module. Then EmailService depends on OrderQueryPort instead of the full OrderService, dissolving the cycle.

```
[ OrderService ] ──▶ [ EmailService ] ──▶ [ OrderService ] (cycle)
```

becomes

```
[ OrderService ] ──▶ [ EmailService ] ──▶ [ OrderQueryPort ] ──▶ [ OrderService ]
```

Alternatively, use **event listeners**: OrderService publishes an OrderCreated event; EmailService subscribes to that event instead of directly calling OrderService. This pub/sub decouples the services entirely:

```
OrderService → EventBus → EmailService
```

Breaking cycles simplifies module boundaries and improves application startup reliability.

4.6.4 Monolithic Packaging Pitfalls

Monolithic packaging groups unrelated features and layers into a single deployable artifact—often a massive WAR, EAR, or JAR. While simple to build and deploy, monoliths tend toward high coupling: UI code imports deep domain classes, domain classes import infrastructure, and endless cross-layer dependencies accumulate. This packaging inhibits incremental releases, as any change—no matter how small—requires redeploying the entire application.

Strategies to mitigate monolithic pitfalls include the **Strangler Fig Pattern**: extract individual features into microservices or separate modules behind stable facades, gradually replacing monolith functionality. For example, migrate the checkout feature into its service, leaving the core monolith intact but routing /checkout/* URLs to the new service.

```
Client → API Gateway ──▶ [ Checkout Service ]
              └──▶ [ Monolith for other features ]
```

Alternatively, introduce **modular monolith** packaging: structure the monolith as separate modules with explicit dependencies, enforce acyclic imports, and build them as independent JARs deployed in one runtime. This preserves the single-deployable advantage while reaping modularity benefits. Over time, the most volatile modules can be extracted into microservices or serverless functions, reducing monolith scope and coupling.

4.6.5 Success Story: Modularizing a Legacy Monolith

A large FinTech company inherited a 10-year-old monolith supporting account management, payments, reporting, and notifications. The codebase comprised 500K lines of Java, with rampant coupling—metrics showed average Ce = 15 and LCOM4 = 4. Shipments of new features took weeks due to regression risks and brittle dependencies.

Step 1: Baseline Metrics & Graphs Using NDepend, they generated a package dependency graph revealing several high-coupling hubs: com.bank.accounts and com.bank.payments. Instability–Abstractness plots placed critical modules in the Zone of Pain.

Step 2: Define Bounded Contexts Architects mapped business domains to modules: Accounts, Payments, Reporting, Notifications. They created separate Maven modules for each, with explicit dependencies only on a shared domain-common module.

Step 3: Extract Modules Over six sprints, they refactored code into new modules. For Accounts, they extracted entities and use-cases into accounts-core, implemented adapters in accounts-infra, and updated the monolith to depend on them. A PlantUML package diagram:

```
package com.bank.accounts.core
package com.bank.accounts.infra
package com.bank.common
com.bank.accounts.infra --> com.bank.accounts.core
com.bank.accounts.core --> com.bank.common
```

Step 4: CI/CD & Quality Gates They added NDepend checks to Jenkins, failing builds if cycles or high coupling appeared. Code reviews enforced refactoring into modules, not new cross-module imports.

Results Within three months, average Ce dropped from 15 to 5, LCOM4 improved to mostly 1–2, and build times decreased by 40%. Feature delivery time for payment enhancements halved, and developer satisfaction rose measurably in internal surveys. The modularized monolith paved the way for a gradual extraction of the Payments module into an independent microservice, further reducing coupling and improving scalability.

Conclusion

Mastering cohesion and coupling transforms an entangled codebase into a modular, maintainable ecosystem where changes remain localized and features can be composed with confidence. By applying clear packaging strategies—whether by layer, by feature, or through micro-modules—and by continually monitoring metrics with static analysis and CI integration, you ensure that components stay focused on their core responsibilities and dependencies stay intentional. The case studies and anti-patterns highlighted in this chapter demonstrate both the cost of neglect and the payoff of disciplined refactoring. Armed with these insights, you are now prepared to incorporate domain-driven design principles into your architecture, crafting bounded contexts and aggregates that align technical structure with business intent. In the next chapter, we'll see how Clean Architecture and DDD work hand in hand to model complex domains into robust, cohesive components.

Chapter 5. Domain-Driven Design Inside Clean Architecture

Capturing the true complexity of your business domain in code requires more than just clever design patterns—it demands a close partnership between developers and domain experts, a shared vocabulary, and a deliberate modeling process. In this chapter, we explore how Domain-Driven Design (DDD) elevates your Clean Architecture by guiding you to identify the most valuable subdomains, articulate clear boundaries around each context, and embed the ubiquitous language directly into your code. You'll learn to distinguish core, supporting, and generic subdomains; craft aggregates that enforce invariants; and leverage tactical patterns—entities, value objects, domain services, factories, and repositories—to keep your domain logic pure. We also dive into modeling techniques like Event Storming and context mapping to align teams and systems, and examine how domain events and anti-corruption layers knit multiple contexts together without contaminating your core model.

5.1 Strategic Domain-Driven Design

5.1.1 Core, Supporting & Generic Subdomains

Domain-Driven Design emphasizes categorizing a business domain into distinct subdomains to focus modeling efforts where they matter most. The **core subdomain** contains the system's differentiating business capabilities—those that deliver the greatest competitive advantage or revenue. In an e-commerce application, core might include order processing, payment authorization, and inventory reservation. Surrounding the core are **supporting subdomains**—areas like reporting, analytics, or customer service workflows that enable the core but are not themselves differentiators. Supporting subdomains often benefit from domain experts but may use patterns and structures derived from the core model. The outermost ring is the **generic subdomain**, comprising commodity capabilities such as authentication, email sending, or logging. These generic concerns are ripe for off-the-shelf solutions, SaaS providers, or internal shared platforms. By mapping functionality to these subdomain types, teams know where to invest deep analysis and where to reuse proven components. Core subdomains justify strategic investments in expert workshops, custom DSLs, or specialized libraries. Supporting subdomains can sometimes be tackled by dedicated teams or outsourced to specialists. Generic subdomains often require minimal modeling; instead, integrate robust third-party tools and adapt them via anti-corruption layers if necessary. This division reduces wasted effort and aligns development focus with business value. Teams should revisit subdomain boundaries regularly as product strategy evolves or market conditions change. Clear subdomain boundaries also inform technology choices: heavy DDD tooling for the core, lightweight frameworks for supporting areas, and managed services for generic concerns.

Domain Driven Designs

Strategic design

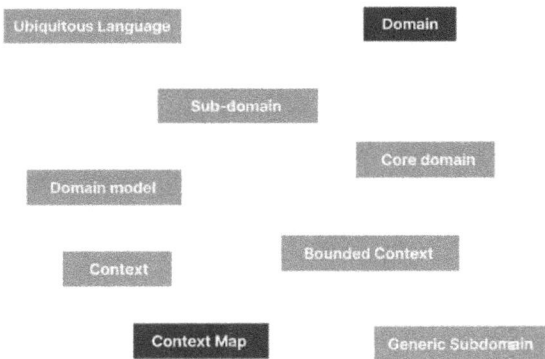

Ubiquitous Language

Domain

Sub-domain

Core domain

Domain model

Context

Bounded Context

Context Map

Generic Subdomain

Tactical patterns

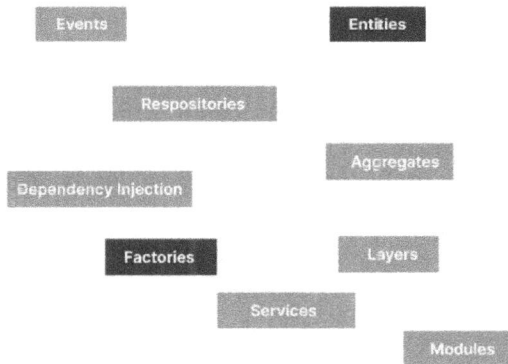

Events

Entities

Respositories

Aggregates

Dependency Injection

Factories

Layers

Services

Modules

5.1.2 Bounded Contexts & Context Mapping

Bounded contexts are the primary strategic unit in Domain-Driven Design, defining clear boundaries within which a particular model applies and terms have specific meanings. Within each bounded context, the ubiquitous language is consistent and the domain model remains coherent. Multiple bounded contexts may coexist in a system, each capturing a different viewpoint or concern—such as Catalog, Sales, and Shipping in an e-commerce platform. Context mapping documents the relationships between these contexts, prescribing patterns for integration. Common patterns include **Customer-Supplier**, where one context's published model is consumed by another, and **Conformist**, where the customer context must adapt to the supplier's model without influencing it. The **Shared Kernel** pattern establishes a small shared model subset that two teams co-own, requiring tight governance to prevent drift. The **Anti-Corruption Layer** protects a core context from external models by translating between languages at the boundary. Visualizing these relationships on a context map helps teams understand integration responsibilities and data flows. For example, a Customer context might publish customer account events, which the Order context consumes as a conformist consumer.

Using context maps, teams negotiate model ownership, integration contracts, and synchronization mechanisms. They decide which context adapts or publishes the canonical view, avoiding semantic confusion. Context mapping also surfaces potential anti-patterns like overlapping models or undefined ownership. As business requirements evolve, context maps guide the decomposition or merging of contexts. Maintaining an up-to-date context map fosters organizational alignment: each team knows its domain responsibility and integration obligations. Documenting context maps alongside code in a living document repository ensures new team members quickly grasp system structure. Regular context-map reviews should be part of architectural governance, especially when new features cross context boundaries. Ultimately, bounded contexts and context mapping form the strategic backbone for scaling Domain-Driven Design in complex systems.

5.1.3 Distilling the Ubiquitous Language

At the heart of Domain-Driven Design is the ubiquitous language—a shared vocabulary developed by domain experts and developers to describe concepts unambiguously. Distilling this language begins with collaborative workshops, where domain experts narrate real-world scenarios using their terminology. Developers capture these terms in code: class names, method names, and module boundaries reflect the ubiquitous language, reinforcing clear communication. For example, instead of a generic process(), a method might be named calculateShippingCost() or authorizePayment(), mirroring business conversations.

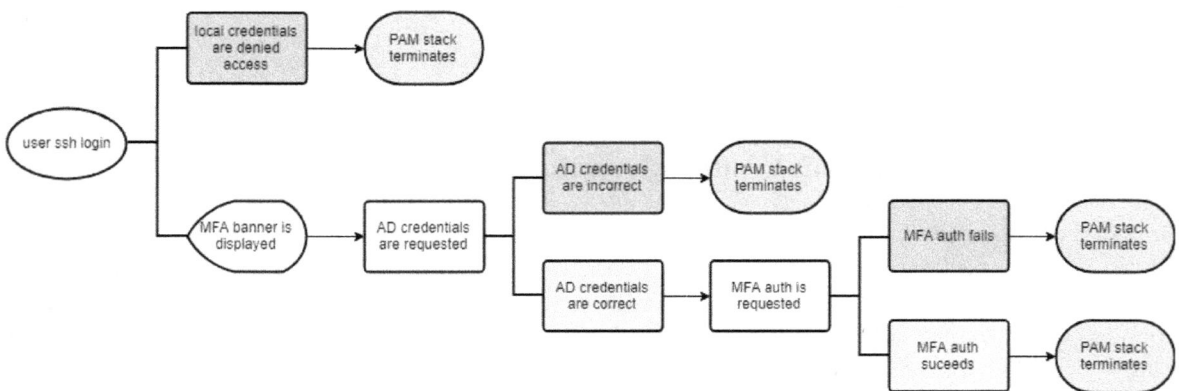

PAM based multi-factor authentication example

Embedding the language in the codebase prevents semantic drift as the system evolves; every time a developer reads or writes code, they reinforce domain terms. To support consistency, automated linters can enforce naming conventions—flagging identifiers that deviate from approved domain terms. Rich documentation, generated from source code comments and API specifications, serves as living reference for both technical and non-technical stakeholders. Pam Baker's Domain Language YAML file can provide a centralized glossary:

When naming events, commands, and responses, follow patterns like VerbNoun or NounEvent to maintain uniformity. Domain terms should avoid technical jargon—using "Shipment" rather than "DeliveryTask"—so business stakeholders recognize code concepts immediately. It's equally important to eliminate synonyms that cause confusion; decide between "client" and "customer" early and enforce one term. Over time, code reviews should include checks for ubiquitous language compliance, catching outliers before they proliferate. As new features arise, update the glossary and incorporate new terms via a pull-request process that includes domain expert approval. This living language strategy ensures that code remains a precise reflection of business intent, reducing miscommunications, accelerating onboarding, and improving maintainability.

5.1.4 Aligning Teams to Context Boundaries

Aligning organizational structure with bounded contexts accelerates delivery and reduces communication overhead. Each bounded context becomes a team's sphere of responsibility, end-to-end—from requirements gathering to deployment. A team that owns the Order context, for example, is accountable for the order entity model, use-case interactors, repository adapters, and any supporting infrastructure. This "vertical slice" ownership eliminates the need for handoffs between UI, backend, and operations teams for order-related features. Moreover, it fosters deep domain expertise within the team: developers become fluent in the ubiquitous language and business rules of their context. Teams collaborate via context maps and published language contracts, establishing clear integration points. When cross-context coordination is necessary—such as shipping integration with payments—teams negotiate customer-supplier agreements or implement anti-corruption layers.

Dedicated teams also optimize capacity planning and sprint prioritization, aligning backlogs with context boundaries. Shared contexts—like authentication—may be owned by a platform team, ensuring coherent reusable services. Regular "context chamber" meetings allow teams to review integration risks, context mapping changes, and shared kernel evolutions. Performance reviews and incentives tied to context-level metrics (e.g., lead time, defect rate) reinforce ownership. This model, often called the **Team Topologies** approach, prevents knowledge silos and reduces cognitive load. As the organization grows, new contexts become new teams, avoiding scaling bottlenecks. Aligning teams to bounded contexts thus transforms DDD from a modeling exercise into an organizational design principle that drives sustainable delivery.

5.2 Tactical DDD Patterns

5.2.1 Entities vs. Value Objects

Entities and value objects solve distinct modeling problems: identity vs. value semantics. Entities are domain objects with a persistent identity that endures beyond state changes. For example, a Customer entity is identified by a UUID or database key; changing customer name or address does not change its identity. Entities encapsulate mutable state and enforce invariants through methods. In contrast, value objects are immutable, self-validating types with no conceptual identity: two Money objects with equal amount and currency are interchangeable. Modeling value objects as immutable types simplifies equality, hashing, and thread safety. In code, we define a Kotlin data class for Money:

```
data class Money(val amount: BigDecimal, val currency: Currency) {
 init { require(amount >= BigDecimal.ZERO) { "Amount cannot be negative" } }
}
```

Here, equality is structural, and we can freely share instances. For entities, we implement a class with an explicit ID and mutating behaviors:

```
public class Customer {
 private final UUID id;
 private String name;
 public Customer(UUID id, String name) {
  this.id = id;
  this.name = name;
 }
 public void changeName(String newName) {
  if (newName.isEmpty()) throw new IllegalArgumentException();
  this.name = newName;
 }
}
```

The id field distinguishes one instance from another, regardless of other property values. Entities often implement equals() and hashCode() based on identity only, not on all fields. In repositories, entities are rehydrated by ID, while value objects are built from data fields. It's crucial to avoid confusion: value objects belong inside aggregates and have no lifecycle outside their aggregate root. Entities may hold references to other entities or to collections of value objects, forming the aggregate boundary.

Here, Order is an entity, OrderLine is a value object inside the aggregate. Properly distinguishing these types ensures model integrity, simplifies persistence semantics, and guides domain experts when describing business rules.

Value Objects vs Entities at a Glance

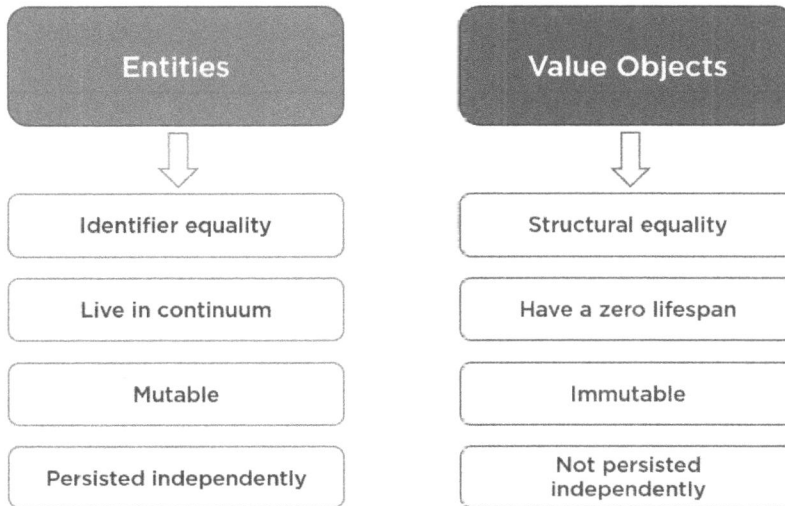

Entities	Value Objects
Identifier equality	Structural equality
Live in continuum	Have a zero lifespan
Mutable	Immutable
Persisted independently	Not persisted independently

5.2.2 Aggregates & Aggregate Roots

Aggregates define consistency boundaries within which business invariants hold. An aggregate root is the only entity in the boundary that external code can reference; all interactions with child entities or value objects go through the root. This simplifies transactional modeling: when persisting an aggregate, repositories only save the root, and associated data is cascaded. For example, an Order aggregate root might contain a collection of OrderLine value objects and a ShippingAddress. The root enforces invariants such as non-negative total, unique line items, and correct status transitions. In code, an Order entity might look like:

```
public class Order {
 private UUID id;
 private List<OrderLine> lines = new ArrayList<>();
 private OrderStatus status;
 public void addLine(OrderLine line) {
  if (status != NEW) throw new IllegalStateException();
  lines.add(line);
 }
 public Money total() {
  return lines.stream()
     .map(OrderLine::subtotal)
     .reduce(Money.ZERO, Money::add);
 }
 public void confirm() {
```

```
if (total().isZero()) throw new BusinessException("Cannot confirm empty order");
status = CONFIRMED;
   }
}
```

Here, Order is the aggregate root, and OrderLine is a child inside the boundary. External code never directly instantiates or modifies OrderLine—all operations go through Order. This containment enforces invariants consistently. Aggregates should be as small as possible to avoid large, unwieldy transaction scopes; a rule of thumb is one aggregate per business transaction. Aggregates are saved and loaded via a single repository, such as OrderRepository.findById(), which returns the fully initialized root.

Bounded contexts often align with aggregate clusters, grouping related aggregates under the same business boundary. Identifying aggregate roots requires asking: "What entity needs a unique identity, and which invariants require transactional integrity?" Overloading aggregate roots with too many responsibilities leads to bottlenecks and complex concurrency controls; splitting aggregates when invariants don't span across them can improve performance. Ensuring each aggregate maintains its own consistency simplifies scaling, as different aggregates can be handled in parallel without cross-aggregate locking. Aggregates are fundamental building blocks in both DDD and Clean Architecture, anchoring your domain model and guiding repository and service design.

5.2.3 Domain Services

Domain services encapsulate operations that involve multiple entities or value objects but do not naturally belong to any single entity. They represent domain logic that cannot be neatly modeled as a method on an aggregate root. For instance, a CurrencyConversionService might convert between currencies using live exchange rates, a process not intrinsic to any one entity. Domain services live in the core domain layer, depend only on domain primitives, and should be named using domain terms—e.g., InvoiceCalculationService rather than MathHelper. A typical domain service interface in Java might look like:

```
public interface CurrencyConversionService {
  Money convert(Money source, Currency targetCurrency);
}
```

The implementation, perhaps ForexApiCurrencyConversionService, lives in the adapter layer and implements the interface by calling an external API. Domain services enforce business invariants, such as rounding rules or rate refresh policies. They are stateless and should not maintain mutable internal state—any required state, like a cache of rates, is injected via constructor or accessed through repositories. Tests for domain services use mocks or fakes for dependencies, enabling fast verification of logic. Overuse of domain services can signal an Anemic Domain Model; if too much logic lives outside entities, consider whether behaviors belong on aggregates. When a service interacts with multiple aggregates, it orchestrates calls to those aggregates via their public methods and repositories, maintaining aggregate boundaries. The service method signatures should refer only to domain abstractions, not infrastructure classes. A simple sequence diagram clarifies a domain service interaction:

Client → CurrencyConversionService.convert()
Service → ExchangeRateRepository.findRate()
Service → Money.add()
Service → return converted Money

Domain services often collaborate with domain events to publish outcomes, such as a PaymentProcessedEvent after a PaymentService completes. They play a crucial role in use-case orchestrations, ensuring complex business operations remain testable and decoupled from technical concerns.

5.2.4 Factories

Factories encapsulate the complex logic required to create domain objects in a valid state, especially aggregates that have multiple invariants. They live in the domain layer—or close to it—and expose expressive methods like OrderFactory.createFromCart(cart) that hide the details of identifier generation, default values, and invariant checks. Factories help keep constructors simple and focused, avoiding telescoping constructor parameters or exposing partially initialized objects. For example, an OrderFactory in Java might look like:

```java
public class OrderFactory {
 public static Order create(UUID id, List<Item> items, Optional<Promotion> promo) {
  Order order = new Order(id);
  items.forEach(order::addLine);
  promo.ifPresent(order::applyPromotion);
  order.calculateTotals();
  return order;
 }
}
```

Here, the factory ensures that calculateTotals() and any promo application happen before the order leaves the factory. Factories also encapsulate collaboration with auxiliary services—such as OrderNumberGenerator or DateProvider—injected into the factory via constructor or static context. In more complex domains, factories may implement the **Factory Method** or **Abstract Factory** patterns, allowing families of related objects to be produced polymorphically. For instance, different geographic regions might require region-specific invoice templates, so you might have an InvoiceFactory interface with implementations per region. In test scenarios, you can swap in a TestOrderFactory that seeds orders with deterministic IDs, enhancing reproducibility. Diagrammatically, object creation via factory is:

```
Client → OrderFactory.create()
Factory → PREPARE Order entity
Factory → MULTIPLE calls to entity methods
Factory → returns fully initialized Order
```

By centralizing creation logic, factories reduce duplication across application services and repositories, ensuring consistent initialization. They also assist in migrating legacy code: encapsulate awkward constructors behind a factory, then refactor constructors without changing calling code. In Clean Architecture, factories form part of the core domain, with adapter layers invoking them rather than using new. This approach maintains purity of business rules and simplifies evolution of creation policies over time.

5.2.5 Repositories

Repositories act as collection-like interfaces for retrieving and persisting aggregates, hiding the details of data access. They belong in the domain layer as ports (interfaces) and are implemented in the adapter layer to use specific persistence technologies. A repository interface might be:

```
public interface OrderRepository {
 Optional<Order> findById(UUID id);
 void save(Order order);
 List<Order> findByCustomerId(UUID customerId);
}
```

Implementations—such as JpaOrderRepository or MongoOrderRepository—live in the outer layers and depend on framework libraries (JPA, MongoTemplate). By coding against the OrderRepository interface, application services and domain code remain independent of SQL, ORM, or document-store semantics. Repositories should return fully loaded aggregates; lazy loading risks exposing persistence context to the domain. Transaction management is typically applied at the service or application service level via annotations (e.g., @Transactional) rather than inside the repository. Repositories may throw domain-agnostic exceptions—wrap technology exceptions into infrastructure errors or domain exceptions as appropriate. When a new persistence mechanism is introduced, only the repository adapter changes; domain code is untouched. A UML sequence diagram for repository usage:

```
[ Use-Case ] → OrderRepository.findById()
OrderRepository → Database
Database → OrderRepository : OrderData
OrderRepository → Use-Case : OrderAggregate
```

For complex queries, consider using **Specification** objects or **Query Objects** to encapsulate criteria without polluting the repository interface. In distributed systems, repositories may also be proxies to remote services or event stores, but the interface contracts remain the same. Unit tests mock repository interfaces to verify business logic without hitting the database. Integration tests use in-memory or containerized databases to validate mappings. Over time, consistent repository patterns across aggregates simplify developers' mental models and promote reuse of query and mapping logic.

5.3 Domain Events & Event Modeling

5.3.1 Defining Domain Events

Domain events represent things that have occurred in the domain that other parts of the system may need to react to. They capture facts rather than intentions—a PaymentReceived event declares that payment has been successfully captured, not that payment should be captured. Domain events belong in the core domain model, defined as immutable data structures. In Java, a simple event class might be:

```
public final class PaymentReceived {
private final UUID paymentId;
private final BigDecimal amount;
private final Instant timestamp;


public PaymentReceived(UUID paymentId, BigDecimal amount, Instant timestamp) {
this.paymentId = Objects.requireNonNull(paymentId);
this.amount = Objects.requireNonNull(amount);
this.timestamp = Objects.requireNonNull(timestamp);
}


// getters...
}
```

Here, all fields are final, enforcing immutability. Events should include enough context for handlers to act without needing further data lookups; for example, include the order ID, customer ID, or relevant metadata. Versioning domain events early is crucial for backward compatibility. One strategy is to include a version field or use schema evolution tools like Avro with a schema registry. Systems consuming events can use this version to adapt deserialization logic. Domain events are not commands—they reflect completed actions that may trigger subsequent processes. In an event-driven architecture, events flow through an event bus, message queue, or event store. Recording domain events also facilitates audit trails: you can replay events to reconstruct state or debug issues. Inline with event-sourcing patterns, events become the source of truth, persisting in an append-only log. Even if you don't adopt full event sourcing, capturing domain events alongside state changes enables eventual consistency between contexts and microservices. This structure decouples producers and consumers, improving scalability and resilience.

5.3.2 Event Storming Workshops

Event Storming is a highly collaborative workshop technique for discovering domain events, commands, and aggregates using sticky notes on a wall. Domain experts, developers, UX designers, and testers gather to rapidly visualize business processes by placing orange sticky notes—each representing a domain event—on a timeline. Commands are represented on blue notes, mapping user or system intentions that trigger events. Aggregates are outlined with yellow notes, grouping related events and commands into coherent clusters. The workshop begins with a high-level walkthrough of key domain flows—such as checkout or account registration—and proceeds to flesh out details iteratively. Facilitators guide participants to ask "What happens next?" and "What triggered this?" to ensure completeness. As events and commands accumulate, the group identifies aggregates and bounded contexts, drawing context boundaries with marker pens or colored tape.

The map quickly highlights areas of complexity—clusters of events indicating rich business processes—and gaps where domain rules may be missing. After event identification, participants assign commands to roles, discuss relevant policies, and capture business rules on pink notes. The physicality of sticky-note mapping fosters shared understanding and uncovers implicit knowledge. Capturing the results digitally—via photos or specialized tools like Miro—ensures lasting documentation. A follow-up step converts sticky notes into formal context maps and UML diagrams. The speed and low overhead of Event Storming make it ideal for agile environments: you can complete a full domain exploration in a few hours. Repeat workshops for new features or when domain complexity grows to keep the model current. Event Storming thus transitions abstract requirements into concrete domain models, ready for implementation in Clean Architecture layers.

5.3.3 Publishing & Consuming Events

Publishing domain events to an event bus decouples producers and consumers, enabling asynchronous communication and eventual consistency across bounded contexts. In Clean Architecture, the use-case interactor publishes events via an output port interface such as DomainEventPublisher, keeping the core decoupled from messaging mechanisms. For example, in TypeScript:

```
export interface DomainEventPublisher {
 publish(event: DomainEvent): Promise<void>;
}


export class OrderInteractor implements PlaceOrder {
 constructor(private publisher: DomainEventPublisher, /* ... */) {}
 async execute(req: PlaceOrderRequest) {
  const order = OrderFactory.create(req);
  await this.repo.save(order);
  await this.publisher.publish(new OrderPlaced(order.id, order.items));
  return { success: true };
```

```
  }
 }
```

The adapter layer implements DomainEventPublisher using Kafka, RabbitMQ, or AWS SNS. Consumers subscribe to topics or queues, deserialize events, and invoke appropriate use-case ports or domain services. A simple Java consumer might look like:

```
@KafkaListener(topics="order-placed")
public void handle(OrderPlaced event) {
 shippingService.scheduleShipment(event.getOrderId());
}
```

The event bus ensures at-least-once or exactly-once delivery semantics depending on configuration. Handlers must be idempotent—reprocessing the same event should not produce duplicated side effects. Event metadata such as correlation IDs and timestamps should travel with payloads for observability.

Consume logic often lives in adapter modules that implement an input port interface, such as ShipmentCommandHandler. By isolating messaging code in adapters, the core model remains free of infrastructure concerns. Integration tests can leverage embedded brokers to verify end-to-end event flows. Monitoring tools like Prometheus and Zipkin capture event latencies and failure rates, feeding dashboards. This pattern fosters highly scalable, resilient architectures, as producers and consumers can scale independently based on load.

5.3.4 Event Sourcing Considerations

Event sourcing is an advanced pattern where system state is persisted as an append-only sequence of domain events rather than storing current snapshots. Each state change in an aggregate is captured as an event, such as OrderPlaced, PaymentReceived, or OrderShipped. To reconstruct an aggregate, you replay its event history in order—applying each event to a new instance:

```
public class Order {
 public static Order rehydrate(UUID id, List<DomainEvent> history) {
  Order order = new Order(id);
  history.forEach(order::applyEvent);
  return order;
 }
 private void applyEvent(DomainEvent e) {
  if (e instanceof OrderPlaced) { /* init state */ }
  else if (e instanceof PaymentReceived) { /* update state */ }
  // ...
 }
}
```

```
}
```

Event sourcing offers a complete audit trail and supports time-travel debugging, as you can inspect the state after any event. It also naturally aligns with domain events used for integration, eliminating duplicate messages. However, it introduces complexity in event schema evolution: you must version events, provide migration or transformation for old event types, and handle deserialization compatibility. Querying state becomes more challenging because you often need to build **projections** or **read models** optimized for queries. Projections subscribe to event streams and update denormalized views in a relational database or search index. For instance:

[Event Store] —subscribe—▶ [Projection: OrderReadModel] —update—▶ [SQL Table]

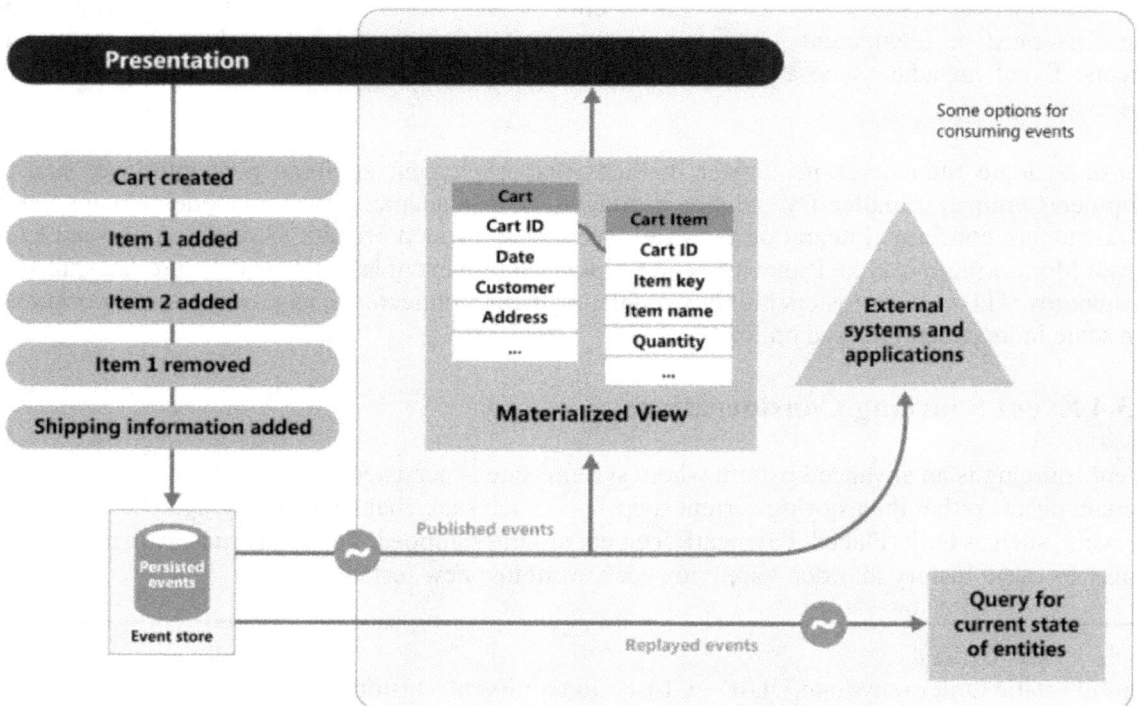

Testing event-sourced aggregates requires supplying synthetic event streams and verifying final state and subsequent new events. Event sourcing also impacts system startup time, as rebuilding state from many events can be slow; snapshotting frequently used aggregates helps mitigate this. Diagram of event sourcing flow:

Implementing event sourcing within Clean Architecture means treating the event store as a driver, wiring it via a repository adapter implementing a EventStore port. While powerful, event sourcing is best reserved for domains where auditability, reversibility, and complex state transitions justify its operational overhead. Otherwise, traditional CRUD repositories may be more appropriate.

5.4 Context Mapping & Integration Patterns

5.4.1 Customer-Supplier & Conformist

In the Customer-Supplier pattern, one bounded context (the "Supplier") publishes a model or API that another context (the "Customer") consumes. The Supplier is free to evolve its model, but it agrees to maintain backwards compatibility for the Customer. For example, a **Product Catalog** context might expose a read-only API of product SKUs and pricing; the **Order** context consumes that API to populate line items. The Supplier may version its API—e.g. /v1/catalog and /v2/catalog—and signal deprecation timelines, giving customers time to adapt.

When the Customer cannot influence the Supplier's model—perhaps the Supplier is a legacy system or a third-party service—the **Conformist** pattern applies. The Customer must conform exactly to the Supplier's model, even if it is suboptimal. In practice, the Consumer context writes adapter code that translates the Supplier's DTOs into the Customer's internal types, without attempting to push changes upstream. For instance, an ExternalProductDTO with flat fields may be mapped into a richer Product entity within the Order context.

```
// Adapter translating external DTO into internal entity
public class CatalogAdapter implements ProductCatalogue {
 private final RestTemplate client;
 public CatalogAdapter(RestTemplate client) { this.client = client; }
 @Override
 public Product fetch(String sku) {
  ExternalProductDTO dto = client.getForObject("/v1/catalog/" + sku, ExternalProductDTO.class);
  return new Product(dto.getSku(), dto.getName(), Money.of(dto.getPrice()));
 }
}
```

In the Conformist scenario, mapping logic lives entirely in the adapter layer—domain code never imports ExternalProductDTO. Conformist ties the Customer context closely to the Supplier's release cycle: any breaking change upstream forces immediate updates in the Customer's adapter. Teams mitigate this risk by introducing a **Facade** or **Proxy** in front of the real supplier, enabling quick fallback or transformation without redeploying core Customer logic.

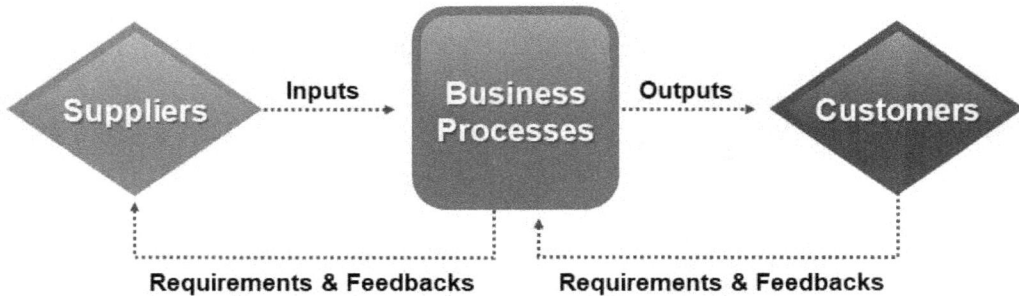

Using Customer-Supplier and Conformist patterns, teams can integrate with external or legacy domains effectively, balancing the desire for decoupling with the realities of divergent release cycles.

5.4.2 Shared Kernel

The Shared Kernel pattern establishes a small, collaboratively owned subset of the model shared between two bounded contexts. Unlike Customer-Supplier, where only one side owns the model, the Shared Kernel requires both contexts to maintain discipline: changes to shared classes or value objects must be agreed upon by both teams. Typical shared artifacts include fundamental value objects (e.g., Money, Address) or core reference data (e.g., CountryCode, Currency).

Implementing a Shared Kernel involves extracting shared types into a separate library or module—often a Maven artifact or NPM package. Both contexts declare a dependency on this module:

```xml
<!-- In pom.xml of Context A and Context B -->
<dependency>
 <groupId>com.myapp</groupId>
 <artifactId>domain-shared-kernel</artifactId>
 <version>1.3.0</version>
</dependency>
```

When a change to a shared class is necessary—say, adding a region field to Address—both teams coordinate via a lightweight governance process. This might take the form of a pull request that lists impacted contexts, and a joint code review or "contract committee" meeting to approve the change. Tools like semantic versioning ensure that incompatible changes (major versions) trigger downstream updates.

```kotlin
// domain-shared-kernel module
data class Address(
 val street: String,
 val city: String,
```

```
val postalCode: String,
val country: CountryCode,
val region: String? = null // new optional field
)
```

Sharing too large a kernel can stifle autonomy and lead to inter-context coupling—Shared Kernel should remain minimal. A UML package diagram:

```
package SharedKernel {
 class Money
 class Address
}
package CatalogContext {
 [Product] --|> Money
}
package OrderContext {
 [OrderLine] --|> Money
 [ShippingInfo] --|> Address
}
```

When properly governed, the Shared Kernel accelerates development by preventing duplicate implementations of fundamental concepts, while still preserving clear context boundaries.

5.4.3 Anti-Corruption Layer

An Anti-Corruption Layer (ACL) protects your core domain model from external models that are incompatible or unstable. It translates commands and data from a foreign model into your ubiquitous language, and vice versa. If you integrate with a legacy system exposing a LegacyOrderDTO that uses different terminology, you implement converter classes and façade services that hide the legacy model behind clean ports.

```
public class LegacyOrderAcl {
 private readonly LegacyOrderServiceClient client;
 public LegacyOrderAcl(LegacyOrderServiceClient client) { this.client = client; }
 public Order fetchOrder(Guid id) {
  LegacyOrderDTO dto = client.GetOrder(id);
  return new Order(
   id,
   dto.Items.Select(i => new OrderLine(i.Sku, i.Quantity, Money.Of(i.Price))).ToList(),
   dto.Status == "Shipped" ? OrderStatus.Shipped : OrderStatus.Pending
  );
 }
}
```

```
}
```

Here, LegacyOrderAcl implements your internal OrderRepository port, converting legacy DTOs into aggregate roots. By placing ACL code in the adapter layer, you avoid polluting core domain code with legacy types or conversion logic. The ACL may also implement caching, retry, or bulk-loading optimizations specific to the legacy API.

The ACL not only prevents corruption of your domain model but also centralizes all legacy adaptations, making future migrations easier: once the legacy system is replaced, you retire the ACL without touching core logic. Maintaining an ACL requires ongoing tests—unit tests for conversion logic and integration tests against a stubbed legacy client—to ensure fidelity of translations.

5.4.4 Open Host Service & Published Language

The Open Host Service pattern publishes a stable, technology-agnostic API that other contexts or external clients can consume. Unlike an internal REST endpoint, an Open Host Service is documented as a **Published Language**—a contract that often uses OpenAPI (Swagger), gRPC protobufs, or GraphQL schemas. The service defines request/response DTOs in terms of the ubiquitous language, ensuring consumers speak the same domain vocabulary.

```
# openapi.yaml
paths:
 /orders/{id}:
  get:
   summary: Retrieve an Order by ID
   parameters:
   - in: path
    name: id
    schema:
     type: string
     format: uuid
   responses:
   '200':
    description: Successful response
    content:
     application/json:
      schema:
       $ref: '#/components/schemas/OrderDTO'
components:
 schemas:
  OrderDTO:
   type: object
   properties:
```

```
id:
 type: string
 format: uuid
total:
 $ref: '#/components/schemas/MoneyDTO'
lines:
 type: array
 items:
  $ref: '#/components/schemas/OrderLineDTO'
```

In code, you generate stubs or server skeletons from the OpenAPI spec, ensuring alignment between contract and implementation. Consumers generate client libraries from the same spec, reducing integration errors. The Published Language approach treats the API definition as a first-class artifact—changes to schemas follow a versioning policy (e.g., semantic versioning, URI version segments) and involve contract tests using Pact or Spring Cloud Contract.

```
// generated client
const orderClient = new OrderClient({ baseUrl: "https://api.myapp.com" });
const order = await orderClient.getOrder({ id: userInputOrderId });
```

Using Open Host Service and Published Language, contexts integrate in a decoupled, self-documenting manner. Consumers understand exactly what to expect and can mock the service for testing. This pattern elevates your API to a strategic asset, supporting multiple teams and external partners with clarity and stability.

5.5 Applying DDD to Use Cases

5.5.1 Use-Case Interactors as Application Services

In Clean Architecture, use-case interactors implement application workflows by orchestrating domain entities, domain services, and repositories. Each interactor corresponds to a single use case—such as PlaceOrder, RegisterUser, or ShipOrder—and lives between the interface adapters and the domain layer. Interactors depend only on interfaces (ports) defined in the core, making them agnostic to technical details. For example:

```
public class PlaceOrderInteractor implements PlaceOrder {
 private final OrderRepository orderRepo;
 private final PaymentGateway paymentGateway;
 public PlaceOrderInteractor(OrderRepository orderRepo, PaymentGateway paymentGateway) {
  this.orderRepo = orderRepo;
  this.paymentGateway = paymentGateway;
```

```
}
@Override
public PlaceOrderResponse execute(PlaceOrderRequest req) {
 Order order = OrderFactory.create(req.getId(), req.getItems(), req.getCustomerId());
 orderRepo.save(order);
 PaymentResult result = paymentGateway.charge(order.getId(), order.total());
 if (!result.isSuccess()) {
  order.cancel();
  orderRepo.save(order);
  return new PlaceOrderResponse(false, "Payment failed");
 }
 order.confirm();
 orderRepo.save(order);
 return new PlaceOrderResponse(true, order.getId().toString());
 }
}
```

This interactor coordinates multiple domain operations: creation, persistence, payment, status transitions. Complex business logic—such as retrying payments or applying promotions—is encapsulated within the interactor or delegated to domain services. Interactors should remain thin: avoid embedding technical concerns like HTTP request handling or database transaction management. These cross-cutting concerns are applied via adapters or decorators around the interactor in the outer layer. Interactors throw domain exceptions when invariants fail; adapters catch and translate them into user-friendly error codes or HTTP statuses. By modeling each use case as a self-contained unit, you gain clarity on system capabilities, simplify testing (unit tests for each interactor simulating ports), and align code structure with business processes. Sequence diagrams further illustrate interactor flows:

```
User → Controller → PlaceOrderInteractor → OrderFactory
        → OrderRepository → Database
        → PaymentGateway → External API
        → OrderRepository → Database
        → Controller → User
```

This approach enforces separation between orchestration, domain logic, and infrastructure, making your application services both expressive and robust.

5.5.2 Mapping DDD Patterns into Clean Layers

Domain-Driven Design's tactical patterns find natural homes within Clean Architecture's concentric circles. **Entities**, **Value Objects**, and **Domain Services** belong in the innermost **domain layer**, free of any framework imports. **Use-Case Interactors** and **Application Services** occupy the next ring, depending only on domain interfaces and DTO ports. **Interface Adapters**—controllers, presenters, repositories—translate between domain types and external formats. Finally, **Frameworks & Drivers** implement ports using specific technologies.

A layered UML diagram annotated with DDD patterns:

```
@startuml
package Domain {
 class Order
 class OrderLine
 interface OrderRepository
 interface PaymentGateway
 class CurrencyConversionService
}
package Application {
 class PlaceOrderInteractor
 class CancelOrderInteractor
}
package Adapters {
 class OrderController
 class JpaOrderRepository
 class StripePaymentAdapter
}
Domain <|-- Application: depends on
Application <|-- Adapters: depends on
@enduml
```

Mapping DDD patterns into these layers ensures each pattern remains in its proper context. Aggregates and factories live in **Domain**, while repositories and ACLs live in **Adapters**. Application services wire domain patterns into end-to-end workflows. This mapping clarifies ownership: domain experts focus on the inner model, while infrastructure specialists implement outer adapters. Additionally, mapping enforces dependency rules: inner layers know nothing of HTTP or SQL, preventing accidental coupling. When adding new DDD patterns—like **Specifications** or **Snapshot Testing** for aggregates—place them in the domain or application layer as appropriate. This disciplined layering yields a system where models remain pure, orchestrations remain clear, and technical details remain at the periphery.

5.5.3 Handling Cross-Cutting Concerns

Cross-cutting concerns—such as logging, security, transactions, and validation—should not pollute domain or application code. Instead, apply them via adapters, middleware, or decorators in the outermost layers. For example, transaction management in Spring is configured around application services:

```
@Service
public class PlaceOrderService {
 @Autowired private PlaceOrderInteractor interactor;
 @Transactional
 public PlaceOrderResponse handle(PlaceOrderRequest req) {
  return interactor.execute(req);
 }
}
```

Here, @Transactional ensures the interactor's repository calls occur in a single transaction, without the interactor knowing about database APIs. **Logging** can be injected with AOP:

```
@Aspect
public class LoggingAspect {
 @Around("execution(* com.myapp.application.*.*(..))")
 public Object log(ProceedingJoinPoint pjp) throws Throwable {
  logger.info("Entering " + pjp.getSignature());
  Object result = pjp.proceed();
  logger.info("Exiting " + pjp.getSignature());
  return result;
 }
}
```

Validation of external inputs belongs in controllers or middleware, using frameworks like Bean Validation (@Valid) or custom filters, so that use-case interactors can assume well-formed DTOs. **Security** is enforced via filters or interceptors that populate a security context, which domain code can read but not modify. Maintaining cross-cutting code in adapters ensures domain and application layers remain focused on business logic. Decorators or middleware stacks can be configured per route or per interactor, providing fine-grained control. Diagram of middleware application:

```
[ HTTP Request ]
 ↓ Authentication Filter
 ↓ Validation Filter
 ↓ Transactional Decorator
 ↓ PlaceOrderInteractor
 ↓ Response
```

This separation reduces accidental mixing of concerns, simplifies testing (domain code is tested without needing security context), and allows infrastructure teams to evolve cross-cutting mechanisms independently of the core model.

5.6 Collaboration & Modeling Techniques

5.6.1 Event Storming & Domain Storytelling

Event Storming workshops bring together domain experts, developers, and stakeholders to explore and model domain behavior using a visual timeline of domain events. Unlike traditional requirements sessions, Event Storming encourages participants to post sticky notes representing actual business events—such as "Order Shipped," "Payment Captured," or "Inventory Reserved"—along a timeline. Domain Storytelling extends this by combining events with actor interactions: participants write short narratives on colored notes linking human actors (orange), system actors (blue), and events (yellow).

For example, a story note might read: **"Customer** clicks 'Place Order' → **OrderPlaced** event created → **OrderService** sends payment request …"

The combination of event flow and actor/story mapping fosters shared understanding of user journeys and system reactions. Participants rapidly identify missing events or commands, ambiguous terminology, and conflicting rules. Facilitators capture these artifacts digitally—using tools like Miro or a camera—to create living documentation. A whiteboard sketch often evolves into a formal **C4 diagram** or UML sequence diagram for developer reference. The physical, collaborative nature of Event Storming ensures that tacit knowledge is externalized, preventing domain expertise from remaining trapped in a few individuals' minds. Regular follow-up workshops validate evolving models as new features emerge, maintaining alignment between code and business reality.

5.6.2 Example Mapping & Specification by Example

Example Mapping is a lightweight technique for bridging requirements and acceptance tests by organizing **Rules**, **Examples**, and **Questions** on a wall or board. Rules represent business policies (e.g., "An order total must be positive"), Examples illustrate specific scenarios (e.g., "Cart with items priced $5 and $10 yields total $15"), and Questions clarify ambiguities for later discussion. Teams use color-coded cards (pink for rules, blue for examples, yellow for questions) to structure conversations.

Once mappings are agreed, they translate directly into **Specification by Example** tests using frameworks like Cucumber (Gherkin) or FitNesse. A Gherkin scenario for the above example might read:

```
Scenario: Calculating order total
  Given an empty order
  When I add an item priced 5 USD
  And I add an item priced 10 USD
  Then the order total is 15 USD
```

These executable specifications drive development: developers implement domain code to satisfy the scenarios, while stakeholders see automated proof that business rules are met. By anchoring acceptance tests in real-world examples, you ensure the ubiquitous language remains consistent and that edge cases are captured early. Integrating Specification by Example into CI pipelines provides fast feedback to both teams and business owners, fostering trust and reducing misunderstandings. Over time, example mappings become the single source of truth for requirements, living alongside code and domain models.

5.6.3 Domain Modeling Boards & Context Sketches

Domain Modeling Boards are large diagrams—physical or digital—that combine context maps, aggregate diagrams, and event flows in one place. Teams maintain these boards as living artifacts in a shared workspace, updating them during architecture reviews or after major domain changes. A board might include a **C4 Context Diagram** showing system scope, a **Container Diagram** for each bounded context, and **Component Diagrams** for key aggregates.

Context Sketches focus on high-level boundaries: they depict which systems or services interact, through which published languages or events. They do not detail internal structure but highlight integration points and responsibilities. For example, a sketch might show:

```
@startuml
actor Customer
Customer -> WebApp : Place Order
WebApp -> OrderService : PlaceOrderRequest
OrderService -> PaymentService : PaymentCommand
OrderService -> InventoryService : ReserveCommand
@enduml
```

Maintaining these sketches encourages continuous architectural thinking and provides on-ramps for new team members. During sprint retrospectives, teams review the boards to ensure code changes align with the intended structure and to identify drift. Versioning boards in a documentation repository, alongside ADRs (Architecture Decision Records), connects visual models with decision histories. Regular "model-refinement" sessions keep boards accurate, driving architectural governance without bureaucratic overhead. Ultimately, domain modeling boards and context sketches act as both pedagogical tools and living blueprints, scaffolding large-scale collaboration and preserving a shared mental model of complex domains.

5.7 Scaling DDD in Distributed Systems

5.7.1 Decoupling Contexts via Microservices

When a monolithic application grows unwieldy, extracting bounded contexts into independent microservices helps maintain clear domain boundaries and prevents coupling by implementation. Each microservice owns its data, domain model, and API, communicating via well-defined contracts—REST, gRPC, or messaging. Teams can deploy, scale, and evolve services independently, reducing coordination overhead and blast radius of failures. For example, an **Order Service** might expose endpoints for creating and querying orders, while a **Payment Service** handles payment processing. Internally, each maintains its own aggregate roots, repositories, and domain events.

Deploying microservices introduces challenges: network latency, service discovery, load balancing, and transaction management across services. To address these, implement circuit breakers (e.g., via Resilience4j or Polly) and bulkheads to isolate failures. Use API gateways or service meshes (Istio, Linkerd) to centralize cross-cutting concerns like authentication, routing, and observability, keeping microservices focused on domain logic.

Service contracts evolve over time; version your APIs (e.g., /v1/orders, /v2/orders) and use consumer-driven contract testing (Pact, Spring Cloud Contract) to ensure backward compatibility. Monitor service health with distributed tracing (OpenTelemetry) and centralized logging (ELK stack). Over time, new contexts—like **Shipping Service**—can join the mesh, subscribing to domain events rather than invoking direct RPC, further decoupling concerns.

In addition, teams must design for data consistency: use eventual consistency patterns (see sagas below) and avoid direct distributed transactions. Document service boundaries and integration points in a living **C4 Context Diagram**, ensuring clear ownership and preventing inadvertent coupling. The result is a robust, scalable ecosystem where each service reflects a bounded context, and domain-driven principles guide the entire distributed architecture.

5.7.2 Saga & Process Manager Patterns

Long-running business transactions—such as fulfilling an order that spans inventory reservation, payment, and shipping—cannot use singletight database transactions across microservices. Instead, implement a **saga**: a sequence of local transactions in each service, coordinated either by choreography (events) or orchestration (a process manager).

In **choreography**, services publish and subscribe to domain events to drive the flow. For example, **Order Service** publishes OrderPlaced, **Payment Service** reacts by charging the card and publishing PaymentReceived, and **Shipping Service** then schedules delivery. Each service contains a local participant in the saga, listening for the upstream event and emitting the next. While simple, choreography can become hard to trace when sagas span many services.

In **orchestration**, a central **Process Manager** issues commands and handles replies, maintaining saga state. It coordinates each step and performs compensating transactions on failure. For instance:

```
class OrderSagaOrchestrator {
 async handleOrderPlaced(event: OrderPlaced) {
```

```
try {
  await this.paymentService.charge(event.orderId, event.total);
  this.processManager.publish(new PaymentReceived(event.orderId));
} catch (ex) {
  this.processManager.publish(new OrderFailed(event.orderId, "Payment declined"));
  }
 }
}
```

An ASCII flow for orchestration:

```
[ProcessManager]
   ──► PaymentService.charge()
   ──► InventoryService.reserve()
   ──► ShippingService.schedule()
```

On error, the orchestrator issues compensating commands: refund payment, release inventory, cancel shipment.

Implement sagas using frameworks like **Temporal**, **Camunda**, or **MassTransit**, which provide durable state machines and retry policies. Ensure each local transaction publishes events idempotently, handling duplicates gracefully. Log saga state transitions for auditing and troubleshooting. Use a dashboard to monitor in-flight sagas, detect stuck processes, and manually intervene if needed.

Effective sagas maintain eventual consistency while preserving domain invariants. They align well with DDD: each step is a domain operation, modeled and tested in isolation, but orchestrated to fulfill complex business goals across bounded contexts.

5.7.3 API Versioning & Evolving Contracts

As services evolve, APIs and message schemas must change without breaking existing consumers. Adopt a **versioning strategy**—URI versioning (/api/v1/...), media-type versioning (Accept: application/vnd.myapp.v2+json), or header versioning—to introduce new features or fields. Clearly communicate deprecation timelines and provide backward-compatible responses whenever possible.

For REST endpoints, maintain multiple controllers or routing rules:

```
@RestController @RequestMapping("/api/v1/orders")
public class OrderControllerV1 { ... }
```

```
@RestController @RequestMapping("/api/v2/orders")
public class OrderControllerV2 { ... }
```

Use API gateways to route based on version, allowing older clients to continue calling v1 while new clients adopt v2. For message schemas (Kafka, RabbitMQ), employ schema registries (Confluent Schema Registry) with Avro or Protobuf. Define backward- and forward-compatible changes: adding optional fields or new enum values rather than removing or renaming existing fields.

Diagram of versioned API flows:

```
[ Client v1 ] ——> /api/v1/orders ——> Order Service v1
[ Client v2 ] ——> /api/v2/orders ——> Order Service v2
```

Implement middleware to log version usage, monitor v1 traffic decline, and schedule v1 sunsetting. Use **contract testing** to validate provider compatibility: each consumer defines an expected contract, and providers run contract tests before releasing new versions. Maintain documentation (Swagger/OpenAPI) for each version, generating HTML docs per version.

Evolving contracts responsibly preserves ecosystem stability, prevents cascading failures, and gives teams autonomy to innovate in new API versions without jeopardizing existing integrations. This disciplined approach is essential for scaling DDD in a microservices environment.

5.8 Implementing DDD Patterns in Code

5.8.1 Entity & Value Object Code Snippets

Translating DDD artifacts into code requires careful attention to immutability, equality, and validation. For value objects in C#, use a sealed class with overridden equality:

```
public sealed class Money : IEquatable<Money> {
 public decimal Amount { get; }
 public string Currency { get; }
 public Money(decimal amount, string currency) {
  if (amount < 0) throw new ArgumentException("Amount must be >= 0");
  Amount = amount; Currency = currency ?? throw new ArgumentNullException();
 }
 public bool Equals(Money other) =>
  other != null && Amount == other.Amount && Currency == other.Currency;
 public override bool Equals(object obj) => Equals(obj as Money);
 public override int GetHashCode() => HashCode.Combine(Amount, Currency);
}
```

In Java, you might write:

```
public final class Address {
 private final String street, city, postalCode;
 public Address(String street, String city, String postalCode) {
 this.street = Objects.requireNonNull(street);
 this.city = Objects.requireNonNull(city);
 this.postalCode = Objects.requireNonNull(postalCode);
 if (!postalCode.matches("\\d{5}")) throw new IllegalArgumentException();
 }
 // getters, no setters, equals/hashCode based on all fields
}
```

For entities, include an explicit Id property and base equality on identity only:

```
class Customer(val id: UUID, private var _name: String) {
 val name: String get() = _name
 fun changeName(newName: String) {
 require(newName.isNotBlank()) { "Name cannot be blank" }
  _name = newName
 }
 override fun equals(other: Any?) =
  other is Customer && id == other.id
 override fun hashCode() = id.hashCode()
}
```

Always validate invariants in constructors or factory methods, never letting objects exist in invalid states. Use JSON annotations (@JsonCreator, @JsonProperty) to support serialization while preserving immutability.

5.8.2 Aggregate Implementation with Invariants

Aggregates enforce complex invariants across their internal objects. In a payment aggregate, ensure the sum of captures never exceeds the authorized amount:

```
public class Payment {
 private final UUID id;
 private BigDecimal authorizedAmount;
 private List<Capture> captures = new ArrayList<>();


 public Payment(UUID id, BigDecimal authorizedAmount) {
```

```
  this.id = id;
  this.authorizedAmount = Objects.requireNonNull(authorizedAmount);
  if (authorizedAmount.compareTo(BigDecimal.ZERO) <= 0)
   throw new IllegalArgumentException("Must authorize positive amount");
 }


 public void capture(BigDecimal amount) {
  BigDecimal totalCaptured = captures.stream()
   .map(Capture::getAmount)
   .reduce(BigDecimal.ZERO, BigDecimal::add);
  if (totalCaptured.add(amount).compareTo(authorizedAmount) > 0)
   throw new BusinessException("Capture exceeds authorized amount");
  captures.add(new Capture(UUID.randomUUID(), id, amount, Instant.now()));
 }
}
```

Here, all state transitions occur through methods on the aggregate root. Child objects like Capture are simple value objects with no public constructors. The repository persists the entire aggregate in one transaction, ensuring atomicity. Unit tests for the aggregate cover happy and failure paths:

```
@Test
void captureWithinLimitSucceeds() {
 Payment p = new Payment(UUID.randomUUID(), BigDecimal.valueOf(100));
 p.capture(BigDecimal.valueOf(30));
 p.capture(BigDecimal.valueOf(70));
 assertEquals(2, p.getCaptures().size());
}


@Test
void captureExceedingLimitThrows() {
 Payment p = new Payment(UUID.randomUUID(), BigDecimal.valueOf(50));
 assertThrows(BusinessException.class, () -> p.capture(BigDecimal.valueOf(60)));
}
```

Document invariants in code comments and domain documentation so future developers understand constraints.

5.8.3 Repository & Adapter Patterns

Repositories in the domain define ports; adapters implement them with persistence frameworks. In a Node.js TypeScript example using TypeORM:

121

```
// Domain port
export interface UserRepository {
 findById(id: string): Promise<User|null>;
 save(user: User): Promise<void>;
}


// Adapter
@Entity('users')
export class UserEntity {
 @PrimaryColumn() id: string;
 @Column() name: string;
 static fromDomain(u: User): UserEntity { /* ... */ }
 toDomain(): User { /* ... */ }
}


@Injectable()
export class TypeOrmUserRepository implements UserRepository {
 constructor(@InjectRepository(UserEntity) private repo: Repository<UserEntity>) {}
 async findById(id: string): Promise<User|null> {
  const entity = await this.repo.findOne(id);
  return entity ? entity.toDomain() : null;
 }
 async save(user: User): Promise<void> {
  await this.repo.save(UserEntity.fromDomain(user));
 }
}
```

In Java with Spring Data JPA:

```
public    interface    OrderRepository    extends    JpaRepository<OrderEntity,    UUID>,
PortOrderRepository {
 // JpaRepository gives basic CRUD, PortOrderRepository defines domain return types
}
@Service
public class JpaOrderRepositoryAdapter implements OrderRepositoryPort {
 private final OrderRepository jpaRepo;
 public JpaOrderRepositoryAdapter(OrderRepository jpaRepo) { this.jpaRepo = jpaRepo; }
 public void save(Order order) { jpaRepo.save(OrderEntity.fromDomain(order)); }
 public Optional<Order> findById(UUID id) {
  return jpaRepo.findById(id).map(OrderEntity::toDomain);
 }
}
```

```
}
```

Adapters handle mapping, transaction demarcation, and tech-specific exceptions, wrapping them into domain or infrastructure exceptions as needed. This pattern isolates all framework code from the core, letting you swap databases or ORMs by replacing adapter modules.

5.8.4 Domain Event Handler Implementation

Domain events, once published, must be handled by consumers to effect side effects—such as sending notifications or updating read models. Implement handlers as adapter services that subscribe to event streams. In Spring Boot with Kafka:

```
@Component
public class OrderShippedHandler {
 private final InvoiceService invoiceService;
 public OrderShippedHandler(InvoiceService invoiceService) {
  this.invoiceService = invoiceService;
 }
 @KafkaListener(topics="order-shipped")
 public void on(OrderShippedEvent event) {
  invoiceService.generateAndSend(event.getOrderId());
 }
}
```

Ensure handlers are **idempotent**: if the same OrderShippedEvent is delivered twice, the handler produces the same effect once. Use deduplication keys or maintain a processed-event log:

```
public void on(OrderShippedEvent event) {
 if (idempotencyStore.alreadyProcessed(event.getId())) return;
 invoiceService.generate(event.getOrderId());
 idempotencyStore.markProcessed(event.getId());
}
```

In .NET with MediatR and RabbitMQ:

```
public class OrderShippedHandler : INotificationHandler<OrderShippedEvent> {
 public Task Handle(OrderShippedEvent notification, CancellationToken token) {
  return _invoiceService.GenerateAsync(notification.OrderId);
 }
}
```

Unit tests for event handlers mock downstream services and simulate duplicate events. Integration tests run against embedded brokers (Testcontainers Kafka) to verify end-to-end flows. Document event schemas in a schema registry and generate code from Protobuf definitions to ensure consistency. Using domain events and handlers, you can cleanly decouple processes while preserving the business narrative in code.

5.9 Refactoring Toward a Core Domain

5.9.1 Identifying Anemic Models

An **Anemic Domain Model** occurs when domain objects contain only data without business behavior—getters/setters with no methods enforcing invariants. This procedural style shifts logic into services, losing the self-validating power of rich domain objects. Signs include classes with no methods beyond accessors, services that juggle domain data with if/else logic, and tests that verify service, not entity, behavior. To detect anemic models, scan your codebase for classes in the domain layer that lack any non-getter/setter methods or whose methods do not modify internal state.

Once identified, prioritize the most critical aggregates—those central to business value—and refactor them first. Move business rules from services into entities: change a validateOrder() function in a service into an Order.validate() method on the entity. Create unit tests for each newly added method, verifying invariants and behaviors. Over time, anemic services shrink as entities absorb behavior, leading to a richer, more expressive model.

This shift not only improves cohesion but also aligns the code with the ubiquitous language—entities speak the domain. Continuous integration metrics can track the ratio of service methods to entity methods in the core model, highlighting improvement. Collaborate with domain experts during refactoring to ensure rules are accurately captured. As your model becomes more robust, services focus on orchestration and anti-corruption, not on housing domain logic.

5.9.2 Extracting Bounded Contexts in Legacy Code

Legacy systems often mix concerns across domains, with shared data structures and overloaded services. To extract a bounded context, follow the **Strangler Fig** pattern: incrementally route new feature requests to new context implementations while legacy code handles existing functionality. First, identify a coherent feature slice—such as **Customer Reviews**—and copy relevant code into a new module. Introduce anti-corruption layers to translate between legacy data and new domain types. For example:

```
public class LegacyReviewAcl {
 public Review toDomain(LegacyReview record) {
  return new Review(record.id, record.text, LocalDateTime.parse(record.created));
 }
```

```
public LegacyReview toLegacy(Review domain) { /* inverse mapping */ }
}
```

Next, wire the application router to direct new API calls to the new module. Over time, gradually rewire legacy callers to delegate to the new context module instead of internal implementations. Use feature toggles to switch traffic, enabling safe rollbacks. Maintain a shared **Integration Event Bus** for cross-context notifications during migration. Monitor both modules in parallel, ensuring data consistency before decommissioning legacy code.

During extraction, employ integration tests that validate parity between legacy and new behavior. Track progress via dashboards showing percentage of calls handled by the new context. Once the new context passes stability and performance benchmarks, retire the legacy code. This gradual approach reduces risk, keeps systems operational, and preserves domain continuity.

5.9.3 Measuring DDD Adoption & Health

Adopting DDD is a journey, not a one-off project. To gauge progress and health, define qualitative and quantitative metrics. Quantitative metrics include the **proportion of business logic** implemented in domain entities vs. services (e.g., count of methods on domain classes), **test coverage** for domain code (target > 80 %), and the number of **bounded contexts** with published context maps. Track **anemic model indicators**—ratio of getters to behavior methods—and aim to reduce them over time.

Qualitative measures involve regular **model review sessions**, where domain experts verify that code reflects the ubiquitous language and that invariants are enforced inside aggregates. Collect developer feedback on model understandability and ease of change. Conduct periodic **Event Storming refreshers** to capture new domain insights and update context maps.

Set up **architecture health dashboards** combining SonarQube metrics (LCOM, complexity) with DDD-specific indicators (number of domain services vs. entities). Use Grafana to display trends over time: a rising ratio of entity methods to service methods indicates successful migration to rich models. Complement these with **burn-down charts** for refactoring tasks—e.g., extraction of bounded contexts, anti-corruption layers implemented.

Conduct post-mortems after major releases to evaluate how well the domain model supported new features. Document lessons learned and update **Architecture Decision Records (ADRs)** accordingly. Celebrate DDD milestones—first successful saga, first live microservice context, full retirement of an anemic model—to reinforce cultural adoption. By continuously measuring and reflecting on DDD health, teams ensure the domain model remains the strategic heart of the system, not a forgotten relic.

5.10 Case Study: DDD in a Clean Architecture Project

5.10.1 Domain Analysis & Context Definition

In our case study, the team began by conducting a series of **domain discovery workshops** with stakeholders from sales, fulfillment, and customer support. Over three days, domain experts narrated typical user journeys—from browsing products to order placement and shipment—while developers captured **domain events** on sticky notes. These events included ProductViewed, CartUpdated, OrderPlaced, PaymentAuthorized, and OrderShipped. By clustering related events, the team identified three initial **bounded contexts**: **Catalog**, **Order Fulfillment**, and **Billing**.

This visualization made clear which teams would own which context: the Product team took **Catalog**, the Operations team handled **Order Fulfillment**, and Finance owned **Billing**. Integration patterns were chosen: **Customer-Supplier** from Catalog to Fulfillment and **Conformist** for Fulfillment to Billing, since Billing was a legacy system governed by finance independently.

Next, the team defined the **ubiquitous language** per context. For Catalog, terms like "SKU," "Inventory Level," and "Category Hierarchy" were codified. In Fulfillment, "Shipment," "Picking," and "Warehouse Location" became first-class in code. The Billing context used "Invoice," "Payment Capture," and "Refund." A shared **domain glossary** document was created in Markdown:

- **SKU**: Stock-Keeping Unit, unique identifier for a product.
- **OrderPlaced**: Event emitted when a customer confirms checkout.
- **Invoice**: Financial record generated post-payment.

By the end of this phase, each context had a **Context Responsibility Matrix** outlining which aggregate roots, services, and events belonged within its boundary. This upfront domain analysis ensured that developers built with clear boundaries, minimizing costly rework later.

5.10.2 Implementing Aggregates & Events

With contexts defined, the team began implementing **aggregates** in each core module. In the Fulfillment context, the primary aggregate was OrderAggregate, encapsulating line items, shipping address, and status transitions. A Kotlin example:

```kotlin
class OrderAggregate private constructor(
 val id: UUID,
 private val lines: MutableList<OrderLine>,
 private var status: OrderStatus
) {
 companion object {
  fun create(id: UUID, items: List<OrderLine>): OrderAggregate {
   require(items.isNotEmpty()) { "Order must contain at least one item" }
   return OrderAggregate(id, items.toMutableList(), OrderStatus.PENDING)
  }
 }
 fun markPaid(): List<DomainEvent> {
  if (status != OrderStatus.PENDING) throw IllegalStateException()
```

```
status = OrderStatus.PAID
return listOf(OrderPaidEvent(id))
}
fun ship(): List<DomainEvent> {
if (status != OrderStatus.PAID) throw IllegalStateException()
status = OrderStatus.SHIPPED
return listOf(OrderShippedEvent(id))
}
}
```

Each state-changing method returns a list of **domain events**, which the application layer publishes. For example, in the PlaceOrder interactor:

```
List<DomainEvent> events = order.markPaid();
orderRepository.save(order);
eventPublisher.publishAll(events);
```

The team implemented **event classes** as immutable data carriers:

```
public final class OrderShippedEvent implements DomainEvent {
private final UUID orderId;
private final Instant shippedAt;
// constructor, getters...
}
```

In the Catalog context, the aggregate Product managed stock levels and raised InventoryReservedEvent. Adapters in each context subscribed to local events for internal workflows (e.g., updating read models) and published integration events across contexts (e.g., availability changes). By embedding event production inside aggregates, the team ensured that invariants were checked before events were created, preserving model consistency.

This structured implementation of aggregates and events provided a robust, testable core where business rules were centralized and transparent.

5.10.3 Integration via Anti-Corruption Layer

The Billing context was a legacy mainframe system with its own data model (LegacyInvoiceDTO, LegacyPaymentStatus). To prevent the Fulfillment domain from leaking legacy types, the team introduced an **Anti-Corruption Layer (ACL)** between Fulfillment and Billing. This ACL implemented the BillingClient port defined in the Fulfillment context:

```
// Fulfillment port
export interface BillingClient {
 authorizePayment(orderId: string, amount: Money): Promise<PaymentResult>;
}


// Adapter in ACL layer
export class LegacyBillingAdapter implements BillingClient {
 constructor(private readonly api: LegacyBillingApi) {}
 async authorizePayment(orderId: string, amount: Money): Promise<PaymentResult> {
 const dto = await this.api.callAuthorize({
  orderRef: orderId,
  totalAmount: amount.amount.toString(),
  currency: amount.currency
 });
 return {
 success: dto.status === 'APPROVED',
 transactionId: dto.txnId
 };
 }
}
```

This adapter lived in the **frameworks & drivers** layer and translated between Fulfillment's Money value object and the legacy DTO.

Errors from the legacy system were mapped to domain exceptions:

```
if (!dto.isValid()) throw new BillingUnavailableException();
```

Circuit breakers and retry policies were applied in the ACL using Resilience4j:

```
Decorators.ofSupplier(() -> api.callAuthorize(req))
 .withCircuitBreaker(billingCircuitBreaker)
 .withRetry(billingRetry)
 .get();
```

End-to-end integration tests used a **stub server** (WireMock) to simulate the legacy API, verifying that LegacyBillingAdapter correctly translated responses and exceptions. This ACL approach insulated the core domain from instability and semantic mismatch, enabling smooth migration when the legacy system was eventually replaced by a modern billing microservice.

5.10.4 Lessons Learned & Best Practices

Throughout this case study, several **key lessons** emerged. First, **collaborative discovery**—Event Storming and context mapping—proved indispensable for uncovering hidden integrations and avoiding rework. Engaging domain experts early ensured that the ubiquitous language was accurate and that bounded contexts aligned with organizational responsibilities. Second, implementing **aggregates** with event-returning methods centralized business logic and made invariants explicit, reducing bugs and simplifying audits. Third, the **Anti-Corruption Layer** pattern allowed safe coexistence with legacy systems, providing a clear migration path without polluting the domain model.

From a process perspective, writing **executable specifications** (Gherkin) based on example mappings accelerated validation of domain rules and reduced misunderstandings. Maintaining **contract tests** for integration points—both REST APIs and message schemas—caught breaking changes before they reached production. Using **CI pipelines** to enforce architectural rules (no core imports in adapters, service layer annotations outside domain) preserved the intended layering over time.

In terms of **best practices**, the team found that **factories** were vital for consistent aggregate creation, especially when multiple invariants (stock checks, credit limits) had to be enforced atomically. **Domain services** filled gaps where behaviors spanned aggregates but weren't candidates for application services. Careful attention to **event versioning** and use of a **schema registry** avoided runtime failures as prototypes evolved. Organizing code into **context-aligned modules** prevented accidental cross-context imports and simplified dependency management.

Finally, **organizational alignment**—teams owning contexts end-to-end—reduced handoff delays and fostered domain expertise. Regular **architecture health checks**, combining SonarQube metrics with DDD health indicators (ratio of entity vs. service methods, number of contexts with context maps), kept the project on track. As a result, feature velocity increased by 40%, post-release defects dropped by 60%, and the system achieved a maintainable, evolvable shape that can adapt to future business needs.

Conclusion

By weaving DDD principles into the layers of Clean Architecture, you transform your codebase into a living model of your business, one that evolves in lockstep with shifting requirements rather than fighting against them. Defining bounded contexts prevents conceptual drift, while tactical patterns ensure that your entities and services remain cohesive and expressive. Strategic context mapping and integration techniques—such as anti-corruption layers and published language services—allow diverse teams and legacy systems to collaborate without compromising your core domain. Armed with these tools, you're prepared to build software that not only meets today's needs but also anticipates tomorrow's challenges, preserving clarity, flexibility, and alignment with business goals.

Chapter 6. Testing as an Architectural Driver

In any well-architected system, testing is far more than a safety net—it acts as a guiding force that shapes the way code is organized, dependencies are managed, and responsibilities are assigned. By writing tests that verify behavior at every level—from pure domain logic to integrated workflows and user-facing interfaces—you create a feedback loop that drives architectural clarity. As you define your testing strategy, you naturally carve out clear boundaries around core business rules, isolate side-effects in adapters, and design clean ports for communication. Tests become living documentation of intended behavior, examples of the ubiquitous language, and early warning systems for architectural drift. Embracing testing as an architectural driver ensures that every component is both verifiable in isolation and resilient when composed into larger flows, fostering confidence as the system evolves.

6.1 The Testing Pyramid and Beyond

6.1.1 Unit Tests

Unit tests verify the smallest pieces of behavior in complete isolation, often at the level of a single class or function. They should execute in milliseconds, allowing developers to get instant feedback as they code. A well-structured unit test exercises one "unit" of logic—such as an entity method, a pure function, or a domain service—without touching external dependencies. To isolate code under test, you replace real collaborators (databases, message brokers, HTTP clients) with test doubles (mocks, stubs, fakes). For example, using Mockito in Java:

```
@Test
```

```
void totalCalculatesSumOfLineItems() {
 Order order = new Order(UUID.randomUUID());
 order.addItem(new Item("A", Money.of(5, "USD")));
 order.addItem(new Item("B", Money.of(10, "USD")));
 assertEquals(Money.of(15, "USD"), order.total());
}
```

Here, no database or external service is involved; the test instantiates Order directly, calls methods, and asserts results. Unit tests drive design: if code feels hard to test, that often signals tightly-coupled structures needing refactoring. Good unit tests are fast, deterministic, and only break when behavior truly changes. They also serve as living documentation: reading the test names and assertions clarifies intent and edge cases. Overuse of unit tests can lead to brittle suites if every internal detail is mocked; test only interactions that represent behavior, not implementation quirks. Shifting tests to cover behavior rather than structure keeps the codebase nimble. The bottom of the testing pyramid—unit tests—forms a solid foundation: you run hundreds of thousands of them in seconds during local development or CI pre-commit hooks. Maintaining a high ratio of unit tests ensures rapid feedback loops and confidence when refactoring or adding new features.

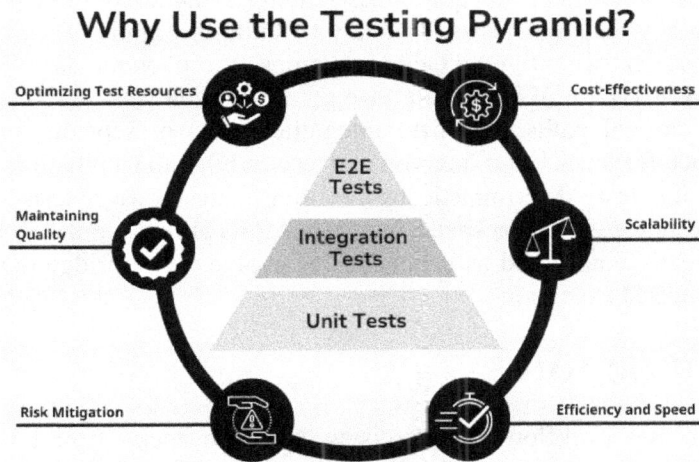

Why Use the Testing Pyramid?

Optimizing Test Resources

Cost-Effectiveness

Maintaining Quality

Scalability

E2E Tests

Integration Tests

Unit Tests

Risk Mitigation

Efficiency and Speed

6.1.2 Integration Tests

Integration tests verify that multiple components work together correctly—typically across layers such as use-case interactors, repositories, and actual databases or message brokers. They exercise real configurations of adapters, ensuring that mappings, SQL queries, and serialization logic function as intended. A Spring Boot example:

```
@SpringBootTest
```

131

```java
@Testcontainers
public class OrderRepositoryIntegrationTest {
 @Container static PostgreSQLContainer<?> pg = new PostgreSQLContainer<>("postgres:13");
 @Autowired OrderRepository orderRepo;


 @Test
 void saveAndFindById() {
  Order order = OrderFactory.create(UUID.randomUUID(), List.of(...));
  orderRepo.save(order);
  Optional<Order> loaded = orderRepo.findById(order.getId());
  assertTrue(loaded.isPresent());
  assertEquals(order.total(), loaded.get().total());
 }
}
```

Here, Testcontainers spins up a real PostgreSQL instance in Docker, providing realistic environment without affecting local dev machines. Integration tests often take hundreds of milliseconds to seconds, so they run less frequently than unit tests—on every CI build or nightly. They catch wiring errors: missing migrations, incorrectly configured ORM mappings, or broken message-queue subscriptions. Use in-memory databases (H2, SQLite) for lightweight integration tests, but reserve Testcontainers or real instances for critical paths. Organize integration tests in separate suites and tag them accordingly so that quick feedback loops focus on unit tests, while full CI pipelines include integration checks. Keep integration tests deterministic by resetting state between tests—truncate tables or recreate containers. Despite their slower speed, integration tests provide confidence that your adapters and ports remain correctly configured as dependencies evolve. They bridge the gap between pure domain logic and real-world execution.

6.1.3 End-to-End (E2E) Tests

E2E tests simulate real user workflows by exercising the entire stack—from UI to database—often through HTTP or browser automation. They validate that all layers integrate seamlessly under production-like conditions. For example, a Cypress test might add an item to a shopping cart and verify the subtotal:

```javascript
describe('Shopping Cart', () => {
 it('calculates cart total correctly', () => {
  cy.visit('/products/123');
  cy.get('button.add-to-cart').click();
  cy.visit('/cart');
  cy.get('.total').should('contain', '$15.00');
 });
```

```
});
```

E2E suites ensure that routing, JavaScript front-end code, controllers, services, and databases collaborate to deliver the correct result. These tests are the slowest, often running in seconds to minutes, so they're typically executed nightly or on release branches rather than on every commit. Maintain E2E tests in a separate pipeline stage and target high-value scenarios—shopping flows, user sign-up, payment processing—rather than every edge case. Flaky E2E tests can erode trust; invest in robust selectors, complete environment setups, and retries only where legitimate. Use headless browsers or remote browser farms (e.g., Selenium Grid, Cypress Cloud) to parallelize and scale. Collect logs and screenshots on failures to diagnose UI, network, or backend errors. Although heavyweight, E2E tests catch integration slip-ups that unit and integration tests can't, acting as a final verification before releasing to production.

6.1.4 Exploratory & Mutation Testing

Beyond scripted tests, **exploratory testing** empowers QA and developers to manually probe the system for unexpected behaviors. Testers follow chartered paths, perform boundary testing, and use techniques like pair testing to uncover gaps not covered by automated suites. Tools like **Session-Based Test Management** (SBTM) structure sessions with goals and heuristics, recording observations and defects. Exploratory testing complements automation by finding usability issues, race conditions, and security vulnerabilities that code-driven tests may miss.

Mutation testing assesses test suite effectiveness by introducing small code changes (mutants) and checking if tests fail. For Java, tools like **PIT** generate mutants—e.g., replacing == with !=—and report the **mutation score**, the percentage of mutants killed. A high score (> 90 %) indicates tests robustly capture intended behavior; low scores reveal inadequate or missing tests. In JavaScript, **Stryker** performs similar mutation analysis, guiding teams to write more meaningful assertions. Mutation testing is resource-intensive but can run periodically or on critical modules to validate test quality.

```
# Example PIT command
mvn org.pitest:pitest-maven:mutationCoverage
```

Interpreting mutation reports helps identify under-tested code paths, especially error handling and boundary conditions. Combining exploratory and mutation testing elevates overall quality: exploratory uncovers novel issues, while mutation ensures automated suites remain trustworthy over time. Together, they drive architectural improvements—poorly tested modules often correlate with high coupling or low cohesion, signaling design refactoring opportunities.

6.2 Test-Driven Development & Clean Architecture

6.2.1 Red-Green-Refactor Cycle

Test-Driven Development (TDD) proceeds in three repeating steps: **Red**, **Green**, **Refactor**. First, write a minimally failing test (Red). Next, write the simplest code to make it pass (Green). Finally, refactor the code to improve design while ensuring tests still pass (Refactor). This cycle encourages incremental design evolution and prevents over-engineering. For example, a Python TDD sequence:

```python
# test_money.py
def test_negative_amount_raises():
  with pytest.raises(ValueError):
    Money(-5, 'USD')
```

Running this yields a failure. Next, add code to pass the test:

```python
# money.py
class Money:
  def __init__(self, amount, currency):
    if amount < 0: raise ValueError("Negative not allowed")
    self.amount, self.currency = amount, currency
```

Tests now pass (Green). Finally, refactor—extract validation logic into a separate method—while keeping all tests green. Over time, the Red-Green-Refactor cycle drives both test coverage and design improvements, embedding testability and clean layering from the start. TDD also builds a comprehensive regression suite that enforces architectural boundaries: tests outside a layer must use public ports, not internal classes. By writing tests first, developers think through APIs and dependencies, naturally applying Clean Architecture principles—pure domain functions, inverted dependencies, and adapter isolation.

6.2.2 Behavior-Driven Development (BDD)

Behavior-Driven Development extends TDD by focusing on business outcomes and collaboration between technical and non-technical stakeholders. Using a ubiquitous language, teams write **Gherkin** scenarios that read like executable specifications:

```gherkin
Feature: Checkout
 Scenario: Successful purchase
  Given a shopping cart with items priced 5 USD and 10 USD
  When the customer checks out
  Then an order is created with total 15 USD
```

> And the payment is captured

These scenarios serve as acceptance criteria and drive the development of step definitions:

```
@When("the customer checks out")
public void checkout() {
 response = restTemplate.postForEntity("/api/checkout", cart, CheckoutResponse.class);
}
```

BDD scenarios live in the application or adapter layer, testing the behavior of use-case endpoints. They validate both workflow orchestration and domain rules, acting as high-level integration tests that still provide readable documentation. Because Gherkin uses domain terms (checkout, order, payment), business stakeholders can review and refine specifications before code is written. BDD bridges the gap between requirements and tests, ensuring alignment and reducing miscommunication. Over time, the collection of scenarios becomes a living requirements document that doubles as an automated test suite.

6.2.3 Designing for Testability vs. Testing for Design

"Design for Testability" involves crafting code with hooks—interfaces, dependency injection, small methods—that make writing tests straightforward. In Clean Architecture, this means defining clear ports for dependencies, avoiding static methods, and keeping side-effects at the periphery. Conversely, "Testing for Design" uses tests themselves to drive architectural decisions: tests fail because a class is too large or a method has hidden dependencies, prompting refactoring. For example, if testing a service method requires constructing a complex graph of objects, that test difficulty signals the code under test violates SRP and DIP. Developers then refactor—extract interfaces, break classes apart—guided by the failing tests. This feedback loop ensures that the architecture evolves to support testability, while tests validate the architecture. In practice, teams combine both approaches: proactively design modules to be easily testable, and rely on tests to reveal design shortcomings. Over time, this symbiotic relationship yields a codebase that is both highly testable and robustly architected.

6.2.4 Tests as Living Documentation

Well-written tests describe what the system does in language close to the domain model, serving as executable documentation. Test method names like shouldRejectOrderWithInsufficientInventory() encapsulate both the condition and expected outcome. Code comments quickly go stale, but tests must pass, so they remain up-to-date. Tools like Javadoc or Sphinx can extract code examples from tests to include in API docs, ensuring examples work. In BDD, the Gherkin scenarios themselves become documentation pages that non-technical stakeholders can read. When onboarding new developers, the test suite provides immediate examples of how to create orders, calculate totals, or integrate with external services. Diagrams—such as sequence diagrams generated from tracing tests—further illustrate flows. This living documentation approach closes the gap between code and design, making the system's behavior transparent and reducing the learning curve for new team members.

6.3 Unit Testing the Core Domain

6.3.1 Testing Entities & Value Objects

Entities and value objects embody pure domain logic with no external dependencies, making them ideal candidates for unit testing. Since they contain no I/O, tests are trivial to write and run instantly. For an immutable Money value object in C#:

```
[Test]
public void Money_EqualsBasedOnValue() {
 var m1 = new Money(10, "USD");
 var m2 = new Money(10, "USD");
 Assert.AreEqual(m1, m2);
}
[Test]
public void Money_NegativeAmount_Throws() {
 Assert.Throws<ArgumentException>(() => new Money(-5, "USD"));
}
```

Testing entities involves verifying invariants and state transitions. For a Java Order entity:

```
@Test
void cannotAddItemAfterConfirmation() {
 Order order = Order.create(UUID.randomUUID(), List.of(item));
 order.confirm();
 assertThrows(IllegalStateException.class, () -> order.addItem(item));
}
```

Value object tests emphasize immutability, equality, and self-validation, while entity tests focus on lifecycle methods (confirm(), cancel()) and proper exception throwing on rule violations. Achieving high coverage on domain classes ensures that core business rules remain reliable as the system evolves. Since these tests require no test doubles or container setup, they compose the majority of the fast, reliable base layer of the testing pyramid.

6.3.2 Mocking Repositories & Ports

When unit testing application services or domain services that depend on external interfaces (ports), you replace real implementations with mocks or stubs. For example, using Mockito:

136

```
@Test
void placeOrder_SavesAndPublishesEvent() {
 OrderRepository repo = mock(OrderRepository.class);
 DomainEventPublisher pub = mock(DomainEventPublisher.class);
 PlaceOrderInteractor svc = new PlaceOrderInteractor(repo, pub);
 PlaceOrderResponse resp = svc.execute(new PlaceOrderRequest(...));
 verify(repo).save(any(Order.class));
 verify(pub).publish(any(OrderPlacedEvent.class));
 assertTrue(resp.isSuccess());
}
```

Here, OrderRepository and DomainEventPublisher are mocked, so the test focuses solely on the interactor's orchestration logic. Use argument captors to inspect the exact objects passed to mocks, ensuring correct state and event contents:

```
ArgumentCaptor<OrderPlacedEvent>                        captor        =
ArgumentCaptor.forClass(OrderPlacedEvent.class);
verify(pub).publish(captor.capture());
assertEquals(orderId, captor.getValue().getOrderId());
```

Mocking ports also tests error handling: simulate repository failures or exceptions to verify that services react appropriately:

```
when(repo.save(any())).thenThrow(new DatabaseException());
assertThrows(ServiceException.class, () -> svc.execute(req));
```

By mocking ports, unit tests remain fast and deterministic, enabling deep coverage cf orchestration paths without external dependencies.

6.3.3 Verifying Domain Services

Domain services encapsulate business logic not naturally belonging to a single entity. Testing them requires mocking any repository or external dependency they use. For instance, a CurrencyConversionService that depends on a ExchangeRateProvider:

```
[Test]
public void Convert_UsesLatestRate() {
 var provider = Mock.Of<IExchangeRateProvider>();
 Mock.Get(provider).Setup(p => p.GetRate("USD", "EUR")).Returns(0.85m);
 var service = new CurrencyConversionService(provider);
```

```
Money result = service.Convert(new Money(100, "USD"), "EUR");
Assert.AreEqual(85, result.Amount);
Assert.AreEqual("EUR", result.Currency);
}
```

Test invalid scenarios—unknown currencies or stale rates—asserting that domain exceptions are thrown. Domain service tests validate complex computations, rounding rules, and policies that span multiple value objects or aggregates. They ensure that service logic remains pure and predictable, independent of infrastructure. Because domain services live in the core, their tests import only domain modules, reinforcing architectural boundaries and reducing test suite complexity.

6.3.4 Factories & Composition Root in Unit Tests

Factories often orchestrate the creation of aggregates with multiple invariants. Unit tests for factories verify that objects are created in a valid state and that factory logic handles optional parameters correctly. For example:

```
@Test
void createOrder_WithPromotion_AppliesDiscount() {
 Promotion promo = new PercentagePromotion(0.1);
 Order order = OrderFactory.createWithPromo(id, items, promo);
 assertEquals(expectedTotal, order.total());
}
```

Testing factories may require faking auxiliary services—like OrderNumberGenerator or DateProvider—by injecting predictable implementations. The **Composition Root** in tests manually wires factories and dependencies:

```
@BeforeEach
void setup() {
 numberGen = () -> "ORD-123";
 dateProv = () -> Instant.parse("2025-01-01T00:00:00Z");
 orderFactory = new OrderFactory(numberGen, dateProv);
}
```

By centralizing factory wiring, tests remain DRY and clearly show how dependencies are injected. This approach also documents expected collaborators for factory logic and ensures that domain creation policies remain consistent across tests. Factories tested thoroughly enable reliable aggregate instantiation in both unit and integration scenarios.

6.4 Integration Testing Interface Adapters

6.4.1 Controller & Gateway Tests

Integration tests for controllers (or gateways) validate that HTTP endpoints correctly invoke use-case interactors, handle request parsing/validation, and return appropriate responses and status codes. These tests use real application contexts—bootstrapping Spring Boot with @WebMvcTest or Node.js Express with Supertest—while often mocking downstream adapters. In Spring:

```
@WebMvcTest(OrderController.class)
class OrderControllerITest {
 @Autowired MockMvc mvc;
 @MockBean PlaceOrder placeOrder;


 @Test
 void postOrders_Returns201AndLocation() throws Exception {
  when(placeOrder.execute(any()))
   .thenReturn(new PlaceOrderResponse(UUID.randomUUID(), true));
  mvc.perform(post("/orders")
   .contentType(MediaType.APPLICATION_JSON)
   .content("{\"customerId\":\"123\",\"items\":[{\"sku\":\"A\",\"qty\":1}]}"))
   .andExpect(status().isCreated())
   .andExpect(header().string("Location", startsWith("/orders/")));
 }
}
```

This verifies JSON binding, endpoint mapping, and status/header logic in one shot. In Node.js with Supertest:

```
const request = require('supertest');
const app = require('../app'); // Express app


jest.mock('../usecases/placeOrder');
const { placeOrder } = require('../usecases/placeOrder');


test('POST /orders returns 201', async () => {
 placeOrder.mockResolvedValue({ orderId: 'abc', success: true });
 const res = await request(app)
```

```
.post('/orders')
.send({ customerId: '123', items: [{ sku: 'A', qty: 1 }] });
expect(res.status).toBe(201);
expect(res.header.location).toMatch(/^\/orders\/abc/);
});
```

Key practices include resetting mocks between tests, seeding required application configuration, and verifying error paths (e.g., invalid JSON yields 400). Controller tests also double-check global exception handlers or advice (e.g., mapping domain exceptions to proper HTTP codes).

6.4.2 DTO & Mapper Validation

Data Transfer Objects (DTOs) shuttle data between adapters and core layers, often undergoing transformations via mapping frameworks (MapStruct, AutoMapper, manual mappers). Integration tests should verify that mapping logic preserves field values, enforces validation annotations, and handles missing or extra fields gracefully. For example, testing a MapStruct mapper in Java:

```
@Mapper
public interface OrderMapper {
 OrderDto toDto(Order order);
 Order toEntity(OrderDto dto);
}


// Integration Test
class OrderMapperITest {
 @Test
 void roundTripMapping_PreservesTotals() {
  Order order = OrderFactory.create(...);
  OrderDto dto = Mappers.getMapper(OrderMapper.class).toDto(order);
  Order result = Mappers.getMapper(OrderMapper.class).toEntity(dto);
  assertEquals(order.getTotal(), result.getTotal());
  assertEquals(order.getLines().size(), result.getLines().size());
 }
}
```

Additionally, test DTO validation using Bean Validation:

```
@Test
void missingCustomerId_ReturnsValidationError() throws Exception {
 mvc.perform(post("/orders")
  .content("{\"items\":[{\"sku\":\"A\",\"qty\":1}]}")
```

```
  .contentType(APPLICATION_JSON))
  .andExpect(status().isBadRequest())
  .andExpect(jsonPath("$.errors.customerId").exists());
}
```

In .NET with AutoMapper and FluentValidation:

```
[Test]
public void MapperConfiguration_IsValid() {
 var config = new MapperConfiguration(cfg => cfg.AddProfile<OrderProfile>());
 config.AssertConfigurationIsValid();
}
```

And for validator:

```
[Test]
public void OrderDtoValidator_FailsOnEmptyItems() {
 var validator = new OrderDtoValidator();
 var result = validator.Validate(new OrderDto { CustomerId = "123", Items = null });
 Assert.IsFalse(result.IsValid);
 Assert.IsTrue(result.Errors.Any(e => e.PropertyName == "Items"));
}
```

A diagram of the mapping flow:

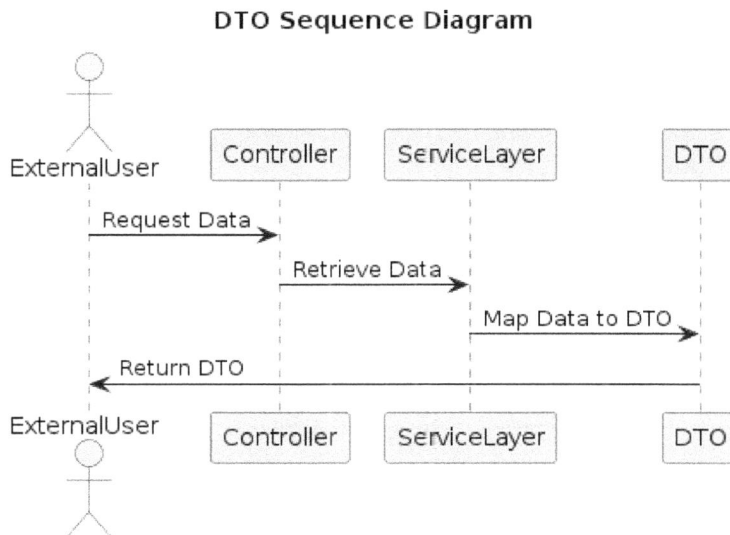

DTO Sequence Diagram

Comprehensive DTO and mapper tests prevent subtle data loss, ensure strong typing, and maintain alignment between API contracts and domain expectations.

6.4.3 Database Integration (In-Memory & Testcontainers)

Integration tests involving the database verify that repository adapters correctly map aggregates to tables/collections, execute queries, and handle transactions. Two main approaches exist: **in-memory databases** (H2, SQLite) and **containerized real databases** (Testcontainers). In-memory DBs are fast and require minimal setup:

```
@SpringBootTest
@AutoConfigureTestDatabase(replace = Replace.ANY)
class InMemoryRepositoryTest {
 @Autowired OrderRepository orderRepo;


 @Test
 void saveAndRetrieveOrder() {
  Order order = OrderFactory.create(...);
  orderRepo.save(order);
  assertTrue(orderRepo.findById(order.getId()).isPresent());
 }
}
```

However, dialect differences (H2 vs. PostgreSQL) can mask SQL compatibility issues. Testcontainers launches a real database in Docker for high-fidelity tests:

```
@Testcontainers
@SpringBootTest
public class PostgresRepositoryTest {
 @Container static PostgreSQLContainer<?> pg = new PostgreSQLContainer<>("postgres:14");
 @DynamicPropertySource
 static void props(DynamicPropertyRegistry r) {
  r.add("spring.datasource.url", pg::getJdbcUrl);
  r.add("spring.datasource.username", pg::getUsername);
  r.add("spring.datasource.password", pg::getPassword);
 }
 // ...
}
```

This approach catches schema or SQL nuances but runs slower due to container startup (~5–10s). A diagram of life cycle:

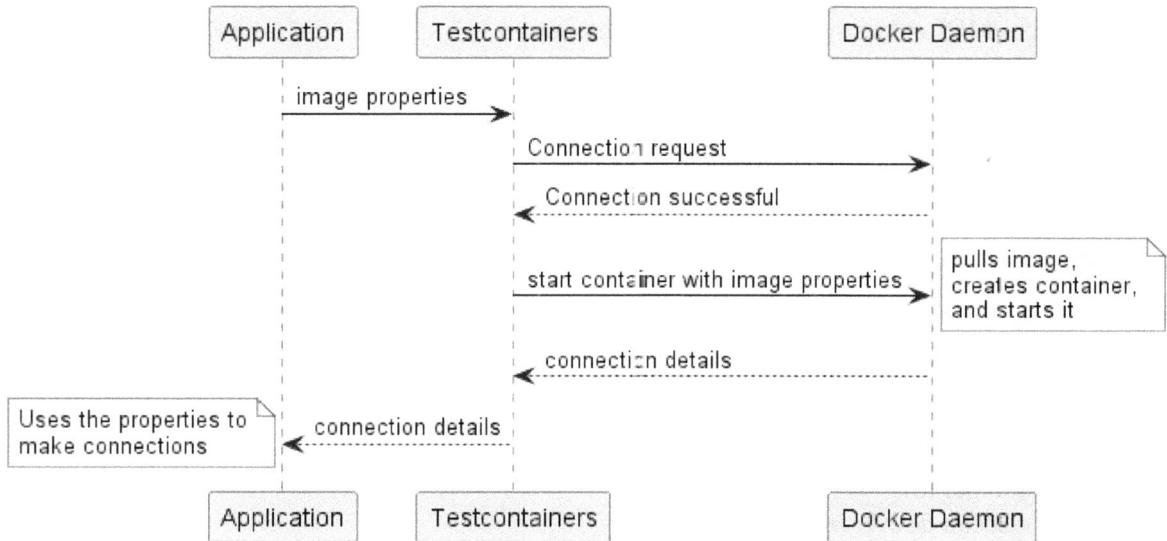

Best practice: use in-memory tests for rapid local TDD feedback, and Testcontainers tests in CI or nightly builds to catch real-DB issues. Always clean up state between tests—truncate tables or recreate schemas—to avoid test interdependence. Monitoring query performance in integration tests can also surface N+1 issues or missing indexes before production.

6.4.4 Messaging & Event Bus Integration

When your architecture relies on asynchronous messaging—Kafka, RabbitMQ, Azure Service Bus—integration tests must verify adapter wiring, message serialization, and handler routing. **Embedded brokers** or **Testcontainers** provide realistic test environments. For Kafka in Java:

```
@EmbeddedKafka(partitions = 1, topics = { "orders" })
@SpringBootTest
public class KafkaAdapterIntegrationTest {
 @Autowired KafkaTemplate<String, OrderPlacedEvent> template;
 @Autowired OrderEventListener listener;
 @Test
 void publishesAndConsumesOrderPlaced() throws Exception {
  template.send("orders", new OrderPlacedEvent(...)).get();
  listener.getLatch().await(10, TimeUnit.SECONDS);
  assertEquals(expectedId, listener.getLastEvent().getOrderId());
 }
}
```

The OrderEventListener is a Spring Kafka consumer stub with a CountDownLatch to await message consumption. For RabbitMQ in Node.js using Testcontainers:

```
const { RabbitMQContainer } = require('testcontainers');
let container, channel;
beforeAll(async () => {
 container = await new RabbitMQContainer().start();
 const conn = await amqp.connect(container.getAmqpUrl());
 channel = await conn.createChannel();
});
afterAll(() => container.stop());


test('publishes and consumes event', async () => {
 await channel.assertQueue('orders');
 // simulate publisher
 await channel.sendToQueue('orders', Buffer.from(JSON.stringify({ orderId: '123' })));
 // consumer under test
 const msg = await new Promise(resolve =>
  channel.consume('orders', m => resolve(m), { noAck: true }));
 const event = JSON.parse(msg.content.toString());
 expect(event.orderId).toBe('123');
});
```

These tests ensure end-to-end messaging pipelines function correctly, including serialization format (JSON, Avro, Protobuf) and consumer deserialization. Integration tests for messaging also simulate error conditions: invalid payloads, broker downtime, and retries. Diagram of messaging integration test:

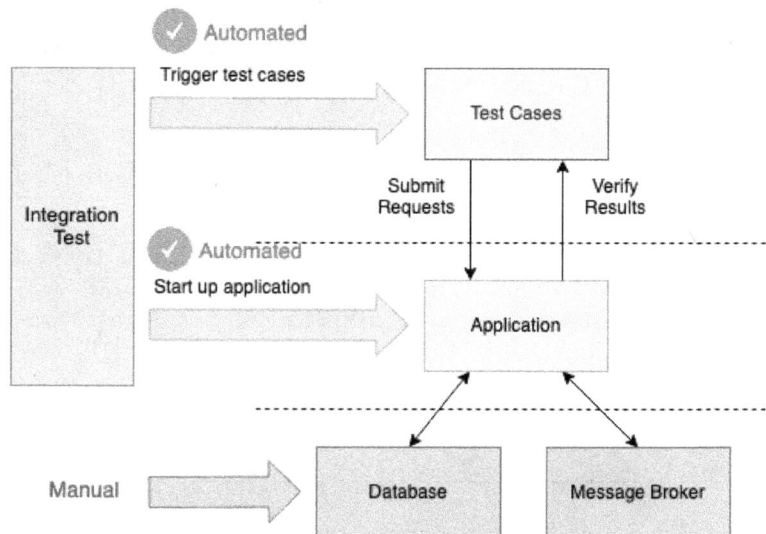

By testing messaging adapters in isolation with embedded brokers, you validate the contract between services, catch configuration errors early, and ensure robust asynchronous communication in production.

6.5 Acceptance & UI Testing

6.5.1 API Contract Tests (Pact, OpenAPI)

API contract tests verify that service providers adhere to the expectations of their consumers without requiring full end-to-end environments. **Consumer-Driven Contracts** (CDC) tools like Pact allow each consumer to publish a pact file that defines expected request/response interactions. In a JavaScript consumer test:

```
const { Pact } = require('@pact-foundation/pact');
const path = require('path');


describe('Order Service Pact', () => {
 const provider = new Pact({
  consumer: 'FrontendApp',
  provider: 'OrderService',
  port: 1234,
  dir: path.resolve(process.cwd(), 'pacts'),
 });


 beforeAll(() => provider.setup());
 afterAll(() => provider.finalize());


 it('gets order by ID', async () => {
  await provider.addInteraction({
   state: 'order 123 exists',
   uponReceiving: 'a GET request for order 123',
   withRequest: { method: 'GET', path: '/orders/123' },
   willRespondWith: { status: 200, body: { id: '123', total: 50 } }
  });
  const order = await getOrder('123'); // call to provider mock
  expect(order.total).toBe(50);
 });
});
```

The generated pact file is then used by the provider in its CI pipeline to verify the interactions:

```
pact-provider-verifier pacts/frontendapp-orderservice.json \
 --provider-base-url=http://localhost:8080
```

OpenAPI contract tests use the OpenAPI schema as the single source of truth. Tools like **Dredd** or **springdoc-openapi-validator** validate that the implemented endpoints conform to the published OpenAPI spec. Running against a running instance:

```
dredd openapi.yaml http://localhost:8080
```

Contract tests ensure backward compatibility: any breaking change in the provider causes test failure, preventing integration surprises. They also serve as living documentation of API behavior, improving trust between teams. Finally, contract test results can be visualized in dashboards to track consumer-provider compatibility over time.

6.5.2 UI Component & Selenium/WebDriver Tests

Testing UI components in isolation ensures front-end code behaves correctly without spinning up the full backend. In React, tools like **Jest** and **React Testing Library** provide fast, deterministic tests:

```
test('CartButton shows correct count', () => {
 render(<CartButton count={3} />);
 expect(screen.getByText('Cart (3)')).toBeInTheDocument();
});
```

These tests verify rendering, event handlers, and accessibility attributes. For full browser tests, **Selenium** or **Playwright** automate real user interactions:

```
WebDriver driver = new ChromeDriver();
driver.get("https://app.local/login");
driver.findElement(By.name("username")).sendKeys("user");
driver.findElement(By.name("password")).sendKeys("pass");
driver.findElement(By.id("submit")).click();
assertTrue(driver.findElement(By.id("welcome")).isDisplayed());
driver.quit();
```

Selenium tests catch CSS regressions, layout issues, and real-world browser behaviors. Use page object patterns to encapsulate UI locators:

```
public class LoginPage {
 WebDriver driver;
```

```
By userField = By.name("username"), passField = By.name("password"), submitBtn =
By.id("submit");
public void login(String u, String p) {
 driver.findElement(userField).sendKeys(u);
 driver.findElement(passField).sendKeys(p);
 driver.findElement(submitBtn).click();
 }
}
```

Component tests run in milliseconds and live in dev workflows; Selenium tests take seconds and run in CI or nightly. Parallelize browser tests across containers or cloud services (BrowserStack, Sauce Labs) to reduce time. Combine headless mode for speed and headed mode for debugging failures with screenshots and videos. UI tests validate not only functionality but also user experience and accessibility, ensuring a polished front-end.

6.5.3 Full End-to-End Scenarios

E2E tests cover complete user workflows across UI, API, and backend, simulating real usage paths. Tools like **Cypress** or **Playwright** drive headless browsers, invoking real services and verifying business outcomes. A Cypress example:

```
describe('Checkout Flow', () => {
 it('completes purchase and shows confirmation', () => {
 cy.visit('/products/123');
 cy.get('button.add-to-cart').click();
 cy.visit('/cart').contains('Checkout').click();
 cy.get('input[name="cardNumber"]').type('4111111111111111');
 cy.get('button.submit-payment').click();
 cy.url().should('include', '/confirmation');
 cy.contains('Thank you for your order');
 });
});
```

E2E tests validate integrations across layers, including authentication, payment gateways (stubbed or sandboxed), and database state. They guard against regression in critical flows like onboarding or purchases. However, they are fragile if run against unstable environments—use clean data resets and feature toggles to control test conditions. Record network traffic to stub third-party calls where necessary. Organize E2E test suites by user journeys and rank them by business priority, running the most critical tests on every push and the rest nightly. Monitor failures with screenshots/logs and integrate with Slack or email for immediate visibility. While heavyweight, E2E scenarios provide the highest confidence that the system works end-to-end as intended.

6.5.4 Performance & Load Tests as Acceptance Criteria

Performance and load testing ensure the system meets non-functional requirements under expected traffic. Define performance acceptance criteria—e.g., "95th percentile response time < 200 ms under 1000 RPS"—and automate tests using tools like **k6**, **Gatling**, or **JMeter**. A simple k6 script:

```
import http from 'k6/http';
import { check, sleep } from 'k6';


export let options = {
 vus: 50,
 duration: '1m',
 thresholds: {
  http_req_duration: ['p(95)<200'],
  http_req_failed: ['rate<0.01']
 }
};


export default function () {
 let res = http.get('https://api.myapp.com/orders/123');
 check(res, { 'status 200': r => r.status === 200 });
 sleep(1);
}
```

This defines a test with 50 virtual users over one minute, checking that 95 % of requests complete under 200 ms. Integrate performance tests into CI pipelines—on release branches or nightly builds—and store metrics in a time-series database (InfluxDB) with Grafana dashboards to track trends over time. Use thread dumps and flame graphs to diagnose hotspots. Conduct tests against production-like environments with realistic data volumes and network conditions. Performance tests also validate scaling behavior: ramp up users to measure throughput curves and identify saturation points. Incorporate load tests into definition of done for critical features, ensuring that new code does not degrade performance. By treating performance and load tests as acceptance criteria, teams build systems that are not only correct but also performant and reliable in production.

6.6 Test Doubles & Patterns

6.6.1 Mocks vs. Stubs vs. Fakes vs. Spies

Mocks, **stubs**, **fakes**, and **spies** are four categories of test doubles serving different testing needs:

1. **Stub**: Provides canned responses for method calls without behavior verification. Use stubs to simulate simple, side-effect-free dependencies.
2. **Mock**: A stub with built-in verification of interactions—asserting which methods were called, how many times, and with what arguments. Libraries like Mockito (Java) or Sinon (JavaScript) support mocks.
3. **Fake**: A lightweight implementation of an interface with working logic, often in-memory. For example, an in-memory UserRepository storing data in a HashMap. Fakes give realistic behavior without external dependencies.
4. **Spy**: Wraps a real object, allowing you to call actual methods while still verifying interactions or overriding select behaviors. Useful when you want partial mocking.

Type	Behavior	Verification	Example Usage
Stub	Returns predefined data	No	Stub HTTP client returning JSON
Mock	Returns data + verifies calls	Yes	Verify repository.save() invoked
Fake	Simplified real implementation	Optional	In-memory DB instead of real SQL
Spy	Uses real object + inspect calls	Yes	Spy on service to confirm method use

Selecting the right double depends on test goals: use fakes for integration-like unit tests, mocks for behavior verification, and stubs to isolate trivial dependencies. Over-mocking can lead to brittle tests tied to implementation details; favor fakes or partial mocks where appropriate. Always reset doubles between tests to avoid state leakage. Understanding these patterns ensures your test suite is both expressive and maintainable.

6.6.2 Dependency Injection for Test Double Injection

Dependency Injection (DI) frameworks make swapping real implementations for test doubles straightforward. In Spring Boot tests, use @TestConfiguration to override beans:

```
@TestConfiguration
static class TestConfig {
@Bean
public PaymentGateway paymentGateway() {
 return new FakePaymentGateway();
}
}
```

```
@SpringBootTest
@Import(TestConfig.class)
class PaymentServiceTest { ... }
```

In .NET Core, override registrations in a custom WebApplicationFactory:

```
builder.ConfigureServices(services => {
 services.RemoveAll<IPaymentGateway>();
 services.AddSingleton<IPaymentGateway, FakePaymentGateway>();
});
```

In Node.js with InversifyJS:

```
const testContainer = new Container();
testContainer.bind<IPaymentGateway>('PaymentGateway').toConstantValue(new
FakePaymentGateway());
```

Manual DI without a container relies on factory parameters or builder patterns. For instance:

```
def create_order_service(repo=None, gateway=None):
  return OrderService(repo or InMemoryRepo(), gateway or FakeGateway())
```

Passing doubles explicitly simplifies tests and clarifies dependencies. Centralizing test double injection in composition roots or test fixtures prevents repetition and ensures consistency. By leveraging DI, you keep production wiring separate from test wiring, maintaining clean architecture while enabling full control over test environments.

6.6.3 Test Fixtures & Setup/Teardown Strategies

Test fixtures prepare and clean up the environment for each test or test suite. In JUnit 5:

```
@BeforeEach
void setUp() {
 database.clean(); // truncate tables
}


@AfterAll
```

```
static void tearDownAll() {
 container.stop(); // shut down Testcontainers
}
```

In pytest:

```
@pytest.fixture(autouse=True)
def clean_db(db_session):
 db_session.rollback()
 yield
 db_session.close()
```

Fixtures can be scoped per test (function), per class/module (module), or per session (session), balancing isolation with performance. For web tests, spin up test servers before suite and tear down afterward:

```
beforeAll(async () => {
 await server.start();
});
afterAll(async () => {
 await server.stop();
});
```

When fixtures depend on each other, define explicit dependencies to guarantee correct order. Use factory fixtures to produce test data:

```
@pytest.fixture
def user_factory(db_session):
 def factory(**kwargs):
  user = UserModel(**kwargs)
  db_session.add(user); db_session.commit()
  return user
 return factory
```

Avoid hidden state by resetting singletons or static contexts in teardown. Fixture lifecycle diagrams clarify setup order:

```
Suite Start
 ├── BeforeAll fixtures
 ├── For each test:
```

```
    ├─ BeforeEach fixtures
    └─ AfterEach fixtures
  └─ AfterAll fixtures
```

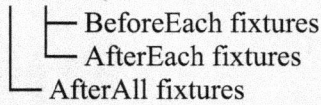

Well-structured fixtures reduce boilerplate, improve test clarity, and ensure isolation, preventing flaky or interdependent tests.

6.6.4 In-Memory vs. Embedded System Doubles

In-Memory doubles simulate dependencies entirely in memory: in-memory databases, caches, or simple collections. They run in microseconds and are ideal for fast integration-style unit tests. However, they may not catch issues with driver behavior, SQL dialect, or serialization quirks. **Embedded system doubles**—containers for real databases (Testcontainers), embedded Kafka, or in-process servers (WireMock)—provide higher fidelity at the cost of slower startup times (seconds).

Use in-memory doubles during local development and TDD to maintain rapid feedback. Reserve embedded doubles for CI pipelines or nightly suites to validate real-world scenarios. For example, an embedded Kafka tests:

```
@EmbeddedKafka(partitions = 1, topics = "orders")
class KafkaIntegrationTest { ... }
```

In Node.js:

```
const { KafkaContainer } = require('testcontainers');
const kafka = await new KafkaContainer().start();
```

Choose the level of fidelity based on test goals: mock clients and in-memory queues for pure logic tests; embedded containers for adapter verification. Document these choices in your testing guidelines so team members know when to use each approach. A decision matrix helps:

Scenario	In-Memory	Embedded
Pure domain logic	✓	✗
Repository mapping	✗	✓

Messaging format verification	✗	✓
Rapid local feedback	✓	✗

Balancing in-memory and embedded doubles ensures comprehensive coverage while preserving developer productivity.

6.7 Contract & Consumer-Driven Testing

6.7.1 REST/gRPC Contract Testing

Consumer-driven contract testing ensures that each service provider fulfills the expectations of its consumers without launching full end-to-end environments. In HTTP/REST architectures, tools like **Pact** or **Spring Cloud Contract** let consumers define expected request and response pairs, which are then published as contracts. Providers import these contracts and verify against their live endpoints during CI, catching breaking changes before deployment. For example, a Pact consumer test in JavaScript might declare:

```
const { Pact } = require('@pact-foundation/pact');
await provider.addInteraction({
 state: 'order exists',
 uponReceiving: 'a GET /orders/123',
 withRequest: { method: 'GET', path: '/orders/123' },
 willRespondWith: { status: 200, body: { id: '123', total: 42 } }
});
```

On the provider side, a JUnit test uses the generated Pact file:

```
@Provider("OrderService")
@PactFolder("pacts")
public class OrderServicePactTest {
 @TestTarget
 public final Target target = new HttpTarget(8080);
}
```

This two-way verification means consumers and providers collaborate on API evolution, promoting safe refactoring.

In gRPC ecosystems, contract testing occurs at the Protobuf level: consumers generate stubs from .proto files and write integration tests against a mock server (e.g., using **grpc-mock**). Providers incorporate the same .proto definitions and run **protoc**-generated verification tests to ensure implemented services match RPC signatures and message schemas. A simple gRPC contract test in Go:

```
srv := grpcmock.NewMockServer()
srv.AddUnaryRPC("/order.OrderService/GetOrder",
grpcmock.NewResponse(&orderpb.Order{Id: "123", Total: 42}))
conn, _ := grpc.Dial(srv.Address(), grpc.WithInsecure())
client := orderpb.NewOrderServiceClient(conn)
resp, err := client.GetOrder(context.Background(), &orderpb.GetOrderRequest{Id: "123"})
assert.NoError(t, err); assert.Equal(t, int32(42), resp.Total)
```

By verifying both REST and gRPC contracts in CI, teams reduce integration failures and solidify API compatibility.

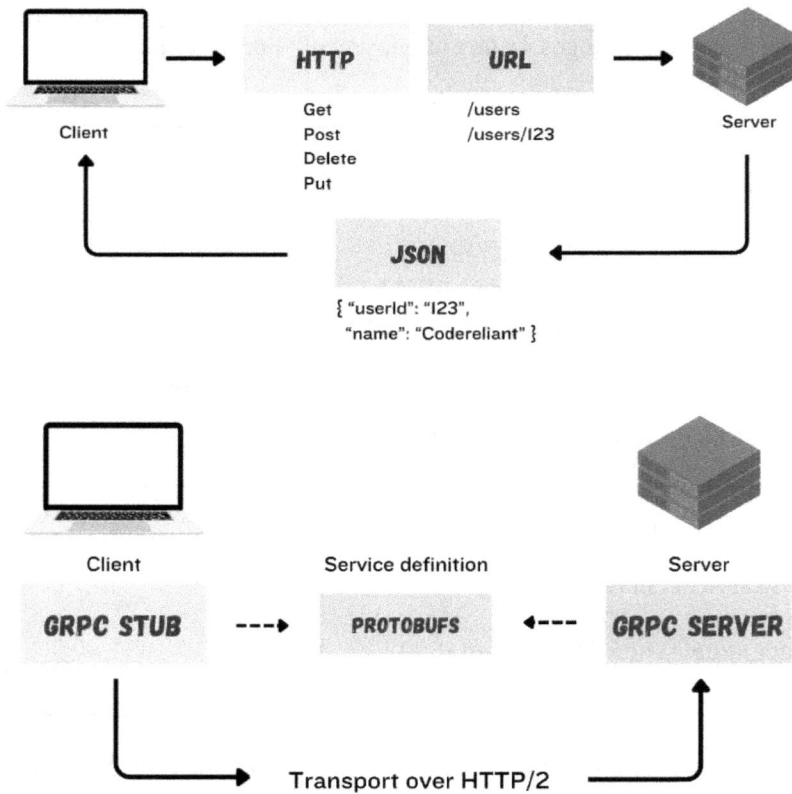

6.7.2 Messaging Schema Contracts

Event-driven systems rely on well-defined message schemas to communicate asynchronously between services. Whether using **Avro**, **Protobuf**, or **JSON Schema**, schema contracts define the structure, types, and optional fields of events. Publishing schemas to a **Schema Registry** (e.g., Confluent Schema Registry) centralizes versioning, compatibility rules, and discovery. Producers register schemas under a subject (e.g., order-placed), and consumers fetch the latest compatible version at runtime or during CI.

For Avro-based messaging, a schema might look like:

```
{
 "namespace": "com.myapp.events",
 "type": "record",
 "name": "OrderPlaced",
 "fields": [
  {"name": "orderId","type": "string"},
  {"name": "total","type": "double"},
  {"name": "timestamp","type": {"type":"long","logicalType":"timestamp-millis"}}
 ]
}
```

When a producer publishes an OrderPlaced event, it serializes according to the registered schema, including a schema ID in the message header. Consumers validate incoming data against the schema, ensuring robustness against malformed or unexpected fields.

During testing, **Schema Registry mock servers** or **embedded registries** (Testcontainers) allow integration tests to act against a real registry. In Java with Kafka and Avro:

```
EmbeddedKafkaCluster cluster = new EmbeddedKafkaCluster(1);
cluster.start();
ConfluentSchemaRegistry                 registry              =              new
ConfluentSchemaRegistry(cluster.getZookeeperConnect());
int id = registry.register("order-placed-value", avroSchema);
Producer<String, GenericRecord> producer = createAvroProducer(cluster, registry);
```

Tests can assert that invalid messages are refused or produce serialization exceptions, safeguarding consumer logic. Maintaining backward and forward compatibility—by only adding new optional fields or following the **proposed compatibility rules**—prevents runtime errors during rolling upgrades. A diagram of message flow with schema validation:

APIs for REST Calls   Schemas for Events

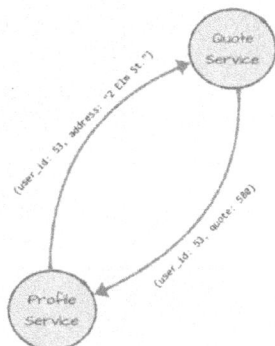

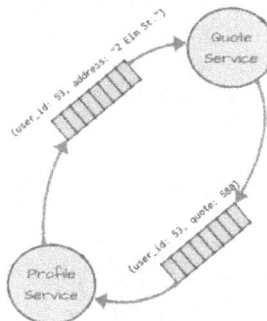

By enforcing messaging schema contracts, teams ensure asynchronous integrations remain stable and evolvable as systems scale.

6.7.3 Stub Servers & Canary Releases

Stub servers simulate external dependencies—APIs, legacy systems, or third-party services—with predefined responses, enabling integration and acceptance tests without relying on live endpoints. Tools like **WireMock**, **Mountebank**, and **Hoverfly** allow you to record real traffic or manually define stubs:

```
WireMockServer stub = new WireMockServer(options().port(8089));
stub.stubFor(get(urlEqualTo("/inventory/sku-A"))
 .willReturn(aResponse().withStatus(200).withBody("{\"stock\":10}")));
```

Your tests point at the stub (http://localhost:8089/inventory/sku-A) instead of the real service, isolating variability and network failures. Stubs support fault injection (timeouts, 500 errors) to test resilience and retry logic.

Canary releases complement stubbing by directing a small percentage of real traffic to a new service version before full rollout. Infrastructure tools—Kubernetes **Canary Deployments**, AWS **CodeDeploy**, or Istio **Traffic Shifting**—enable gradual traffic migration. For example, Istio VirtualService configuration:

```
apiVersion: networking.istio.io/v1alpha3
kind: VirtualService
metadata: { name: order-service }
spec:
```

```
hosts: ["order-service"]
http:
- route:
 - destination: { host: order-service, subset: stable, weight: 90 }
 - destination: { host: order-service, subset: canary, weight: 10 }
```

While 10 % of calls hit the canary subset, monitor logs, errors, and performance. Canary releases guard production against undiscovered issues in new code, acting as high-fidelity tests under real-user conditions. Metrics and logs collected during the canary phase inform rollout decisions: if errors spike, automatically rollback via CI/CD pipelines. Diagrams illustrating stubbing vs. canary:

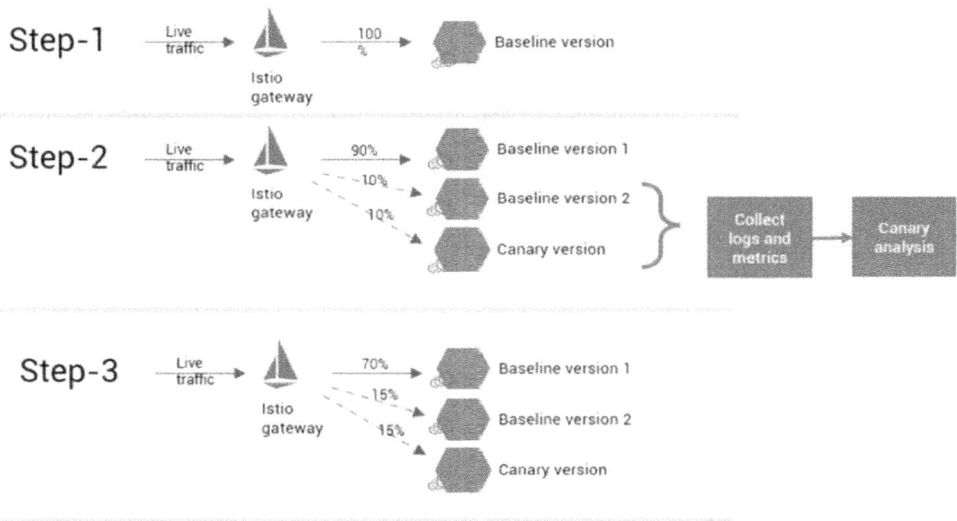

Combining stub servers for pre-prod testing and canary releases for production validation offers a comprehensive safety net for architectural changes and deployments.

6.7.4 Versioning & Compatibility of Contracts

Evolution of both REST/gRPC APIs and messaging schemas demands disciplined versioning and compatibility management. For synchronous APIs, adopt **semantic versioning** in URI paths (/v1/..., /v2/...) or media types (application/vnd.myapp.v2+json). Deprecate old versions with clear documentation and sunset schedules. In code:

```
@RequestMapping("/api/v1/orders")
public class OrderControllerV1 { ... }


@RequestMapping("/api/v2/orders")
```

```
public class OrderControllerV2 { ... }
```

Maintain both controllers in parallel, sharing business logic via application services where possible.

For messaging schemas, use the Schema Registry's compatibility settings: **BACKWARD**, **FORWARD**, or **FULL**. Backward compatibility allows new readers (consumers) to read old data; forward allows old readers to read new data; full covers both. When adding a new optional field:

```
{"name":"discount","type":["null","double"],"default":null}
```

This change is backward and forward compatible, and tests verify that both old and new consumers handle messages correctly. Breaking changes—removing fields or altering types—require schema marker increases (major version) and coordination across producers and consumers. Canary testing with a mock consumer can validate that new schemas do not break existing consumers before propagation. A compatibility matrix diagram:

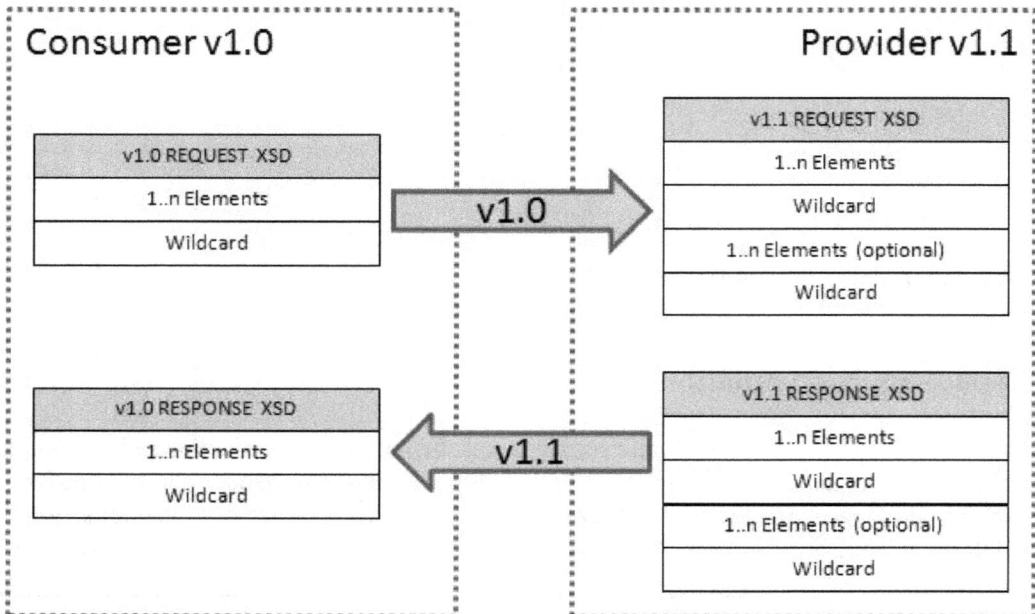

Service Forwards Compatibility

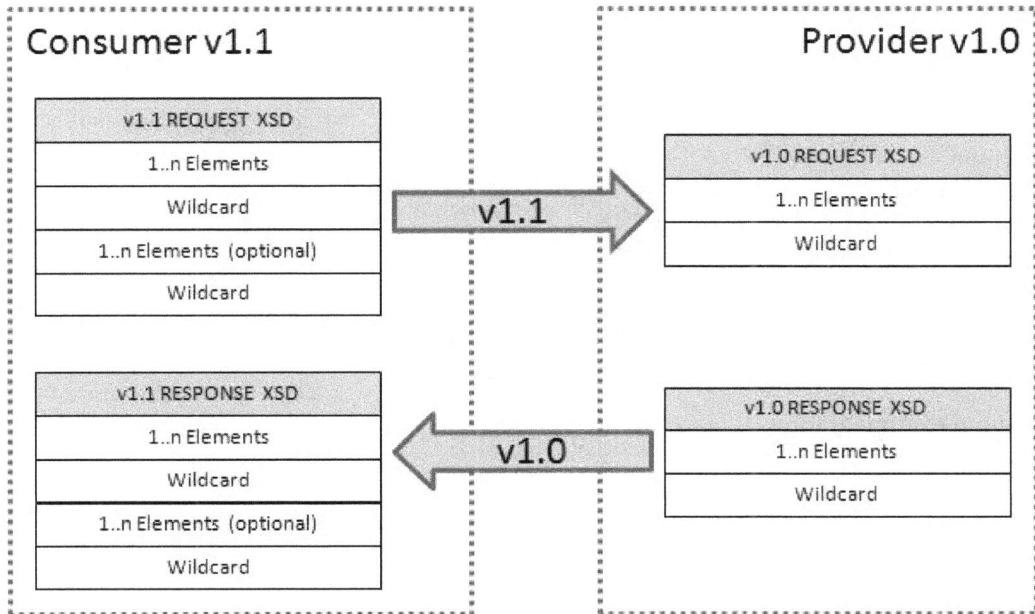

Maintain a **changelog** for each contract, detailing added fields, changed semantics, and deprecation notes. By enforcing strict versioning and compatibility rules, systems can evolve contracts without disrupting live integrations, preserving stability amidst continuous delivery.

6.8 Continuous Integration & Test Automation

6.8.1 CI Pipeline Test Stages

A robust CI pipeline orchestrates multiple test stages—**Linting**, **Unit Tests**, **Integration Tests**, **Contract/CDC Tests**, **E2E Tests**, and **Performance Tests**—executed in sequence or parallel to balance speed and coverage. A typical GitHub Actions workflow:

```
jobs:
 lint:
  runs-on: ubuntu-latest
  steps:
   - uses: actions/checkout@v2
   - run: npm run lint


unit-tests:
```

```
  needs: lint
  runs-on: ubuntu-latest
  steps:
   - run: npm test:unit


integration:
  needs: unit-tests
  runs-on: ubuntu-latest
  services:
   postgres:
    image: postgres:14
    env: POSTGRES_DB: testdb
  steps:
   - run: npm test:integration


contract:
  needs: integration
  runs-on: ubuntu-latest
  steps:
   - run: npm run pact:verify


e2e:
  needs: contract
  runs-on: ubuntu-latest
  services:
   selenium/standalone-chrome: {}
  steps:
   - run: npm test:e2e


perf:
  if: github.ref == 'refs/heads/main'
  needs: e2e
  runs-on: ubuntu-latest
  steps:
   - run: npm run perf:test
```

Each stage produces artifacts—coverage reports, pact files, performance metrics—stored for analysis. Fail-fast configuration stops execution on critical test failures, conserving resources. Annotate PRs with test results, highlighting regressions immediately. Build matrix configurations (e.g., Java 11/17, Node 14/16) ensure cross-environment compatibility. Pipeline stages mirror the testing pyramid, allowing granular feedback: developers see unit test failures in minutes, integration issues soon after, and E2E regressions in the final stage. This layered approach ensures rapid feedback while safeguarding system integrity before merging or deployment.

6.8.2 Managing Flaky & Slow Tests

Flaky tests—those that nondeterministically pass or fail—erode developer trust and impede CI pipelines. Common causes include reliance on external networks, shared state, or race conditions. To manage flakiness: identify and quarantine flaky tests by tagging them (e.g., @Flaky in JUnit, test.skip in Jest), then prioritize fixing. Implement retries with caution—tools like **JUnit's RetryRule** or **Mocha's this.retries()**—to filter out transient failures, but treat retries as a temporary measure while addressing root causes.

Slow tests—particularly large integration or E2E suites—delay feedback loops. Shift slow tests to nightly or pre-release pipelines, and focus on fast tests in pull-request checks. Use test coverage and mutation scores to identify critical modules needing faster, more focused tests. Profile test execution times (e.g., JUnit's -DtrimStackTrace=false or Jest's --detectOpenHandles) to pinpoint bottlenecks. Optimize slow tests by mocking heavy dependencies, using in-memory databases for local runs, or parallelizing tests (see next subsection).

Maintain a **Flaky Test Dashboard**—a test analytics tool or simple spreadsheet—to track failure rates, flakiness trends, and resolution times. Assign ownership of flaky tests to developers, with SLAs for fixes. Continuous monitoring and triage ensure that flaky and slow tests are kept under control, preserving pipeline reliability and developer productivity.

6.8.3 Parallelizing & Sharding Test Suites

Parallel execution of tests maximizes resource utilization and minimizes feedback time. Modern test frameworks—JUnit 5 (junit.jupiter.execution.parallel.enabled=true), pytest (-n auto), Jest (--runInBand=false), Mocha with parallel—support parallel test runs by default or with configuration. Sharding splits a large test suite into "shards" (groups) distributed across multiple CI agents. A GitLab CI example:

```
stages:
 - test
test:
 stage: test
 parallel: 4
 script:
 - npm test -- --grep "$CI_NODE_INDEX/$CI_NODE_TOTAL"
```

Here, CI_NODE_INDEX and CI_NODE_TOTAL divide tests among four parallel runners. For JUnit, use the **Surefire** plugin's forkCount and reuseForks:

```
<configuration>
 <parallel>methods</parallel>
 <threadCount>8</threadCount>
</configuration>
```

A diagram of test sharding:

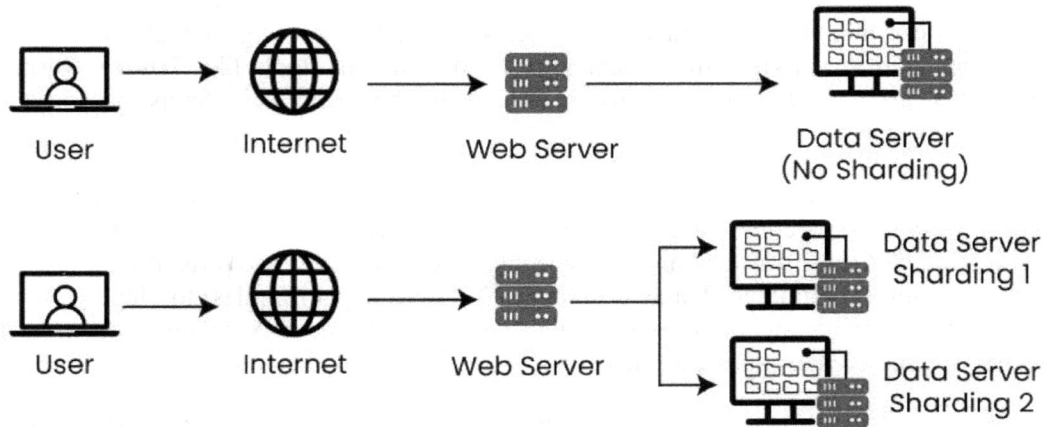

Balance shard sizes by historical timing data to avoid "slowest shard dominates" issues. Aggregate results from all shards into a unified report—Jacoco's merged coverage or Jest's combined output. Secure environment caching (Docker images, dependencies) to keep startup times low. Parallelization transforms lengthy test suites into sub-minute pipelines, enabling fast merge cycles and sustained developer flow.

6.8.4 Automating Test Environment Provisioning

Modern CI pipelines automate provisioning of test environments—databases, message brokers, external services—using container orchestration or infrastructure-as-code. **Docker Compose** files spin up multi-container test stacks locally and in CI:

```
version: '3.8'
services:
 db:
  image: postgres:14
  environment: { POSTGRES_DB: testdb }
 kafka:
  image: confluentinc/cp-kafka:latest
  ports: ["9092:9092"]
 app:
  build: .
```

```
depends_on: [db, kafka]
```

CI jobs run docker-compose up -d before tests and docker-compose down after, ensuring consistent environments. For end-to-end tests, **Kubernetes namespaces** or **Kind** clusters provide closer production parity:

```
kind create cluster --name test-cluster
kubectl apply -f test-namespace.yaml
helm install test-app ./chart --namespace test
```

Infrastructure provisioning tools like **Terraform** or **Pulumi** script cloud resources (databases, queues) for larger integration tests, with automated teardown to avoid bill shocks. Dynamic environment orchestration—via ephemeral feature environments—lets teams test PRs in isolation. Tools such as **Garden**, **Tilt**, or **Skaffold** accelerate local environment iterations by watching code changes and refreshing containers. Automated provisioning ensures that developers and CI pipelines run tests against identical, reproducible stacks, eliminating "it works on my machine" discrepancies and boosting confidence in test results.

6.9 Measuring Quality & Coverage

6.9.1 Code Coverage Metrics & Pitfalls

Code coverage metrics quantify the percentage of source code exercised by automated tests, typically reported as **Line**, **Branch**, and **Function** coverage. Tools like **JaCoCo**, **Coverage.py**, and **Istanbul** integrate into CI to generate reports. A sample JaCoCo configuration for Maven:

```
<plugin>
 <groupId>org.jacoco</groupId>
 <artifactId>jacoco-maven-plugin</artifactId>
 <version>0.8.8</version>
 <executions>
  <execution>
   <goals><goal>prepare-agent</goal></goals>
  </execution>
  <execution>
   <id>report</id>
   <phase>verify</phase>
   <goals><goal>report</goal></goals>
  </execution>
 </executions>
</plugin>
```

While high coverage correlates with lower risk, "100 % coverage" can be misleading. Tests might execute code without asserting meaningful behavior—so-called **assert-less tests**. Coverage ignores **test quality**: branches that merely log errors count as covered even if no assertions verify outcomes. Aim for critical business logic to have high coverage, but allow utility or trivial code to have lower thresholds. Set coverage **quality gates** in CI—e.g., fail if coverage drops by more than 1 %—to prevent regressions. Use coverage heatmaps (IDE plugins like IntelliJ's coverage view) to identify untested areas. Finally, combine coverage analysis with **mutation testing** (next section) to gauge test effectiveness rather than raw coverage numbers alone.

6.9.2 Mutation Testing for Test Effectiveness

Mutation testing injects small changes ("mutants") into production code—such as negating conditions or altering arithmetic—and runs the test suite to see if tests catch the error. Tools like **PIT** for Java or **Stryker** for JavaScript automate this process. A PIT example:

```
mvn org.pitest:pitest-maven:mutationCoverage \
 -Dmutators=NO_NEGATE_CONDITIONALS \
 -DoutputFormats=HTML
```

The mutation report shows a **mutation score** (% of mutants killed by tests). A low score indicates inadequate assertions or missing tests for edge cases. Mutation testing guides developers to write tests that cover both happy paths and failure modes—such as exception handling and alternative branches. However, mutation testing is computationally expensive and slows CI; schedule it for nightly or weekly runs. For JavaScript projects, configure Stryker:

```
npx stryker run --reporters clear,dots,html
```

Review the HTML report to pinpoint surviving mutants and augment tests accordingly. Incorporating mutation testing into your quality dashboard ensures that your test suite not only executes code paths but truly validates behavior and guards against regressions, driving continuous improvement in test robustness.

6.9.3 Static Analysis & Test Smell Detection

Static analysis tools—SonarQube, CodeClimate, ESLint, or pylint—identify **test smells** and anti-patterns that compromise test maintainability. Common smells include **assert-less tests**, **sleep-based waits**, **hard-coded data**, and **excessive mocking**. For example, SonarQube rules can flag tests longer than a threshold or those with no assertions:

```
sonar.junit.smells.assertlessTest=true
sonar.junit.smells.sleepInTest=true
```

ESLint's **no-floating-promises** rule catches un-awaited async tests in JavaScript:

```
"rules": {
 "no-floating-promises": "error"
}
```

Integrate these rules into CI to block PRs with new test smells. IDE plugins like IntelliJ's **Test Smell Detector** provide immediate feedback. Address flagged smells by adding assertions, replacing sleeps with proper synchronization (e.g., await or polling loops), and parameterizing hard-coded fixtures. Regular static analysis keeps the test suite clean, fast, and reliable, preventing technical debt in test code from undermining overall architecture quality.

6.9.4 Dashboards & Reporting

Centralized dashboards give teams visibility into code quality, test coverage, mutation scores, and pipeline health. Tools like **SonarQube**, **Azure DevOps**, or **GitLab** aggregate metrics across branches and time. Embed coverage badges in README files:

```
![Coverage](https://img.shields.io/sonar/coverage/my-app.svg)
```

Use **Grafana** to visualize performance test trends, mutation scores, and test durations via Prometheus exporters. A sample Prometheus exporter snippet in Python:

```
from prometheus_client import Gauge, start_http_server
coverage_gauge = Gauge('code_coverage', 'Code coverage %')
coverage_gauge.set(85.3)
start_http_server(8000)
```

Services like **Coveralls** and **Codecov** upload coverage reports and highlight pull-request changes. Track **flaky test rates**, **build durations**, and **failure trends** in dashboards to identify hotspots. Automated alerts—Slack notifications for coverage drops or mutation score regressions—keep the team informed. Regularly review dashboards in sprint retrospectives to celebrate improvements or plan remediation. By making quality metrics highly visible, teams cultivate a data-driven culture that values both functionality and maintainability, ensuring that testing continues to drive architectural decisions.

6.10 Testing in Distributed & Microservice Architectures

6.10.1 Testing Sagas & Orchestrations

Testing sagas and process managers in a microservices environment requires simulating long-running, cross-service workflows and their compensating transactions. In a choreography-based saga, each service listens for upstream events and publishes downstream events, so tests must start by publishing an initial event—such as OrderPlaced—to the event bus and then assert that the expected sequence of events occurs. For example, using an embedded Kafka and a test consumer in Java:

```java
@SpringBootTest
@Testcontainers
public class OrderSagaChoreographyTest {
 @Autowired KafkaTemplate<String, DomainEvent> template;
 @Autowired EmbeddedKafkaBroker broker;
 @Autowired TestConsumerService consumer;


 @Test
 void fullOrderSaga_FiresExpectedEvents() throws Exception {
 // Publish initial event
 template.send("order-placed", new OrderPlaced(orderId, items));
 // Wait for PaymentReceived
 DomainEvent payment = consumer.awaitEvent("payment-received", 10, TimeUnit.SECONDS);
 assertTrue(payment instanceof PaymentReceived);
 // Wait for ShippingScheduled
 DomainEvent        shipping        =        consumer.awaitEvent("shipping-scheduled",        10,
TimeUnit.SECONDS);
 assertTrue(shipping instanceof ShippingScheduled);
 }
}
```

In orchestration-based sagas, a central process manager issues commands and listens for replies. Tests for an orchestrator simulate command handling and verify that each step is triggered correctly, including compensations on failure:

```
it('compensates when payment fails', async () => {
 paymentService.charge.mockRejectedValue(new PaymentDeclinedError());
 await orchestrator.handleOrderPlaced({ orderId });
 expect(inventoryService.release).toHaveBeenCalledWith(orderId);
 expect(notificationService.notifyFailure).toHaveBeenCalledWith(orderId);
});
```

Diagrams illustrate both patterns:

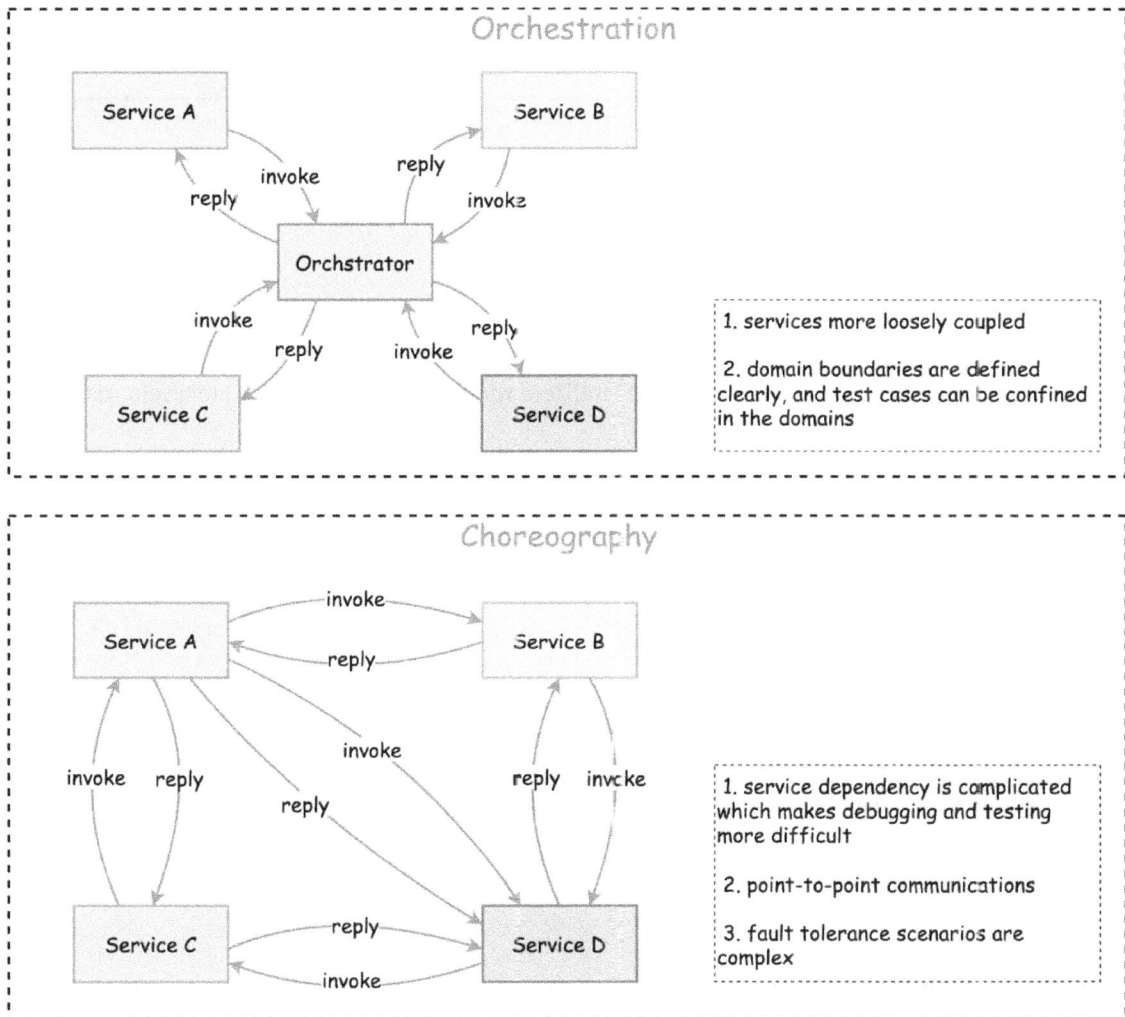

Key testing strategies include using **in-memory event buses** or **embedded containers** to avoid external dependencies, injecting test hooks into process managers to observe internal state transitions, and verifying that compensating transactions (e.g., refund, inventory release) fire when exceptions occur. Tests should cover happy-path sagas, partial failures, and idempotency (replaying the same event should not cause duplicate actions). By weaving saga tests into your CI pipeline, you ensure that complex distributed workflows remain reliable as services evolve.

6.10.2 Contract Testing for Event-Driven Systems

In event-driven microservices, services communicate via asynchronous messages, so ensuring producers and consumers agree on message formats is critical. **Contract testing** for events involves generating and verifying message schemas at build time. For Avro-based Kafka, consumers define a **consumer contract** by writing tests against a mock broker using the same schema:

```
@EmbeddedKafka(partitions = 1, topics = "order-events")
public class OrderEventsConsumerContractTest {
 @Autowired KafkaTemplate<String, GenericRecord> producer;
 @Autowired OrderEventsConsumer consumer;


 @Test
 void consumerHandlesValidOrderPlacedEvent() throws Exception {
  GenericRecord event = new GenericData.Record(schemaRegistry.getLatestSchema("order-placed-value"));
  event.put("orderId", orderId.toString());
  event.put("total", 100.0);
  producer.send("order-events", event).get();
  consumerLatch.await(5, TimeUnit.SECONDS);
  assertEquals(orderId, consumer.getLastOrderId());
 }
}
```

On the producer side, CI runs a **provider verification** that reads consumer-published contracts (Pact files or Avro schemas) and sends sample messages to a stub consumer to ensure compatibility. For JSON-based messaging, **Pact for asynchronous messaging** can define the expected structure of events:

```
{
"description": "OrderPlaced event",
"provider": "order-service",
"consumer": "inventory-service",
"message": {
 "body": {
  "eventType": "OrderPlaced",
  "orderId": "123",
  "items": [{"sku":"A","qty":2}]
 }
 }
}
```

Provider tests then load the pact and assert that serialized messages conform. A high-level diagram:

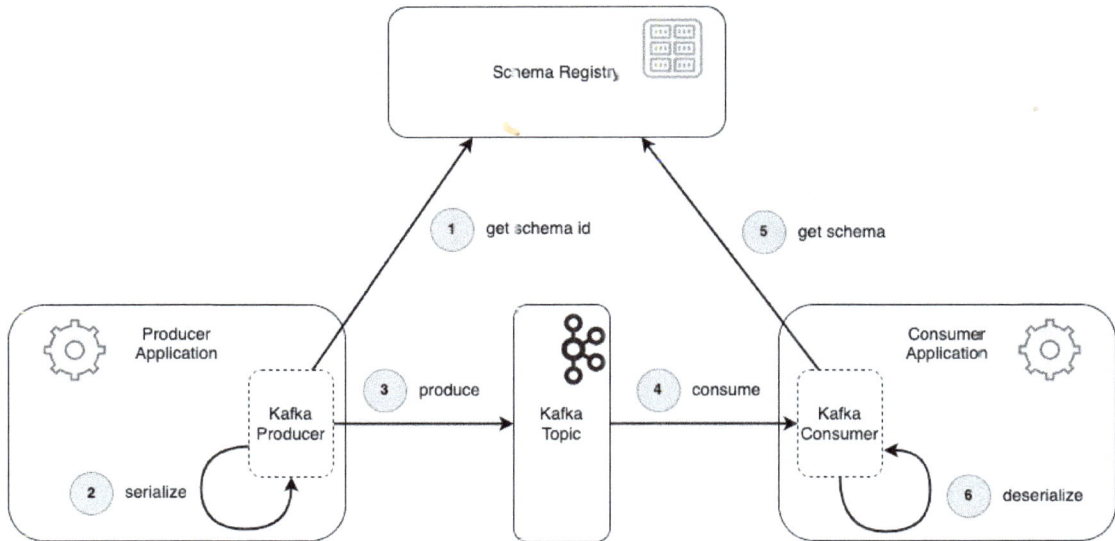

This approach catches schema drift early, prevents runtime deserialization errors, and documents message contracts centrally. Versioned contracts ensure that both old and new message formats are supported for a transition period, enabling safe rolling deployments.

6.10.3 Chaos Engineering & Resilience Tests

Chaos engineering introduces controlled failures into production-like environments to validate system resilience and failure handling. Tools like **Chaos Monkey**, **Gremlin**, or **LitmusChaos** can randomly terminate instances, throttle network traffic, or inject latency. A typical chaos test might terminate a payment microservice while a high-volume order placement test is running, then assert that orders either queue for later processing or fail gracefully:

```
# gremlin chaos experiment
apiVersion: chaos.gremlin.com/v1alpha1
kind: Attack
metadata:
 name: kill-payment-service
spec:
 target: "service == 'payment-service'"
 mode: "one"
 length: 60s
 actions:
  file:
  - kill
```

Chaos Engineering

Purpose: focuses on proactively testing the resilience of systems by introducing controlled failures or disruptions. Goal is to uncover weaknesses in the system's architecture, infrastructure, or design.

Methodology: deliberately injecting faults, such as network latency, service failures, or increased database response times, into a system to observe how it behaves under stress.

Example Tools: Chaos Monkey, Gremlin, Chaos Toolkit, Pumba, LitmusChaos.

Testing

Purpose: aims to verify that a system meets its functional requirements and performs as expected under normal conditions.

Methodology: encompasses various types such as unit testing, integration testing, system testing, and acceptance testing. These tests are typically automated and cover different aspects of the system, including functionality, performance, security, and usability.

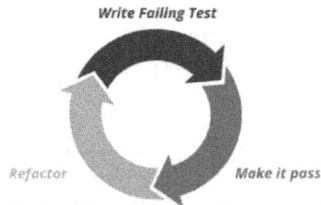

Example Tools: JUnit, Selenium, Postman, Apache JMeter, OWASP ZAP.

Resilience tests validate retry policies, circuit breakers, and fallback behaviors. For example, using Resilience4j and its **retry** annotation:

```
@Retry(name = "paymentRetry", fallbackMethod = "paymentFallback")
public PaymentResult capture(PaymentRequest req) { ... }
```

Test code simulates intermittent failures and asserts that after three retries, control flows to the fallback:

```
when(paymentClient.charge(any())).thenThrow(new TimeoutException());
assertDoesNotThrow(() -> service.capture(req));
verify(fallbackHandler).handleFallback(any());
```

Chaos experiments should be automated in staging environments with telemetry dashboards (Prometheus, Grafana) to detect anomalies. Rescue plans—automated rollbacks or traffic rerouting—validate operational runbooks before true incidents occur. By proactively testing failure modes, teams build confidence that their distributed architecture can withstand real-world disturbances.

6.10.4 End-to-End Tracing & Observability

Distributed tracing ties together calls across microservice boundaries, allowing tests and production monitoring to follow the flow of a request—encompassing HTTP, messaging, database queries, and background jobs. Instrument code with **OpenTelemetry** SDKs, propagating trace context via headers or message metadata:

```
// Java OpenTelemetry instrumentation
Tracer tracer = GlobalOpenTelemetry.getTracer("order-service");
Span span = tracer.spanBuilder("PlaceOrder' ).startSpan();
try (Scope scope = span.makeCurrent()) {
 orderRepo.save(order);
 httpClient.get("/inventory/reserve");
} finally {
 span.end();
}
```

In Node.js:

```
const tracer = opentelemetry.trace.getTracer('payment-service');
await tracer.startActiveSpan('charge', async span => {
 await axios.post('/payment', req);
 span.end();
});
```

End-to-end tests verify that traces appear in back-end systems (Jaeger, Zipkin) with correct spans and tags. A test might call the API then query the tracing backend's API to assert the presence of a trace spanning multiple services:

```
trace = get_trace(trace_id)
assert any(span.name == 'charge' for span in trace.spans)
```

Diagram of a trace:

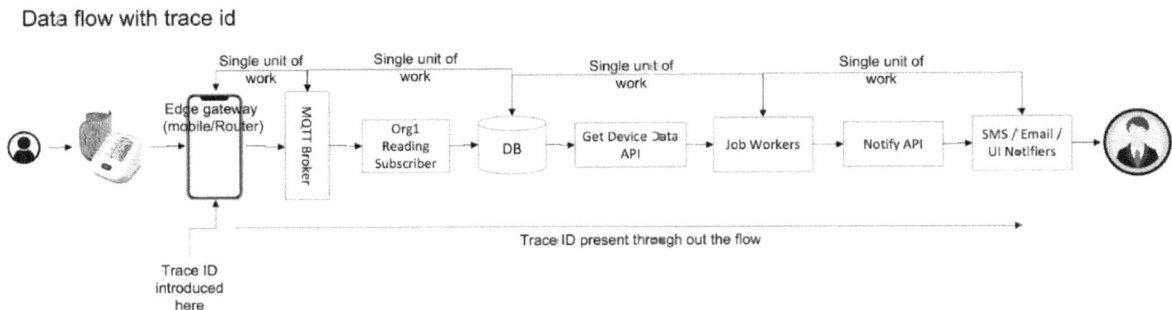

Logs should correlate with traces via **trace IDs** and **span IDs**, enabling test-driven validation of observability pipelines. Automated checks for trace completeness and latency SLAs ensure that monitoring exists before incidents occur. Observability tests complement functional tests by validating that when the system runs, it produces the necessary signals for debugging and alerting, closing the loop on both code correctness and operational readiness.

6.11 Anti-Patterns in Testing

6.11.1 Over-Mocked & Brittle Tests

Over-mocking occurs when tests mock too many collaborators or internal calls, coupling tests tightly to implementation details rather than behavior. For instance, mocking every repository method call in a service test:

```
when(repo.findById(any())).thenReturn(Optional.of(order));
when(repo.save(any())).thenReturn(order);
...
verify(repo).findById(orderId);
verify(repo).save(order);
```

Such tests break whenever refactoring merges or splits internal calls, even if external behavior remains unchanged. Brittle tests often arise from **white-box testing**, where tests assert internal state or call counts instead of outcomes. For example, verifying two calls to repo.findById() rather than asserting the returned result contains expected data.

Symptoms include frequent test failures unrelated to business logic, high maintenance overhead, and low developer confidence. To remedy, refactor tests to use **fakes** or **in-memory implementations** for dependencies, verify only observable behaviors, and avoid asserting on mock interactions unless part of the contract (for example, retries). Use **spies** sparingly—only when verifying side-effects that cannot be observed otherwise. A resilient test focuses on "the system under test outputs X given input Y" rather than "method A called method B three times." Diagrams of brittle vs. robust tests:

```
Brittle: Service → mock(repo)→ assert(repo interaction)
Robust: Service → fake(repo)→ assert(service output)
```

By reducing over-mocking and focusing on behavior, tests become more maintainable and resilient to internal refactoring, enabling developers to improve implementation without fear of breaking tests that shouldn't care about the details.

6.11.2 Excessive Reliance on E2E Tests

Relying too heavily on end-to-end tests can slow development feedback loops, as E2E suites are slow, brittle, and often flaky due to network or UI timing issues. When a team treats E2E tests as the primary safety net, minor UI changes can break dozens of tests, blocking build pipelines and frustrating developers. Over time, teams may skip or ignore broken E2E tests, reducing their value.

Symptoms include increasing test durations (minutes to hours), frequent false positives, and test backlogs. To avoid this, apply the **testing pyramid**: maximize unit and integration tests, reserve E2E tests for a handful of high-value user journeys, and run them in parallel or nightly. Break large E2E flows into smaller, more focused scenarios. Use **headless mode**, **network stubbing**, and **containerized environments** to stabilize tests.

Diagram of test distribution:

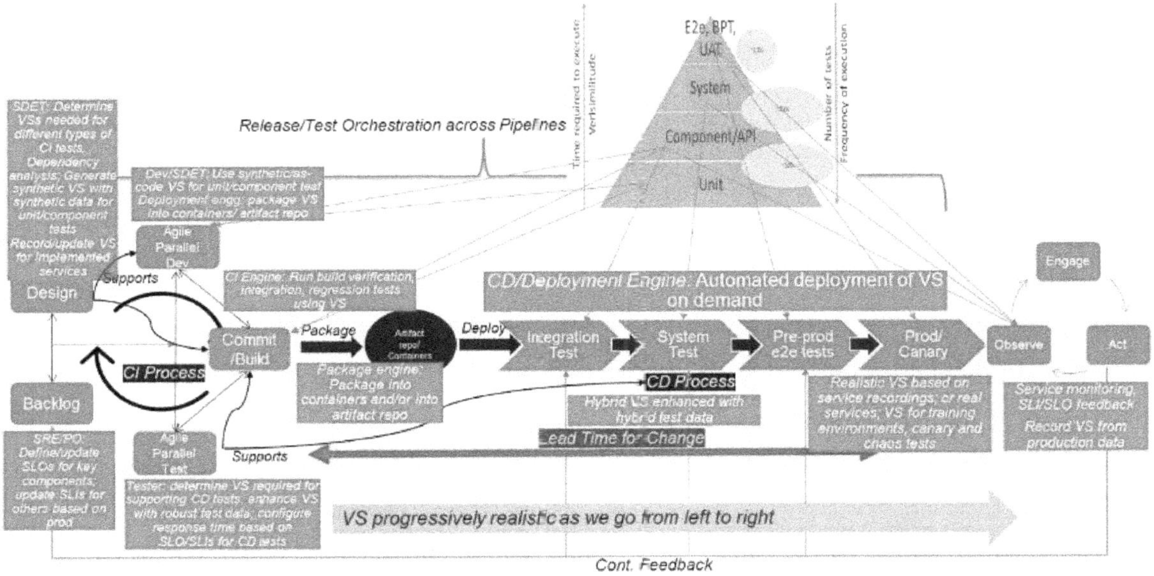

By shifting most checks to faster layers and limiting E2E to core paths, teams maintain rapid feedback and prevent pipeline bottlenecks. E2E tests then serve as a final confirmation rather than the primary guardrail, improving both speed and reliability.

6.11.3 Test Data Smells & Hard-Coded Fixtures

Hard-coded test data—static JSON strings, SQL dumps, or inline object literals—leads to duplication, brittleness, and difficulty evolving tests when the domain model changes. For instance:

```
Order order = new Order(UUID.fromString("00000000-0000-0000-0000-000000000001"),
List.of(new Item("A", 1, 10)));
```

When the Order constructor changes, dozens of tests break. Instead, use **builder** or **factory** patterns to centralize test data creation:

```
Order order = OrderBuilder.anOrder()
.withId(orderId)
.withItem("A", 1, 10)
.build();
```

Builders encapsulate defaults, reduce duplication, and allow tests to specify only relevant variations. For large fixtures, use **fixture libraries** (e.g., AutoFixture in .NET, Fixture Monkey in Java) or **seed data** scripts that populate databases consistently. Abstract test data into **external YAML/JSON** files when readability or reuse across languages is needed, and load them via parsers:

```
order:
 id: 00000000-0000-0000-0000-000000000001
 items:
 - sku: A
  qty: 1
  price: 10
```

Load with:

```
order = Order.from_dict(load_fixture('order.yaml'))
```

By removing hard-coded literals, tests become easier to maintain, more expressive, and resilient to refactoring. Ensure fixture code lives alongside tests, not in production, to avoid accidental dependencies.

6.11.4 Coupling Tests to Implementation Details

Tests that reach through layers—accessing private fields, calling helper methods, or instantiating classes that should be hidden by ports—violate architectural boundaries and become brittle. For example, a test that directly instantiates a repository adapter instead of using the repository port:

```
PostgresOrderRepository repo = new PostgresOrderRepository(dataSource);
Order order = new Order(...);
repo.save(order);
```

This bypasses the OrderRepository interface and ignores any caching or transactional decorators applied at the port level. Better tests exercise behavior via ports or use-case services:

```
orderRepo.save(order);
assertEquals(order, orderRepo.findById(order.getId()).get());
```

174

Similarly, tests should not import internal utility classes or mock private methods via reflection. Keep tests aligned with public APIs and domain ports; this enforces clean architecture and ensures test stability as internal implementation changes. Coupling tests only to the published port boundaries promotes test longevity, validates architecture contracts, and prevents tests from becoming a drag on refactoring.

6.12 Best Practices & Guidelines

6.12.1 Testing Boundaries, Not Layers

Tests should target **architectural boundaries**—the seams between layers—rather than testing each layer in isolation. By focusing on ports (interfaces) and adapters, you validate the contracts that glue layers together. For example, test the public API of a use-case interactor via its interface, rather than testing private helper methods. Integration tests should use real adapters but exercise application ports:

```
OrderService orderService = new OrderService(orderRepo, paymentGateway);
orderService.placeOrder(request);
```

This approach ensures that tests remain relevant even if the internal layering changes. By verifying boundary contracts—such as the JSON schema at the controller boundary or the SQL schema at the repository boundary—tests catch misconfigurations when wiring evolves.

Testing boundaries minimizes duplication, keeps tests aligned with system use cases, and supports refactoring of internal layers without breaking tests that assert on architectural contracts.

6.12.2 Keeping Tests Maintainable & Fast

Maintainable tests follow **DRY** principles: extract common setup into fixtures or builders, centralize configuration (e.g., spinning up containers), and avoid complex logic in test code. Use **naming conventions**—e.g., shouldDoX_whenConditionY()—to improve readability. Tests should be deterministic and side-effect-free: reset shared state, avoid randomness unless seeded, and isolate time-dependent code via clock-injectable utilities.

Fast tests accelerate developer feedback: aim for unit tests under 50 ms each, integration tests under 500 ms, and limit E2E tests to core scenarios. Profile test suites to identify slow tests and optimize or relocate them to slower pipelines. Parallelize test execution and leverage in-memory doubles for local development.

Monitor test flakiness: track failure rates and resolve flaky tests promptly. A **test linting** stage can enforce rules—no sleeps, no long running tests in unit suites. Regularly prune or refactor outdated tests to prevent rot. By investing in maintainability and performance, you ensure that the test suite remains a boon rather than a burden, enabling continuous delivery and high developer productivity.

6.12.3 Balancing Speed vs. Coverage

Achieving the right balance between test suite speed and coverage requires strategic allocation of test types. Prioritize broad **unit test** coverage for core business logic, supplemented by **integration tests** on critical adapter interactions. Reserve **E2E tests** for end-user workflows that no other tests cover. Use **coverage thresholds** wisely—set high standards for domain and application code, but allow lower coverage for generated code or trivial adapters.

Employ **test coverage heatmaps** to identify untested high-complexity areas and focus investment there. Use **mutation testing** to audit test effectiveness rather than raw coverage. Shift tests between pipelines based on their duration: local dev runs primarily unit tests, CI pre-merge runs unit + fast integration + contract tests, nightly runs the full suite including E2E and performance tests.

By tailoring test execution to context, you deliver fast feedback when it matters and thorough verification before releases, maximizing both speed and safety.

6.12.4 Cultivating a Quality-First Culture

Technical practices alone cannot guarantee quality; teams must embrace a **quality-first mindset**. Encourage **collective ownership** of tests: developers write both production and test code, code reviews include test reviews, and pairing sessions spread test expertise. Establish **Definition of Done** that includes test coverage, passing static analysis, and performance baselines.

Celebrate test improvements—refactoring brittle tests, raising mutation scores, reducing pipeline time—in team retrospectives. Provide **training and workshops** on effective testing patterns, mocking strategies, and debugging techniques. Integrate **test smells** into developer onboarding and highlight common anti-patterns.

Invest in **developer ergonomics**: curated libraries of fixtures and builders, CI feedback into IDEs (e.g., SonarLint, Pact plugin), and dashboard alerts for regressions. Leadership support is crucial: allocate time for test debt repayment, resist the urge to skip tests for deadlines, and reward engineers for maintaining high-quality test suites.

A quality-first culture recognizes that tests are as valuable as production code: they document behavior, drive design, and safeguard against regression. By institutionalizing testing as a core facet of development, teams build software that is not only functional but robust, maintainable, and aligned with business outcomes.

Conclusion

When testing permeates every layer of your application, it transforms from a chore into a powerful design tool. Unit tests prompt you to keep domain entities focused and self-validating; integration tests encourage clean contracts between adapters and ports; end-to-end scenarios validate that the pieces form a coherent whole under real-world conditions. By balancing fast, isolated checks with broader, scenario-based verifications, you guard against regressions without sacrificing agility. Over time, this disciplined approach to testing not only uncovers defects early but also reinforces clean architecture principles—dependency rules, separation of concerns, and clear module boundaries—ensuring your software remains maintainable, scalable, and aligned with business intent.

Chapter 7. Data Persistence & Repositories

Data persistence is the backbone of any real-world application: it gives life to your domain model by safely storing and retrieving state, enforcing business invariants, and enabling scale and performance optimizations. In a clean architecture, the persistence layer is carefully decoupled from core business logic, interacting through purpose-built interfaces that encapsulate storage concerns without leaking implementation details. Whether you're working with relational tables, document collections, in-memory caches, or streaming logs, the repository abstraction lets you treat your domain entities as coherent objects while hiding the intricacies of SQL dialects, ORM mappings, or NoSQL query patterns. Thoughtful transaction management, unit-of-work coordination, and careful schema evolution practices ensure data integrity even as systems grow, while caching, batching, and sharding techniques help meet demanding performance and availability requirements. By making data access an explicit, well-governed concern, you create a foundation that is both flexible to change and robust under load.

7.1 Persistence Fundamentals

7.1.1 Data Storage Models

Modern applications have a rich landscape of storage technologies, each optimized for different data access patterns. **Relational databases** (e.g., PostgreSQL, MySQL) organize data into tables with fixed schemas, enforcing **ACID** guarantees—atomicity, consistency, isolation, durability—via transactions. They excel at complex joins, strong referential integrity, and ad-hoc querying through SQL. Typical use cases include financial ledgers, customer records, and any domain requiring strict consistency.

Document stores (e.g., MongoDB, Couchbase) persist data as semi-structured JSON documents, allowing fields to vary across records. This schema-flexibility supports rapid iteration and denormalized views, embedding related data in one document. You might model an Order with embedded OrderLine sub-documents to avoid joins and improve read performance:

```
// MongoDB Order document
{
 "_id": "order123",
 "customerId": "cust456",
 "lines": [
  { "sku": "A", "qty": 2, "price": 5.0 },
  { "sku": "B", "qty": 1, "price": 10.0 }
 ],
 "status": "PENDING"
}
```

Key–value stores (e.g., Redis, DynamoDB in simple mode) map opaque keys to binary blobs or JSON, offering extreme performance and horizontal scalability. They're ideal for caching session data, feature flags, or simple lookup tables where the application logic manages structure.

Graph databases (e.g., Neo4j, Amazon Neptune) represent entities as nodes and relationships as edges, optimized for traversals like social networks or recommendation engines. A Cypher query to find friends-of-friends might look like:

```
MATCH (u:User {id:'u1'})-[:FRIEND]->(f)-[:FRIEND]->(fof)
WHERE fof.id <> 'u1'
RETURN DISTINCT fof
```

Columnar (e.g., ClickHouse) and **time-series** (e.g., InfluxDB) stores use storage layouts optimized for analytical queries or high-frequency data points, respectively. Columnar stores accelerate scans over few columns, while time-series databases handle massive write rates with retention policies.

Choosing among these models depends on your domain's consistency needs, query patterns, and scalability requirements. Often, a **polyglot** architecture leverages multiple stores in harmony (see 7.1.3). Understanding each model's trade-offs enables you to tailor persistence strategies that match use-case semantics, whether strong ACID for payments or eventual consistency for analytics.

7.1.2 ACID vs. BASE Trade-Offs

Relational systems emphasize **ACID**: a transaction either fully succeeds or fully fails (atomicity), transitions the database from one valid state to another (consistency), isolates concurrent transactions (isolation), and survives crashes once committed (durability). Isolation levels—READ COMMITTED, REPEATABLE READ, SERIALIZABLE—control phenomena like dirty reads or phantom reads. SERIALIZABLE provides the strongest guarantees but at the cost of locking and throughput.

In contrast, **BASE** ("Basically Available, Soft state, Eventual consistency") architectures prioritize availability and partition tolerance over strict consistency. NoSQL datastores may accept writes on any node, replicate asynchronously, and allow reading stale data briefly before convergence. This model suits globally distributed caches, social feeds, or IoT telemetry, where slight staleness is acceptable.

The **CAP theorem** states a distributed system can guarantee at most two of Consistency, Availability, and Partition tolerance. In practice, network partitions are inevitable, so systems must choose between consistency and availability. For example, Cassandra opts for AP with tunable consistency; PostgreSQL streaming replicas opt for CP, sacrificing availability on partition.

Selecting ACID vs. BASE involves evaluating business invariants. If processing a payment, strong consistency is paramount; if storing website analytics, eventual consistency may suffice. Some systems blend models using transactions for critical paths and background jobs for analytics, preserving user experience while ensuring data integrity where it matters most.

```
// Spring transaction example
@Service
public class OrderService {
 @Transactional(isolation = Isolation.SERIALIZABLE)
 public void placeOrder(Order order) { /* ... */ }
}
```

By understanding ACID and BASE, you can design a persistence layer that balances correctness, performance, and resilience according to real-world needs.

7.1.3 Polyglot Persistence

No single datastore fits all workloads, so **polyglot persistence** combines multiple technologies, each chosen for its strengths. A typical e-commerce platform might use:

1. **Relational DB** for transactional consistency of orders and payments.
2. **Document store** for user profiles with dynamic fields.
3. **Search engine** (Elasticsearch) for full-text product search and filtering.
4. **Key–value cache** (Redis) for session data and rate limits.

Data flows between stores can happen via asynchronous replications or **Change Data Capture** (CDC) pipelines. For example, capturing PostgreSQL WAL entries to feed Elasticsearch indices ensures search is eventually consistent with the transactional store.

Adapters encapsulate interactions with each store, presenting a unified repository interface to the core:

```
public class UnifiedProductRepository implements ProductRepository {
 private final SqlProductRepo sql;
 private final ESProductRepo es;
 public Product find(String id) {
  Optional<Product> p = sql.findById(id);
  if (p.isPresent()) return p.get();
  return es.findById(id);
 }
}
```

This facade hides polyglot complexity behind a single port. Careful coordination avoids **cross-store joins**: instead, denormalization or materialized views pre-compute combined data.

Polyglot architectures demand robust **anti-corruption layers** to translate between models, consistent schema evolution strategies per store, and monitoring of replication lags. When applied judiciously, polyglot persistence empowers systems to meet diverse performance and consistency requirements without overloading a single technology.

7.2 Ports & Adapters for Data Access

7.2.1 Defining Repository Ports

In Clean Architecture, data access begins with **ports**—interfaces defined in the core domain or application layer that describe required persistence operations without prescribing technology. A well-designed port is **intention-revealing** and minimal, focused on the business' unit of work. For example:

```
// in core layer
public interface OrderRepository {
 Order load(OrderId id);
 void save(Order order);
}
```

This interface uses domain types (Order, OrderId) and hides all SQL or ORM details. Port granularity should align with **aggregate** boundaries; you typically offer save and load per aggregate root, rather than low-level CRUD on every table. For common queries (e.g., retrieving pending orders), consider query-specific ports or methods:

```
List<Order> findByStatus(OrderStatus status);
```

Avoid **fat** ports with dozens of methods; instead, use the **Specification** pattern (7.3.2) to compose queries. By depending on abstractions, core logic remains decoupled from frameworks—facilitating both testability (mocks, fakes) and flexibility in switching implementations. Document each port's contract—transactional expectations, exception semantics—in code comments to guide adapter developers and ensure consistent behavior across implementations.

7.2.2 Implementing Adapter Repositories

Adapters reside in the outermost layer, wiring ports to concrete technologies. For a JPA-based adapter:

```
@Repository
public class JpaOrderRepository implements OrderRepository {
 @PersistenceContext private EntityManager em;


 @Override
 public Order load(OrderId id) {
  OrderEntity e = em.find(OrderEntity.class, id.toString());
  return e.toDomain();
 }


 @Override
 @Transactional
 public void save(Order order) {
  OrderEntity e = OrderEntity.from(order);
  em.merge(e);
 }
}
```

Here, OrderEntity maps using JPA annotations (@Entity, @Id). The adapter translates between domain and persistence models via toDomain() and from(). All framework imports remain within the adapter; the core never sees EntityManager.

Exception handling is critical: catch PersistenceException and wrap it in a domain-agnostic adapter exception:

```
catch (PersistenceException ex) {
 throw new RepositoryException("Failed to save order", ex);
}
```

This prevents low-level exceptions from "leaking" into domain logic. Adapter code also configures caching, batching, or custom SQL via @Query annotations. By isolating all data-access logic within adapters, you preserve core purity and enable multiple implementations (e.g., a test double or an alternative NoSQL adapter) to coexist seamlessly.

7.2.3 Abstracting Multiple Data Stores

When using **polyglot persistence**, you may need a single port implemented by multiple adapters, or a facade that routes calls to the right store. For instance:

```
public class ProductRepositoryFacade implements ProductRepository {
 private final SqlProductRepo sql;
 private final MongoProductRepo mongo;

 public Product load(ProductId id) {
 Optional<Product> p = sql.load(id);
 if (p.isPresent()) return p.get();
 return mongo.load(id); // fallback
 }

 public void save(Product product) {
 sql.save(product);
 mongo.save(product); // denormalize to document store
 }
}
```

Alternatively, use the **Strategy pattern** to select a store at runtime based on configuration or data age:

```
public class ConfigurableOrderRepository implements OrderRepository {
 private final Map<String, OrderRepository> implementations;
 public Order load(OrderId id) {
 String store = config.get("order.store"); // "sql" or "cache"
 return implementations.get(store).load(id);
 }
}
```

A diagram of this arrangement:

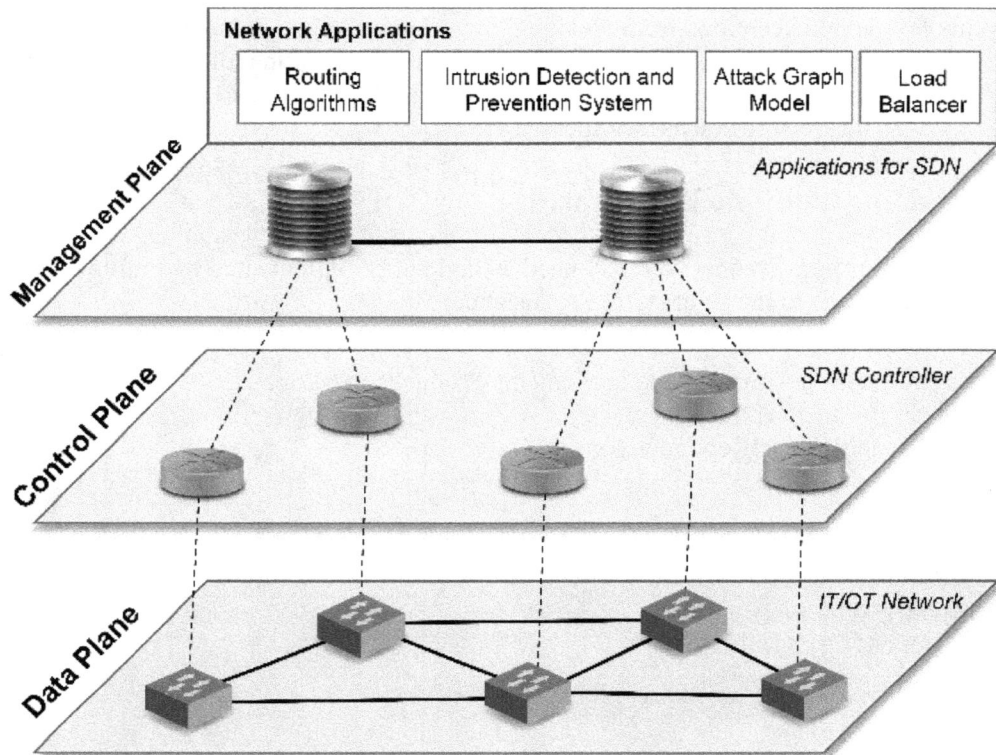

Network Applications: Routing Algorithms, Intrusion Detection and Prevention System, Attack Graph Model, Load Balancer — Applications for SDN (Management Plane); SDN Controller (Control Plane); IT/OT Network (Data Plane)

Adapters for each store implement the same port, while a facade or strategy picks among them. This pattern enables seamless migration between stores, blue/green deployments of new persistence technologies, and combining transactional and analytical stores without polluting core business logic.

7.3 The Repository Pattern

7.3.1 Interface Design & Naming

A clean repository interface balances generic CRUD capabilities with domain-specific intention. Generic methods—save(), load(), delete()—cover basic persistence, while tailor-made methods capture business queries:

```
public interface OrderRepository {
 Optional<Order> findById(OrderId id);
 void save(Order order);
 List<Order> findByStatus(OrderStatus status);
 OrderId nextOrderId();
}
```

findByStatus expresses an important domain query, while nextOrderId encapsulates ID-generation logic. Avoid **anemic** repositories that push business logic into service layers; if complex querying or filtering arises, consider the **Specification** pattern rather than proliferating methods.

Return types matter: use Optional<T> instead of nulls, Stream<T> for lazily-fetched results, and Page<T> for paginated queries. Clearly document each method's semantics—are calls idempotent? Is caching applied? Does the method participate in a transaction? Adhering to naming conventions (findByX, loadAll, countByY) makes repository behavior predictable and discoverable. Well-designed interfaces form the contract between domain and infrastructure, enabling independent evolution of both sides.

7.3.2 Query Methods & Specification Pattern

Over time, the number of repository methods can explode as business requirements add new filters and sorts. The **Specification** pattern centralizes query logic into reusable, composable predicates. In Java, using Spring Data JPA:

```
public      interface      OrderRepository      extends      JpaRepository<OrderEntity,      String>,
JpaSpecificationExecutor<OrderEntity> {}


// Specification for "pending" orders over $100
Specification<OrderEntity> highValuePending = (root, q, cb) ->
 cb.and(
  cb.equal(root.get("status"), "PENDING"),
  cb.gt(root.get("total"), 100)
 );


// Using the spec
List<Order> results = repo.findAll(highValuePending)
        .stream()
        .map(OrderEntity::toDomain)
        .collect(Collectors.toList());
```

Specifications can be combined with and(), or(), and not(), enabling arbitrary complex queries without changing repository interfaces. Alternately, use **QueryDSL** or **Jooq** for a typesafe, fluent API:

```
JPAQuery<OrderEntity> query = new JPAQuery<>(entityManager);
QOrderEntity order = QOrderEntity.orderEntity;
List<Order> orders = query.select(order)
 .from(order)
 .where(order.status.eq("PENDING"))
```

```
.and(order.total.gt(100)))
.fetch()
.stream()
.map(OrderEntity::toDomain)
.collect(Collectors.toList());
```

This approach prevents method bloat, keeps interfaces stable, and localizes query definitions. Business rules expressed as specifications also serve as living documentation of domain predicates.

7.3.3 Paging, Sorting & Projection

Handling large datasets requires pagination and sorting to limit memory usage and improve responsiveness. Repository ports can accept **pageable** parameters:

```
Page<Order> findByCustomerId(CustomerId id, Pageable page);
```

Clients pass PageRequest.of(pageNumber, pageSize, Sort.by("createdAt").descending()) to retrieve a specific slice:

```
Pageable pageable = PageRequest.of(0, 20, Sort.by("createdAt").descending());
Page<Order> page = orderRepo.findByCustomerId(custId, pageable);
```

Implementations use SQL LIMIT/OFFSET or cursor-based pagination for efficiency. Cursor pagination (seek method) avoids large offsets:

```
SELECT * FROM orders
 WHERE customer_id = ?
  AND created_at < :lastTimestamp
 ORDER BY created_at DESC
 LIMIT 20;
```

Projection lets you fetch only required fields into DTOs, reducing I/O and memory. In Spring Data:

```
interface OrderSummary {
 String getId();
 BigDecimal getTotal();
}


List<OrderSummary> findByCustomerId(CustomerId id, Pageable page);
```

Under the hood, the JPA provider generates SELECT id, total FROM orders …, mapping results to the projection interface. Combined pagination, sorting, and projection form a powerful toolset for building responsive, scalable APIs that serve user-facing lists without loading entire aggregates into memory.

7.4 Unit of Work & Transaction Management

7.4.1 Unit of Work Pattern

The **Unit of Work (UoW)** pattern tracks changes to multiple domain objects during a business transaction, batching insert, update, and delete operations into a single commit. In ORM frameworks like Hibernate, the Session or EntityManager acts as the UoW:

```
EntityManager em = ...;
em.getTransaction().begin();
OrderEntity order = em.find(OrderEntity.class, id);
order.setStatus("SHIPPED");
em.merge(order);      // UoW tracks this as "dirty"
em.getTransaction().commit(); // flushes all changes in one go
```

Custom UoW implementations maintain lists of new, changed, and removed objects, applying them in the correct order. Pseudocode:

```
public class UnitOfWork {
 private List<Entity> newEntities = new ArrayList<>();
 private List<Entity> dirtyEntities = new ArrayList<>();
 private List<Entity> removedEntities = new ArrayList<>();


 public void registerNew(Entity e) { newEntities.add(e); }
 public void registerDirty(Entity e) { dirtyEntities.add(e); }
 public void registerRemoved(Entity e) { removedEntities.add(e); }


 public void commit() {
  insertNew(); updateDirty(); deleteRemoved();
  clear();
 }
}
```

Using UoW ensures atomicity across multiple repositories and aggregates without scattering transaction logic throughout the domain.

7.4.2 Defining Transaction Boundaries

Determining where transactions begin and end is crucial for data integrity and performance. Best practice places transaction demarcation at the **service layer** (application services or interactors), encompassing all repository calls required for a use case:

```
@Service
public class PlaceOrderService {
 @Transactional
 public void placeOrder(PlaceOrderRequest req) {
  Order order = orderFactory.create(req);
  orderRepository.save(order);
  paymentGateway.charge(order);
  // all-or-nothing: either both save and charge succeed, or rollback
 }
}
```

In Spring, @Transactional on a class or method creates a transaction context. **Propagation** settings define behavior when nested transactions occur:

- REQUIRED (default) joins an existing transaction
- REQUIRES_NEW suspends the outer transaction and starts a new one
- SUPPORTS runs within a transaction if one exists

Use **read-only** transactions (@Transactional(readOnly=true)) for lookup methods to optimize performance and hint to the ORM to skip dirty checks. Avoid placing transactions at the repository method level, as it can lead to partial commits if multiple repository calls occur within one service method. Clear transaction boundaries make rollback semantics predictable and simplify error handling.

7.4.3 Distributed Transactions & Sagas

When a single business operation spans multiple microservices or disparate databases, traditional two-phase commit (2PC) via XA transactions can guarantee atomicity but introduces complexity, blocking resources during network partitions. Instead, **sagas** implement **eventual consistency** through a series of local transactions and compensating actions.

In the **choreography** style (see 6.10.1), each service emits an event upon successful local commit; downstream services react and emit subsequent events. If a failure occurs mid-workflow, compensating events undo prior steps. In the **orchestration** style, a central saga orchestrator issues commands and invokes compensating commands on failure. Pseudocode for an orchestrator:

```
public class OrderSaga {
```

```
public void handle(OrderPlaced e) {
 try {
  paymentService.charge(e.orderId, e.amount);
  shippingService.schedule(e.orderId);
 } catch (PaymentFailed ex) {
  inventoryService.release(e.orderId);
  orderService.cancel(e.orderId);
 }
 }
}
```

Each local service uses its own transaction for critical updates, ensuring autonomy and resilience. Compensating transactions must be idempotent and carefully designed to restore system invariants. Monitoring tools track in-flight saga instances, detect hangs, and allow manual intervention. While sagas sacrifice strict ACID across services, they offer a scalable, decoupled alternative for long-running business processes, aligning with Clean Architecture's principle of separating concerns and managing dependencies explicitly.

7.5 ORM, Data Mapper & Active Record

7.5.1 ORM Trade-Offs

Object-Relational Mapping (ORM) frameworks like Hibernate or Entity Framework seek to bridge the gap between in-memory domain objects and relational tables. They provide an **identity map** that ensures each database row corresponds to a single in-memory object instance, enabling features like transparent caching and change tracking. With change tracking, you can modify your domain entities and simply call save(), relying on the ORM to generate the appropriate INSERT, UPDATE, or DELETE statements in a single flush.

However, ORMs introduce complexity: **lazy loading** of associations can trigger unexpected SQL queries (the "N+1 selects" problem) when iterating collections. For example, iterating order.getLines() outside of a transaction may fire one query per line item if not fetched eagerly or via a fetch-join. Tuning involves balancing eager vs. lazy strategies, using batch-fetch sizes, or employing explicit fetch plans.

Furthermore, ORMs often generate verbose SQL or inefficient JOIN patterns under complex mappings. Debugging these issues requires careful inspection of the generated SQL and occasional fallback to native queries. The second-level cache can mitigate perfect-storm load, but misconfiguration can lead to stale data if cache invalidation isn't tuned correctly.

ORMs support sophisticated features—inheritance mapping, optimistic locking with version columns, interceptors, and custom user types—but each adds cognitive load and potential performance pitfalls. In systems where you only need simple CRUD, a **lightweight data mapper** (e.g., MyBatis, Dapper) may be preferable, offering direct control over SQL with minimal impedance mismatch.

Active Record patterns (e.g., Ruby on Rails, Laravel Eloquent) embed persistence logic inside domain entities themselves, simplifying small applications but risking **anemic domain** violations as business logic and data access intermingle. In Clean Architecture, it's often better to keep persistence concerns in adapters rather than polluting your core models.

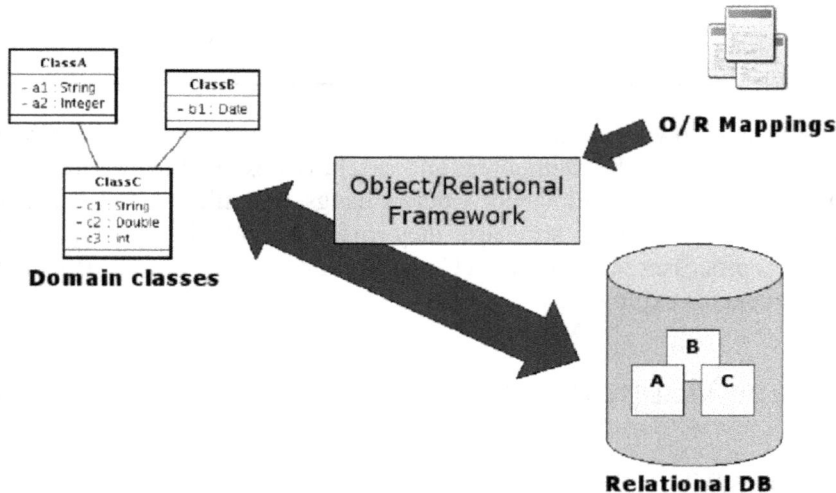

When selecting an ORM, evaluate your domain complexity, query patterns, and team expertise. For transactional systems with rich object graphs, an ORM can dramatically accelerate development once mastered. For high-performance or analytics workloads, consider dedicated data mappers or direct SQL/NoSQL drivers to maintain predictability and avoid hidden query generation.

```
// Hibernate example: mapping a Money value object
@Embeddable
public class Money {
 @Column(name="amount") private BigDecimal amount;
 @Column(name="currency") private String currency;
 // equals(), hashCode(), business validation...
}


// Entity using Money
@Entity
public class OrderLine {
 @Embedded private Money unitPrice;
 @Column private int quantity;
}
```

7.5.2 Mapping Configuration Patterns

ORM frameworks offer multiple mapping configuration approaches: **annotations**, **XML**, and **fluent API**. Annotations co-locate mapping metadata with code, improving discoverability:

```
@Entity
@Table(name="orders")
public class OrderEntity {
 @Id @GeneratedValue private Long id;
 @Column(name="created_at") private LocalDateTime createdAt;
 @OneToMany(mappedBy="order", cascade=CascadeType.ALL, fetch=FetchType.LAZY)
 private List<OrderLineEntity> lines = new ArrayList<>();
}
```

XML mappings decouple code from configuration, useful when you can't or don't want to modify entity classes. However, they introduce external files that can drift out of sync.

A **fluent API** (e.g., Hibernate's ModelMapper or Entity Framework's OnModelCreating) lets you configure mappings in Java/C# code:

```
modelBuilder.Entity<Order>(o => {
 o.ToTable("orders");
 o.HasKey(x => x.Id);
 o.Property(x => x.CreatedAt).HasColumnName("created_at");
 o.HasMany(x => x.Lines)
  .WithOne(l => l.Order)
  .HasForeignKey(l => l.OrderId)
  .OnDelete(DeleteBehavior.Cascade);
});
```

For complex value objects—like Money or Address—you often need **custom converters** or **attribute converters**. In JPA:

```
@Converter(autoApply=true)
public class MoneyConverter implements AttributeConverter<Money, String> {
 public String convertToDatabaseColumn(Money money) {
  return money.getAmount() + ":" + money.getCurrency();
 }
 public Money convertToEntityAttribute(String dbData) {
  String[] parts = dbData.split(":");
  return new Money(new BigDecimal(parts[0]), parts[1]);
 }
```

```
}
```

Conventions-over-configuration tools (e.g., Spring Data) infer table and column names from entity and field names, reducing boilerplate but risking surprise when defaults change. Always document mapping overrides and validate them with integration tests.

```
@startuml
entity OrderEntity {
 *id : Long
 *createdAt : LocalDateTime
}
entity OrderLineEntity {
 *id : Long
 *orderId : Long
 *unitPrice : String
}
OrderEntity ||--o{ OrderLineEntity : lines
@enduml
```

Mapping configuration patterns should align with team skills: annotations for small projects, fluent API for centralized configuration, XML for decoupled mapping, and custom converters for complex types. Consistent conventions and code reviews help maintain mapping correctness as the domain model evolves.

7.5.3 Lazy vs. Eager Loading Strategies

Association fetching strategies—**lazy** or **eager**—directly impact both performance and memory consumption. Lazy loading defers loading of related entities until accessed, reducing initial query cost but risking the N+1 problem if multiple accesses occur in a loop:

```
Order order = orderRepo.load(id);    // loads only Order
for (OrderLine line : order.getLines()) { // triggers separate query per line
 System.out.println(line.getUnitPrice());
}
```

To avoid this, you can configure eager fetching via mapping metadata:

```
@OneToMany(fetch=FetchType.EAGER, mappedBy="order")
private List<OrderLine> lines;
```

However, eager loading can fetch large object graphs even when unnecessary, wasting memory and bandwidth. A middle ground is **fetch joins** in queries:

```
String jpql = "SELECT o FROM OrderEntity o JOIN FETCH o.lines WHERE o.id = :id";
OrderEntity order = em.createQuery(jpql, OrderEntity.class)
        .setParameter("id", id)
        .getSingleResult();
```

This retrieves both Order and OrderLine in a single SQL join, avoiding N+1 while controlling exactly which associations load.

In Criteria API or QueryDSL:

```
QOrderEntity o = QOrderEntity.orderEntity;
JPAQuery<OrderEntity> query = new JPAQuery<>(em);
OrderEntity order = query.select(o)
 .from(o).leftJoin(o.lines).fetchJoin()
 .where(o.id.eq(id)).fetchOne();
```

For collection-heavy associations, consider **batch fetching**:

```
hibernate.default_batch_fetch_size=100
```

This groups lazy loads into batches, reducing the number of queries from N+1 to ~N/batchSize+1.

Lazy Loading vs Eager Loading

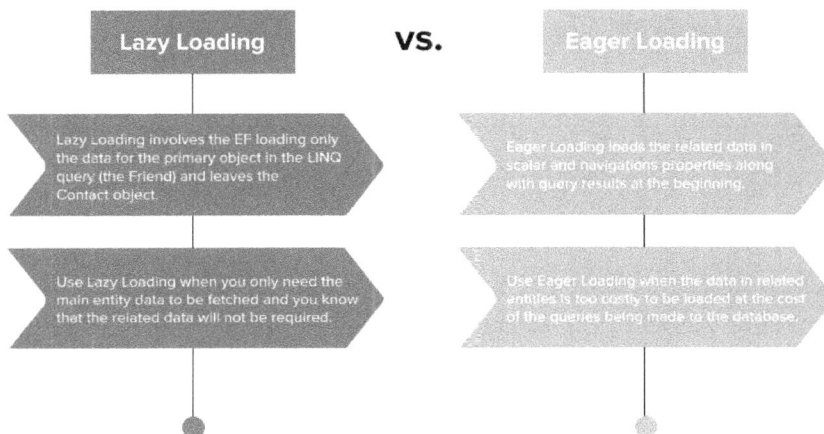

Choosing the right strategy depends on your use case: use lazy loading for rarely accessed associations, eager for always-needed data (e.g., display DTOs), and fetch joins or batch fetching for controlled eager access. Profile your application with SQL logs or metrics to detect problematic fetch patterns, and adjust mappings or queries accordingly to balance performance and simplicity.

7.6 NoSQL & Specialized Datastores

7.6.1 Document Databases

Document databases like MongoDB store data as JSON/BSON documents, offering schema flexibility and horizontal scalability. When modeling aggregates, it's common to embed related data directly:

```
{
"_id": "order123",
"customerId": "cust456",
"lines": [
  { "sku": "A", "qty": 2, "unitPrice": 5.0 },
  { "sku": "B", "qty": 1, "unitPrice": 10.0 }
],
"status": "PENDING"
}
```

Embedding improves read performance—fetching the entire aggregate requires a single document read—at the cost of potential document bloat if collections grow unbounded. For large child lists, you may choose **referencing** instead:

```
// Order document
{ "_id":"order123","customerId":"cust456","status":"PENDING" }
// Separate OrderLine collection
{ "orderId":"order123","sku":"A","qty":2,"unitPrice":5.0 }
```

Schema evolution in schemaless stores still requires discipline: use **application-level versioning** or **migration scripts** to transform documents. For example, to add a new field discount, write a migration:

```
db.orders.updateMany({}, { $set: { discount: 0 } });
```

Indexing nested fields ensures performance:

```
db.orders.createIndex({ "lines.sku": 1 });
```

Mapping between domain models and documents relies on **object mappers** (e.g, Spring Data MongoDB):

```
@Document("orders")
public class OrderDocument {
 @Id private String id;
 private String customerId;
 private List<OrderLineDocument> lines;
 // toDomain(), fromDomain()...
}
```

Aggregations—grouping, filtering, sorting—use the database's **aggregation framework**, akin to a map-reduce pipeline:

```
db.orders.aggregate([
  { $match: { status: "SHIPPED" }},
  { $unwind: "$lines" },
  { $group: { _id: "$lines.sku", totalSold: { $sum: "$lines.qty" }}}
]);
```

By modeling aggregates as documents and leveraging native query and aggregation capabilities, you can build rich, high-performance data layers. However, you must carefully plan partition keys (shard keys) in sharded clusters to balance load and avoid hotspots.

7.6.2 Key-Value & In-Memory Stores

Key–value stores such as Redis and Memcached excel at ultra-low-latency lookups and simple data structures. They often serve as caches in a **cache-aside** pattern: the application checks the cache first, falling back to the primary store on a miss, then populating the cache:

```
public Order getOrder(String id) {
 String key = "order:" + id;
 Order o = cache.get(key);
 if (o == null) {
  o = orderRepo.load(id);
  cache.set(key, o, Duration.ofMinutes(5));
 }
 return o;
}
```

Other patterns include **write-through** (writes go to cache and primary store) and **read-through** (cache automatically fetches from the store). High-availability modes—Redis Sentinel or cluster mode—ensure resilience.

Key–value stores also support advanced data structures: lists, sets, sorted sets, and hashes. For example, storing a user's session as a hash:

```
HSET session:abc123 userId 42 expiresAt "2025-06-01T00:00:00Z"
EXPIRE session:abc123 3600
```

Distributed caches require careful invalidation strategies: timeouts, explicit eviction on updates, or cache versioning. Use **CAS** (compare-and-set) operations for safe updates in concurrent environments. In-memory grids—Hazelcast, Apache Ignite—provide distributed maps and compute capabilities, enabling data locality and collocated processing.

By offloading frequent reads and session state to key–value stores, you reduce pressure on primary databases and improve application responsiveness, while patterns and TTL policies guard against stale data.

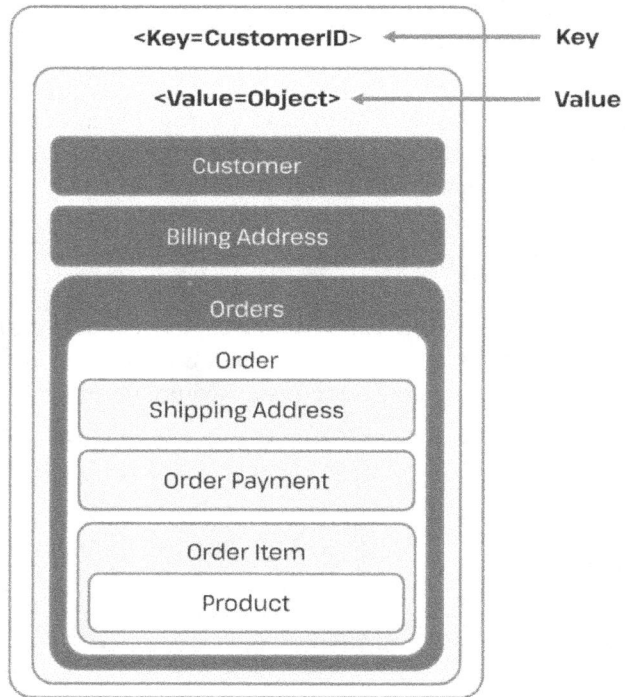

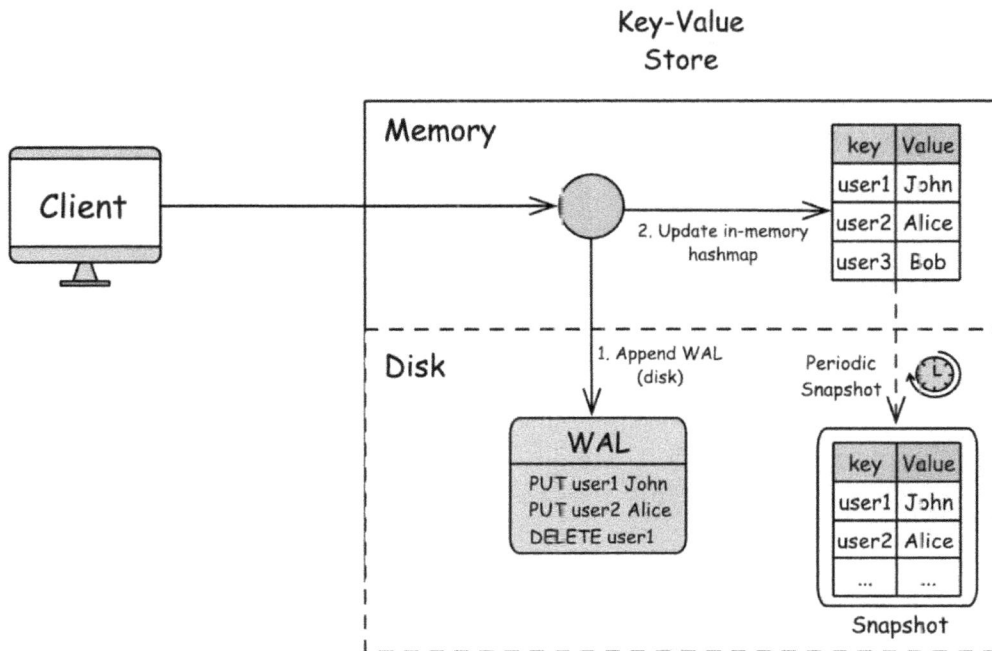

Key-Value Store

7.6.3 Graph Databases & Search Engines

Graph databases like Neo4j or Amazon Neptune model entities (:User, :Product) as nodes and relationships (:FRIEND, :PURCHASED) as first-class edges. They optimize for traversals and pattern matching that are cumbersome in relational or document stores. A Cypher query to find friends-of-friends with at least one common interest:

```
MATCH        (u:User        {id:"u1"})-[:FRIEND]->(f)-[:INTERESTED_IN]->(topic)<-
[:INTERESTED_IN]-(fof)
WHERE fof.id <> "u1"
RETURN DISTINCT fof, collect(topic) AS sharedTopics
```

Integration with Clean Architecture occurs in an adapter implementing a SocialGraph port. For example:

```
public interface SocialGraph {
 List<User> findFriendsOfFriends(UserId id);
}


@Component
public class Neo4jSocialGraph implements SocialGraph {
```

```
@Autowired private Session session;
public List<User> findFriendsOfFriends(UserId id) {
 Result r = session.run(MY_CYPHER_QUERY, Map.of("id", id.toString()));
 // map Result to List<User>
 }
}
```

Search engines like Elasticsearch or Solr provide full-text search, faceted navigation, and analytics over large document sets. You index domain data into an inverted index:

```
PUT /products/_doc/1
{
 "name": "Wireless Mouse",
 "description": "Ergonomic design with long battery life",
 "price": 29.99
}
```

Then perform a match query:

```
GET /products/_search
{
 "query": {
  "multi_match": {
   "query": "ergonomic mouse",
   "fields": ["name", "description"]
  }
 }
}
```

Adapter code using the Java High-Level REST Client:

```
SearchRequest req = new SearchRequest("products");
req.source(new SearchSourceBuilder()
.query(QueryBuilders.multiMatchQuery("ergonomic mouse", "name", "description")));
SearchResponse resp = client.search(req, RequestOptions.DEFAULT);
```

Graph and search stores expand your data-access toolkit for specialized queries—social networks, recommendations, or product discovery—that would be inefficient in traditional datastores. By encapsulating access behind well-defined ports, your core logic remains agnostic, enabling experimentation and evolution of underlying technologies without disrupting domain code.

7.7 Performance, Caching & Batching

7.7.1 Second-Level & Query-Level Caches

ORMs like Hibernate offer **second-level caches** to store entity or collection data across sessions, reducing database load for frequently accessed data. You configure cache regions per entity:

```
<cache usage="READ_WRITE" region="orders"/>
<cache usage="READ_ONLY" region="productCatalog"/>
```

And annotate entities:

```
@Entity
@Cacheable
@org.hibernate.annotations.Cache(usage = CacheConcurrencyStrategy.READ_WRITE)
public class OrderEntity { ... }
```

On a cache hit, Hibernate returns the entity without firing SQL. **Query caches** store the results of named queries or criteria executions:

```
List<Order> orders = session.createQuery("from Order where status = :st", Order.class)
.setParameter("st", "PENDING")
.setCacheable(true)
.list();
```

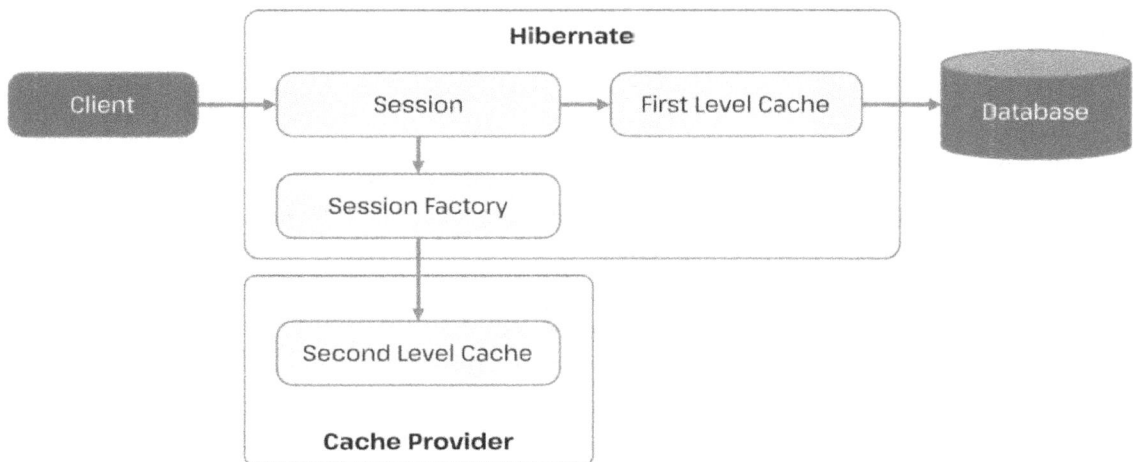

Subsequent identical queries fetch results from cache and then resolve entities from the second-level cache, improving performance. However, stale data risk arises if cache invalidation isn't aligned with data changes; use **time-to-live** (TTL) or **explicit evictions** (sessionFactory.getCache().evict*(...)) to control freshness. Distributed caches like **Hazelcast** or **Infinispan** can back Hibernate's second-level cache across a cluster, but require configuration of replication and consistency policies. Monitoring cache hit ratios and query latencies reveals caching effectiveness, guiding region sizing and eviction policies.

By judiciously applying second-level and query-level caches, you can dramatically reduce database contention for read-heavy workloads while maintaining acceptable staleness and consistency semantics.

7.7.2 Batch Operations & Bulk APIs

Batching multiple write operations reduces round-trips and leverages DB optimizations. In JPA/Hibernate, enable JDBC batching:

```
hibernate.jdbc.batch_size=50
hibernate.order_inserts=true
hibernate.order_updates=true
```

And within a transaction:

```
for (int i = 0; i < orders.size(); i++) {
 em.persist(orders.get(i));
 if (i % 50 == 0) {
 em.flush();
 em.clear();
 }
}
```

This sends 50 inserts in one JDBC batch, speeding up data loads and ETL tasks. For updates, similar batching applies to merge(). Bulk APIs in document stores (MongoDB):

```
List<WriteModel<Document>> writes = lines.stream()
 .map(line -> new InsertOneModel<>(new Document(...)))
 .collect(Collectors.toList());
collection.bulkWrite(writes, new BulkWriteOptions().ordered(false));
```

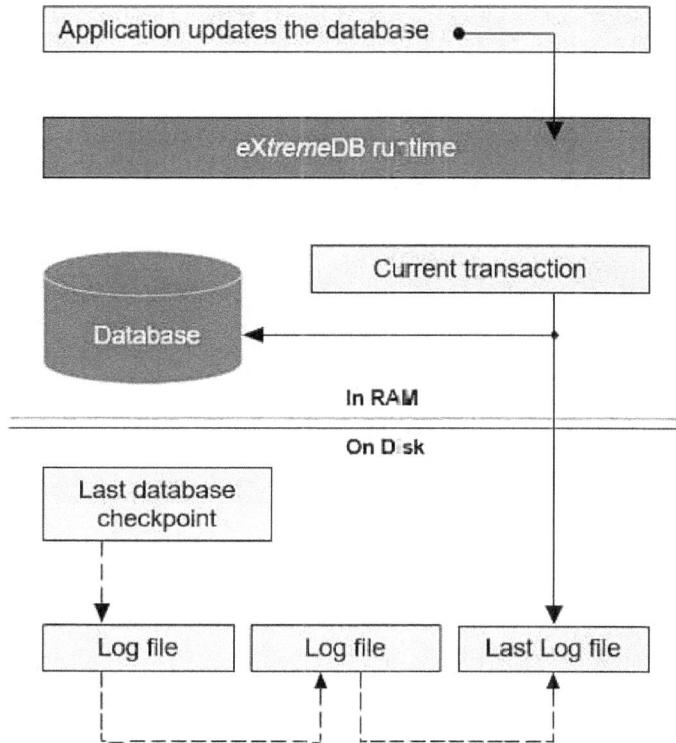

ordered(false) allows the DB to parallelize writes and skip failed documents, improving throughput. Bulk deletion and replacement also exist. When batching, watch for **driver memory usage** and **transaction log** growth—chunk operations into manageable sizes and commit periodically to bound resource consumption.

Throttling may be needed to avoid overwhelming the storage engine; use back-pressure or sleep intervals between batches. Logging batch performance metrics (CPU, I/O, latency) informs optimal batch sizes for production hardware.

Batch operations and bulk APIs are indispensable for high-volume data pipelines, ensuring that domain-driven operations scale to meet real-world throughput demands without excessive boilerplate.

7.7.3 Sharding & Partitioning

When a single database instance can no longer handle data volume or throughput, **horizontal partitioning** (sharding) splits data across multiple nodes. Choose a **shard key**—often a hash of a user ID, tenant ID, or geographical region—to distribute load evenly:

```
Shard 1: userId % 4 == 0
Shard 2: userId % 4 == 1
Shard 3: userId % 4 == 2
Shard 4: userId % 4 == 3
```

In application code, implement a **shard router** adapter:

```
public DataSource route(String tenantId) {
 int shard = hash(tenantId) % 4;
 return dataSources.get(shard);
}
```

Use consistent hashing to add or remove shards with minimal data movement. **Range partitioning** groups contiguous key ranges (e.g., timestamps) onto separate nodes, useful for time-series archives.

Key-value datastores like Cassandra handle sharding automatically via ring architectures and partitioners. You define **partition keys** in table schemas:

```
CREATE TABLE orders (
 customer_id text,
 order_id timeuuid,
 total decimal,
 PRIMARY KEY ((customer_id), order_id)
);
```

Here, all orders for a customer route to the same node, supporting efficient per-customer queries.

Sharding complicates cross-shard joins; to aggregate across shards, use middleware or orchestrate in application code with scatter-gather. Multi-tenant isolation benefits from separate databases or schemas per tenant, simplifying backups and compliance but increasing operational overhead.

Monitoring per-shard metrics—latency, storage growth, hotspotting—guides rebalancing strategies. Sharding and partitioning, when aligned with domain access patterns, unlock massive scale while preserving query performance for targeted workloads.

Diagram of sharded topology:

Replication

E-Commerce DB
(customers and orders)

E-Commerce DB
(customers and orders)

E-Commerce DB
(customers and orders)

Keeping the copy of same
data on multiple servers.

Table Partitioning

Orders DB
(March)

Orders DB
(January)

Orders DB
(February)

Splitting a large table into smaller
parts based on data cohesion

Table Sharding

Customers (A-G)

Customers
(All)

Customers (H-P)

Customers (Q-Z)

Splitting a large table row wise

Database Federation

Customers DB

Orders DB

Disparate DBs functioning as one DB

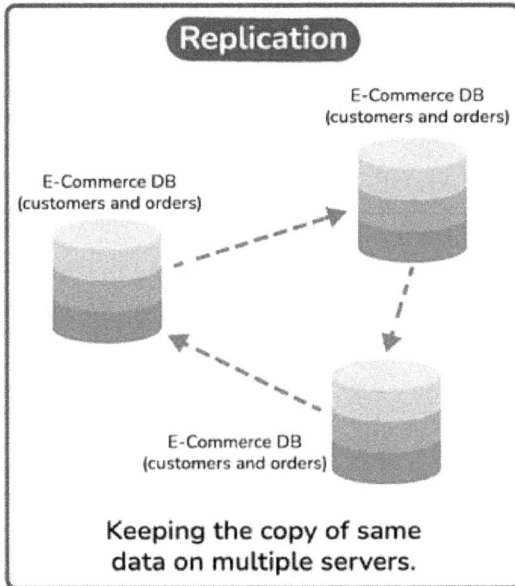

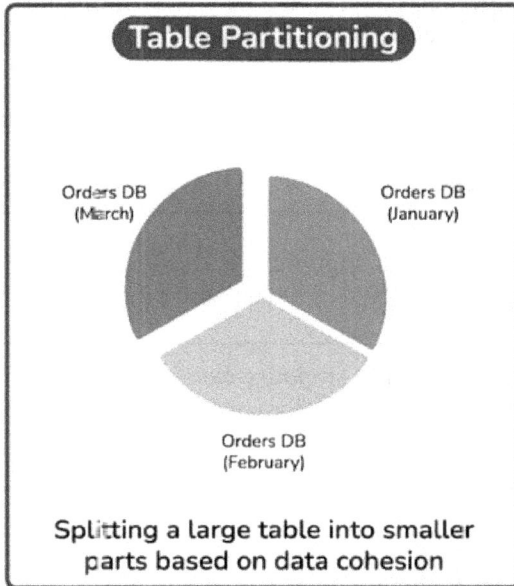

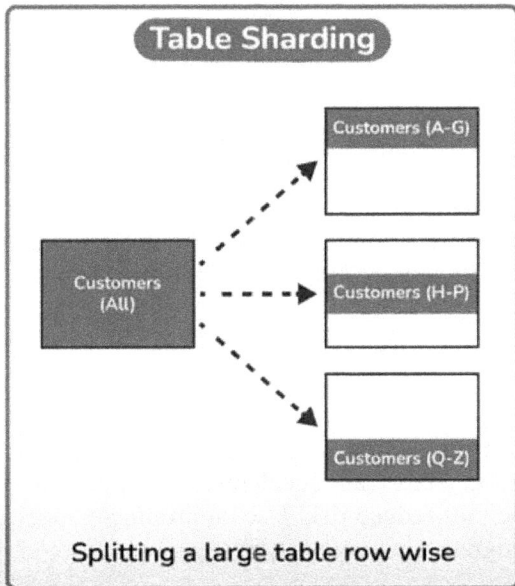

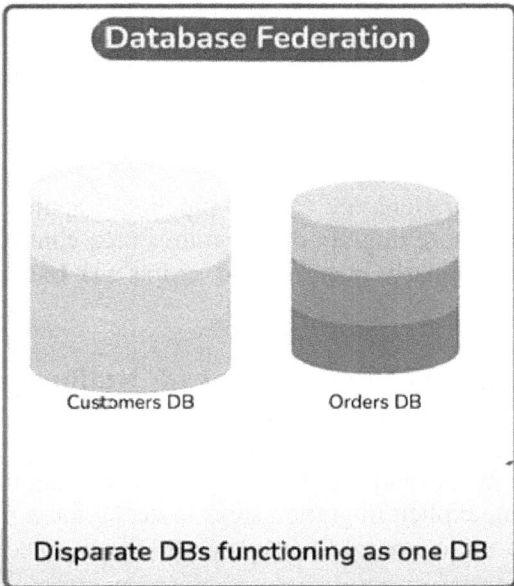

7.8 Database Migrations & Schema Evolution

7.8.1 Migration Tools & Best Practices

Schema migrations adapt your database as the application evolves. **Flyway** and **Liquibase** are popular tools that manage versioned change scripts. With Flyway, SQL files named V1__create_orders.sql, V2__add_discount_column.sql are applied in order. Example:

```
-- V2__add_discount_column.sql
ALTER TABLE orders ADD COLUMN discount DECIMAL DEFAULT 0 NOT NULL;
```

Flyway tracks applied migrations in a schema_version table, preventing reapplication. Liquibase uses XML/JSON/YAML/SQL formats with a <changeSet> identifier:

```
<changeSet id="3-add-shipping-date" author="dev">
 <addColumn tableName="orders">
  <column name="shipping_date" type="timestamp"/>
 </addColumn>
</changeSet>
```

Best practices include:

1. **Idempotent** scripts that can run safely on existing schemas.
2. **Small, incremental** changes—one logical change per script—for easy rollback.
3. **Descriptive naming** to aid tracing history.
4. **Testing migrations** against clean and long-lived schemas in dedicated environments.

Automate migrations in CI/CD pipelines, applying them to dev/test databases before code deployment. Store migration scripts in source control alongside application code to ensure version alignment. Regularly clean up old scripts via **baseline** operations after stable releases to reduce clutter.

7.8.2 Managing Environments & Rollbacks

Different environments—development, staging, production—often run migrations at different cadences. In **development**, auto-migrate on application start can accelerate iteration, but in **production**, explicit migration steps in deployment pipelines reduce risk. Use environment-specific configurations to control Flyway's cleanDisabled and migration timeout settings.

Rollback strategies vary:

- **Undo scripts** (Liquibase supports <rollback>): writing inverse change sets (e.g., DROP COLUMN).
- **Point-in-time restore**: revert the entire database to a backup taken before migration.
- **Feature toggles**: deploy schema-and-code changes in stages, using toggles to deactivate new columns or tables before migrating.

Destructive changes (column drops, type changes) demand precaution: introduce new columns, backfill data, switch the code path to use the new column, then drop the old column in a later migration. This **expand-contract pattern** ensures backward and forward compatibility. Automated tests verify both the presence and absence of schema elements, and manual runbooks define emergency rollback procedures.

By treating migrations as first-class artifacts and planning rollbacks explicitly, you reduce the risk of downtime and data loss during schema evolution.

7.8.3 Backward/Forward Compatibility

Zero-downtime deployments often require database schemas that support both old and new application versions simultaneously. The **expand-contract** pattern facilitates this: first **expand** the schema in a backward-compatible way (add columns or tables), then deploy new code that reads and writes using the expanded schema, and finally **contract** by removing legacy elements once no longer needed.

For example, to rename a column amount to total_amount:

1. Migration: ALTER TABLE orders ADD COLUMN total_amount DECIMAL; UPDATE orders SET total_amount = amount;
2. Deploy code reading/writing both amount and total_amount.
3. Migration: ALTER TABLE orders DROP COLUMN amount;
4. Deploy code referencing only total_amount.

Throughout this process, both versions of the application operate correctly. View-based compatibility can also help: create a **view** orders_view that unifies old and new columns:

```
CREATE VIEW orders_view AS
SELECT id, COALESCE(total_amount, amount) AS total
FROM orders;
```

Both old and new code reference orders_view for reads, insulating them from schema drift.

Feature flags further smooth transitions: code paths reading from new columns behind flags that can be toggled at runtime. Automated compatibility tests exercise both code paths against the staging database, asserting that data consistency and query performance remain acceptable. By rigorously applying backward/forward compatibility patterns, you achieve zero-downtime deployments and continuous evolution of your data model, keeping pace with business demands without sacrificing system availability.

7.9 Testing Data Access

7.9.1 In-Memory vs. Containerized Databases

Testing persistence can use either lightweight in-memory databases or full-fidelity containerized instances; each approach has distinct trade-offs. **In-memory databases** such as H2 (for Java) or SQLite (for many languages) run entirely in process, start in milliseconds, and require minimal configuration. They excel for rapid developer feedback and TDD cycles: your JUnit or pytest suite spins up an in-memory schema via Hibernate or SQLAlchemy and executes DDL automatically. For example, in Spring Boot:

```
spring.datasource.url=jdbc:h2:mem:testdb;DB_CLOSE_DELAY=-1
spring.datasource.driverClassName=org.h2.Driver
spring.jpa.hibernate.ddl-auto=create-drop


@SpringBootTest
public class InMemoryOrderRepositoryTest {
 @Autowired OrderRepository orderRepo;
 @Test void saveAndLoadOrder() {
 Order order = new Order(...);
 orderRepo.save(order);
 assertTrue(orderRepo.findById(order.getId()).isPresent());
 }
}
```

Benefits include near-zero setup and cleanup overhead—each test class can start with a fresh schema. However, dialect differences between H2 and your production DB (PostgreSQL, MySQL) may hide SQL compatibility issues: functions, data types, or optimizer hints can behave differently.

Containerized databases via Testcontainers or Docker Compose provide high-fidelity testing against the same engine as production. Testcontainers for Java:

```
@Container static PostgreSQLContainer<?> pg = new PostgreSQLContainer<>("postgres:14");
@DynamicPropertySource
static void props(DynamicPropertyRegistry r) {
 r.add("spring.datasource.url", pg::getJdbcUrl);
}
```

This spins up a real PostgreSQL instance in Docker, executes migrations (Flyway/Liquibase), and runs tests against actual SQL behavior. You catch schema drift, SQL syntax errors, and performance regressions early. The trade-off is slower startup (5–10 s) and greater resource usage, so containerized tests typically run in CI or nightly pipelines rather than on every local change.

A hybrid strategy combines both: developers run in-memory tests locally for speed, while CI pipelines include containerized tests to validate real-DB behavior. Diagram:

VMs   **Containers**

Ensure your test suite can switch easily via profiles or environment variables. Automate schema migrations for both setups to keep them in sync. By blending in-memory and containerized approaches, you attain both rapid feedback and production-grade confidence in your data access code.

7.9.2 Mocking vs. Embedded Fakes

When unit testing code that depends on repositories, you can choose **mocks** or **embedded fakes** to simulate data stores. **Mocks** (e.g., Mockito, Sinon) verify interactions: that save() was called with a correctly populated Order or that findById() returns a preset object. A Mockito example:

```
OrderRepository repo = mock(OrderRepository.class);
when(repo.findById(id)).thenReturn(Optional.of(order));
PlaceOrderService svc = new PlaceOrderService(repo, /*...*/);
svc.placeOrder(req);
verify(repo).save(any(Order.class));
```

Mocks confirm that your code invokes the repository correctly, but they don't validate persistence logic or repository contract. Over-mocking can lead to brittle tests tied to internal calls.

Embedded fakes provide a lightweight, in-memory implementation of the repository interface, without involving real databases. For example, a simple Java fake:

```
public class InMemoryOrderRepo implements OrderRepository {
 private final Map<OrderId, Order> store = new ConcurrentHashMap<>();
 public Optional<Order> findById(OrderId id) { return Optional.ofNullable(store.get(id)); }
 public void save(Order order) { store.put(order.getId(), order); }
}
```

Using this fake, unit tests exercise both your service logic and the repository's basic behavior, catching mapping or integration errors earlier. Fakes typically run faster than embedded containers and provide reasonable fidelity for business logic tests.

Deciding between mocks and fakes depends on your test goals:

- **Mocks** for pure orchestration tests, verifying interactions.
- **Fakes** for higher-confidence tests that include simple data access logic.

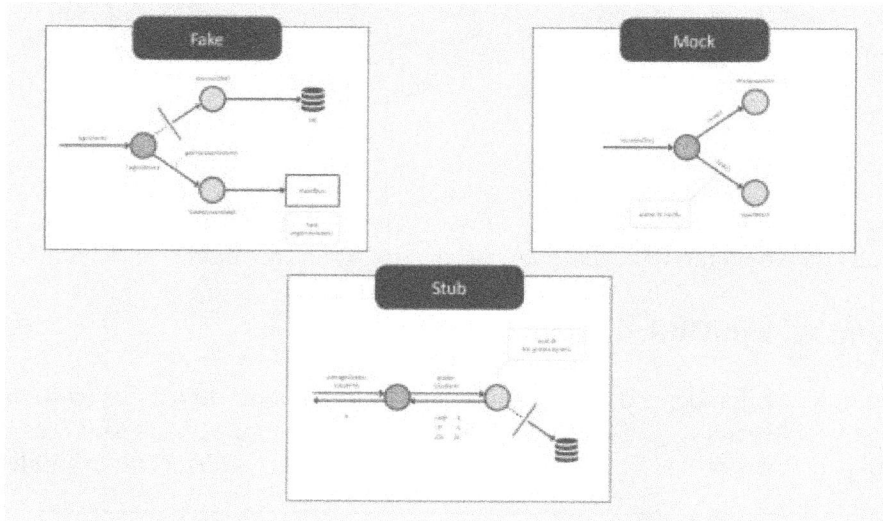

Avoid mixing strategies in the same suite; choose one per test class to maintain clarity. Both approaches keep your core logic decoupled from frameworks, supporting fast, deterministic tests.

7.9.3 Migration & Seed Data Tests

Validating database migrations and seed data is critical to ensure schema changes don't break application expectations. **Migration tests** apply your versioned migration scripts (Flyway, Liquibase) against a fresh database and then run assertions on the resulting schema. For example, using Flyway's Java API in a JUnit test:

```
@Test
void migrationsApplyCleanly() {
 Flyway flyway = Flyway.configure().dataSource(pg.getJdbcUrl(), user, pw).load();
 MigrateResult res = flyway.migrate();
 assertEquals(3, res.migrationsExecuted);
}
```

This guarantees that migrations up to version N execute without errors.

Seed data tests verify that initial data—required lookup tables, default configurations—loads correctly and matches domain expectations. After migrations, execute your seed scripts:

```
INSERT INTO roles (id, name) VALUES (1,'ADMIN'),(2,'USER');
```

Then test:

```
@Test
void seedDataPresent() {
 List<Role> roles = roleRepo.findAll();
 assertTrue(roles.stream().anyMatch(r -> r.getName().equals("ADMIN")));
}
```

Integration tests combining migrations and seeding catch regressions when migration scripts change or seed data drifts. In CI pipelines, spin up a fresh containerized DB, apply migrations, load seeds, and run the full test suite, ensuring your test environments mirror production initialization exactly.

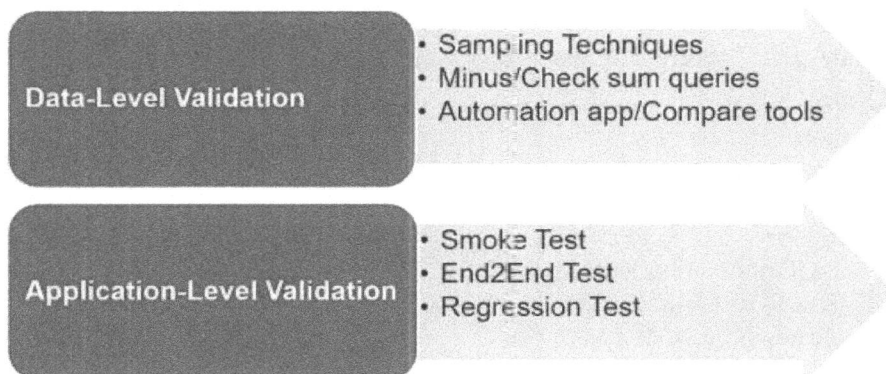

Diagram of migration & seed testing:

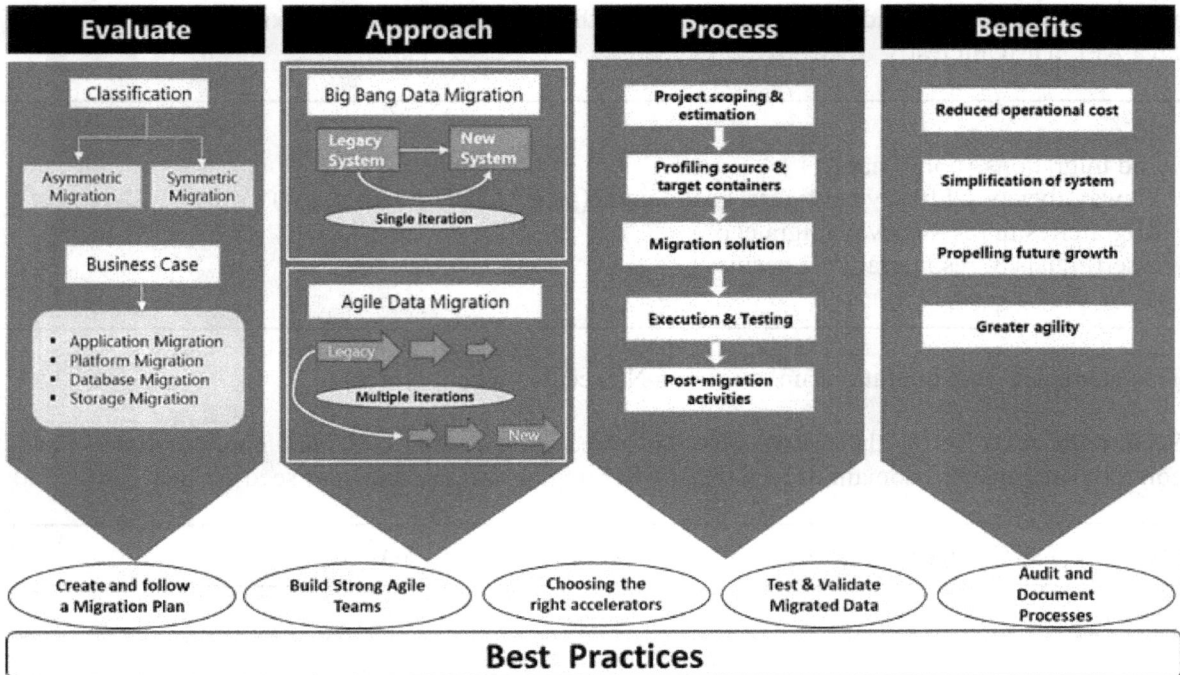

Automate rollback of migrations and reseeding between test runs to maintain idempotence. Versioned seed data scripts should live alongside migration scripts in source control. Regularly review and prune obsolete seeds to keep test environments lean and relevant.

7.10 Anti-Patterns & Best Practices

7.10.1 Anemic Repositories & Fat Services

An **anemic repository** exposes low-level CRUD operations without capturing domain intent, pushing business logic into service layers. For instance:

```
// Anemic repository
public interface UserRepo { UserEntity findById(String id); void update(UserEntity u); }
// Fat service
public class UserService {
 public void changeEmail(String id, String newEmail) {
  UserEntity u = userRepo.findById(id);
  if (!isValidEmail(newEmail)) throw ...;
```

```
  u.setEmail(newEmail);
  userRepo.update(u);
  }
}
```

Here, validation and invariant enforcement live in the service rather than within domain or repository boundaries. The service quickly becomes bloated ("fat") with logic that should belong to domain entities or specialized domain services.

Refactor by pushing logic into domain or repository abstractions:

```
public interface UserRepository {
 Optional<User> load(UserId id);
 void save(User user);
}


public class User {
 private final UserId id;
 private Email email;
 public void changeEmail(Email newEmail) {
  if (!newEmail.isValid()) throw new DomainException(...);
  this.email = newEmail;
 }
}
```

Service becomes:

```
public class UserService {
 public void changeEmail(UserId id, Email newEmail) {
  User user = userRepo.load(id).orElseThrow(...);
  user.changeEmail(newEmail);
  userRepo.save(user);
 }
}
```

Repositories remain **rich enough** to handle persistence of complete aggregates, while services orchestrate interactions. This inversion keeps business rules close to data and repositories small but intention-rich.

Eliminating anemic repositories and fat services improves cohesion and separates infrastructure concerns (data access) from domain behaviors, aligning with Clean Architecture principles.

7.10.2 Leaky Abstractions

A **leaky abstraction** occurs when repository interfaces expose framework or infrastructure-specific types, forcing domain layers to import unwanted dependencies:

```
// Leaky port
public interface OrderRepository {
 List<OrderEntity> findByCustomer(Session session, String customerId);
}
```

Here, the Session (Hibernate API) leaks into the port, coupling core logic to the ORM. To fix, ensure ports depend only on domain types:

```
public interface OrderRepository {
 List<Order> findByCustomer(CustomerId id);
}
```

Adapters handle any required session management internally. Another example is returning ResultSet or Cursor from ports, which drags JDBC or driver types into domain code. Instead, map low-level results to domain aggregates within the adapter:

```
List<Order> findByCustomer(CustomerId id) {
 try (Connection c = ds.getConnection();
   PreparedStatement ps = c.prepareStatement(SQL)) {
 ...
 return domainMapper.mapAll(rs);
 }
}
```

Leaky abstractions complicate testing—domain or service tests must now mock or instantiate framework objects. They also hinder portability: switching from Hibernate to JPA, or SQL to NoSQL, becomes onerous.

Maintaining pure ports and adapters preserves decoupling, testability, and the ability to evolve persistence technologies without breaking core logic.

7.10.3 Chatty Data Access

Chatty data access arises when code issues many small queries instead of batch or coarse-grained operations, causing performance degradation due to round-trip overhead. The classic **N+1 query** problem occurs when loading an aggregate with a parent and its children:

```
Order order = orderRepo.load(orderId);
for (OrderLine line : order.getLines()) {
 // Each call triggers a separate SELECT
 Product p = productRepo.load(line.getProductId());
 }
```

This issues 1 query for the order, plus N queries for each line's product, leading to poor performance at scale.

To combat chatty access, employ **fetch joins** or **batch loading**. In JPA:

```
Order order = em.createQuery(
 "SELECT o FROM Order o JOIN FETCH o.lines WHERE o.id = :id", Order.class)
 .setParameter("id", orderId).getSingleResult();
```

Alternatively, use a single query for products:

```
List<Product> products = em.createQuery(
 "SELECT p FROM Product p WHERE p.id IN :ids", Product.class)
 .setParameter("ids", lineIds).getResultList();
```

In document databases, embed frequently accessed sub-documents to avoid separate reads. For caches, use **multi-get** operations:

```
Map<String, Order> orders = redis.mget("order:1", "order:2", "order:3");
```

Monitoring database logs or using an APM tool (New Relic, Datadog) reveals excessive queries. Refactor code and repository methods to use bulk operations or optimized queries. Eliminating chatty data access is essential to meet latency SLAs and reduce resource consumption, ensuring your persistence layer scales efficiently under load.

Conclusion

Mastering data persistence in the context of clean architecture means more than picking a favorite database—it requires designing clear ports for all storage interactions, implementing adapters that translate between domain aggregates and physical schemas, and applying patterns that manage transactions and optimize throughput. You've seen how to balance strong consistency with eventual consistency, when to introduce polyglot stores, and how to automate schema migrations without downtime. You've learned to test repositories in isolation and in realistic environments, to catch mapping errors before they reach production. With these principles in hand, your applications can evolve their data layer without entangling business logic, ensuring that growth in both features and data volume never compromises maintainability or performance.

Chapter 8. Resilient Services & Microservice Topologies

In a world where systems span continents, handle unpredictable traffic, and integrate a multitude of services, resilience is no longer optional—it's a foundational requirement. As you break a monolith into microservices, you inherit the complexity of distributed systems: network failures, cascading errors, and partial outages become everyday realities. To thrive in this environment, you must build services that anticipate failure, contain faults, and recover gracefully without user impact. This chapter explores how to weave resilience into every layer of your architecture—from wiring timeouts and circuit breakers into client calls to isolating failures through bulkheads and rate limits, from packaging services behind intelligent gateways to orchestrating chaos experiments that validate your defenses. You'll learn how thoughtful topology choices—pod counts, service meshes, and deployment strategies—combine with runtime guards and observability to create a system that continues to serve, even when pieces falter.

8.1 Principles of Service Resilience

8.1.1 Fault Tolerance vs. Graceful Degradation

Fault tolerance is the ability of a system to continue operating correctly in the presence of partial failures. At its core, a fault-tolerant service implements redundancy, retries, and fallback logic so that if one component fails, another steps in seamlessly. For example, a payment service might retry a failed authorization request up to three times before giving up. Graceful degradation, by contrast, accepts that some functionality may be unavailable under duress but ensures the system still provides the most critical features. In an e-commerce site, if the recommendation engine goes down, the product detail pages still load without suggestions. Fault tolerance often relies on automated recovery mechanisms—circuit breakers, bulkheads, and health checks—whereas graceful degradation involves designing alternate user flows and degraded feature sets. A concrete code example shows a fallback method:

```
@CircuitBreaker(name="payment", fallbackMethod="fallbackAuthorize")
public PaymentResult authorize(PaymentRequest req) { … }


public PaymentResult fallbackAuthorize(PaymentRequest req, Throwable t) {
 return PaymentResult.deferred("Service unavailable, try later");
}
```

Here, if the circuit is open, calls immediately go to the fallback, ensuring fast failures. Diagrammatically:

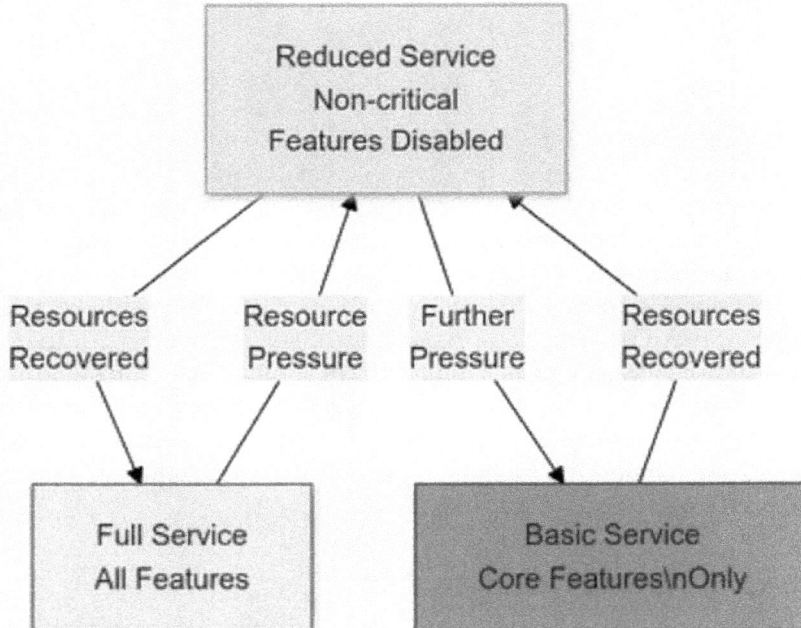

Both approaches share the same goal—minimizing user impact—but differ in whether degraded features remain available or core functionality is preserved at reduced capacity. Testing both scenarios ensures users experience controlled responses under failure. Logging and metrics track when fault tolerance or graceful degradation paths are used, informing capacity planning and feature prioritization. Ultimately, balancing the two yields a robust system that stays responsive even when parts fail.

8.1.2 Designing for Failure

Designing for failure begins with the assumption that any component—network, disk, or service—can and will fail. You model services to expect timeouts, dropped connections, and unexpected exceptions, then design every remote call behind a timeout wrapper and circuit breaker. For example, configuring an HTTP client:

```
HttpClient client = HttpClient.newBuilder()
.connectTimeout(Duration.ofSeconds(2))
.build();
```

Combine this with a bulkhead pattern to isolate failing calls:

```
Bulkhead bulkhead = Bulkhead.ofDefaults("paymentBulkhead");
```

Every layer should validate inputs defensively, and components should fail fast when preconditions are violated. You introduce chaos monkeys to inject random failures during development and staging—killing pods, disabling network interfaces—to ensure systems recover gracefully. Documentation of failure modes and recovery behaviors becomes part of the design, alongside architecture decision records (ADRs). Dependency graphs annotate which services are critical and which are optional; critical paths get extra redundancy and monitoring. A PlantUML sequence emphasizes defensive design:

```
@startuml
participant Client
participant ServiceA
participant ServiceB
Client -> ServiceA: request()
ServiceA -> ServiceB: remoteCall()
alt ServiceB times out
 ServiceA -> ServiceA: fallbackLogic()
 ServiceA --> Client: degradedResponse
else success
 ServiceA -> ServiceA: normalProcessing()
 ServiceA --> Client: standardResponse
end
@enduml
```

Every remote call is wrapped in try/catch, and resources are released in finally blocks. You instrument latencies and error rates to trigger automated alerts when thresholds are exceeded. This mindset ensures that failure isn't an afterthought, but a first-class citizen in your service design.

8.1.3 Observability-Driven Resilience

Observability is the ability to infer system health from logs, metrics, and traces. Resilience without observability is blind—you must know which components are failing, how often, and under what conditions. Instrument every service with standardized metrics: request count, error count, latency histograms. In Spring Boot with Micrometer:

```
@Autowired MeterRegistry registry;
Counter failureCounter = registry.counter("payments.failures")
;
```

Emit structured logs with correlation IDs so traces can be reconstructed across services:

```
log.info("Authorize payment", kv("orderId", orderId), kv("traceId", traceId()));
```

Distributed tracing (OpenTelemetry) stitches together trace spans:

```
Span span = tracer.spanBuilder("authorizePayment").startSpan()
;
```

Dashboards visualize service dependencies and error hotspots. Alerting rules notify on high error rates or circuit-breaker tripping. Observability drives resilience by closing the loop: if a cache miss rate spikes, add capacity; if bulkheads are saturated, tune limits. Run regular game-days to validate alert pipelines and on-call procedures. Use anomaly detection on metrics to preemptively catch slow degradation. This data-driven approach ensures your resilience mechanisms are effective and tuned to real-world conditions.

8.2 Fault Containment Patterns

8.2.1 Circuit Breaker

The circuit-breaker pattern prevents cascading failures by monitoring remote call failures and, after a threshold, "opening" the circuit to block further calls for a cool-down period. Using Resilience4j:

```
CircuitBreaker cb = CircuitBreaker.of("payment", CircuitBreakerConfig.custom()
 .failureRateThreshold(50)
 .waitDurationInOpenState(Duration.ofSeconds(30))
 .slidingWindowSize(20)
 .build());
Supplier<PaymentResult> decorated = CircuitBreaker
 .decorateSupplier(cb, () -> paymentClient.charge(req));
```

When more than 50% of the last 20 calls fail, the breaker opens, and subsequent calls throw CallNotPermittedException immediately. After 30 s, it transitions to half-open state—allowing a trial call to test recovery.

Circuit breakers decouple client load from unstable services, enabling fail-fast behavior and self-healing. Registries allow monitoring breaker state across all services, while event consumers log state transitions. Effective configuration balances sensitivity to transient errors with responsiveness to true outages.

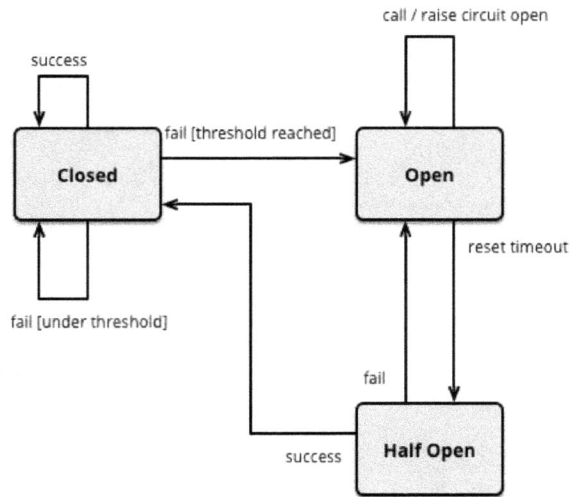

8.2.2 Bulkhead Isolation

Bulkheads isolate failures by partitioning resources (threads, connections) into separate pools. A bug in one feature cannot exhaust the entire service. Using Resilience4j's ThreadPoolBulkhead:

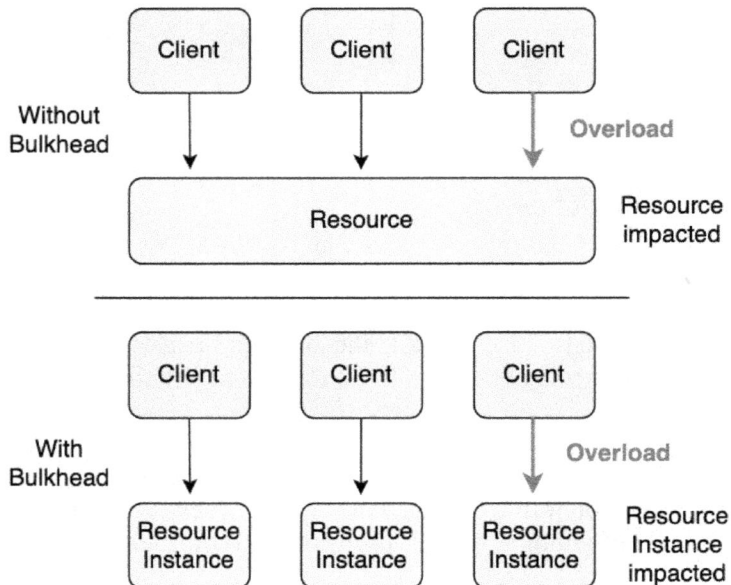

```
ThreadPoolBulkheadConfig config = ThreadPoolBulkheadConfig.custom()
 .maxThreadPoolSize(10)
 .coreThreadPoolSize(5)
 .queueCapacity(20)
 .build();
ThreadPoolBulkhead bulkhead = ThreadPoolBulkhead.of("ordersPool", config);
```

Each command runs in the ordersPool; if threads and queue are full, calls are rejected immediately, preserving capacity for other operations. Diagram:

Bulkheads reduce contention between critical and non-critical tasks. Failures in one pool trigger fallback without starving other flows. Combine with circuit breakers to maximize fault containment.

8.2.3 Fail-Fast & Fail-Safe

Fail-fast design stops operations at the first sign of trouble, returning errors immediately rather than waiting for timeouts. This improves responsiveness under failure. For example, before calling a downstream service, check its health status:

```
if (!healthRegistry.get("inventory").isUp()) {
 throw new ServiceUnavailableException();
}
inventoryClient.reserve(...);
```

Fail-safe design aims to keep the system running by degrading functionality. A booking service might accept orders without immediate inventory reservation, marking them as pending and retrying later. Pseudocode:

```
try {
 inventoryClient.reserve(order);
} catch (Exception e) {
 order.markPending();
 orderRepo.save(order);
}
```

Combined, fail-fast prevents resource waste, while fail-safe preserves user experience with degraded features. Logging and metrics distinguish between fast-fail and degraded flows, guiding future resiliency investments.

8.2.4 Timeout Wrapping

Every remote call should enforce timeouts at application and network levels. In WebClient (Spring):

```
WebClient.builder()
 .clientConnector(new ReactorClientHttpConnector(
 HttpClient.create().responseTimeout(Duration.ofSeconds(2))
))
 .build();
```

In plain Java HTTP client:

```
HttpRequest.newBuilder(uri)
 .timeout(Duration.ofSeconds(2))
 .build();
```

Timeouts prevent threads from hanging indefinitely. Wrap calls with fallback logic:

```
try {
 return client.call(req).block(Duration.ofSeconds(2));
} catch (TimeoutException te) {
 return fallbackHandler.handleTimeout(req);
}
```

Choosing appropriate timeouts balances failure detection speed with tolerance for transient slowness. Collect latency percentiles to tune settings accurately.

8.3 Traffic Control & Stability

8.3.1 Rate Limiting & Throttling

Rate limiting prevents clients or services from overwhelming downstream systems by capping request rates. A token-bucket algorithm is common: tokens accumulate at a fixed rate, and each request consumes a token. In Bucket4j (Java):

```
Bandwidth limit = Bandwidth.simple(100, Duration.ofMinutes(1));
Bucket bucket = Bucket4j.builder().addLimit(limit).build();
if (bucket.tryConsume(1)) {
 processRequest();
} else {
 return Response.status(429).build();
}
```

Throttling can be client-focused (per IP/API key) or global. You store token buckets in distributed caches (Redis) to enforce limits across instances:

```
GridBucketState state = bucket.getAvailableTokens();
redis.set(key, state);
```

Effective limits match SLA requirements and resource capacity. Burst capacity allows short spikes without dropping legitimate traffic. Monitoring rejected request rates informs rate limit adjustments. Document quotas and return Retry-After headers for well-behaved clients.

8.3.2 Load Shedding

When downstream services saturate, load shedding drops low-priority requests to maintain core functionality.

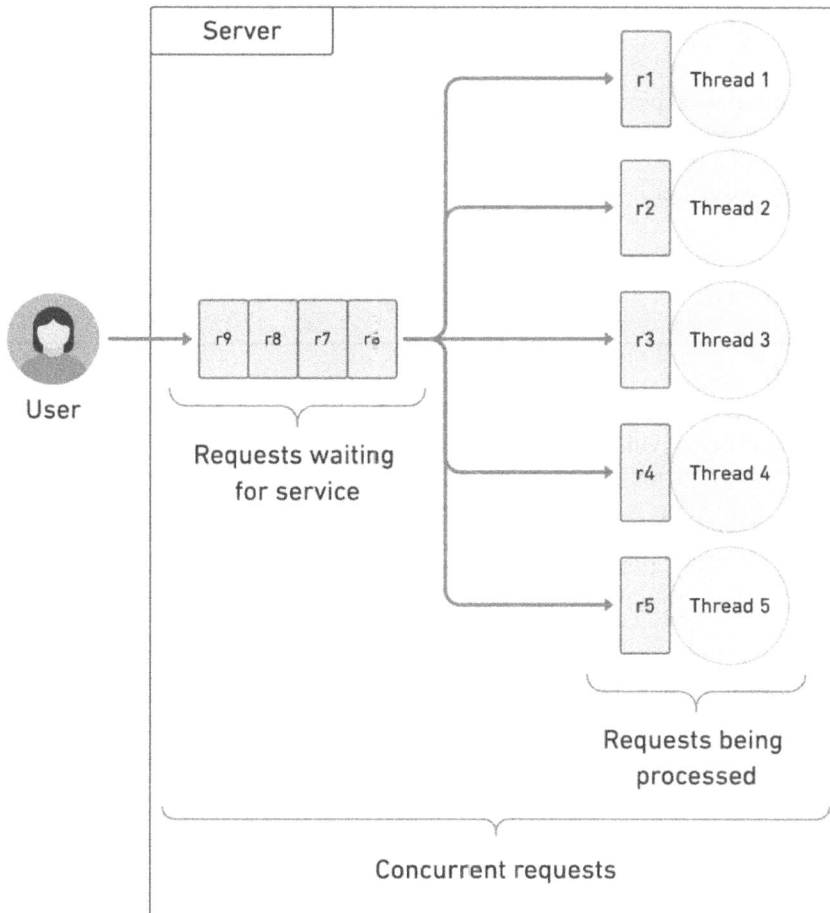

For instance, if service latency exceeds a threshold, automatically reject analytics or non-critical API calls:

```
if (healthRegistry.get("payment").getResponseTime() > 500) {
  return Response.status(503).entity("Service busy").build();
}
```

Circuit breakers can act as dynamic load-sheds: open when failure rates spike. More advanced policies defer to queue depths or CPU/memory metrics. A simple shedding rule:

```
if (threadPoolBulkhead.getMetrics().getQueueDepth() > 50) {
  throw new RejectedExecutionException();
}
```

Load shedding maintains responsiveness for high-value traffic at the cost of best-effort features. Communicate shedding via HTTP 503 and graceful UI messaging.

8.3.3 Adaptive Backpressure

Adaptive backpressure signals senders to slow down when consumers can't keep up. In reactive streams (Project Reactor):

```
Flux.range(1, 1000)
  .onBackpressureBuffer(100, BufferOverflowStrategy.DROP_OLDEST)
  .subscribe(value -> process(value));
```

Here, if the subscriber lags, the buffer holds up to 100 items; older items are dropped beyond that. TCP's built-in flow control is another form of backpressure. In HTTP/2 or gRPC, window sizes throttle data flow.

Backpressure feedback informs upstream services to reduce request rates, avoiding overload. Implement in messaging systems (Kafka) via consumer lag monitoring: if lag > threshold, pause producers temporarily. Dashboards tracking buffer usage, queue depths, and lag metrics trigger scaling events or shedding. Adaptive policies evolve with traffic patterns, ensuring stability even under unpredictable load surges.

8.4 API Gateways & Backend-for-Frontend

8.4.1 Gateway Responsibilities

An API gateway centralizes cross-cutting concerns—routing, authentication, SSL termination, rate limits, and monitoring—away from individual services. It exposes a unified facade to clients, decoupling clients from internal topologies. Responsibilities include request validation, path rewriting, load balancing, response caching, and protocol translation (REST→gRPC). A typical Spring Cloud Gateway configuration:

```
spring:
 cloud:
  gateway:
   routes:
   - id: order
   uri: lb://ORDER-SERVICE
   predicates:
   - Path=/orders/**
   filters:
   - StripPrefix=1
   - Retry=3
```

The gateway can also aggregate multiple service calls into a single response, reducing client-side complexity. It enforces global security policies—JWT validation, OAuth2 token introspection—ensuring consistent access control. Health checks on downstream services update routing weights or circuit-breaker state. Centralizing these features simplifies service code, offloading infrastructure to the gateway tier.

8.4.2 Request Routing & Aggregation

Gateways route requests based on predicates—paths, headers, query params—and can fan-out to multiple backends, then merge responses. Aggregation at the gateway:

```
app.get('/catalog/:id', async (req, res) => {
 const prod = await fetch(`http://product/${req.params.id}`);
 const inv = await fetch(`http://inventory/${req.params.id}`);
 res.json({ ...prod, stock: inv.stock });
});
```

For example, a catalog-detail endpoint might fetch product data and inventory simultaneously:

```
spring:
 cloud:
  gateway:
   routes:
   - id: productDetail
   uri: http://localhost:8081
   predicates:
   - Path=/v1/product/{id}
   filters:
   - RewritePath=/v1/product/(?<id>.*), /product/${id}
   - DedupeResponseHeader=access-token
```

GraphQL gateways offer more flexible aggregation, letting clients request exactly the fields they need. Aggregation reduces client churn when services evolve, as the gateway shields clients from topology changes. Monitoring aggregated endpoints tracks success rates per constituent call, surfacing hotspots.

8.4.3 BFF for Device-Specific APIs

A Backend-for-Frontend (BFF) creates specialized gateways for different client types—web, mobile, IoT—tailoring payloads, caching, and aggregation. For mobile where bandwidth is limited, the BFF might compress responses, send fewer fields, or batch calls. In Node.js:

```
const express = require('express');
const mobileApi = express.Router();


mobileApi.get('/user/profile', async (req, res) => {
 const profile = await userService.getProfile(req.user.id);
 const settings = await settingsService.getMobileSettings(req.user.id);
 res.json({ profile, settings });
});
app.use('/mobile', mobileApi);
```

Each BFF lives alongside the main gateway but contains client-specific logic—authentication flows, A/B testing flags, localization. BFFs improve developer velocity by isolating changes to one gateway without affecting others. They also enable granular scaling based on client usage patterns.

8.4.4 Security, Authentication & Quotas

Gateways enforce security policies using JWT tokens or OAuth2 introspection:

```
spring:
 security:
  oauth2:
   resourceserver:
    jwt:
     issuer-uri: https://auth.example.com
```

They verify scopes and roles before routing to services, centralizing authorization rules. Quotas per client or API key prevent abusive usage:

```
spring:
 cloud:
  gateway:
   filters:
   - name: RequestRateLimiter
    args:
     redis-rate-limiter.replenishRate: 10
     redis-rate-limiter.burstCapacity: 20
```

Gateways also inject security headers—CORS, CSP—and sanitize inputs to guard against injection attacks. TLS termination at the gateway offloads SSL work from services. Auditing and access logs capture client identity, endpoints accessed, and response codes for compliance. This consistent security posture across all entry points closes vulnerablities that might arise if each service handled auth individually.

8.5 Service Discovery & Load Balancing

8.5.1 Client-Side Discovery

Client-side discovery embeds the logic for finding healthy service instances directly in the client. The client queries a service registry (e.g., Eureka, Consul) to retrieve a list of available endpoints, then applies a load-balancing algorithm (round-robin, least connections, random) before invoking one. In Spring-Cloud Netflix Eureka:

```
@Service
public class OrderClient {
@Autowired private RestTemplate restTemplate;
@LoadBalanced
@Bean
public RestTemplate restTemplate() { return new RestTemplate(); }
public Order getOrder(String id) {
 // "order-service" is the logical service name
 return restTemplate.getForObject("http://order-service/orders/{id}", Order.class, id);
 }
}
```

Behind the scenes, Ribbon intercepts the RestTemplate call, queries Eureka for instances of order-service, and picks one. If the chosen instance fails, Ribbon retries according to its retry policy. Client-side discovery requires that clients depend on registry clients and load-balancer libraries, but it offers fine-grained control over routing decisions—clients can filter instances by zone or metadata.

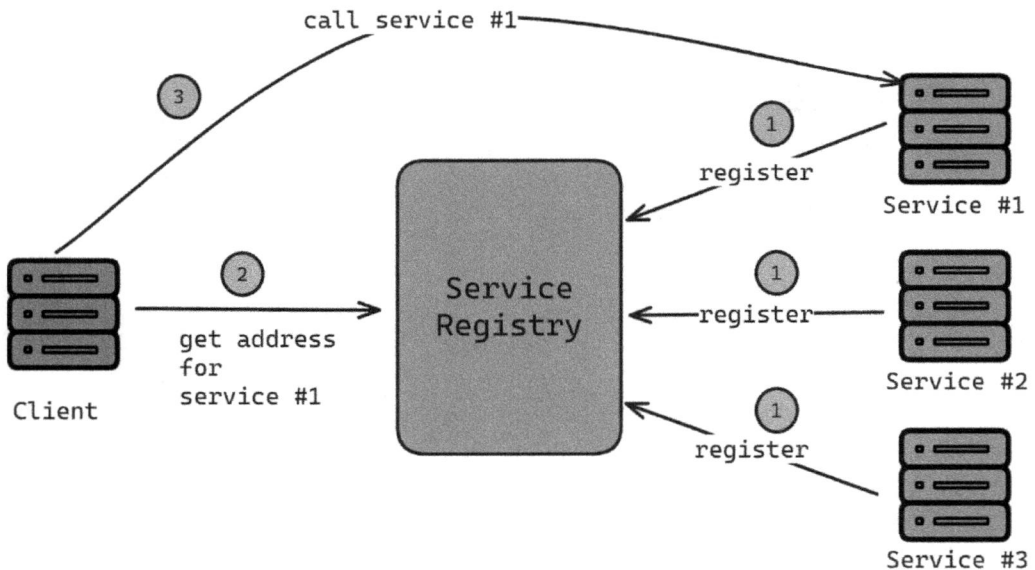

ScalableThread.com

While powerful, client-side discovery can complicate clients and duplicate logic across services. It also requires that each client maintain and refresh its own view of the registry, adding memory and CPU overhead. To mitigate this, clients often cache registry data with short TTLs and subscribe to registry change events. Because retries and load-balancing live in the client, you gain the ability to plug in custom rules—e.g., weight by instance load or latency—but you must test those rules thoroughly to avoid uneven traffic distribution. Overall, client-side discovery is ideal when you need low-latency routing decisions or advanced routing logic embedded in clients.

8.5.2 Server-Side Discovery

In server-side discovery, clients make requests to a well-known load balancer or API gateway, which then performs service discovery and load balancing on behalf of clients. This shifts complexity away from clients into a centralized proxy layer (e.g., Kubernetes Service, AWS ALB, NGINX). For example, in Kubernetes:

```
apiVersion: v1
kind: Service
metadata:
 name: order-service
spec:
 selector:
  app: order
 ports:
 - port: 80
   targetPort: 8080
 type: ClusterIP
```

Clients simply call http://order-service/orders/{id}, and the Kubernetes kube-proxy distributes traffic among pods matching the app=order label. The service IP remains stable, decoupling clients from pod lifecycles. A high-level diagram:

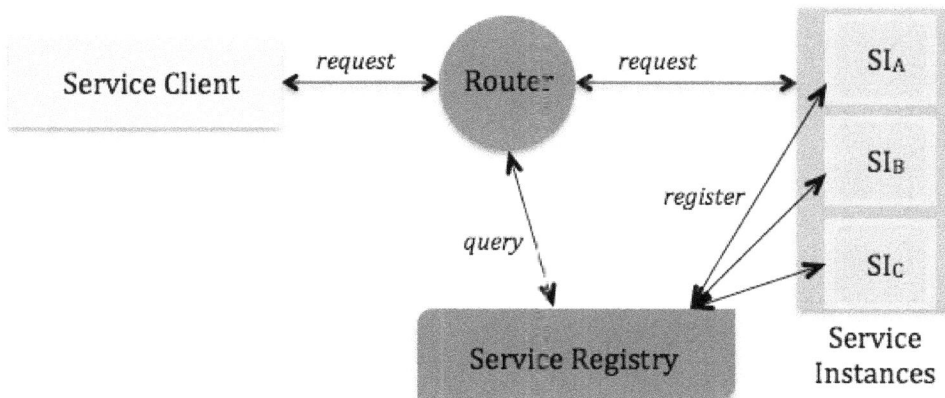

Server-side discovery centralizes routing logic, reducing client dependencies—but pushes scaling and resilience concerns into the network layer. Health checks (readiness/liveness probes) ensure that only healthy pods receive traffic. When new pods come online, Kubernetes updates its endpoint list automatically, providing near-real-time load balancing. This model simplifies client code and fosters uniform routing policies—TLS termination, authentication, and rate limits can be applied at the service level in an Ingress controller or load balancer. However, it can introduce network hops and require robust networking infrastructure to avoid becoming a single point of failure.

8.5.3 DNS-Based & Consul-Based Discovery

DNS-based discovery leverages DNS SRV or A records to encode service endpoints. Clients perform DNS lookups on service names, receiving IP addresses of healthy instances. In Consul, services register themselves with health checks:

```
// POST to /v1/agent/service/register
{
 "Name": "order-service",
 "ID": "order-1",
 "Address": "10.0.0.5",
 "Port": 8080,
 "Check": {
  "HTTP": "http://10.0.0.5:8080/health",
  "Interval": "10s"
 }
}
```

Consul's DNS interface then allows clients to resolve order-service.service.consul to healthy IPs. A typical SRV record lookup returns:

```
$ dig SRV _order-service._tcp.service.consul
;; ANSWER SECTION:
_order-service._tcp.service.consul. 10 IN SRV 1 1 8080 10.0.0.5.
_order-service._tcp.service.consul. 10 IN SRV 1 1 8080 10.0.0.6.
```

DNS propagation delays must be managed—low TTLs (e.g., 10 s) help but increase DNS traffic. Consul also offers an HTTP API for more dynamic discovery:

```
GET /v1/health/service/order-service?passing=true
```

Clients parse SRV records to obtain host, port, and weight, then apply client-side load balancing. Diagram:

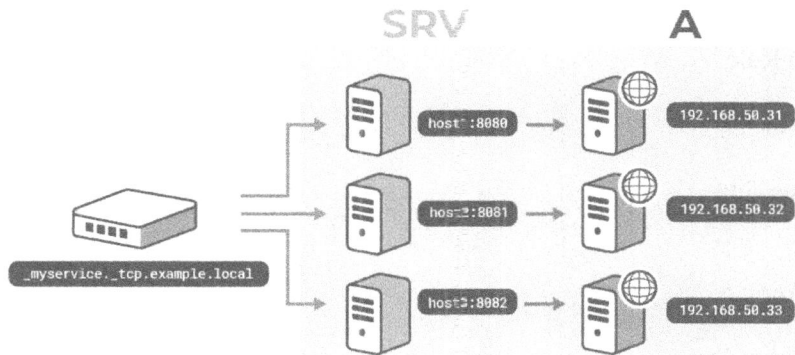

Clients can choose DNS or HTTP API based on their capabilities. DNS-based discovery is widely supported and easily integrated into any language, but suffers from potential caching by intermediate resolvers. Consul's API ensures fresh data but duplicates client-side logic, similar to Eureka.

8.5.4 Health Checks & Integration with Circuit Breakers

Health checks are the first line of defense in identifying unhealthy instances and maintaining service resilience. Kubernetes defines **liveness** and **readiness** probes:

```
livenessProbe:
 httpGet:
  path: /actuator/health/live
  port: 8080
 initialDelaySeconds: 30
 periodSeconds: 10


readinessProbe:
 httpGet:
  path: /actuator/health/ready
  port: 8080
 initialDelaySeconds: 5
 periodSeconds: 5
```

Liveness probes determine if a container should be restarted, while readiness probes control endpoint registration. When a readiness check fails, the instance is removed from service discovery and load balancers, preventing traffic to a degraded or corrupt state.

Integrating health checks with circuit breakers ensures that an instance tripped open is also marked unhealthy at the service mesh or gateway level. In Istio:

```
apiVersion: networking.istio.io/v1alpha3
kind: DestinationRule
metadata:
 name: payment-dr
spec:
 host: payment-service
 trafficPolicy:
  outlierDetection:
   consecutiveErrors: 5
   interval: 10s
   baseEjectionTime: 1m
```

Outlier detection automatically ejects unhealthy endpoints after 5 consecutive errors, tying into the mesh's health management. The mesh's sidecar proxies perform active and passive checks, combining metrics and health endpoints to make routing decisions.

Diagram of integration:

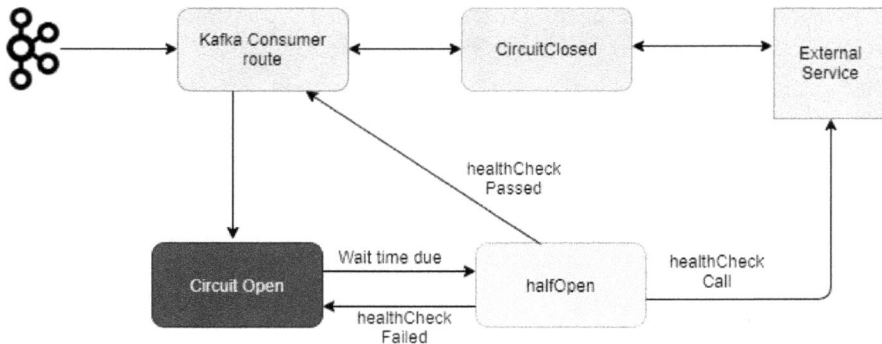

A cohesive health-check strategy combined with circuit-breaker and bulkhead patterns ensures that failures are detected, isolated, and do not ripple through the system. Metrics from health checks feed into service-level dashboards, alerting on degraded capacity or failing endpoints, enabling operations teams to intervene before users notice impact.

8.6 Service Mesh & Sidecar Architectures

8.6.1 Sidecar Proxies (Envoy, Linkerd)

A service mesh uses a sidecar proxy deployed alongside each application container, offloading network-level concerns—service discovery, load balancing, TLS, retries—to the mesh rather than application code. Envoy, for example, runs as a separate container in the same pod:

```
apiVersion: v1
kind: Pod
metadata:
 name: payment-pod
spec:
 containers:
 - name: payment-app
  image: myorg/payment:1.0
  ports: [{ containerPort: 8080 }]
 - name: envoy
  image: envoyproxy/envoy:v1.18.3
  args: ["-c","/etc/envoy/envoy.yaml"]
  ports: [{ containerPort: 15001 }]
```

All outbound traffic from payment-app is redirected via the Envoy sidecar on port 15001. Envoy's configuration (xDS API) is managed by a control plane (Istio Pilot).

Linkerd offers a lighter-weight Rust/Go sidecar with similar features. The sidecar intercepts incoming requests, applies policies—circuit breaking, rate limiting—and emits detailed metrics (latency histograms, success rates) to a telemetry back end (Prometheus).

Sidecars enforce mTLS automatically, encrypting all inter-pod traffic without modifying application code. Retry and timeout policies are defined centrally, ensuring consistency across services. By abstracting networking concerns into sidecars, developers focus on business logic, while the mesh ensures robust, uniform connectivity.

8.6.2 Ambassador & Adapter Patterns

The ambassador pattern extends the sidecar concept to legacy or non-meshed services. An ambassador cache or proxy sits next to a legacy service, speaking mesh protocols to neighbors while translating to the legacy protocol:

```
apiVersion: apps/v1
kind: Deployment
metadata: { name: legacy-ambassador }
spec:
 template:
  spec:
   containers:
```

```
- name: legacy-proxy
  image: envoyproxy/envoy:v1.18
  args: ["-c","/etc/envoy/legacy-envoy.yaml"]
- name: legacy-service
  image: myorg/legacy:2.3
```

The envoy config translates mesh-inbound gRPC calls into the legacy service's HTTP interface. This adapter approach allows incremental migration: new services speak mesh, while legacy code remains untouched behind ambassadors.

Another variation uses a **sidecar adapter** injecting a library into the application process for languages that cannot use a separate container. This adapter intercepts HTTP client calls and applies mesh logic in-process.

Ambassadors streamline mesh adoption in brownfield environments, providing a bridge between modern and legacy topologies. They also serve as test harnesses for mesh policies—observability, security—before rewriting legacy services. A deployment diagram:

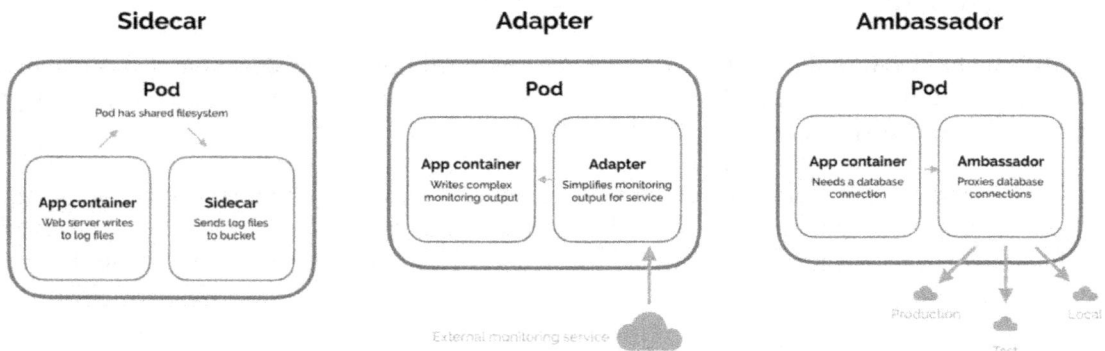

This pattern decouples migration concerns from core application bundles and paves the path toward full mesh integration.

8.6.3 Control Plane vs. Data Plane

A service mesh splits into a **data plane**—the lightweight proxies (Envoy, Linkerd) handling per-request decisions—and a **control plane**—the management layer that distributes configuration. The control plane (Istio Pilot, Linkerd Controller) watches service registries, config maps, and policy definitions, then pushes xDS updates to sidecars.

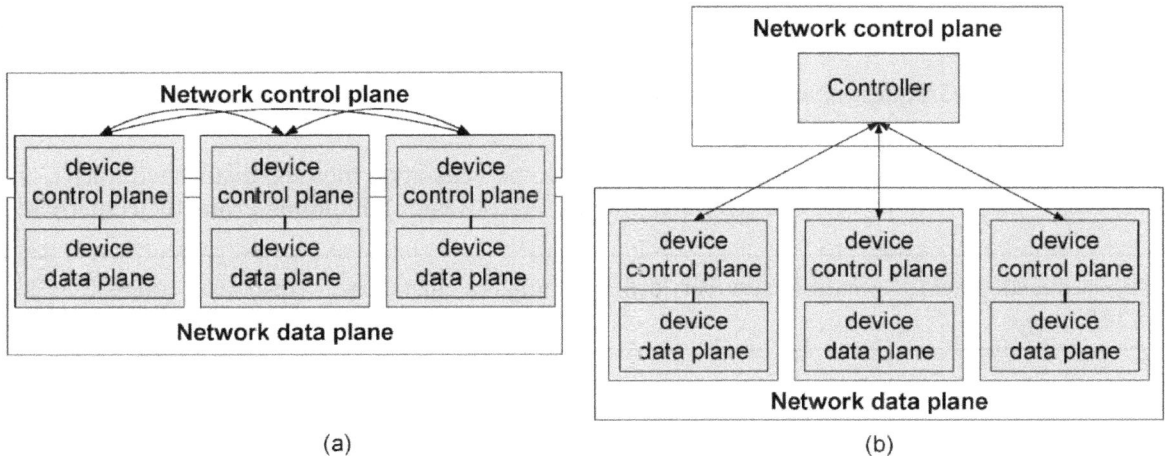

(a)   (b)

The data plane runs in each pod, intercepting all inbound and outbound traffic, enforcing policies with minimal latency. Sidecars cache configurations from the control plane, reducing churn.

Operations teams interact with the control plane via CLI (istioctl) or YAML manifests, defining routing rules, circuit breakers, and telemetry sinks. The control plane aggregates health metrics from sidecars, providing a centralized view of mesh state.

Separating planes lets you scale control-plane components independently from application pods, tuning HA settings for management services without affecting data-path performance. It also secures the mesh by restricting sensitive config operations to control-plane nodes.

8.6.4 Policy Enforcement & Telemetry

Service meshes enforce fine-grained policies—access control, quotas, retry budgets—at the network edge without modifying application code. Istio's AuthorizationPolicy:

```
apiVersion: security.istio.io/v1beta1
kind: AuthorizationPolicy
metadata: { name: order-policy }
spec:
 selector: { matchLabels: { app: order } }
 rules:
 - from:
  - source:
    principals: ["cluster.local/ns/default/sa/payments-service"]
```

This policy allows only the payments-service identity to call order-service, leveraging mTLS certificates for authentication. Quota policies throttle requests:

```
apiVersion: config.istio.io/v1alpha2
kind: QuotaSpec
metadata: { name: request-count }
```

Telemetry is automatically collected by sidecars—Prometheus-style metrics, distributed traces, and access logs—exported to backends (Grafana, Jaeger, Elasticsearch). Example Prometheus metrics:

```
istio_requests_total{destination_service="order.default.svc.cluster.local",response_code="200"}
12345
```

Logs include trace and span IDs:

```
2025-05-14T12:00:00Z INFO [svc=order svc_ver=1.2.3 trace_id=abcd1234] GET /orders/1 200
15ms
```

This uniform policy and telemetry model ensures every service complies with corporate policies and emits the data needed for alerting, dashboards, and root-cause analysis—core tenets of resilient microservice architectures.

8.7 Deployment Topologies & Scaling

8.7.1 Single vs. Multiple Instances (Pods/VMs)

Deploying a single instance of a service simplifies development but creates a single point of failure. For resilience and scaling, you run multiple instances (pods in Kubernetes or VMs in VM clusters) behind load balancers. A Kubernetes Deployment spec:

```
apiVersion: apps/v1
kind: Deployment
metadata: { name: order-service }
spec:
 replicas: 3
 selector: { matchLabels: { app: order } }
 template:
  metadata: { labels: { app: order } }
  spec:
   containers:
   - name: order
     image: myorg/order:1.0
     ports: [{ containerPort: 8080 }]
```

With replicas: 3, Kubernetes ensures three pods are always running. The corresponding Service:

```
kind: Service
spec:
 selector: { app: order }
 ports: [{ port: 80, targetPort: 8080 }]
```

distributes traffic evenly across pods. Multi-instance deployments enable **horizontal autoscaling**: by monitoring CPU or custom metrics, the cluster can scale from 3 to 10 pods under load:

```
apiVersion: autoscaling/v2beta2
kind: HorizontalPodAutoscaler
spec:
 scaleTargetRef: { kind: Deployment, name: order-service }
 minReplicas: 3
 maxReplicas: 10
 metrics:
 - type: Resource
  resource: { name: cpu, target: { type: Utilization, averageUtilization: 70 } }
```

Single-Node

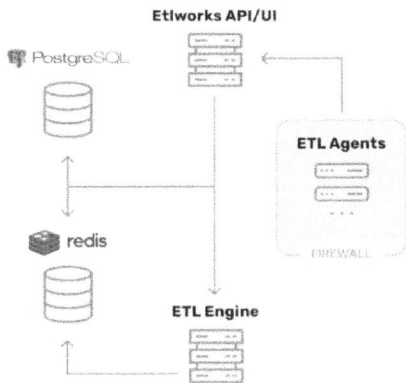

Multi-Node

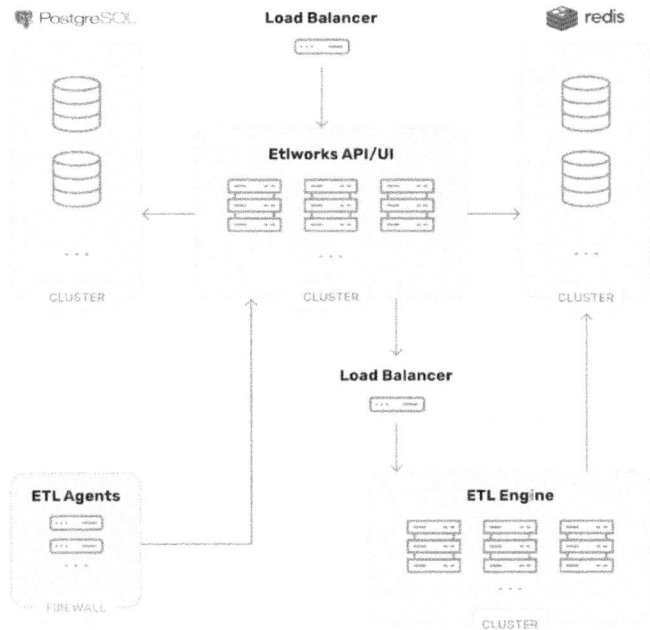

Multiple instances provide both resilience—if one pod crashes, others serve traffic—and capacity to handle spikes. For VM clusters, similar autoscaling groups exist (AWS ASG, Azure VMSS).

Scaling decisions must account for stateful aspects: stateless services scale easily, whereas stateful services (caches, databases) require careful sharding or leader election. Multi-instance topologies underpin high availability and horizontal scaling, core to microservice resilience.

8.7.2 Blue/Green & Canary Deployments

Blue/green deployments run two parallel environments—blue (current) and green (new)—with a router switching traffic upon successful validation. In Kubernetes, using an Ingress with a selector:

```
apiVersion: networking.k8s.io/v1
kind: Ingress
spec:
 rules:
 - host: api.example.com
  http:
   paths:
   - path: /orders
    backend:
     service:
      name: order-service-green
      port: { number: 80 }
```

Traffic shifts from order-service-blue to order-service-green by updating the Ingress backend. In Helm, values toggle replica sets between active and standby.

Canary deployments gradually shift a percentage of traffic to the new version, monitoring metrics before full rollout. With Istio VirtualService:

```
spec:
 http:
 - route:
  - destination: { host: order-service, subset: blue, weight: 90 }
  - destination: { host: order-service, subset: green, weight: 10 }
```

Metrics (error rate, latency) on the green subset inform automated promotion or rollback decisions. A typical workflow:

1. Deploy green subset alongside blue.
2. Shift 10% traffic, observe for 10 minutes.
3. If metrics are stable, shift to 50%, then 100%.

4. Remove blue subset.

Diagram: Blue/Green Deployments

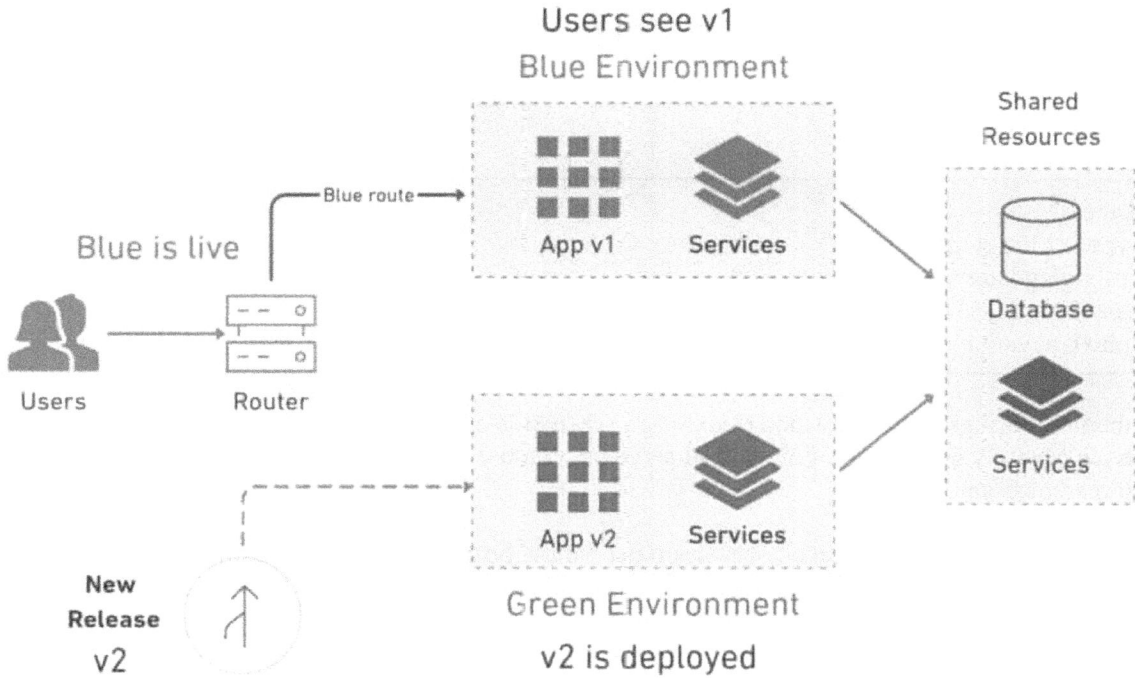

Diagram: Canary Deployments

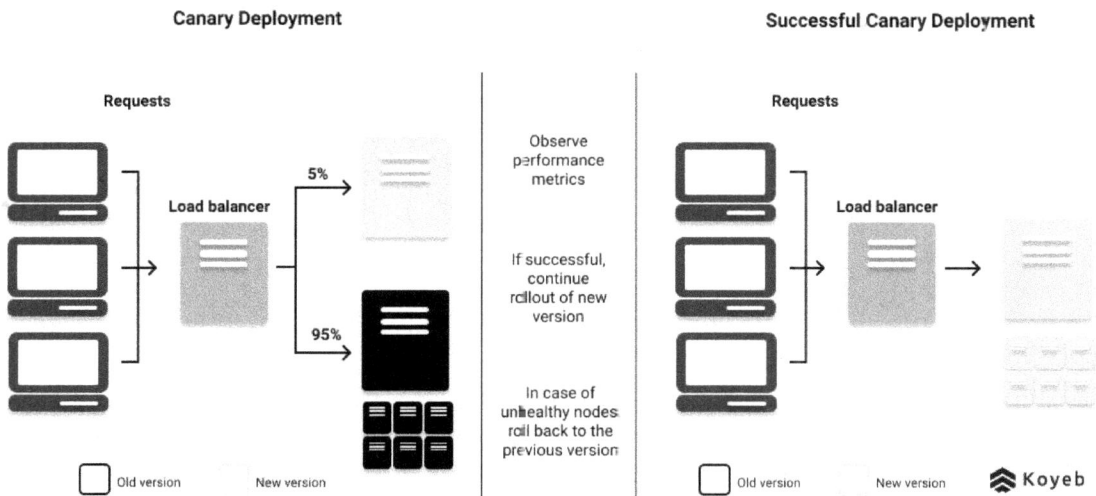

Blue/green and canary strategies minimize risk, allowing rapid rollback if the new version exhibits regressions. Automation pipelines orchestrate promotion based on health metrics, delivering both safety and agility.

8.7.3 Rolling Updates & Version Compatibility

Rolling updates replace pods incrementally to avoid downtime, combining maxUnavailable and maxSurge parameters:

```
strategy:
 type: RollingUpdate
 rollingUpdate:
  maxSurge: 1
  maxUnavailable: 1
```

Kubernetes brings up one new pod (maxSurge), then kills one old pod (maxUnavailable), maintaining service capacity throughout. For stateful services, you use **StatefulSets** with careful update policies and readiness gates.

Version compatibility is critical: services must handle both old and new versions during the update window. Employ backward- and forward-compatible schemas (see 7.8), API contracts, and feature flags. For example, deprecate fields rather than removing them immediately, and use compatibility middleware in sidecars or gateways.

A sequence diagram of a rolling update:

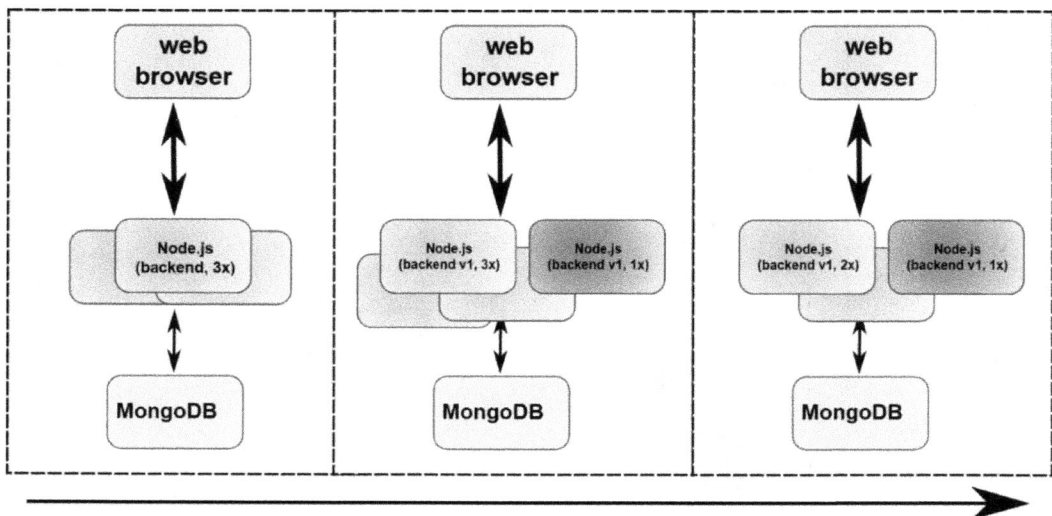

As time goes on, v2 backends replace v1 backends.

Monitoring during rolling updates ensures that metrics (error rate, latency, pod restarts) remain within thresholds. Automated canary checks can gate the progression of rolling updates, combining patterns to deliver zero-downtime, low-risk deployments.

8.7.4 Geographic & Multi-Region Clusters

To serve global users with low latency and regional fault isolation, you deploy clusters across multiple regions or cloud zones. Traffic directs users to the nearest region via DNS routing (GeoDNS) or anycast IPs. For example, AWS Route 53 geolocation routing:

```
{
 "Type": "A",
 "Name": "api.example.com",
 "SetIdentifier": "us-east-1",
 "GeoLocation": { "Region": "us-east-1" },
 "ResourceRecords": [{ "Value": "1.2.3.4" }]
}
```

Each region runs its own Kubernetes cluster, with cross-region replication for data stores (multi-master Cassandra, global DynamoDB tables). Data sovereignty and compliance concerns must be addressed—some data cannot leave certain jurisdictions.

Inter-region service calls use mTLS and optimized WAN links; routers like HAProxy with external DNS ensure failover if a region goes down.

Global Kubernetes management tools (Anthos, Rancher) unify operations across clusters. CI/CD pipelines target multiple clusters, ensuring consistent versions. Disaster recovery plans include region-wide failovers and cross-region backups. Multi-region architectures provide resilience against regional outages and deliver improved performance to geographically dispersed users.

8.8 Chaos Engineering & Resilience Testing

8.8.1 Designing Chaos Experiments

Chaos engineering validates resilience by proactively injecting failures and observing system behavior. Each experiment tests a **hypothesis**: "If we kill 30% of payment-service instances, overall order throughput remains above 90 % SLA." Designing experiments involves:

1. Defining blast radius (scope of failure).
2. Selecting steady-state metrics (error rates, latency, throughput).
3. Introducing failure (kill pods, network blackhole).
4. Observing impact and verifying hypothesis.

Example chaos scenario using LitmusChaos:

```
apiVersion: litmuschaos.io/v1alpha1
kind: ChaosEngine
metadata: { name: pod-kill-chaos }
spec:
 appinfo:
  appns: default
  applabel: "app=order"
 chaosServiceAccount: litmus-admin
 experiments:
 - name: pod-delete
  spec:
   components:
    env:
     - name: TOTAL_CHAOS
      value: "2"
```

This deletes 2 random order pods and monitors recovery. Good experiments include both lasting failures (pod kills) and transient faults (CPU/memory stress). Always run chaos in staging first, with alert rules in place to abort if safety thresholds are breached. Document each experiment in a **chaos playbook**, specifying roll-back procedures and expected outcomes.

8.8.2 Automating Failure Injection

Automated failure injections integrate into CI/CD or runbooks. Tools like **Gremlin** provide APIs to programmatically trigger attacks—shutdowns, packet drops, CPU spikes. A Gremlin script to throttle network:

```
{
 "name": "throttle-payment-service",
 "target": {
  "type": "label",
  "where": "app=payment-service"
 },
 "command": {
  "type": "network",
  "specification": {
   "egress": {
    "throttle": 50,
    "latency": 100
   }
  }
}
```

```
    }
}
```

You invoke these scripts via CI jobs or cron-triggered pipelines to ensure regular resilience tests. Embedding chaos in nightly builds or smoke-test stages catches regressions early—if a new version becomes brittle under failure, the pipeline fails. Automating injection and recovery reduces manual steps, enabling continuous validation of fault tolerance.

8.8.3 Monitoring Blast Radius

Blast radius is the scope of impact from an injected failure. Effective monitoring requires observing service-level and system-level metrics before, during, and after experiments. Use dashboards tracking:

- Error rates per service
- Request latencies (p95, p99)
- Instance counts and restart rates
- Circuit-breaker state transitions
- Resource utilization (CPU, memory, network)

Annotate chaos events in time series databases (Prometheus) for correlation:

```
increase(istio_requests_total{response_code="500"}[5m]) # errors during chaos
```

Quantify recovery time (MTTR) and error impact, feeding results into post-mortems and resilience scorecards. Smaller blast radii—faults contained to non-critical paths—indicate stronger resilience.

8.8.4 GameDays & Post-Mortem Analysis

GameDays are scheduled simulations where teams run chaos experiments in a production-like environment, practicing incident response and verifying runbooks. Participants monitor dashboards, receive alerts, execute rollbacks or mitigation scripts, and communicate status updates. After the exercise, teams conduct a post-mortem to capture:

- What went well?
- What failed?
- Gaps in monitoring or runbooks?
- Action items and ownership.

A typical post-mortem template includes timeline, impact summary, root causes, corrective actions, and prevention measures. For example:

Timestamp	Event	Impact	Action Taken
10:00 UTC	2 pods killed	20 % error rate spike	Killed surplus pods
10:05 UTC	Alert triggered	PagerDuty on-call	Switched traffic via Ingress
10:10 UTC	Metrics steady	System stabilized	Completed GameDay

GameDays foster resilience culture, ensuring teams are prepared for real incidents. Regularly rotating scenarios—database failover, region outage, API degradation—build muscle memory and uncover hidden dependencies. Document lessons learned in ADRs and training materials, continuously raising your organization's resilience maturity.

8.9 Observability & Health Endpoints

8.9.1 Liveness, Readiness & Startup Probes

Kubernetes probes ensure that only healthy pods receive traffic and that failing pods are restarted or removed promptly. **Liveness probes** check that the application is alive—if this fails, kube-let kills the container and restarts it. **Readiness probes** indicate whether the app is ready to serve traffic; failing readiness removes the pod from service endpoints without killing it, allowing it to finish background work. **Startup probes** guard against slow-starting applications: before the startup probe succeeds, liveness and readiness probes are disabled, preventing premature restarts during initialization.

A typical Deployment excerpt:

```
spec:
 containers:
 - name: api
  image: myorg/api:2.0
  ports: [{ containerPort: 8080 }]
  startupProbe:
   httpGet:
    path: /health/startup
    port: 8080
   failureThreshold: 30
   periodSeconds: 10
```

```
livenessProbe:
 httpGet:
  path: /health/live
  port: 8080
 initialDelaySeconds: 5
 periodSeconds: 10
 failureThreshold: 3
readinessProbe:
 httpGet:
  path: /health/ready
  port: 8080
 initialDelaySeconds: 5
 periodSeconds: 5
 failureThreshold: 2
```

Here, the startup probe allows up to 5 minutes (30×10 s) for initialization before marking the pod dead. Only after successful startup do liveness and readiness checks commence.

On the application side, health endpoints often use frameworks like Spring Boot Actuator:

```
@Configuration
public class HealthConfig {
 @Bean
 public HealthIndicator startupHealth() {
  return () -> // check migrations done
   isMigrated ? Health.up().build() : Health.down().withDetail("migrated", false).build();
 }
}
```

The /health endpoint at /health/startup, /health/live, and /health/ready map to different indicators.

Probes must be fast and side-effect-free: long-running checks can cause flapping. Use dedicated endpoints that only check critical subsystem readiness (DB connectivity, cache warm-up). Properly tuned probes reduce downtime and prevent traffic from hitting unhealthy instances, forming the foundation of a resilient control plane.

8.9.2 Metrics Collection (Prometheus, Micrometer)

Metrics provide quantitative insight into system behavior—throughput, error rates, latency distributions—which drive alerting, capacity planning, and SLO verification. **Micrometer** offers a vendor-neutral facade in Spring applications, emitting metrics in Prometheus format:

```
@Autowired MeterRegistry registry;


@PostConstruct
public void initMetrics() {
 registry.counter("orders.placed", "region", "us-east").increment();
 Timer.builder("payment.latency")
   .description("Time to process payment")
   .tags("gateway", "stripe")
   .publishPercentileHistogram()
   .register(registry);
}


public void recordPayment(Duration duration) {
 registry.timer("payment.latency", "gateway", "stripe").record(duration);
}
```

In application.yml:

```
management:
 metrics:
  export:
   prometheus:
    enabled: true
 endpoints:
  web:
   exposure:
    include: prometheus,health,info
```

Prometheus scrapes /actuator/prometheus at defined intervals:

```
scrape_configs:
 - job_name: 'api'
  static_configs:
   - targets: ['api-service:8080']
```

Collected metrics feed Grafana dashboards. Use **counters** for event counts, **gauges** for instantaneous values (e.g., queue depth), **timers** or **histograms** for latency distributions (p50, p95, p99). Tag metrics with dimensions—service, region, endpoint—to slice data meaningfully.

Define **alert rules** for SLO breaches:

```
groups:
- name: service_alerts
 rules:
 - alert: HighErrorRate
 expr: rate(http_requests_total{status=~"5.."}[5m]) > 0.01
 for: 2m
 labels: { severity: "critical" }
 annotations:
  summary: "Error rate >1% for 2 minutes"
```

By instrumenting code with rich, tagged metrics, teams gain real-time observability into system health, enabling data-driven resilience improvements.

8.9.3 Distributed Tracing (OpenTelemetry)

Distributed tracing reveals end-to-end request flows across microservices, exposing latency bottlenecks and error hotspots. **OpenTelemetry** provides APIs and SDKs for tracing in multiple languages. In a Spring Boot service:

```
@Bean
public OpenTelemetrySdk openTelemetry() {
 SdkTracerProvider tracerProvider = SdkTracerProvider.builder()
  .addSpanProcessor(BatchSpanProcessor.builder(
  OtlpGrpcSpanExporter.builder().setEndpoint(OTLP_ENDPOINT).build()
 ).build())
 .build();
 return OpenTelemetrySdk.builder().setTracerProvider(tracerProvider).build();
}


@Autowired
Tracer tracer;


public void placeOrder() {
 Span span = tracer.spanBuilder("PlaceOrder").startSpan();
 try (Scope scope = span.makeCurrent()) {
 // downstream call
 inventoryClient.reserve(...);
 } finally {
 span.end();
 }
}
```

Context propagates automatically over HTTP if you use instrumented HTTP clients (Spring Cloud Sleuth with OpenTelemetry integration). For Node.js with @opentelemetry/sdk-node:

```
const       sdk       =       new       NodeSDK({       traceExporter,       instrumentations:
[getNodeAutoInstrumentations()] });
sdk.start();
const tracer = opentelemetry.trace.getTracer('payment-service');
```

A sequence diagram of a traced request:

```
@startuml
participant Client
participant API
participant Inventory
participant Billing


Client -> API: HTTP POST /orders
activate API
API -> Inventory: RPC reserveItem()
activate Inventory
Inventory --> API: OK
deactivate Inventory
API -> Billing: RPC chargeCard()
activate Billing
Billing --> API: OK
deactivate Billing
API --> Client: HTTP 200
deactivate API
@enduml
```

Traces appear in back ends like Jaeger or Zipkin, showing spans, durations, and attributes. Use sampling to control volume—tail-based sampling can retain slow or error traces. Annotate spans with business context (orderId, userId) for easier debugging. Distributed tracing uncovers cross-service latencies that metrics alone cannot, completing the observability triad.

8.9.4 Correlation IDs & Log Enrichment

Correlation IDs tie together logs, metrics, and traces for a single request, enabling holistic debugging. A correlation ID is generated at the edge (API gateway or web server) and propagated through HTTP headers (e.g., X-Request-ID). In Spring Boot with Sleuth:

```
@Bean
public Sampler defaultSampler() { return Sampler.ALWAYS_ON; }
```

Sleuth generates and injects X-B3-TraceId and X-B3-SpanId into threads and log MDC. A Logback pattern:

```
<pattern>%d{ISO8601}        [%X{traceId},%X{spanId}]        %-5level        %logger{36}
- %msg%n</pattern>
```

A sample log line:

```
2025-05-14T10:00:00Z [abcd1234,ef012345] INFO OrderService - Placed order 1234
```

In Node.js with Winston:

```
const { createLogger, format, transports } = require('winston');
const { v4: uuidv4 } = require('uuid');


function requestIdMiddleware(req, res, next) {
 req.id = req.headers['x-request-id'] || uuidv4();
 res.set('X-Request-ID', req.id);
 next();
}


const logger = createLogger({
 format: format.combine(
  format.timestamp(),
  format.printf(({ timestamp, level, message, meta }) =>
   `${timestamp} [${meta.requestId}] ${level}: ${message}`
  )
 ),
 transports: [ new transports.Console() ]
});
```

Always log the correlation ID and other context (userId, tenantId) in every log entry. In distributed systems, this ID links traces, metrics, and logs. A debug tool can query logs for requestId=abcd1234 across multiple services. Without correlation IDs, reconstructing request flows in logs is nearly impossible. Enriched logs fuel incident response, post-mortems, and capacity planning. Ensure IDs propagate through async boundaries—messaging, thread pools—by capturing and restoring MDC or equivalent context storage.

8.10 Communication Topologies & Patterns

8.10.1 Synchronous Request-Response RPC

Synchronous RPC—typically REST over HTTP or gRPC—offers straightforward request-response semantics but introduces coupling and latency chains. In REST, controllers expose endpoints:

```
@RestController
@RequestMapping("/orders")
public class OrderController {
 @Autowired OrderService service;
 @GetMapping("/{id}")
 public ResponseEntity<OrderDto> get(@PathVariable String id) {
  Order order = service.findById(id);
  return ResponseEntity.ok(OrderMapper.toDto(order));
 }
}
```

Clients issue HTTP calls and block until a response arrives, propagating latency: each downstream call adds to end-to-end response time. To optimize, use parallel calls or request pipelining where possible:

```
CompletableFuture<Inventory> invFut = inventoryClient.get(invId);
CompletableFuture<Price> priceFut  = pricingClient.get(priceId);
CompletableFuture.allOf(invFut, priceFut).join();
```

gRPC provides HTTP/2 multiplexing and strong typing via Protobuf:

```
service OrderService {
 rpc GetOrder (GetOrderRequest) returns (Order);
}
```

Server implementation in Java:

```
public class OrderServiceImpl extends OrderServiceGrpc.OrderServiceImplBase {
 public void getOrder(GetOrderRequest req, StreamObserver<Order> obs) {
  Order order = find(req.getId());
```

```
    obs.onNext(order);
    obs.onCompleted();
  }
}
```

gRPC clients benefit from lower overhead and bi-directional streaming but require mutual TLS or trust management.

Each arrow represents a blocking call. Use timeouts, retries, and circuit breakers to contain latency spikes. Avoid deep call chains; prefer back-end for front-end aggregation or the **gateway pattern** to reduce client-observed latency.

8.10.2 Asynchronous Messaging & Event-Driven

Asynchronous messaging decouples services via queues or topics, enabling loose coupling and resilience under load. Producers publish events without waiting for consumers:

```
public void publishOrderPlaced(OrderPlaced event) {
  kafkaTemplate.send("order-placed", event.getOrderId(), event);
}
```

Consumers subscribe via listeners:

```
@KafkaListener(topics = "order-placed")
public void onOrderPlaced(OrderPlaced e) {
  inventoryService.reserve(e.getOrderId());
}
```

Event-driven topologies use **pub/sub** or **message brokers** (Kafka, RabbitMQ). **Event sourcing** persists events as the source of truth, reconstructing state by replaying them.

Benefits include high throughput and natural retry semantics. Drawbacks include eventual consistency and ordering considerations. For workflows, implement sagas (6.10) to orchestrate multi-service transactions.

Use **dead-letter queues** for poison messages and **idempotent** handlers to cope with duplicate deliveries. Asynchronous designs absorb traffic spikes better, since producers can publish at will and consumers process at their own pace. This topology enhances resilience by decoupling availability between services.

8.10.3 Fan-Out, Pub/Sub & Scatter-Gather

The **fan-out** pattern broadcasts one message to multiple subscribers (pub/sub), useful for notifying many services of a domain event. In RabbitMQ:

```
channel.exchangeDeclare("order-exchange", BuiltinExchangeType.FANOUT);
channel.basicPublish("order-exchange", "", null, orderPlacedJson.getBytes());
```

Each bound queue—inventory, billing, analytics—receives the event. Pub/sub decouples producers from consumers entirely.

Scatter-gather extends fan-out by collecting responses from multiple services. A coordinator publishes a query to a topic and waits for replies on a reply queue:

```
String corrId = UUID.randomUUID().toString();
props = new AMQP.BasicProperties.Builder()
    .correlationId(corrId)
    .replyTo(replyQueueName).build();
channel.basicPublish("", "query-queue", props, queryJson);
```

Consumers process and reply:

```
channel.basicPublish("", props.getReplyTo(),
 new BasicProperties.Builder().correlationId(props.getCorrelationId()).build(),
 responseJson.getBytes());
```

The coordinator gathers responses with matching correlationId until all are received or a timeout occurs.

Use this pattern for aggregating data from multiple microservices—e.g., building a composite view in an API gateway. Manage timeouts and partial results gracefully, returning partial data if some services lag or fail.

8.10.4 Gateway Aggregation vs. Client-Side Composition

Gateway aggregation centralizes composition logic in a backend for front-end (BFF) or API gateway. For a composite endpoint /dashboard, the gateway calls multiple services, merges results, and returns a single payload:

```
app.get('/dashboard', async (req, res) => {
 const [orders, notifications] = await Promise.all([
  fetch(`http://order-service/orders`),
  fetch(`http://notif-service/notifs`)
```

```
]);
 res.json({ orders, notifications });
});
```

Clients benefit from fewer HTTP calls and consistent payloads. However, the gateway can become a bottleneck and single point of logic complexity.

Client-side composition pushes aggregation to the client (web or mobile), which issues parallel requests and assembles the UI model. In React:

```
const [orders, setOrders] = useState([]);
const [notifs, setNotifs] = useState([]);
useEffect(() => {
 Promise.all([
  fetchOrders().then(r => setOrders(r)),
  fetchNotifs().then(r => setNotifs(r))
 ]);
}, []);
```

This reduces server-side load and allows clients to control parallelism and caching, but increases coupling to service contracts and may degrade perceived performance due to multiple round-trips.

Diagram: Gateway Aggregation:

API Gateway

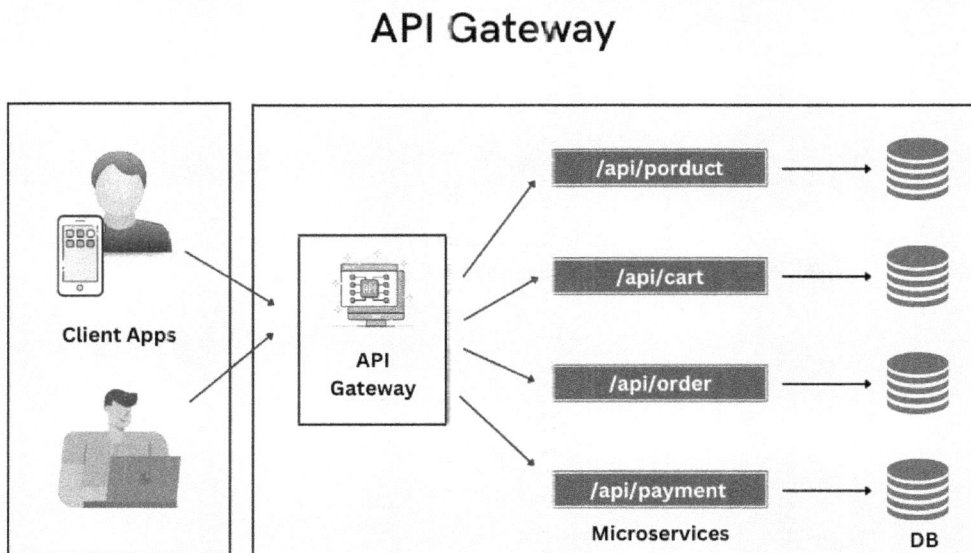

Diagram: Client Composition:

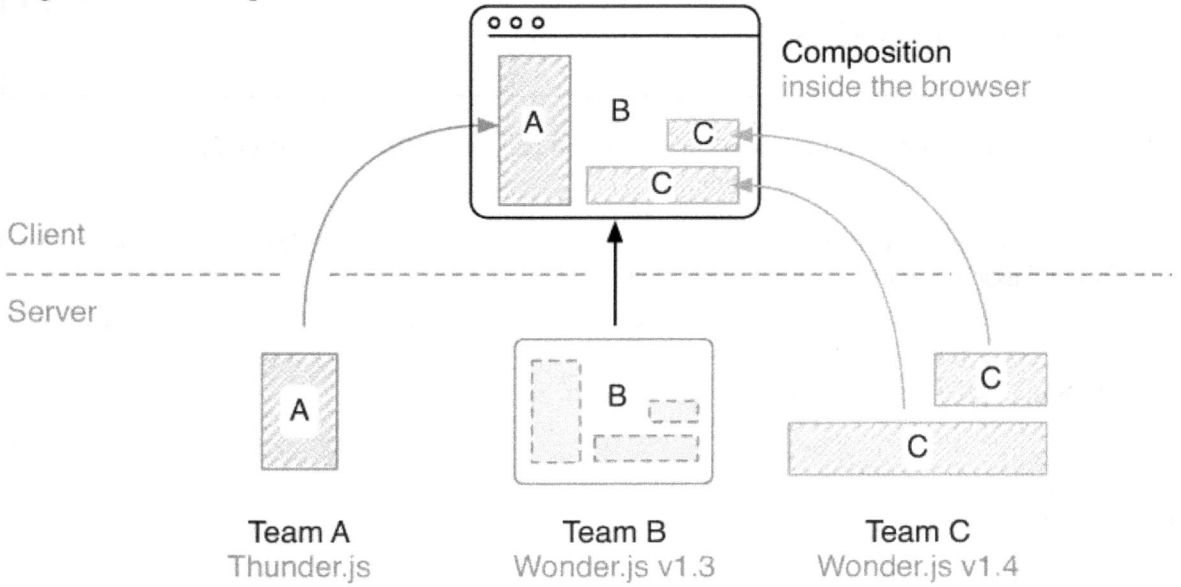

Composition
inside the browser

Client

Server

Team A
Thunder.js

Team B
Wonder.js v1.3

Team C
Wonder.js v1.4

Diagram: Server Composition

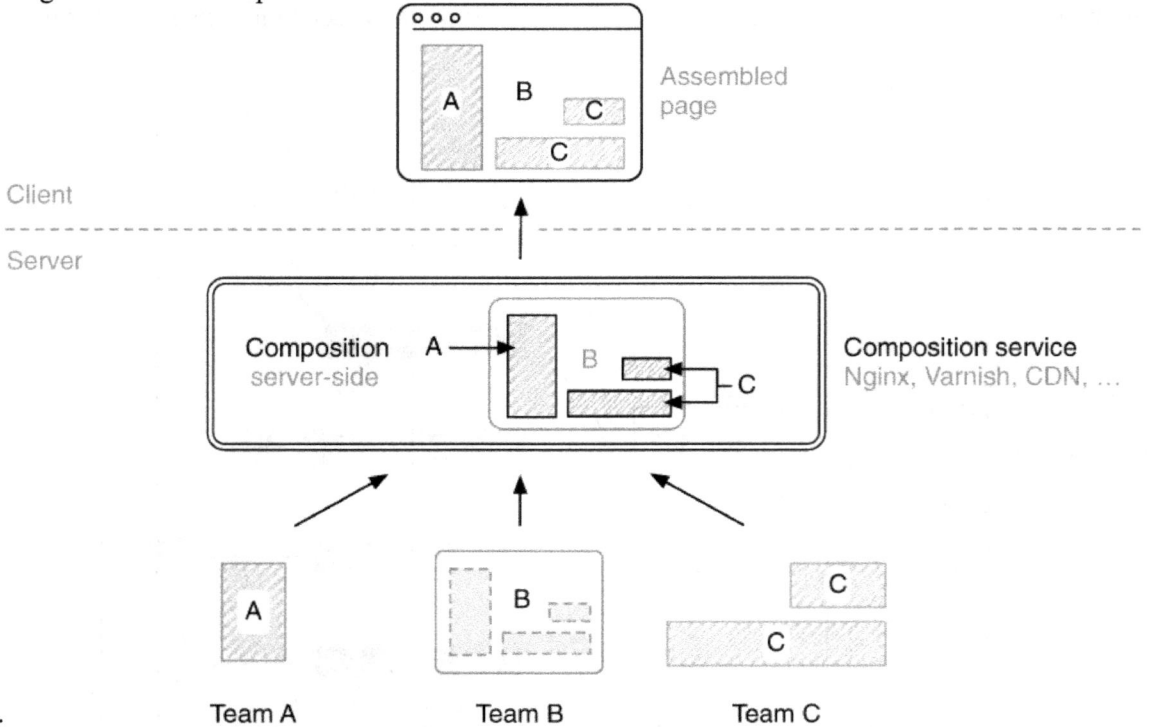

Assembled
page

Client

Server

Composition
server-side

Composition service
Nginx, Varnish, CDN, ...

Team A

Team B

Team C

Choose aggregation when controlling payloads and reducing client complexity is paramount; choose client composition when edge devices can handle parallel calls and you want to avoid an additional server hop. Both patterns solve composition but trade off server load, latency, and coupling differently.

Conclusion

By embracing resilience patterns and microservice topologies as first-class concerns, you transform fragile networks of services into a robust ecosystem capable of surviving both anticipated hiccups and unforeseen failures. Circuits break to prevent floods of errors, bulkheads quarantine faults, and backpressure throttles load to sustain core operations. Gateways and sidecars handle routing, security, and telemetry, while service meshes automate policy enforcement and insights. Deployment strategies—canaries, rolling upgrades, multi-region clusters—ensure that updates glide in without disruption. Crucially, observability and chaos engineering close the feedback loop, turning incidents into learning opportunities and proving that your defenses hold under stress. Armed with these techniques, you can confidently scale, evolve, and maintain a distributed system that not only meets today's demands but anticipates tomorrow's challenges.

Chapter 9. Cross-Cutting Concerns Without Pollution

In any complex system, concerns like logging, security, configuration, and error handling weave their way through nearly every component. If left to be sprinkled directly into business logic, these cross-cutting concerns can obscure intent, introduce hidden dependencies, and hinder both testing and evolution of core features. This chapter shows how to extract such concerns into well-defined layers—via aspects, decorators, filters, or middleware—so that your domain code remains focused on business rules. By embracing techniques that cleanly modularize logging, metrics, validation, and more, you achieve a codebase that's both expressive and resilient to change.

9.1 Aspect-Oriented Foundations

9.1.1 Separation of Concerns via Aspects

Aspect-Oriented Programming (AOP) allows you to encapsulate cross-cutting logic—such as logging, security checks, or transaction management—into reusable "aspects" that weave themselves into your application at well-defined join points. By defining pointcuts (places in the code, like method executions or class instantiations) and advices (the code to run at those points), you cleanly separate concerns without littering business logic with plumbing. For example, using Spring AOP:

```
@Aspect
@Component
public class LoggingAspect {
 @Pointcut("execution(* com.myapp.service.*.*(..))")
 public void serviceMethods() {}
```

```
@Before("serviceMethods()")
public void logEntry(JoinPoint jp) {
 LoggerFactory.getLogger(jp.getTarget().getClass())
  .info("Entering {}.{}() with args {}",
    jp.getSignature().getDeclaringTypeName(),
    jp.getSignature().getName(),
    jp.getArgs());
 }
}
```

Here, every method in com.myapp.service is automatically logged before execution. The aspect defines neither domain logic nor logging code inside the services themselves, leaving your core methods pristine. Under the hood, Spring dynamically creates proxies around the target beans, intercepting calls and invoking advices as configured. This approach encourages reuse—a single @Aspect can apply across hundreds of methods—while maintaining a clean separation of concerns. It also reduces boilerplate and prevents drift, as logging or security policies evolve independently of business code. In performance-sensitive paths, you can control advice execution via pointcut granularity, avoiding unnecessary overhead. Combined with runtime metrics on advice invocation counts and latencies, aspects become a powerful tool to enforce architectural rules consistently. As we move to request pipelines, the same principles guide the use of decorators and filters, forming a cohesive AOP-based strategy for handling cross-cutting concerns.

9.1.2 Decorators, Interceptors & Filters

While AOP focuses on code-level join points, structural patterns like the **Decorator, Interceptor**, and **Filter** enable you to layer behaviors around components or request pipelines. The Decorator pattern wraps a class with additional functionality by composing rather than inheriting:

```
public interface OrderService {
 Order placeOrder(OrderRequest req);
}


public class OrderServiceImpl implements OrderService { ... }


public class OrderServiceLoggingDecorator implements OrderService {
 private final OrderService delegate;
 public OrderServiceLoggingDecorator(OrderService delegate) {
  this.delegate = delegate;
 }
 public Order placeOrder(OrderRequest req) {
```

```
log.info("Placing order {}", req);
Order result = delegate.placeOrder(req);
log.info("Order placed: {}", result.getId());
return result;
}
}
```

Here, OrderServiceLoggingDecorator adds logging without modifying OrderServiceImpl. Interceptor patterns—common in Java EE or JAX-RS—allow chaining multiple interceptors around a method invocation:

```
@Provider
public class AuthenticationFilter implements ContainerRequestFilter {
 public void filter(ContainerRequestContext ctx) {
  String token = ctx.getHeaderString("Authorization");
  if (!authService.isValid(token)) ctx.abortWith(forbidden());
 }
}
```

Filters and interceptors operate at the HTTP request level, pre- and post-processing requests and responses. In web frameworks, filters form a chain where each can modify the request, short-circuit processing, or enrich the response. A simplified flow:

```
[Client] → Filter A → Filter B → Dispatch to Controller → Filter B → Filter A → [Response]
```

By centralizing concerns like authentication, logging, or CORS handling into filters/interceptors, your controllers and services remain free of repetitive code. Decorators shine inside the application layer, whereas filters and interceptors address the transport layer. As we decide which approach to adopt, next we'll compare leading AOP frameworks to choose the right tool for your context.

9.1.3 Choosing Between AOP Frameworks

The Java ecosystem offers multiple AOP implementations—Spring AOP, AspectJ, CDI interceptors, and libraries in other languages—each with its own trade-offs. **Spring AOP** uses proxy-based weaving at runtime, requiring interfaces or @Configurable classes, and supports only method-execution join points. It integrates seamlessly with Spring Boot, has minimal configuration, and performs well for most typical use cases. **AspectJ**, in contrast, provides compile-time and load-time weaving, capable of modifying bytecode to intercept field access, constructor calls, and more. It requires additional build steps or JVM agents but unlocks more powerful pointcuts.

CDI interceptors in Jakarta EE use annotations like @Interceptor and @AroundInvoke, offering portable AOP across Java EE containers. **Micronaut** and **Quarkus** provide compile-time AOP in a

Spring-like programming model, eliminating runtime proxies and reflection for faster startup times. For Node.js, libraries like **AspectJS** bring similar capabilities.

When choosing a framework, consider:

1. **Weaving model** (compile-time vs. runtime vs. load-time).
2. **Pointcut expressiveness** (methods only vs. fields/construction).
3. **Startup performance** (compile-time weaving often faster).
4. **Dependency footprint** (pure-Java libs vs. container support).

A comparative matrix:

Feature	Spring AOP	AspectJ	CDI Interceptors	Micronaut AOP
Weaving	Runtime	Compile/Load-time	Runtime	Compile-time
Join-point types	Methods	Methods, Fields	Methods	Methods
Config complexity	Low	Medium	Medium	Low
Startup cost	Medium	High (Agent)	Medium	Low

Choosing the right AOP framework ensures that your cross-cutting concerns integrate cleanly, with acceptable performance and ease of maintenance. With AOP foundations set, we next turn to one of the most critical concerns: logging and distributed tracing.

9.2 Logging & Distributed Tracing

9.2.1 Structured vs. Text Logs

Traditional text logs—unstructured strings written to files—become difficult to parse and query at scale. **Structured logging**, by contrast, serializes log entries as JSON or key-value pairs, enabling downstream systems to index, filter, and analyze logs efficiently. For example, with Logstash Logback Encoder:

```
<encoder class="net.logstash.logback.encoder.LoggingEventCompositeJsonEncoder">
 <providers>
  <timestamp>
```

```
 <fieldName>timestamp</fieldName>
</timestamp>
<pattern>
 <pattern>
  {"level":"%level","logger":"%logger","thread":"%thread"}
 </pattern>
</pattern>
<arguments/>
<stackTrace/>
</providers>
</encoder>
```

A log line might look like:

```
{"timestamp":"2025-05-
14T12:00:00Z","level":"INFO","logger":"com.myapp.OrderService","thread":"http-nio-8080-
exec-1","message":"Order placed","orderId":"abc123","amount":49.99}
```

Structured logs allow filtering by fields (orderId, amount>100), aggregation (count by logger), and alerting on patterns (errorCode=PAYMENT_FAILURE). They improve reliability of log pipelines (ELK, Splunk) and support machine-driven analysis. In contrast, text logs require brittle regex parsing and are sensitive to format changes. A side-by-side diagram:

```
Text Log:    INFO OrderService - Order placed: abc123
Structured                                                                          Log:
{"level":"INFO","component":"OrderService","event":"OrderPlaced","id":"abc123"}
```

Switching to structured logs is a cross-cutting change best handled via AOP or decorators (see 9.1), so that all log statements automatically emit JSON without manual code changes. With structure in place, logs become a first-class data source in your observability stack. This sets the stage for adding contextual information, like correlation IDs, in the next subsection.

9.2.2 Enriching Logs with Context & Correlation IDs

Adding context—such as user IDs, tenant IDs, and correlation IDs—to every log entry is essential for tracing requests across distributed services. SLF4J's MDC (Mapped Diagnostic Context) lets you inject key-value pairs into the logging context:

```
public void filter(ContainerRequestContext ctx) {
 String traceId = ctx.getHeaderString("X-Request-ID");
 MDC.put("traceId", traceId != null ? traceId : UUID.randomUUID().toString());
```

```
MDC.put("userId", ctx.getHeaderString("User-ID"));
}
```

Your log pattern:

```
<pattern>%d{ISO8601}      [%X{traceId}]      [user=%X{userId}]      %-5level      %logger
- %msg%n</pattern>
```

A sample enriched log:

```
2025-05-14T12:05:00Z [abc123] [user=42] INFO OrderService - Placed order 5678
```

As the request travels between services, each adds or propagates the same traceId, enabling log aggregation tools to group all related entries. In Reactor-based reactive apps, you propagate context via Context:

```
Mono.deferContextual(ctx -> {
 String traceId = ctx.get("traceId");
 MDC.put("traceId", traceId);
 return process();
})
.contextWrite(ctx -> ctx.put("traceId", traceId));
```

A simplified flow:

```
Client → Service A (MDC.put(traceId)) → Service B (MDC.get/put) → Logs with same traceId
```

By enriching logs via filters or aspects, you avoid sprinkling MDC code throughout business methods. This contextual logging bridges to full distributed tracing, covered in the next subsection.

9.2.3 Integrating OpenTelemetry / Zipkin

Distributed tracing captures the full lifecycle of a request across microservices, revealing performance bottlenecks and error propagation. **OpenTelemetry** provides unified APIs for instrumentation, supporting back-ends like Jaeger or Zipkin. In a Spring Boot app:

```
@Bean
public OpenTelemetrySdk openTelemetry() {
 return OpenTelemetrySdk.builder()
```

```
.setPropagators(ContextPropagators.create(
W3CTraceContextPropagator.getInstance()))
.setTracerProvider(SdkTracerProvider.builder()
.addSpanProcessor(BatchSpanProcessor.builder(
ZipkinSpanExporter.builder().setEndpoint("http://zipkin:9411/api/v2/spans").build()
).build())
.build())
.build();
}
```

Annotate methods with spans:

```
@Autowired Tracer tracer;
public void processOrder() {
 Span span = tracer.spanBuilder("OrderProcessing").startSpan();
 try (Scope s = span.makeCurrent()) {
 // business logic
 } finally {
 span.end();
 }
}
```

HTTP client libraries automatically propagate trace context when instrumented. A trace visualization:

```
Client → [OrderService] span1 ——> [InventoryService] span2 ——> [PaymentService] span3
```

Zipkin's UI shows timing breakdowns, errors, and service latencies. This end-to-end view complements logs and metrics, closing the observability loop. After establishing tracing, you'll need robust backends and retention policies to manage the volume, which we address next.

9.2.4 Log Backends & Retention Policies

Choosing the right log backend—Elasticsearch, Splunk, or cloud services—impacts query performance, cost, and compliance. In an ELK stack, Logstash or Filebeat ships structured logs into Elasticsearch indices:

```
output.elasticsearch:
 hosts: ["es1:9200"]
 index: "myapp-logs-%{+yyyy.MM.dd}"
```

Index lifecycle management (ILM) policies automatically roll over daily and delete indices after a retention period:

```
PUT _ilm/policy/log_policy
{ "policy": {
 "phases": {
  "hot": { "actions": {} },
  "delete": { "min_age": "30d", "actions": { "delete": {} } }
 }
 }
}
```

Splunk users configure retention via quotas and cold storage. Secure storage of logs—encrypt at rest and in transit—is essential for sensitive data. Use role-based access to control who can view or delete logs. Archive logs to cheaper object storage (S3, GCS) for long-term compliance, and index recent logs in hot tiers for fast searches.

A flow of the log pipeline:

```
[App Instances] → Filebeat → Logstash → Elasticsearch → Grafana (Kibana)
       ↓
     S3 Archive
```

Balancing retention (for audits) against storage costs requires business input on compliance requirements. With a robust log backend and retention strategy in place, you ensure that logs remain a reliable source of truth over time.

9.3 Metrics & Health Monitoring

9.3.1 Business vs. Technical Metrics

Not all metrics are created equal. **Technical metrics**—CPU usage, memory footprint, request latency—indicate system health and resource utilization, essential for capacity planning and alerting. **Business metrics**—orders per minute, active users, transaction values—reflect actual business outcomes and drive product decisions. Instrumenting both types ensures that the system not only runs smoothly but also meets business goals.

For example, using Micrometer in a Spring Boot service:

```
Counter orderCounter = registry.counter("orders.created", "region", "us-east");
orderCounter.increment();
```

This business metric supplements technical timers:

```
Timer.builder("http.server.requests")
  .publishPercentiles(0.5,0.95,0.99)
  .register(registry);
```

A composite dashboard might display:

Time	CPU %	Heap MB	Orders/min	p95 Latency

Aligning technical and business dashboards helps correlate system performance with revenue impact—for instance, a spike in latency coinciding with dropped orders. Transitioning from metrics to alerting, we next discuss how to expose these metrics to Prometheus for collection.

9.3.2 Instrumenting with Micrometer / Prometheus

Micrometer provides a facade to emit metrics to multiple back-ends; **Prometheus** scrapes and stores them. In application.yml:

```
management:
 endpoints:
 web:
  exposure:
   include: health,info,prometheus
 metrics:
  export:
  prometheus:
    enabled: true
```

Prometheus prometheus.yml config:

```
scrape_configs:
 - job_name: 'myapp'
  metrics_path: '/actuator/prometheus'
  static_configs:
  - targets: ['myapp-service:8080']
```

Define custom counters, gauges, and timers in code:

```
Gauge.builder("inventory.level", inventoryService, svc -> svc.getStock("sku-A"))
  .tags("warehouse","east").register(registry);
```

Histogram buckets provide latency distributions:

```
DistributionSummary summary = DistributionSummary.builder("payload.size")
 .baseUnit("bytes")
 .serviceLevelObjectives(100, 500, 1000)
 .register(registry);
summary.record(payloadLength);
```

Prometheus's powerful query language (PromQL) enables ad-hoc analysis:

```
rate(orders_created[5m])
histogram_quantile(0.95, sum(rate(http_server_requests_seconds_bucket[5m])) by (le))
```

With Prometheus collecting Micrometer metrics, you have a robust, scalable monitoring foundation. Next, we'll turn those metrics into actionable dashboards and alerts.

9.3.3 Dashboarding & Alerting Best Practices

Building effective dashboards requires selecting key metrics, grouping them logically, and providing context. Use **Grafana** to create panels for service health (error rates), performance (latencies), and business KPIs (orders per minute). A dashboard might include:

- Line chart: p95 latency over time
- Bar chart: error count by endpoint
- Gauge: CPU utilization
- Single stat: current active sessions

Organize dashboards by persona—SREs focus on infrastructure metrics, developers on service-level health, product managers on business metrics. Annotate dashboards with deployment events to correlate performance shifts with releases.

Alerting rules should target symptoms, not causes, and include clear runbook links:

```
- alert: HighErrorRate
 expr: rate(http_server_requests_seconds_count{status=~"5.."}[5m]) > 0.01
 for: 2m
 labels: { severity: "page" }
 annotations:
```

```
summary: "5xx error rate >1% for 2m"
runbook: "https://wiki.example.com/alerts#HighErrorRate"
```

Use multi-level alerts: warnings for low-urgency issues, pages for critical system failures. Throttle alert频 to prevent noise, aggregate related alerts into one ticket, and auto-resolve when conditions clear. By following these practices, dashboards become an invaluable tool for both real-time operations and trend analysis. From dashboards and alerts, we move naturally to custom health indicators that enrich standard health endpoints.

9.3.4 Custom Health Indicators

Default health endpoints often check basic components—database connectivity, disk space—but real applications need domain-specific health indicators. In Spring Boot:

```
@Component
public class OrderQueueHealthIndicator implements HealthIndicator {
 @Autowired private QueueService queueService;
 public Health health() {
  int size = queueService.getPendingCount();
  if (size < 1000) {
   return Health.up().withDetail("queueSize", size).build();
  } else {
   return Health.down().withDetail("queueSize", size).build();
  }
 }
}
```

This adds /health details:

```
{
"status": "UP",
"components": {
 "db": { "status": "UP" },
 "orderQueue": { "status": "UP", "details": { "queueSize": 250 } }
 }
}
```

Custom indicators can check cache evictions, third-party API quotas, or feature-flag service availability. Group indicators into readiness and liveness categories: readiness might include schema migrations being up-to-date, while liveness focuses on internal thread health.

Health checks feed into orchestrator probes (9.9), influencing rolling updates and traffic routing. By extending health indicators for domain concerns, you ensure that only genuinely healthy pods serve traffic, closing the loop on robust application monitoring. As monitoring habits mature, the next frontier is externalized configuration and secrets management, covered in the following section.

9.4 Configuration & Secrets Management

9.4.1 The Twelve-Factor App "Config" Principle

The Twelve-Factor App manifesto mandates storing configuration in the environment, separate from code, to support clean separation of builds and deploys. This principle ensures that you can deploy the same artifact across multiple environments—dev, staging, prod—without changes to the binary. Environment variables (DATABASE_URL, REDIS_HOST, API_KEY) carry configuration values. For example, in Spring Boot:

```
spring.datasource.url=${DATABASE_URL}
spring.datasource.username=${DB_USER}
spring.datasource.password=${DB_PASS}
```

In a Docker Compose file:

```
services:
 api:
  image: myorg/api:latest
  environment:
   - DATABASE_URL=jdbc:postgresql://db:5432/app
   - DB_USER=appuser
   - DB_PASS=${APP_DB_PASS}
```

This approach avoids hard-coding secrets or varying configurations in code. Build pipelines inject environment variables at deploy time, and CI/CD systems store them securely in Vault or Kubernetes Secrets. Twelve-Factor also recommends using a config server (see 9.4.2) for complex scenarios—feature flags, dynamic reloading, or hierarchical overrides. By externalizing configuration per this principle, your services become immutable, portable, and easier to manage across environments, setting the stage for robust secret management.

9.4.2 Externalized Config Sources (Env, Vault, Config Server)

Beyond plain environment variables, enterprise applications often rely on centralized config stores—**HashiCorp Vault**, **Spring Cloud Config**, or cloud-native services like AWS SSM Parameter Store. A typical Vault integration in Spring Boot:

```
spring:
 cloud:
  vault:
   authentication: TOKEN
   token: ${VAULT_TOKEN}
   uri: ${VAULT_URI}
   kv:
    enabled: true
    backend: secret
```

The application fetches secrets at startup (and optionally on refresh). Vault's dynamic secrets feature generates short-lived credentials for databases or cloud services, reducing secret sprawl. Spring Cloud Config provides a Git-backed config server:

```
spring:
 cloud:
  config:
   uri: http://config-server:8888
   label: main
```

Clients automatically load application-{profile}.yml from the repo, and /actuator/refresh can reload configs at runtime. Kubernetes ConfigMaps and Secrets mount configuration and certificates as files or environment variables:

```
apiVersion: v1
kind: Secret
metadata: { name: app-secrets }
type: Opaque
data:
 api.key: c2VjcmV0   # base64 of "secret"
```

By externalizing config to dedicated systems, you achieve centralized control, auditing, and dynamic updates without redeploying code. This paves the way for feature toggles and secret rotation in the next subsections.

9.4.3 Feature Flags & Dynamic Toggles

Feature flags let you enable or disable code paths at runtime, supporting safe rollouts, A/B testing, and instant rollbacks. Libraries like **FF4J**, **LaunchDarkly**, or **Unleash** integrate with your application via SDKs:

```
@Autowired FeatureManager featureManager;
public ResponseEntity<?> getDashboard() {
 if (featureManager.isActive("new-dashboard")) {
  return ResponseEntity.ok(newDashboardService.render());
 } else {
  return ResponseEntity.ok(oldDashboardService.render());
 }
}
```

Flags can be scoped by user, region, or percentage, enabling gradual rollouts. A typical flow:

1. Deploy code hidden behind a "dark launch" flag.
2. Enable flag for internal users.
3. Enable for 1 % of users, monitor metrics.
4. Roll out to 100 % once stable.

A feature-flag service UI displays toggle state, change history, and audit logs. Flags live in the same config store (Vault, Config Server), or in a dedicated feature-flag service. Diagram of dynamic toggles:

```
[Config Store] ——flags change——▶ [App Instances] ——apply new behavior
```

With feature flags, you decouple code deploys from feature releases, reducing risk and enabling continuous delivery. Up next, we turn to securing and rotating sensitive secrets.

9.4.4 Encrypting & Rotating Secrets

Storing plaintext secrets in environment variables or config files exposes risk; encryption at rest and regular rotation are essential practices. Vault's Transit secret engine encrypts and decrypts data without storing plaintext:

```
vault write transit/encrypt/mykey plaintext=$(base64 <<< "my-secret")
vault write transit/decrypt/mykey ciphertext="vault:v1:..."
```

Clients integrate via the Vault SDK:

```
String cipher = vaultTransitTemplate.encrypt("mykey", "db-password");
String plain = vaultTransitTemplate.decrypt("mykey", cipher);
```

Automated rotation policies in Vault generate new versions of keys and credentials, invalidating old ones. For database credentials:

```
vault write database/creds/app-role ttl="60m"
```

This returns a username/password pair valid for 60 minutes, rotated automatically. Kubernetes can mount secrets as projected volumes with short TTLs. CI/CD pipelines trigger secret rotation and gracefully reload applications using the Twelve-Factor "config" refresh endpoints. A security-focused flow:

```
[App]─encrypt/─▶[Vault Transit]─▶decrypt─▶[Secret Use]
```

By encrypting secrets in transit and at rest, and rotating them regularly, you minimize the blast radius of leaked credentials and meet compliance requirements without polluting domain code with encryption logic.

9.5 Security, Authentication & Authorization

9.5.1 Pluggable Authentication Providers

In a modular architecture, authentication logic belongs outside the core domain so you can swap providers without touching business code. Define a simple authentication SPI:

```
public interface AuthProvider {
  boolean authenticate(String username, String credential);
  UserDetails loadUser(String username);
}
```

Concrete implementations—LDAP, OAuth token introspection, SAML—reside in separate modules:

```
@Component("ldap")
public class LdapAuthProvider implements AuthProvider { ... }


@Component("oauth")
public class OAuthAuthProvider implements AuthProvider { ... }
```

At startup, a factory or Spring's @Primary selects which bean to wire into security filters. This approach prevents security logic from leaking into services; your OrderService receives a fully authenticated principal. You can add a new provider—Kerberos, certificate-based—by implementing the same interface and adjusting configuration. A Factory:

```
@Service
public class AuthProviderFactory {
 @Autowired Map<String, AuthProvider> providers;
 public AuthProvider get(String id) { return providers.get(id); }
}
```

Configuration in application.yml picks the active provider:

```
security:
 provider: ldap
```

By isolating authentication, you keep domain code clean and enable independent evolution of security mechanisms. Next, we build on authentication to enforce fine-grained access control via roles and attributes.

9.5.2 Role- and Attribute-Based Access Control

Once users are authenticated, authorization decides what they can do. **Role-Based Access Control (RBAC)** assigns users to roles (ADMIN, USER, GUEST), while **Attribute-Based Access Control (ABAC)** uses user, resource, and environmental attributes. Define a simple annotation:

```
@Target({ElementType.METHOD})
@Retention(RetentionPolicy.RUNTIME)
public @interface RequiresRole { String[] value(); }
```

An authorization interceptor checks:

```
@Around("@annotation(req)")
public Object checkRole(ProceedingJoinPoint p, RequiresRole req) throws Throwable {
 UserDetails u = SecurityContext.getCurrentUser();
 for (String role : req.value())
  if (u.getRoles().contains(role)) return p.proceed();
 throw new AccessDeniedException("Missing role: " + Arrays.toString(req.value()));
}
```

For ABAC, pass SpEL expressions:

```
@Target({ElementType.METHOD})
public @interface Requires { String expression(); }
```

And evaluate against a context of attributes. A policy might allow editing an order only if order.ownerId == currentUser.id and time is within business hours. The combination of RBAC and ABAC supports both coarse and fine-grained rules. An access decision flow:

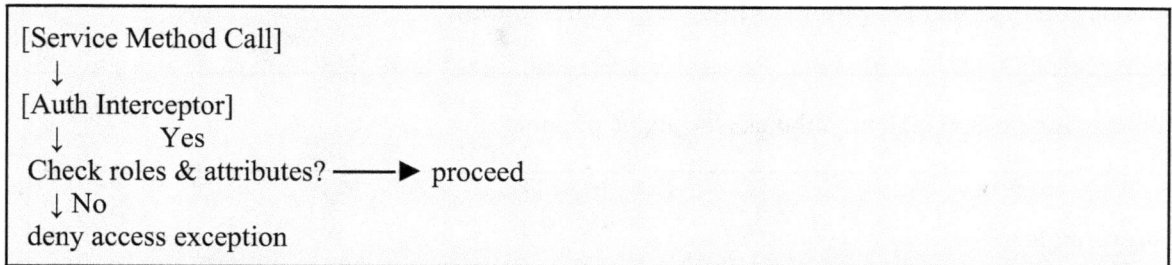

```
[Service Method Call]
   ↓
[Auth Interceptor]
   ↓        Yes
Check roles & attributes? ──────► proceed
   ↓ No
deny access exception
```

By handling authorization through interceptors and annotations, your core services remain free of security checks and easier to test. Next, we'll explore token-based protocols that tie authentication and authorization together.

9.5.3 OAuth2, JWT & Token Management

OAuth2 and JWT are de facto standards for federated authentication and stateless authorization. Your authentication service issues JWTs containing claims:

```
{
"sub":"user123",
"roles":["USER"],
"exp":1710000000
}
```

A Spring Security configuration:

```
http.oauth2ResourceServer()
  .jwt(jwt -> jwt.jwtAuthenticationConverter(jwtAuth -> {
  Collection<GrantedAuthority> ops = ((Jwt) jwtAuth.getToken()).getClaim("roles")
    .stream().map(SimpleGrantedAuthority::new).collect(Collectors.toList());
  return new JwtAuthenticationToken(jwtAuth.getToken(), ops);
  }));
```

Clients include the token in Authorization: Bearer <token>. On each request, the resource server validates signature and expiration using a public key:

```
spring:
 security:
  oauth2:
   resourceserver:
    jwt:
     jwk-set-uri: https://auth.example.com/.well-known/jwks.json
```

Implement **refresh tokens** to obtain new access tokens without re-authentication:

```
@PostMapping("/refresh")
public Token refresh(@RequestBody RefreshRequest req) { ... }
```

Store refresh tokens securely (HttpOnly cookies, encrypted store) and rotate them on use. Support token revocation via a blacklist or short expirations. A sequence flow:

```
[Client] → Auth Server: /login → receives (accessToken, refreshToken)
[Client] → API: Authorization: Bearer accessToken
[API] → Auth Server: refresh if accessToken expired using refreshToken
```

By standardizing on OAuth2 and JWT, your services speak a common language for authentication and authorization. Next, we'll secure inter-service calls with mTLS to prevent token misuse on the wire.

9.5.4 Securing Inter-Service Communication (mTLS)

Even with JWT, network eavesdroppers can steal tokens if TLS isn't mutually authenticated. **Mutual TLS** (mTLS) ensures both client and server present certificates, establishing strong service identities. In Istio or Linkerd, sidecar proxies handle mTLS automatically. In plain Java:

```
SSLContext sslContext = SSLContextBuilder.create()
 .loadKeyMaterial(keyStore, keyPassword.toCharArray())
 .loadTrustMaterial(trustStore, null)
 .build();
HttpClient client = HttpClients.custom().setSSLContext(sslContext).build();
```

Spring's RestTemplate:

```
@Bean
public RestTemplate restTemplate(SSLContext sslContext) {
 HttpClient http = HttpClients.custom().setSSLContext(sslContext).build();
 return new RestTemplate(new HttpComponentsClientHttpRequestFactory(http));
}
```

Servers configure a trust store of allowed client certificates and enforce requestClientCertificate=true. Certificate rotation is managed via an external vault or CA, with short-lived certs distributed to services. A high-level diagram:

```
[Service A] --mTLS handshake--> [Service B]
```

mTLS prevents unauthorized services from connecting, complements JWT by binding tokens to service identities, and protects in-flight secrets. With inter-service communication secured, we turn next to robust error handling and exception management.

9.6 Error Handling & Exception Management

9.6.1 Domain vs. Infrastructure Exceptions

Distinguishing domain exceptions (business rule violations) from infrastructure exceptions (network, database) is critical for proper handling. Domain exceptions—InsufficientInventoryException, InvalidOrderStateException—inherit from a base DomainException, carry meaningful codes, and indicate recoverable business errors. Infrastructure exceptions—DataAccessException, HttpTimeoutException—inherit from SystemException and often trigger retries or fallbacks. Define:

```
public abstract class AppException extends RuntimeException {
 private final String code;
 // constructors...
}


public class DomainException extends AppException { ... }
public class InfrastructureException extends AppException { ... }
```

Services catch and rethrow framework exceptions as InfrastructureException:

```
catch (SQLException ex) {
 throw new InfrastructureException("DB_ERROR", ex);
}
```

Business logic throws DomainException when invariants fail:

```
if (order.isEmpty()) throw new DomainException("ORDER_EMPTY");
```

A flow:

```
Service Call
  ↓
[try]
  ↓
Database → InfrastructureException → Retry/Alert
Business Rule → DomainException → Return 400 to client
```

This separation guides global handlers to respond with appropriate HTTP codes (4xx vs. 5xx) and to trigger different remediation paths. Next, we'll implement those global handlers.

9.6.2 Global Exception Handlers & Problem Details

Frameworks like Spring Boot provide global exception handling via @ControllerAdvice. You can map exceptions to standardized **Problem Details** (RFC 7807) payloads:

```
@ControllerAdvice
public class GlobalExceptionHandler {
 @ExceptionHandler(DomainException.class)
 @ResponseStatus(HttpStatus.BAD_REQUEST)
 @ResponseBody
 public ProblemDetail handleDomain(DomainException ex) {
  ProblemDetail pd = ProblemDetail.forStatus(HttpStatus.BAD_REQUEST);
  pd.setTitle("Business rule violation");
  pd.setDetail(ex.getMessage());
  pd.setProperty("code", ex.getCode());
  return pd;
 }
 @ExceptionHandler(InfrastructureException.class)
 @ResponseStatus(HttpStatus.SERVICE_UNAVAILABLE)
 @ResponseBody
 public ProblemDetail handleInfra(InfrastructureException ex) {
  ProblemDetail pd = ProblemDetail.forStatus(HttpStatus.SERVICE_UNAVAILABLE);
  pd.setTitle("Infrastructure failure");
  pd.setDetail("Please retry later");
  return pd;
 }
}
```

```
}
```

The JSON response:

```
{
"type":"about:blank",
"title":"Business rule violation",
"status":400,
"detail":"ORDER_EMPTY",
"code":"ORDER_EMPTY"
}
```

Clients gain consistent error schemas and can programmatically react based on the code. Global handlers also log exceptions and increment metrics. A sequence:

```
Controller → Service → throw DomainException
  ↓
GlobalExceptionHandler → maps to ProblemDetail → HTTP 400
```

Having a unified error format simplifies client-side error processing and maintains separation of concerns. Building atop this, we next explore how to incorporate retry and backoff policies.

9.6.3 Error Codes, Retries & Backoff Policies

When transient infrastructure errors occur—database deadlocks, timeouts—automatic retries with backoff can often resolve the issue without user impact. Use Resilience4j:

```
Retry retry = Retry.of("dbRetry", RetryConfig.custom()
 .maxAttempts(4)
 .waitDuration(Duration.ofMillis(200))
 .retryExceptions(InfrastructureException.class)
 .build());
Supplier<Order> decorated = Retry.decorateSupplier(retry, () -> repo.load(id));
```

Combine with an exponential backoff:

```
RetryConfig.custom()
 .intervalFunction(IntervalFunction.ofExponentialBackoff(200, 2.0))
```

A retry sequence:

```
Attempt1 → fail → wait 200ms → Attempt2 → fail → wait 400ms → Attempt3 ...
```

In .NET, use Polly:

```
var policy = Policy.Handle<InfrastructureException>()
.WaitAndRetryAsync(3, retryAttempt => TimeSpan.FromMilliseconds(100 * Math.Pow(2,
retryAttempt)));
```

Embed retries at the adapter layer, not in business logic, so services remain oblivious to transient errors. Log each retry attempt using a custom event publisher, and record retry metrics. For persistent failures after max attempts, a fallback or error response is triggered by the global handler. With retries in place, user-facing errors become rarer, and systems recover transparently. Next, we ensure those errors are presented in a user-friendly manner.

9.6.4 User-Friendly Error Responses

While machine-readable problem details serve clients, end users need clear, actionable messages. Map ProblemDetail codes to localized messages:

```
public class ErrorMessageResolver {
 @Autowired MessageSource msgSrc;
 public String resolve(ProblemDetail pd, Locale loc) {
  return msgSrc.getMessage("error."+pd.getProperty("code"), null, loc);
 }
}
```

In a REST controller:

```
@ExceptionHandler(DomainException.class)
public ResponseEntity<ErrorDto> onDomain(DomainException ex, Locale loc) {
 ProblemDetail pd = ...;
 String userMsg = resolver.resolve(pd, loc);
 return ResponseEntity.badRequest().body(new ErrorDto(pd.getCode(), userMsg));
}
```

ErrorDto:

```
{ "code":"ORDER_EMPTY","message":"Your order must contain at least one item." }
```

For HTML UIs, render error pages with friendly instructions:

```
<h1>Oops!</h1><p th:text="${message}"/>
```

Design generic fallback pages advising users to retry or contact support. Always avoid leaking sensitive details (stack traces) in user responses. By localizing and sanitizing error messages, you improve user experience while maintaining security. Transitioning, we next embed validation before the error-handling layer kicks in.

9.7 Validation & Input Sanitization

9.7.1 Declarative Validation (Annotations, DSLs)

Declarative validation keeps parameter checks out of business logic by using metadata on DTOs or entities. In Java, the Bean Validation API (javax.validation) offers annotations:

```
public class CreateOrderRequest {
 @NotNull @Size(min=1)
 private List<@Valid LineItem> items;
 @Pattern(regexp="\\d{5}")
 private String zipCode;
 // getters/setters...
}


public class LineItem {
 @NotNull private String sku;
 @Min(1) private int quantity;
}
```

Spring MVC automatically validates incoming requests when you annotate parameters:

```
@PostMapping("/orders")
public ResponseEntity<?> create(@Valid @RequestBody CreateOrderRequest req) { ... }
```

Violations produce MethodArgumentNotValidException, handled by a global handler to return a detailed field-error list. For richer DSLs, libraries like **FluentValidation** (.NET) or **Vavr Validate** (Java) let you compose rules in code:

```
Validator<CreateOrderRequest> validator = Validator.of(CreateOrderRequest.class)
 .rule(CreateOrderRequest::getZipCode, zip -> zip.matches("\\d{5}"), "Invalid zip");
```

Annotations and DSLs declare intent alongside data definitions, ensuring validation stays close to models and is automatically enforced. After catching structural issues, you can pipeline additional cross-field checks, explored next.

9.7.2 Pipeline-Based Validation Interceptors

Beyond simple annotations, complex validations—cross-field or database-backed—belong in a validation pipeline before business logic execution. In .NET MediatR:

```
public                    class                ValidationBehavior<TRequest,TResponse>               :
IPipelineBehavior<TRequest,TResponse> {
 private readonly IEnumerable<IValidator<TRequest>> _validators;
 public    async    Task<TResponse>    Handle(TRequest    req,    CancellationToken    ct,
RequestHandlerDelegate<TResponse> next) {
  var context = new ValidationContext<TRequest>(req);
  var failures = _validators.Select(v => v.Validate(context)).SelectMany(r => r.Errors).ToList();
  if (failures.Any()) throw new ValidationException(failures);
  return await next();
 }
}
```

Register it so every handler runs through validation interceptors. In Spring WebFlux, a custom HandlerFilterFunction intercepts Web requests:

```
public  Mono<ServerResponse>  filter(ServerRequest  req,  HandlerFunction<ServerResponse>
next) {
 return req.bodyToMono(CreateOrderRequest.class)
  .flatMap(body -> validator.validate(body))
  .flatMap(__ -> next.handle(req));
}
```

This pipeline catches invalid inputs early, returns 4xx, and prevents deeper layers from needing to guard. A pipeline flow:

```
[HTTP Request] → [Validation Interceptor] → [Auth Interceptor] → [Business Handler]
```

By centralizing validation logic in interceptors, you decouple it from both controllers and services, facilitating reuse and consistency. Next, we defend deeper against malicious inputs.

9.7.3 Defense-in-Depth: Sanitizing Inputs

Even after validation, inputs can contain dangerous content—XSS in rich text, SQL injection via poorly-escaped strings. Apply sanitization libraries at the edges. In Java, **OWASP Java HTML Sanitizer** cleans HTML:

```
PolicyFactory policy = Sanitizers.FORMATTING.and(Sanitizers.LINKS);
String safe = policy.sanitize(userInputHtml);
```

For SQL, always use parameterized queries or ORM parameter binding:

```
jdbcTemplate.queryForObject("SELECT * FROM users WHERE name = ?", new Object[]{name}, ...);
```

In Node.js, use **DOMPurify** for frontend XSS prevention and **parameterized queries** with pg:

```
const safeHtml = DOMPurify.sanitize(req.body.comment);
await db.query('INSERT INTO comments(text) VALUES($1)', [safeHtml]);
```

Sanitization at every I/O boundary—HTTP, messaging, batch file imports—guards against injection, cross-site scripting, and other attacks. Logging sanitized vs. raw input lengths aids debugging input issues. This defense-in-depth strategy ensures that even if one layer is bypassed, subsequent layers catch malicious content. Finally, we adapt validation for asynchronous and bulk scenarios.

9.7.4 Validation in Reactive & Batch Flows

Reactive streams and batch jobs require validation strategies that differ from request/response. In Spring WebFlux, leverage Validator and Reactor operators:

```
public Mono<ServerResponse> handle(ServerRequest req) {
 return req.bodyToMono(CreateOrderRequest.class)
  .flatMap(this::validateRequest)
  .flatMap(service::createOrder)
  .flatMap(order -> ServerResponse.ok().bodyValue(order));
}


private Mono<CreateOrderRequest> validateRequest(CreateOrderRequest req) {
 Errors errors = new BeanPropertyBindingResult(req, "order");
 validator.validate(req, errors);
 if (errors.hasErrors()) return Mono.error(new ValidationException(errors));
 return Mono.just(req);
}
```

Use flatMap and onErrorResume to catch and map validation errors to Problem Details. In batch processing (Spring Batch), configure ItemProcessor with a ValidatingItemProcessor:

```
@Bean
public ValidatingItemProcessor<MyItem> processor() {
 ValidatingItemProcessor<MyItem> proc = new ValidatingItemProcessor<>(itemValidator());
 proc.setFilter(true); // skip invalid items
 return proc;
}
```

Invalid items can be logged or routed to a dead-letter queue for manual review. A flow for batch:

```
[Reader] → [ValidatingItemProcessor] → [Writer]
    ↓
   [Invalid Items] → [DLQ/Report]
```

By embedding validation into reactive and batch pipelines, you maintain data quality and prevent downstream failures in asynchronous and high-volume scenarios. With sanitization and validation covered, we next explore caching strategies to optimize performance.

9.8 Caching Strategies

9.8.1 Cache-Aside, Read-Through & Write-Through

Caching patterns decide how data enters and exits the cache. In **cache-aside**, application code explicitly interacts with the cache:

```
public Order getOrder(String id) {
 Order o = cache.get(id);
 if (o == null) {
  o = repo.load(id);
  cache.put(id, o);
 }
 return o;
}
```

Read-through and **write-through** delegate caching to the cache provider. With Caffeine's read-through:

```
LoadingCache<String, Order> cache = Caffeine.newBuilder()
```

```
.expireAfterWrite(5, TimeUnit.MINUTES)
.build(id -> repo.load(id));
```

A simple cache.get(id) will fetch from repo when needed. **Write-through** writes to both cache and DB in one operation, ensuring consistency but potentially increasing write latency. For example:

```
public void saveOrder(Order o) {
 repo.save(o);
 cache.put(o.getId(), o);
}
```

Write-behind queues writes asynchronously to DB, improving throughput. Each pattern has trade-offs in consistency, complexity, and performance. Flow of cache-aside:

```
Client → Cache? → Miss → DB → Cache
```

Moving from explicit to provider-managed caching reduces boilerplate but requires careful eviction policies. Next, we decide between local and distributed caches.

9.8.2 Local vs. Distributed Caches (Caffeine, Redis)

Local caches (Caffeine, Guava) store data in-process, offering ultra-low latency but not shared across instances. Use them for purely ephemeral data (intra-request computations):

```
Cache<String, List<Product>> localCache = Caffeine.newBuilder()
 .maximumSize(10_000)
 .expireAfterAccess(10, TimeUnit.MINUTES)
 .build();
```

Distributed caches (Redis, Hazelcast) share state across all service instances:

```
JedisPool pool = new JedisPool("redis", 6379);
try (Jedis jedis = pool.getResource()) {
 jedis.setex("order:"+id, 300, orderJson);
}
```

Local caches suffer from cold starts and cache misses when scaling out. Distributed caches add network hops and potential single points of failure but provide coherent state. Use local caches for high-speed, low-value data, and distributed for shared session data, feature flags, or computed results used by many instances.

Combining local and distributed (two-level caching) optimizes both latency and hit rate. With cache locations chosen, we establish invalidation and eviction strategies.

9.8.3 Cache Invalidation & Eviction Policies

Cache invalidation prevents stale data. Common strategies: **time-to-live (TTL)** evicts entries after a duration, **least-recently-used (LRU)** evicts least accessed items, and **least-frequently-used (LFU)** evicts the least accessed over time. Caffeine configuration:

```
Caffeine.newBuilder()
.expireAfterWrite(10, TimeUnit.MINUTES)
.maximumSize(10000)
.evictionListener((key, value, cause) -> log.info("Evicted {} cause {}", key, cause))
.build();
```

For distributed caches, use Redis' expire command or volatile-lru eviction policy. Explicit invalidation on data change is critical:

```
public void updateOrder(Order o) {
repo.save(o);
cache.remove(o.getId());
}
```

Invalidate related entries in bulk when a parent entity changes. For event-driven systems, publish cache-invalidations:

```
DB Update → App publishes "order.updated" → Cache Service evicts keys
```

Balancing eviction frequency and TTLs reduces staleness while avoiding cache thrashing. Next, we warm caches and ensure consistency.

9.8.4 Cache Warming & Consistency

Cache warming pre-loads frequently accessed data at startup or after eviction storms. In Spring Boot:

```
@EventListener(ApplicationReadyEvent.class)
public void warmCaches() {
repo.findTop100Orders().forEach(o -> cache.put(o.getId(), o));
}
```

Alternatively, use background jobs to scan hot keys and refresh them periodically. Consistency between cache and DB can be maintained via **write-through** or **cache-aside** with immediate invalidation on writes. For distributed caches, use **Redisson's** RMapCache with RKeys.deleteByPattern() to evict namespaces on changes.

To handle multi-region caches, use a **consistent hashing** overlay so that warmed entries map to appropriate shards. Monitoring cache hit ratios (via Micrometer counters) helps assess warming effectiveness. If hit ratios remain low, adjust pre-loaded dataset or TTLs. By combining warming and strong invalidation policies, caches deliver both performance and freshness, completing our exploration of cross-cutting caching strategies.

9.9 Transaction & Concurrency Control

9.9.1 Local Transactions & Unit of Work

Local transactions ensure that a set of operations against a single datastore either all succeed or all fail, preserving consistency in the face of errors. In an ORM context, the Unit of Work (UoW) tracks all new, changed, and deleted entities in a transactional boundary, flushing them as a single atomic commit. For example, in Spring:

```
@Service
public class OrderService {
 @Transactional
 public void placeOrder(OrderRequest req) {
  Order order = orderFactory.create(req);
  orderRepository.save(order);
  inventoryService.reserve(order.getItems());
  paymentService.charge(order.getTotal());
 }
}
```

Here, if any exception is thrown—say, a payment failure—the entire transaction rolls back, undoing the database insert and any related changes. Under the hood, the EntityManager UoW collects entity state changes and issues batched SQL at commit. The UoW also caches entity identity, ensuring one in-memory instance per database row, avoiding inconsistent representations. Effective UoW implementations minimize database calls by identifying dirty entities and generating optimized SQL only for changed fields. The transactional boundary should be as narrow as possible—spanning only the minimum operations needed—so that long-running work (e.g., remote calls) does not hold database locks unnecessarily. By contrast, manual transaction demarcation (begin, commit, rollback) in code tends to scatter logic; annotations or AOP-based transactions keep code clean and declarative. Monitoring tools can instrument UoW flush durations and SQL counts per transaction, guiding performance tuning. With local transactions and a UoW pattern firmly in place, we now consider how transactional behavior propagates across method calls.

9.9.2 Transaction Propagation & Isolation Levels

Transaction propagation defines how nested or sequential method calls share or create new transactional contexts. Common propagation modes include REQUIRED—join an existing transaction or start a new one—and REQUIRES_NEW—always suspend the current transaction and begin a separate one. For instance:

```
@Transactional(propagation = Propagation.REQUIRES_NEW)
public void auditAction(AuditRecord record) { auditRepo.save(record); }
```

This ensures that audit writes commit even if the calling business transaction ultimately rolls back. Isolation levels (READ_UNCOMMITTED, READ_COMMITTED, REPEATABLE_READ, SERIALIZABLE) balance consistency against concurrency; e.g., SERIALIZABLE prevents phantom reads but can cause deadlocks under high contention. In Spring:

```
@Transactional(isolation = Isolation.REPEATABLE_READ)
public Order loadAndProcess(OrderId id) { ... }
```

Selecting the correct isolation level requires understanding typical conflict rates and read/write patterns. Lower isolation (e.g., READ_COMMITTED) scales better but may expose anomalies like non-repeatable reads; higher isolation increases locking and can throttle throughput under load. Testing different isolation levels in staging with representative workloads reveals deadlock frequency and latency impact. Transaction propagation also covers SUPPORTS, MANDATORY, and NESTED (spring's pseudo-nested savepoints), each serving special use cases—e.g., mandatory transactions enforce that a method must be called within an existing transaction. As we next explore locking strategies, these propagation and isolation settings form the backdrop for controlling concurrency within a single database.

9.9.3 Optimistic vs. Pessimistic Locking

Concurrency control in relational databases typically employs either **optimistic** or **pessimistic** locking. Optimistic locking assumes conflicts are rare; it detects them on commit by checking a version field:

```
@Entity
public class Account {
 @Version private long version;
 private BigDecimal balance;
}
```

If two transactions load the same Account, modify it, and commit, the second commit fails with an OptimisticLockException, prompting a retry. This strategy maximizes concurrency but requires retry logic in the application. Pessimistic locking, conversely, acquires database locks up front:

```
Account account = em.find(Account.class, id, LockModeType.PESSIMISTIC_WRITE);
```

This prevents other transactions from reading (depending on lock mode) or writing the locked row until the lock is released, avoiding retries but reducing throughput under contention. Choosing between them depends on update frequency and conflict likelihood: low-conflict domains favor optimistic locking, while high-conflict scenarios (e.g., inventory decrements under flash sales) benefit from pessimistic locks. Some databases support **select ... for update skip locked**, allowing transactions to lock available rows without blocking:

```
SELECT * FROM orders WHERE status='NEW' FOR UPDATE SKIP LOCKED;
```

This pattern enables worker pools to claim work items without deadlock With locking strategies chosen, we must consider concurrency beyond a single database instance.

9.9.4 Concurrency Control in Distributed Systems

Distributed systems cannot rely on a single database's locking; they require coordination across services. Techniques include **distributed transactions** (two-phase commit) and **eventual consistency** patterns like sagas. Since 2PC can introduce blocking under coordinator failure, more scalable designs use compensating actions: each service executes a local transaction and emits an event; if later stages fail, compensations undo prior work (Chapter 6.10). Another approach uses **optimistic concurrency** with a distributed version vector stored in a replicated store (Cassandra lightweight transactions). For caching or counters, **distributed locks** (e.g., Redis Redlock) guard critical sections:

```
RLock lock = redisson.getLock("orderLock:" + orderId);
if (lock.tryLock(100, 10, TimeUnit.SECONDS)) {
 try { // critical section } finally { lock.unlock(); }
}
```

However, distributed locks have pitfalls: clock skew and partial failures can cause multiple holders. Consensus algorithms like **Raft** (etcd, Consul) offer stronger guarantees for leadership election and distributed locking. For idempotent operations, use **idempotency keys**—clients include a unique key, and services store processed keys to reject duplicates:

```
@PostMapping("/payments")
```

```
public ResponseEntity<?> pay(@RequestBody PaymentRequest req) {
 if (idempotencyStore.contains(req.getKey())) return ResponseEntity.accepted().build();
 processPayment(req);
 idempotencyStore.save(req.getKey());
 return ResponseEntity.ok().build();
}
```

A diagram of a saga-based concurrency control:

```
[Order Service]—(OrderPlaced)→[Payment Service]—(PaymentSuccess)→[Shipping Service]
 ↑
 └—(OrderCanceled via Compensation if any step fails)
```

Distributed concurrency control demands careful design of idempotency, retries, and failure compensation strategies. As we complete this section, our next focus is on auditing and compliance, ensuring all sensitive operations remain traceable and meet regulatory requirements.

9.10 Auditing & Compliance

9.10.1 Audit Trails in the Domain Layer

An audit trail records domain events—who did what, when, and how—in an immutable store, supporting both debugging and regulatory compliance. Instead of scattering logging statements, you capture domain events explicitly:

```
public class Order {
 public void pay(User user, PaymentInfo info) {
  if (!isPaid()) {
   apply(new OrderPaidEvent(id, user.getId(), info.getAmount(), Instant.now()));
  } else {
   throw new DomainException("ORDER_ALREADY_PAID");
  }
 }
 @EventListener
 public void on(OrderPaidEvent ev) {
  auditService.record(ev);
  // update state...
 }
}
```

OrderPaidEvent implements a marker interface, and auditService writes structured records to an append-only store. Domain events include metadata—user ID, correlation ID, timestamp—and carry enough context to reconstruct what happened. Storing them in a dedicated audit database or schema prevents mixing with operational data and allows streamlined querying for compliance reports. A domain-centric audit approach decouples audit concerns from transaction logic: event handlers can run in separate threads or microservices, ensuring minimal impact on core flows. With clear audit events, you can produce chronological timelines of key actions, essential for financial audits or security investigations. As events propagate, audit logs remain immutable; any attempt to alter or delete audit records is itself recorded. Next, we capture domain events in an append-only event log.

9.10.2 Append-Only Event Logs

Append-only event logs underpin both auditing and event sourcing, providing a sequential, immutable record of all state changes. Tools like **Kafka** or **EventStore** offer built-in append-only semantics with high throughput and segment retention. When a domain event occurs, it's serialized and published:

```
kafkaTemplate.send("domain-events", ev.getAggregateId().toString(), ev);
```

Downstream consumers—projections, audit services, or integration bridges—subscribe and process events idempotently. The log's immutable nature guarantees that past events cannot be altered or lost without detection. Event replay allows rebuilding read models or recovering from schema changes. A simple event-sourcing flow:

```
[Aggregate]——ev1,ev2,ev3→[EventLog]→ Rebuild → [ReadModel]
```

Events carry version numbers to detect concurrent modifications; if versions mismatch, the write is rejected, enforcing optimistic concurrency. Snapshotting long event streams prevents unbounded replay costs: periodically write the aggregate's current state to a snapshot store. Retention policies archive old segments to cold storage, ensuring log size remains manageable. With append-only logs in place, we can address stricter data-privacy regulations in the next subsection.

9.10.3 GDPR, CCPA & Data Privacy Considerations

Regulations like GDPR and CCPA impose user rights—data access, rectification, erasure—that challenge immutable logs. To comply with "right to be forgotten," you must either avoid storing personal data in raw form or encrypt personal fields with revocable keys. A pattern:

```java
public class UserEmailChangedEvent implements DomainEvent {
 private final String userId;
 @Encrypted private final String newEmail;
}
```

On erasure request, you rotate the encryption key or delete key material, rendering stored email ciphertext unrecoverable. Alternatively, maintain a separate personal data store that can be purged, while logs reference pseudonymous identifiers. Auditing data access to personal records is itself a privacy requirement: record who queried or exported user data. Build automated workflows: upon user request, redact or anonymize data in read models and caches, then update audit entries to note the erasure.

Implement legal hold exemptions: if data must be retained for litigation, flag records as immutable and exempt from deletion. Regular audits of data life-cycle—automated reviews of personal data retention—ensure continuous compliance. With privacy handled, we define retention and archiving strategies to complete compliance.

9.10.4 Retention Policies & Data Archiving

Regulatory and business requirements dictate how long different data must be kept. For example, financial transactions may require seven-year retention, while logs older than 30 days can be purged. Define retention policies in your storage systems: Elasticsearch ILM, Kafka retention.ms, or S3 lifecycle rules:

```
{
"Rules": [
 { "ID":"seven-year","Prefix":"transactions/","Status":"Enabled",
  "Expiration":{"Days":2555}}
]
}
```

Automate data archival to cost-effective storage: daily snapshots stored in AWS Glacier or Google Archive buckets. Implement data purging jobs that delete expired records and record deletion actions in the audit log. A flow:

```
[Data Ingestion] → [Primary Store] → [Archival Job after retention] → [Archive]
                        ↓
                   [Delete from Primary]
```

Ensure referential integrity: if parent data is archived, either cascade archives of related data or anonymize child records. Provide discovery tools for archived data to support legal or analytical queries. Regularly test restore processes to validate archive integrity. By codifying retention and archiving, you align your architecture with both operational efficiency and legal mandates. Having secured auditing and compliance, we now internationalize our application for global audiences.

9.11 Internationalization & Localization

9.11.1 Externalizing Resource Bundles

To support multiple languages and regions, all user-facing text must be externalized into resource bundles rather than hard-coded. In Java, use ResourceBundle:

```
# messages_en.properties
welcome=Welcome, {0}!
# messages_fr.properties
welcome=Bienvenue, {0} !
```

Load via Spring:

```
@Autowired MessageSource msgSrc;
public String welcome(String user, Locale loc) {
 return msgSrc.getMessage("welcome", new Object[]{user}, loc);
}
```

In Angular, leverage ngx-translate with JSON files:

```
// en.json
{ "welcome": "Welcome, {{name}}!" }
// fr.json
{ "welcome": "Bienvenue, {{name}} !" }
```

A template:

```
<h1>{{ 'welcome' | translate:{name: user.name} }}</h1>
```

Organize bundles hierarchically by module or feature to avoid monolithic files. Version resource files alongside code to maintain alignment. A directory structure:

```
src/main/resources/i18n/
 orders_en.properties
 orders_fr.properties
 errors_en.properties
 errors_fr.properties
```

Continuous localization pipelines extract new keys, send them to translators, and integrate translations via automated PRs. With resource bundles in place, we can focus on formatting values per locale.

9.11.2 Culture-Aware Formatting (Dates, Numbers)

Different locales format dates, numbers, and currencies differently. Leverage locale-aware formatters instead of toString(). In Java:

```
DateTimeFormatter fmt = DateTimeFormatter.ofPattern("dd MMM yyyy", loc);
String formattedDate = LocalDate.now().format(fmt);


NumberFormat nf = NumberFormat.getCurrencyInstance(loc);
String money = nf.format(1234.56);
```

In JavaScript, use Intl API:

```
new Intl.DateTimeFormat('de-DE').format(new Date());
// → "14.5.2025"


new Intl.NumberFormat('en-IN', { style: 'currency', currency: 'INR' })
 .format(123456.78);
// → "□ 1,23,456.78"
```

Embed formatters in UI components and DTO serializers. Avoid mixing raw values and formatted strings; transport data in canonical forms (ISO 8601, JSON numbers) and render formatting in the presentation layer. A flow:

```
[Canonical Data] → [Formatter Service with Locale] → [Localized String]
```

Locale negotiation reads Accept-Language headers or user preferences stored in profiles. With culture-aware formatting set, next we address bidirectional text and layouts.

9.11.3 Right-to-Left & Bidirectional Layout

Languages like Arabic or Hebrew require right-to-left (RTL) rendering and bidirectional text support. In web CSS:

```
html[dir="rtl"] {
 direction: rtl;
```

```
unicode-bidi: embed;
}
.container {
margin-left: auto;
margin-right: 0;
}
```

Dynamically set <html dir="rtl"> based on locale. UI component libraries (Bootstrap, Material) offer RTL mirrored styles. For text containing mixed LTR/RTL, use Unicode control characters ‎ and ‏ or wrap spans with dir attributes:

```
<span dir="rtl">مرحبا</span><span dir="ltr"> World</span>
```

In native applications, platform APIs (Android's setLayoutDirection, iOS' semanticContentAttribute) manage mirroring.

```
[ LTR text ] ← embedded ← [ RTL segment ] ← back to LTR
```

Ensure numeric data remains LTR within RTL contexts by wrapping with 123. Testing with diverse language inputs uncovers layout glitches. With bidirectional layout handled, we next tackle grammatical nuances.

9.11.4 Pluralization, Gender & Context

Natural languages vary in plural forms and gender. English has two forms ("1 item", "2 items"), while Russian has three, and Arabic up to six. Resource bundles support plural rules:

```
# messages_en.properties
cart.items=You have {count, plural, one {# item} other {# items}} in your cart.
```

In ICU message format:

```
{
"cart.items": "You have {count, plural, one {# item} other {# items}} in your cart."
}
```

For gender:

```
# messages_fr.properties
```

```
welcome={gender, select, male {Bienvenue, Monsieur} female {Bienvenue, Madame} other
{Bienvenue}}
```

Use ICU4J or Java's MessageFormat with plural/gender extensions. In JavaScript, libraries like **i18next** support ICU syntax. Contextual keys handle subtle differences:

```
"button.save": "Save",
"button.save_confirmation": "Are you sure you want to save?"
```

Organize keys by context (button., *error.*, label.*) to avoid collisions. Regularly test translations with pseudo-localization—wrapping text in brackets or expanding length to uncover UI truncation issues. Addressing pluralization and gender completes a robust localization strategy. Having internationalized the UI, we turn next to background tasks and scheduling.

9.12 Background Tasks & Scheduling

9.12.1 Cron-Style vs. Event-Driven Scheduling

Background work can run on fixed schedules (cron) or be triggered by events. Cron-style scheduling uses time expressions:

```
@Scheduled(cron = "0 0 2 * * ?") // daily at 2 AM
public void nightlyReport() { reportService.generate(); }
```

Spring's @EnableScheduling manages a thread pool for these tasks. Cron jobs are predictable but static; changing schedules requires redeploying code or externalizing expressions to config. In contrast, **event-driven** scheduling reacts to domain events or external triggers:

```
@KafkaListener(topics = "user-registered")
public void onUserRegistered(UserRegistered ev) {
 onboardingService.start(ev.getUserId());
}
```

This approach scales with workload and avoids idle resources but can lead to burstiness under event floods. Hybrid models use both: cron for housekeeping (cleanup, reports) and event listeners for transactional workflows.

```
┌─────── Cron Scheduler ──→ Nightly Task
└─────── Event Bus ──→ Event Listener
```

Selecting the right mechanism depends on task characteristics—time-based maintenance vs. reactive flows. Next, we integrate these tasks with scalable worker pools.

9.12.2 Task Queues & Worker Pools

For long-running or CPU-intensive jobs, offload work to task queues and worker pools. In Spring Batch:

```
@EnableBatchProcessing
public class BatchConfig {
 @Bean
 public Job importJob(JobBuilderFactory jb, Step s) {
  return jb.get("importJob").start(s).build();
 }
 @Bean
 public Step step(StepBuilderFactory sb) {
  return sb.get("step").<Input,Output>chunk(100)
   .reader(reader()).processor(proc()).writer(writer()).build();
 }
}
```

Chunking processes records in batches with commit intervals. For distributed queues, use RabbitMQ or AWS SQS:

```
@Autowired AmqpTemplate rabbit;
rabbit.convertAndSend("task-queue", taskDto);
```

Workers consume:

```
@RabbitListener(queues = "task-queue")
public void handleTask(TaskDto dto) { taskService.execute(dto); }
```

Configure concurrency—number of threads or containers—to match capacity. Monitor queue depth and processing rate to autoscale workers. Idempotent handlers (next subsection) ensure safe retries.

Proper queue and worker design ensures that background tasks execute reliably and scale independently from the API tier.

9.12.3 Idempotency & Exactly-Once Processing

Messaging and scheduling systems often deliver messages at least once, risking duplicate processing. Designing idempotent tasks is critical: handlers record a unique key per task (message ID, business ID) before executing work:

```
public void handleTask(TaskDto dto) {
 if (processedStore.contains(dto.getId())) return;
 processedStore.save(dto.getId());
 performWork(dto);
}
```

Alternatively, use a database lock on the key to guarantee once-only execution. For true **exactly-once** semantics, use transactional outbox patterns: store task requests in the application database within the same transaction as business data, then publish to the queue via a background poller:

```
INSERT INTO outbox(event_type,payload) VALUES('Task',...');
```

A separate process reads the outbox and sends messages, then marks them as sent—all within a single database transaction. This ensures tasks are published exactly once relative to business data changes.

```
[Business Transaction] ——> insert outbox row ——> commit
 ├—> actual state change
 └—> outbox poller ▲
        └—> publish queue
```

Combining idempotent handlers with transactional outbox guarantees reliable task execution, even under failures and network partitions. Next, we coordinate tasks across distributed locks and leader election.

9.12.4 Distributed Locks & Leader Election

Some scheduled or background tasks must run only on a single node to avoid duplication—e.g., cleanup jobs. Implement distributed locks via Redis, ZooKeeper, or Consul sessions. Using Redisson:

```
RLock lock = redisson.getLock("cleanupLock");
if (lock.tryLock(0, 5, TimeUnit.MINUTES)) {
 try { cleanupService.run(); }
 finally { lock.unlock(); }
}
```

For leader election, frameworks like **Spring Integration** or **Istio** leverage leases:

```
@Test
public void startElection() {
 LeaderInitiator initiator = new LeaderInitiator(registry, "app-election");
 initiator.start();
}
```

Nodes watch the election key; the winner performs scheduled work, while others standby. Kubernetes' **Lease API** provides a native leader election:

```
kubectl apply -f - <<EOF
apiVersion: coordination.k8s.io/v1
kind: Lease
metadata:
 name: myapp-leader
 namespace: default
EOF
```

Controllers use client libraries to acquire and renew the lease. If the leader fails to renew, another node assumes leadership. Distributed locks and leader election ensure singleton task execution without central coordination code in your domain. With this final cross-cutting concern covered, you now have a comprehensive toolkit to manage the needs of a modern, maintainable architecture— keeping your core business logic clean, testable, and free from pollution.

Conclusion

By elevating cross-cutting concerns into dedicated abstractions and avoiding their direct pollution of domain classes, you preserve the clarity and testability of your core logic. Whether through aspect-oriented programming, interceptor pipelines, or sidecar patterns, each concern finds a natural home without tangling dependencies. The result is a maintainable architecture where infrastructure needs—security, observability, configuration, and scheduling—are managed consistently and transparently, allowing teams to innovate on business features with confidence and agility.

Chapter 10. Front-End Clean Architecture

Modern user interfaces have evolved from simple page refreshes to rich, interactive applications that rival their server-side counterparts in complexity. As applications grow, mixing presentation logic, state management, and business rules directly in UI components leads to tangled code, difficult testing, and brittle feature delivery. Front-End Clean Architecture brings the same principles of dependency inversion, separation of concerns, and explicit boundaries—long prized in back-end systems—to the client side. By clearly separating UI rendering from application workflows and domain logic, you gain modularity that supports parallel development, reusability across platforms, and confident refactoring. Whether you're building a web single-page app, a mobile client, or a desktop interface, applying these architectural techniques ensures your front end remains scalable, testable, and resilient as user requirements and underlying services evolve.

10.1 Principles of Front-End Clean Architecture

10.1.1 Layered Separation: UI, Application & Domain

In a clean front-end architecture, we separate responsibilities into distinct layers: the **UI layer** handles rendering and user interactions, the **application layer** orchestrates user flows and use-case logic, and the **domain layer** encapsulates core business rules and entities. The UI layer is thin—components receive data and callbacks via props or context, and never directly manipulate domain objects. Instead, they delegate to application services through well-defined interfaces. The application layer contains controllers or services that interpret UI events (e.g., "Add to cart"), perform validation, coordinate multiple domain actions, and invoke domain operations. These services know neither about rendering libraries nor HTTP clients—they depend only on domain interfaces and application ports.

The domain layer sits at the core, containing entities, value objects, and domain services with no dependencies on UI or network. For example, a Cart entity defines methods like addItem(item: Product, qty: number) and enforces invariants (no negative quantities). This approach ensures that business logic can be exercised in isolation, via unit tests, without bootstrapping UI frameworks or web APIs.

A typical folder structure reflecting these layers:

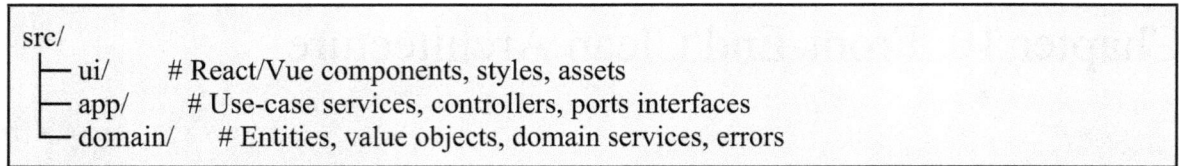

```
src/
├── ui/        # React/Vue components, styles, assets
├── app/       # Use-case services, controllers, ports interfaces
└── domain/    # Entities, value objects, domain services, errors
```

A PlantUML diagram of dependencies:

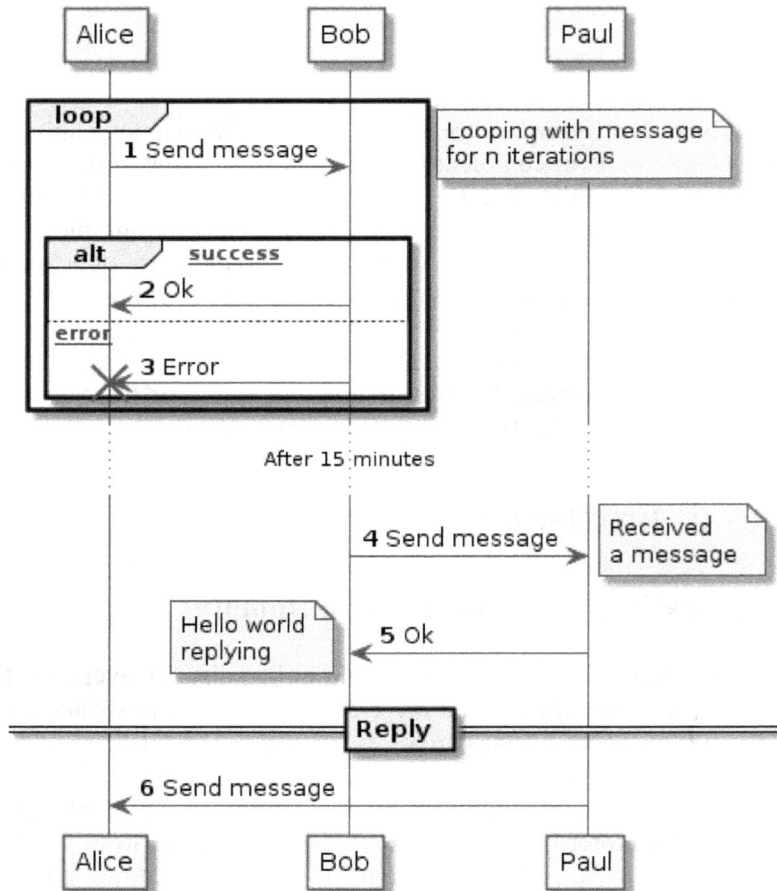

By confining dependencies inward, we maintain a stable core—domain code doesn't change when UI frameworks evolve. This layered separation leads directly to enforcing the dependency rule in browser-based code, which we explore next.

10.1.2 Dependency Rule in the Browser

The **Dependency Rule** mandates that source code dependencies can only point inward, toward higher-level policies. In the browser, this means that UI components must not import domain entities directly; instead, they depend on application layer abstractions. For example, a React component should import an OrderController interface from app/controller.ts, but never import Order or Money classes from domain. At compile time, bundlers (Webpack, Rollup) can enforce these boundaries with aliasing or path constraints:

```
// tsconfig.json
{
 "compilerOptions": {
  "baseUrl": "src",
  "paths": {
   "domain/*": ["domain/*"],
   "app/*": ["app/*"],
   "ui/*": ["ui/*"]
  }
 }
}
```

Lint rules (ESLint's no-restricted-imports) prevent accidental inward violations:

```
// .eslintrc.json
{
 "rules": {
  "no-restricted-imports": [
   "error",
   { "paths": [{ "name": "../domain", "message": "UI must not depend on domain directly." }] }
  ]
 }
}
```

Enforcing this rule ensures that changes to domain code (e.g., refactoring value objects) never ripple into UI code, reducing regression risk. A browser import graph might look like:

```
ui/ProductList.tsx → app/ProductUseCases.ts → domain/Product.ts
```

Rather than:

```
ui/ProductList.tsx → domain/Product.ts
```

By codifying te Dependency Rule, we establish clear contracts between layers. Having enforced architectural boundaries, we now define how to model the glue between the front end and its dependencies via ports and adapters.

10.1.3 Defining Front-End Ports & Adapters

Just as back-end code uses ports and adapters to isolate external concerns, the front end defines **ports** (interfaces) in the application layer for data access, navigation, and persistence, and implements them in adapters in the UI layer. For instance, an IProductService port describes methods returning domain objects:

```
// app/ports/IProductService.ts
import { Product } from "../domain/Product";
export interface IProductService {
 fetchAll(): Promise<Product[]>;
 fetchById(id: string): Promise<Product>;
}
```

The UI layer provides an adapter using HTTP or GraphQL:

```
// ui/adapters/HttpProductService.ts
import { IProductService } from "app/ports/IProductService";
import { Product } from "domain/Product";
export class HttpProductService implements IProductService {
 async fetchAll(): Promise<Product[]> {
  const resp = await fetch("/api/products");
  return (await resp.json()) as Product[];
 }
 async fetchById(id: string): Promise<Product> { … }
}
```

Components or application controllers receive the adapter via dependency injection or context:

```
// ui/contexts/ServiceContext.tsx
export const ServiceContext = createContext<{ productService: IProductService }>(…);
```

```
<ServiceContext.Provider value={{ productService: new HttpProductService() }}>
 <App />
</ServiceContext.Provider>
```

Adapters can be swapped for mocks in tests or alternative implementations (IndexedDB, local mocks) without touching application code. A sequence diagram:

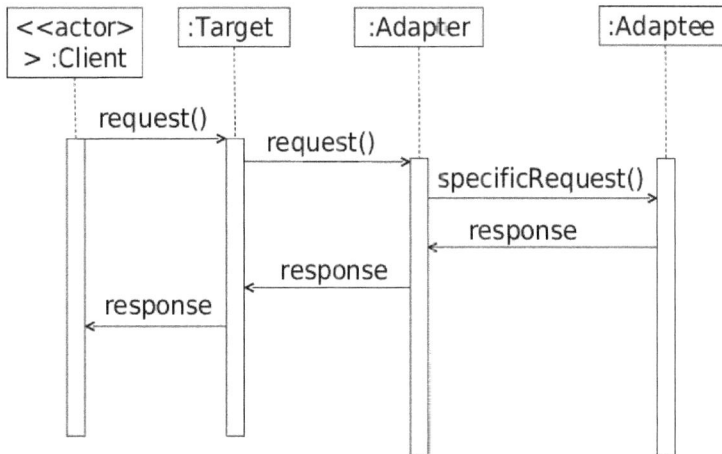

By defining front-end ports and adapters, we keep application and domain code free of UI framework details and network concerns. With abstractions in place, we turn to organizing UI components for maximum reusability.

10.2 Component-Based Architecture

10.2.1 Atomic Design & Design Systems

Atomic Design breaks UI into hierarchical building blocks: **atoms** (buttons, inputs), **molecules** (form fields with labels), **organisms** (navigation bars), **templates**, and **pages**. This methodology encourages consistency and reusability. For example, an Input atom:

```
// ui/components/atoms/Input.tsx
export interface InputProps { value: string; onChange (v:string)=>void; }
export const Input: React.FC<InputProps> = ({value,onChange}) => (
 <input value={value} onChange={e=>onChange(e.target.value)} />
);
```

A molecule composes atoms:

```
// ui/components/molecules/LabeledInput.tsx
import { Input } from "../atoms/Input";
export const LabeledInput: React.FC<{label:string,value:string, onChange:(v:string)=>void}> =
({label,value,onChange}) => (
 <label><span>{label}</span><Input value={value} onChange={onChange}/></label>
);
```

Organisms combine molecules:

```
// ui/components/organisms/LoginForm.tsx
import { LabeledInput } from "../molecules/LabeledInput";
export const LoginForm = () => { /* uses two LabeledInputs and a Button atom */ };
```

Design systems unify these components with shared themes, tokens, and documentation (Storybook).
Tokens define spacing, color, typography:

```
// design-tokens.json
{ "color": { "primary": "#0055FF", "secondary": "#FF5500" }, "spacing": { "sm": "8px", "md":
"16px" } }
```

A Storybook story:

```
// ui/stories/Input.stories.tsx
export default { title: "Atoms/Input", component: Input };
export const Default = () => <Input value="" onChange={()=>{}} />;
```

Atomic Design ensures UI consistency at scale. With components organized, we next distinguish between presentational and container components to encapsulate logic and rendering.

10.2.2 Presentational vs. Container Components

Presentational components focus solely on how things look; they receive data and callbacks via props and avoid side effects or subscriptions. **Container components** handle data fetching, state, and orchestration, passing the results to presentational children. For example:

```
// Presentational
export const ProductListView: React.FC<{products:Product[], onSelect:(id:string)=>void}> =
({products,onSelect}) => (
```

```
<ul>{products.map(p => <li key={p.id} onClick={()=>onSelect(p.id)}>{p.name}</li>)}</ul>
);


// Container
export const ProductList: React.FC = () => {
 const { productService } = useContext(ServiceContext);
 const [products, setProducts] = useState<Product[]>([]);
 useEffect(() => { productService.fetchAll().then(setProducts); }, []);
 return <ProductListView products={products} onSelect={id=>navigate(`/products/${id}`)} />;
};
```

Containers may handle loading and error states, while views render static layouts. This separation simplifies testing: you can unit-test ProductListView by passing dummy props without mocking services. Presentational components live in ui/components/presentational/, while containers live in ui/components/containers/. A diagram:

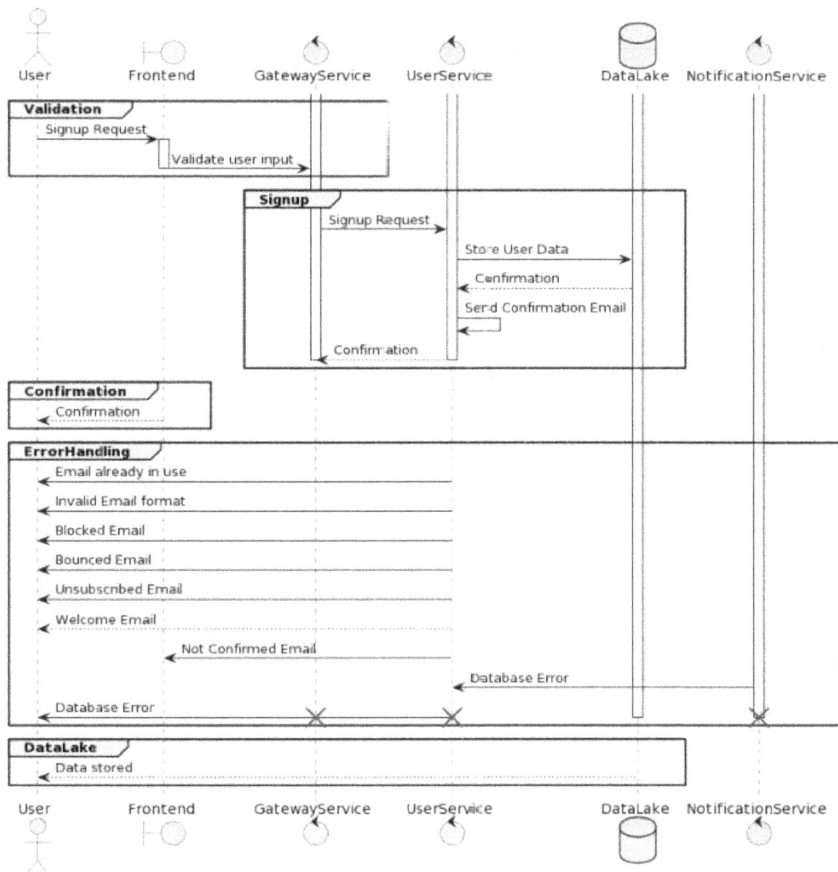

Maintaining this distinction promotes reuse—views can be used in multiple contexts—and aligns with clean architecture's separation of concerns. Having organized components into views and containers, we turn to composition patterns that avoid deep inheritance hierarchies.

10.2.3 Composition over Inheritance

In modern UI frameworks like React or Vue, component composition reigns over class inheritance. Rather than extending base component classes, you compose behavior via props, hooks, or higher-order components (HOCs). For example, a withLoading HOC:

```
function withLoading<P>(Component: React.ComponentType<P>) {
 return (props: P & {isLoading:boolean}) => {
 if (props.isLoading) return <Spinner />;
 return <Component {...props} />;
 };
}
```

You wrap a UserListView:

```
const UserListWithLoading = withLoading(UserListView);
<UserListWithLoading isLoading={loading} users={users} />;
```

Hooks provide another composition mechanism:

```
function useFetch<T>(service: ()=>Promise<T>) {
 const [data, setData] = useState<T|undefined>();
 useEffect(() => { service().then(setData); }, []);
 return data;
}


export const UserList = () => {
 const users = useFetch(()=>userService.fetchAll());
 if (!users) return <Spinner />;
 return <UserListView users={users} />;
};
```

Props like children allow component nesting:

```
<Modal>
 <Form>...</Form>
</Modal>
```

By favoring composition, you avoid rigid inheritance chains and gain flexibility in assembling behaviors. Composition also aligns with clean architecture's emphasis on explicit dependencies and small, reusable modules. With composition patterns established, we can focus on building robust UI libraries for cross-project consistency.

10.2.4 Building Reusable UI Libraries

A reusable UI library packages design system components and utilities for consumption across multiple applications. Using tools like **Lerna**, **Nx**, or **Bit**, you create a monorepo:

```
packages/
    ├── ui-atoms/
    ├── ui-molecules/
    ├── ui-organisms/
    └── themes/
```

Each package exports components and types with strict versioning. In ui-atoms/package.json:

```
{
 "name": "@myorg/ui-atoms",
 "main": "dist/index.js",
 "types": "dist/index.d.ts"
}
```

Build scripts compile TypeScript to ES modules, generate declaration files, and bundle styling (CSS Modules or styled-components). Consumers import:

```
import { Button, Input } from "@myorg/ui-atoms";
```

Use **Storybook** or **Styleguidist** for visual documentation and testing. Automate releases with semantic-release, generating changelogs and publishing to npm. Implement peerDependencies for React to avoid multiple React instances. By treating UI primitives as independent libraries, you ensure consistent look and feel, accelerate feature delivery, and reduce duplication across front-end teams. Transitioning from a well-factored component library, we now address client-side state management to coordinate data across components.

10.3 State Management

10.3.1 Local Component State vs. Global Stores

Managing state on the front end begins with distinguishing between **local component state**—transient, UI-specific data—and **global application state** that multiple components share. Local state lives in hooks (useState) or component properties, ideal for form inputs, toggles, and ephemeral UI flags:

```
const [isOpen, setIsOpen] = useState(false);
```

Global stores—Redux, MobX, Context API—hold application-wide state like authenticated user info, shopping cart contents, or feature flags. For example, using Context:

```
const CartContext = createContext<Cart>([]);
```

Components subscribe to CartContext and re-render on updates. Global state avoids prop drilling but can introduce unnecessary re-renders if not scoped carefully; use selectors or memoization (useMemo) to optimize. Encourage local state where coupling is low, and reserve global stores for truly shared domains.

By consciously placing state, you keep components predictable and prevent spaghetti data flows. With state locations determined, we adopt Flux patterns for more structured global stores.

10.3.2 Flux-Style Containers (Redux, NgRx, MobX)

Flux-style architectures centralize application state in a single store, update it via actions, and notify subscribers through a unidirectional data flow. In Redux:

```
// actions.ts
export const ADD_TO_CART = "ADD_TO_CART";
export interface AddToCart { type: typeof ADD_TO_CART; payload: Product; }


// reducer.ts
export function cartReducer(state: Product[] = [], action: AddToCart) {
 switch(action.type) {
  case ADD_TO_CART: return [...state, action.payload];
  default: return state;
 }
}
```

Dispatch actions:

```
dispatch({ type: ADD_TO_CART, payload: product });
```

Selectors derive slices of state:

```
export const selectCartItems = (state: AppState) => state.cart;
```

NgRx (Angular) and MobX (observable objects) offer similar patterns with different trade-offs: NgRx uses RxJS observables and effects, while MobX uses mutable observables and decorators.

Flux enforces clear state transitions and simplifies debugging with tools like Redux DevTools, which record each action and state diff. With structured global stores, we can model client-side state to reflect domain constructs.

10.3.3 Modeling Domain State on the Client

While back ends use rich domain models, the front end often reduces entities to plain data structures, risking loss of invariants. Instead, mirror domain concepts in client code with TypeScript classes or factories:

```
// domain/Cart.ts
export class Cart {
constructor(private items: CartItem[] = []) {}
add(item: CartItem) {
 if (this.items.find(i=>i.id===item.id)) { /* update qty */ }
 else this.items.push(item);
}
total(): number { return this.items.reduce((sum,i)=>sum+i.price*i.qty, 0); }
}
```

Serialize and deserialize when persisting to Redux or storage:

```
const cart = Cart.fromJSON(storedCart);
```

This approach keeps business rules close to state, enabling clients to enforce domain invariants without round trips. Use factories or builder patterns for complex aggregates. When mapping HTTP responses:

```
const resp = await api.fetchCart();
```

```
const cart = Cart.fromJSON(resp);
```

By maintaining domain models on the client, you reduce mismatch between front and back ends, simplify state transitions, and improve developer ergonomics with IntelliSense and type safety. Having a robust domain model on the client, we next handle asynchronous side effects like API calls.

10.3.4 Handling Side-Effects: Sagas, Epics, Effects

Side effects—API calls, routing, local storage—should be isolated from reducers or components. Redux-Saga leverages generator functions:

```
function* fetchCartSaga() {
try {
 const cart = yield call(api.fetchCart);
 yield put({ type: "FETCH_CART_SUCCESS", payload: cart });
} catch (e) {
 yield put({ type: "FETCH_CART_FAILURE", error: e });
}
}
```

Connect saga to actions:

```
function* rootSaga() {
 yield takeEvery("FETCH_CART_REQUEST", fetchCartSaga);
}
```

Redux-Observable (Epics) uses RxJS:

```
const fetchCartEpic = action$ => action$
.ofType("FETCH_CART_REQUEST")
.mergeMap(() => ajax.getJSON("/api/cart")
.map(response => ({ type: "FETCH_CART_SUCCESS", payload: response }))
.catch(error => of({ type: "FETCH_CART_FAILURE", error }))
);
```

NgRx Effects pattern similarly:

```
fetchCart$ = createEffect(() =>
 this.actions$.pipe(
  ofType(CartActions.fetch),
```

```
mergeMap(() =>
 this.cartService.get().pipe(
  map(cart => CartActions.fetchSuccess({ cart })),
  catchError(err => of(CartActions.fetchFailure({ error: err })))
 )
 )
 )
);
```

Decoupling side effects into sagas, epics, or effects keeps reducers pure and components predictable. Testing side effects becomes simpler: you can invoke sagas or epics with fake stores and assert emitted actions. With effect handlers in place, we transition into data fetching and caching patterns that underlie these effects.

10.4 Data Fetching & Caching

10.4.1 Abstracting Data Services Behind Interfaces

To decouple components from HTTP details, encapsulate all network calls in service classes conforming to application ports (see 10.1.3). For instance, define:

```
// app/ports/IUserApi.ts
export interface IUserApi {
 getUser(id: string): Promise<User>;
 updateUser(u: User): Promise<User>;
}
```

Implement in an adapter:

```
// ui/adapters/AxiosUserApi.ts
import axios from "axios";
export class AxiosUserApi implements IUserApi {
 getUser(id: string) {
  return axios.get(`/api/users/${id}`).then(res => res.data as User);
 }
 updateUser(u: User) {
  return axios.put(`/api/users/${u.id}`, u).then(res => res.data as User);
 }
}
```

Components or effects import only IUserApi, enabling easy swapping for mocks or GraphQL clients. This abstraction prevents UI code from proliferating HTTP logic and supports consistent error handling and request logging in the adapter. A sequence:

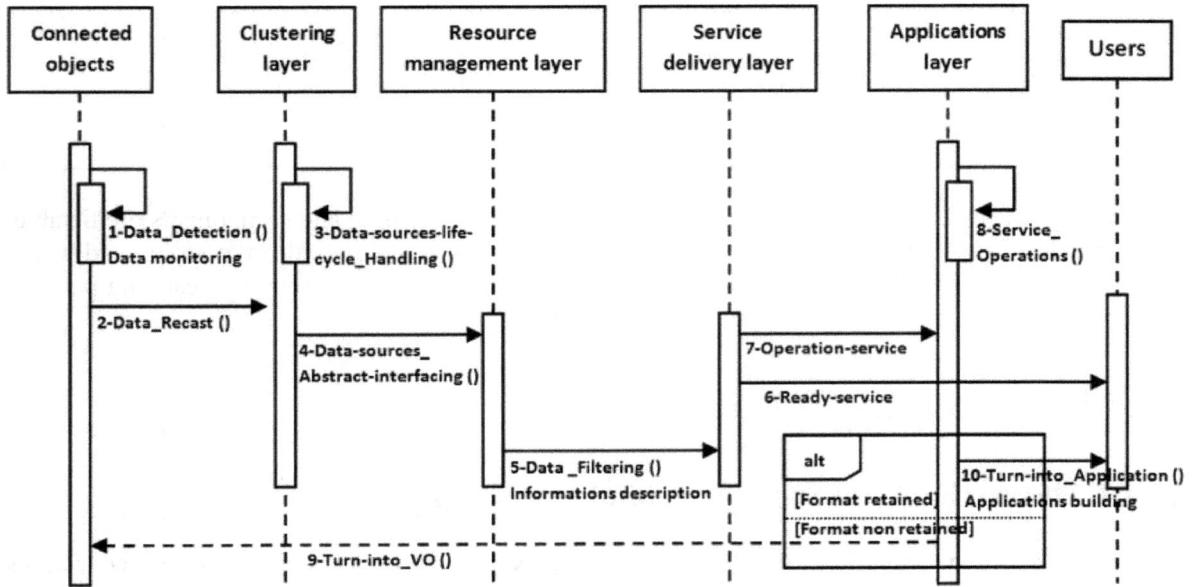

With data services abstracted, we compare transport protocols next.

10.4.2 REST Clients vs. GraphQL Clients

REST clients (Fetch API, Axios) make multiple endpoints calls, while GraphQL clients (Apollo, Relay) allow querying multiple resources in one request. REST pattern:

```
const user = await userApi.getUser("42");
const orders = await orderApi.getByUser("42");
```

GraphQL query:

```
query UserWithOrders($id: ID!) {
 user(id: $id) { id, name }
 orders(userId: $id) { id, total }
}
```

Apollo setup:

```
const client = new ApolloClient({ uri: "/graphcl" });
const { data } = await client.query({ query: GET_USER_WITH_ORDERS, variables: { id } });
```

GraphQL reduces overfetching but can complicate caching and performance monitoring. Clients use normalized caches (Apollo InMemoryCache) to dedupe queries. With REST, you manage multiple service adapters. Your choice depends on API maturity and performance requirements. Next, we examine cache strategies that optimize both protocols.

10.4.3 Cache-Aside, Stale-While-Revalidate & RTK Query

Cache-aside for HTTP:

```
async function fetchProfile(id: string) {
 const cached = cache.get(id);
 if (cached) return cached;
 const profile = await api.getUser(id);
 cache.set(id, profile);
 return profile;
}
```

The **stale-while-revalidate** pattern (used by SWR, React Query) returns cached data immediately while fetching fresh data in background:

```
const { data, isLoading } = useSWR(`/users/${id}`, fetcher);
```

Redux Toolkit Query (RTK Query) integrates caching, invalidation, and polling:

```
export const api = createApi({
 baseQuery: fetchBaseQuery({ baseUrl:'/api' }),
 endpoints: builder => ({
  getUser: builder.query<User, string>({ query: id=>`/users/${id}` }),
 })
});
export const { useGetUserQuery } = api;
```

Components call:

```
const { data, error, isFetching } = useGetUserQuery(id);
```

RTK Query handles caching lifetimes, tag-based invalidation (invalidatesTags), and background re-fetch. These abstractions simplify data fetching and maintain UI responsiveness. Finally, we implement optimistic UI updates to improve perceived performance.

10.4.4 Optimistic Updates & Rollbacks

Optimistic updates immediately reflect user actions in the UI before server confirmation, then revert if the call fails. With React Query:

```
const queryClient = useQueryClient();
const mutation = useMutation(updateUser, {
 onMutate: async newUser => {
  await queryClient.cancelQueries(['user', newUser.id]);
  const previous = queryClient.getQueryData(['user', newUser.id]);
  queryClient.setQueryData(['user', newUser.id], newUser);
  return { previous };
 },
 onError: (err, variables, context) => {
  queryClient.setQueryData(['user', variables.id], context.previous);
 },
 onSettled: (data, error, variables) => {
  queryClient.invalidateQueries(['user', variables.id]);
 }
});
```

This pattern shows instant feedback, improving UX. In Redux-Toolkit:

```
builder.mutation<User, User>({
 query: u => ({ url:`/users/${u.id}`, method:'PUT', body:u }),
 async onQueryStarted(arg, { dispatch, queryFulfilled }) {
  const      patch      =      dispatch(api.util.updateQueryData('getUser',      arg.id,
draft=>{ Object.assign(draft,arg); }));
  try { await queryFulfilled; }
  catch { patch.undo(); }
 }
});
```

Optimistic updates require careful rollback logic and error notifications to the user. You must also consider concurrency: two optimistic updates in flight could overwrite each other. By combining optimistic UI with robust caching and error handling, your application feels snappy while maintaining correctness. Having covered state, data fetching, and caching, the next chapter delves into routing and navigation architectures.

10.5 Routing & Navigation

10.5.1 Declarative vs. Programmatic Routing

Declarative routing describes your application's navigation structure as data, enabling static analysis, tooling, and simpler refactoring. In React Router v6, you define routes as JSX:

```
<Routes>
 <Route path="/" element={<Home />} />
 <Route path="products" element={<ProductList />} />
 <Route path="products/:id" element={<ProductDetail />} />
 <Route path="*" element={<NotFound />} />
</Routes>
```

Here, the routing table lives in one place, and the framework matches URLs to component trees automatically. Declarative routes integrate well with code-splitting (see 10.5.4) and allow tools to visualize navigation graphs. By contrast, programmatic routing uses imperative calls—pushing history entries in response to events:

```
import { useNavigate } from "react-router-dom";
const nav = useNavigate();
button.onClick = () => nav(`/products/${id}`);
```

Programmatic navigation gives full control at runtime—deciding routes based on conditions not known at compile time, such as feature flags or dynamic data. However, overuse can scatter navigation logic throughout components, making it harder to track all possible routes. A balanced approach uses declarative routing for most paths, with programmatic calls confined to well-located hooks or services. In Vue Router, the equivalent is router-link components versus calls to this.$router.push().

A flow diagram:

```
[URL Change] ⇒ Router.matches ⇒ Render New Component
[User Action] ⇒ useNavigate() ⇒ URL Update ⇒ Router.matches
```

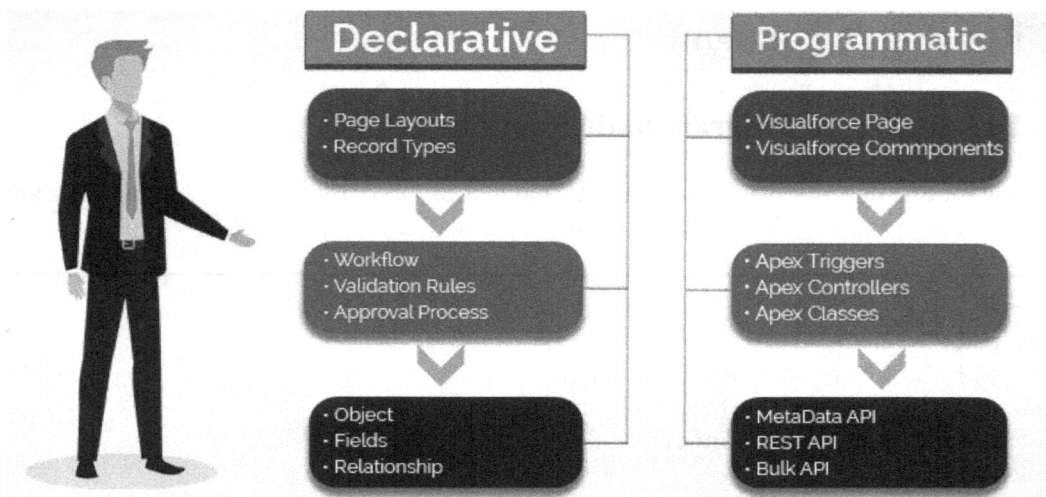

By establishing a clear distinction between the two, you maintain readability and debuggability in your navigation logic. Having declared your routes centrally, you can next structure them in nested and dynamic hierarchies.

10.5.2 Nested & Dynamic Route Configurations

Complex UIs often require nested layouts and parameterized routes. In React Router v6, nested routes render layouts:

```
<Routes>
 <Route path="/" element={<MainLayout />}>
  <Route index element={<Dashboard />} />
  <Route path="users" element={<UsersLayout />}>
   <Route index element={<UserList />} />
   <Route path=":userId" element={<UserProfile />} />
  </Route>
 </Route>
</Routes>
```

<Outlet /> within MainLayout and UsersLayout determines where child routes render; this enables shared headers, sidebars, or tabs. Dynamic segments (:userId) capture URL parts as params:

```
const { userId } = useParams(); // "42"
```

You can further guard or preload nested segments—e.g., fetch user data in the parent layout:

```
function UsersLayout() {
 const { userId } = useParams();
 const user = useFetchUser(userId);
 if (!user) return <Loading />;
 return <Outlet context={{ user }} />;
}
```

This context propagates down to UserProfile, eliminating duplicate fetches. Nesting also scales to deeply hierarchical apps—administration, settings, sub-sections—without duplicating layout code. A tree diagram:

```
/
├─ Dashboard
└─ users/
   ├─ UserList
   └─ :userId/
      ├─ UserOverview
      └─ Settings
```

Dynamic route config can be generated from JSON for CMS-driven sites, enabling preview environments and live updates. With nested and dynamic structures, your application handles complex navigation flows gracefully, ready for securing via route guards.

10.5.3 Route Guards & Permission Checks

Protecting routes based on authentication, roles, or feature flags requires guard logic that intercepts navigation before rendering. In React Router, you wrap protected routes in a guard component:

```
function PrivateRoute({ children }: {children: JSX.Element}) {
 const auth = useAuth(); // { user, loading }
 if (auth.loading) return <Spinner />;
 return auth.user ? children : <Navigate to="/login" replace />;
}
// Usage
<Route path="dashboard" element={<PrivateRoute><Dashboard /></PrivateRoute>} />
```

This pattern centralizes access control and renders fallback UIs during authentication checks. For role-based guards, pass required roles:

```
function RoleRoute({ roles, children }) {
 const { user } = useAuth();
```

```
return user && roles.includes(user.role) ? children : <Forbidden />;
}
```

In Vue Router:

```
router.beforeEach((to, from, next) => {
 if (to.meta.requiresAuth && !auth.isLoggedIn()) next('/login');
 else next();
});
```

Guards can also check feature flags from your flag service, preventing users from accessing unreleased pages. Complex scenarios—multi-tenant authorization, time-based features—benefit from guard factories:

```
function createGuard(predicate) {
 return ({ children }) => predicate() ? children : <NotAllowed />;
}
```

A sequence diagram:

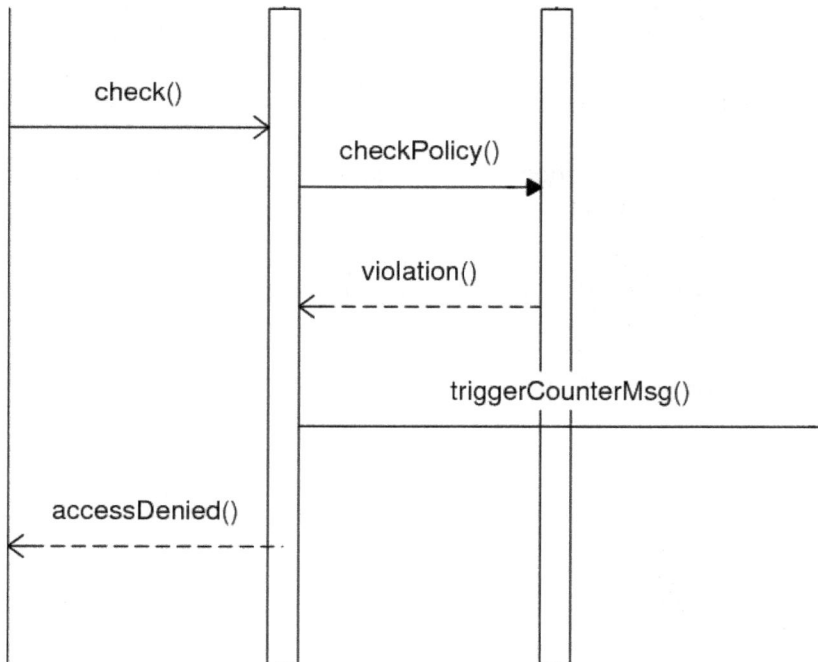

Robust guards ensure only authorized users see sensitive UIs, forming a secure transition into optimizing bundle sizes via code-splitting.

10.5.4 Code-Splitting by Route

Large front-end bundles slow initial load; code-splitting by route defers loading until needed. In React, use React.lazy and Suspense:

```
const ProductDetail = React.lazy(() => import('./ProductDetail'));
<Route path="products/:id" element={
 <Suspense fallback={<Spinner />}>
  <ProductDetail />
 </Suspense>
}/>
```

Webpack automatically creates separate chunks for each dynamic import. Named chunks improve caching:

```
import(/* webpackChunkName: "product-detail" */ './ProductDetail');
```

In Vue Router:

```
const Detail = () => import(/* webpackChunkName: "product-detail" */ './Detail.vue');
{ path: '/detail/:id', component: Detail }
```

Tools like **loadable-components** support server-side rendering and prefetching:

```
const Home = loadable(() => import('./Home'), { fallback: <Spinner /> });
```

You can prefetch likely routes on hover:

```
<Link to="/products/1" onMouseEnter={() => import('./ProductDetail')}>View</Link>
```

By splitting code at route boundaries, you reduce Time To Interactive and deliver fast, scalable navigation. With routing and lazy loading optimized, we turn next to consistent styling and theming strategies.

10.6 Styling & Theming

10.6.1 CSS-in-JS vs. Utility-First CSS

CSS-in-JS libraries (styled-components, Emotion) enable co-located styles with components, dynamic theming, and scoping without class-name collisions:

```
import styled from 'styled-components';
const Button = styled.button`
 background: ${props => props.primary ? 'blue' : 'gray'};
 color: white;
 padding: 0.5rem 1rem;
`;
```

Props drive styling logic, and the library generates unique class names. This approach simplifies conditional styling and theme integration but can increase runtime overhead.

Utility-First CSS frameworks (Tailwind CSS) offer atomic classes that compose together:

```
<button className="bg-blue-500 text-white py-2 px-4 rounded">Click</button>
```

You avoid custom CSS files, relying on a fixed set of utilities. Tailwind eliminates unused styles via PurgeCSS, leading to small bundles. Utility-first promotes consistency—bg-blue-500 always means the same shade of blue—and encourages rapid prototyping. A comparison:

Feature	CSS-in-JS	Utility-First
Dynamic styling	Excellent	Limited (variants)
Bundle size control	Moderate	Excellent
Learning curve	Medium (JS API)	Low (classes)
Theming	Native support	Requires config

Your choice depends on team expertise and application needs. Whichever you pick, you next unify colors, typography, and spacing into a theming system.

10.6.2 Theming via Context / Providers

A central theme object defines design tokens—colors, fonts, spacing—distributed via context or providers. With styled-components:

```
import { ThemeProvider } from 'styled-components';
const theme = {
 colors: { primary: '#0055ff', secondary: '#ff5500' },
 spacing: (n: number) => `${n * 8}px`,
};
<ThemeProvider theme={theme}>
 <App />
</ThemeProvider>
```

Components access theme via props:

```
const Card = styled.div`
 background: ${props => props.theme.colors.primary},
 padding: ${props => props.theme.spacing(2)};
`;
```

In Emotion or Material-UI, similar providers exist. For utility-first, you configure Tailwind's tailwind.config.js:

```
module.exports = {
 theme: {
  colors: { primary: '#0055ff', secondary: '#ff5500' },
  spacing: { 1: '8px', 2: '16px' }
 }
};
```

Switch themes at runtime to support dark mode:

```
<button onClick={()=>setTheme(isDark?light:dark)}>Toggle</button>
```

By centralizing design tokens, you ensure consistency and simplify global style changes. With theming in place, we next isolate styles per component to prevent unintended bleed.

10.6.3 Scoped Styles & Class-Name Strategies

To avoid CSS conflicts, use scoping strategies like **CSS Modules**, **BEM**, or CSS-in-JS's automatic scoping. With CSS Modules:

```
/* Button.module.css */
.btn { padding: 8px; background: blue; }


import styles from './Button.module.css';
<button className={styles.btn}>Click</button>
```

Webpack hashes class names uniquely (Button_btn__3XjKL). BEM (Block-Element-Modifier) uses naming conventions:

```
<button class="button button--primary">Click</button>
```

Modifiers (--primary) adjust appearance. CSS-in-JS inherently scopes by generating unique tokens. Scoped styles reduce global stylesheet size and eliminate cascade unpredictability.

This isolation lets teams work independently on UI modules without collisions. With styles scoped, you can build responsive layouts that adapt to device sizes.

10.6.4 Responsive & Mobile-First Layouts

Mobile-first design begins with base styles for small screens, then uses media queries to adapt for larger viewports:

```
.container { padding: 8px; }
@media(min-width: 640px) {
 .container { padding: 16px; }
}
```

In styled-components:

```
const Wrapper = styled.div`
 display: flex; flex-direction: column;
 @media(min-width: 768px) { flex-direction: row; }
`;
```

Use CSS Grid and Flexbox for fluid layouts:

```
.grid { display: grid; grid-template-columns: 1fr; }
@media(min-width: 1024px) {
 .grid { grid-template-columns: repeat(3, 1fr); }
}
```

Utilities in Tailwind:

```
<div class="p-2 md:p-4 grid grid-cols-1 lg:grid-cols-3"></div>
```

Test layouts on real devices and emulators to catch edge cases. Use flex-wrap, min-width on cards, and relative units (rem, vh) to maintain proportions.

By architecting responsive styles, your application delivers optimal user experiences across devices. Having established robust styling, we next ensure that every piece of code functions correctly through comprehensive testing.

10.7 Testing & Quality Assurance

10.7.1 Unit Testing Components (Jest, Jasmine)

Unit tests validate individual components' behavior in isolation. Use **Jest** (with React) or **Jasmine** (with Angular) to run fast tests without a browser. In Jest:

```
import { render } from '@testing-library/react';
import { Button } from 'ui/components/atoms/Button';


test('calls onClick when clicked', () => {
 const handle = jest.fn();
 const { getByText } = render(<Button onClick={handle}>Click</Button>);
 getByText('Click').click();
 expect(handle).toHaveBeenCalledTimes(1);
});
```

Mock dependencies—ports, services, context—so tests focus on rendering and logic. Snapshot testing captures expected HTML output:

```
const tree = renderer.create(<Button>Save</Button>).toJSON();
expect(tree).toMatchSnapshot();
```

Use **Jasmine** in Angular:

```
it('should render title', () => {
 fixture.detectChanges();
 expect(component.titleElement.nativeElement.textContent).toContain('Welcome');
});
```

Organize tests alongside component files (Button.test.tsx), and run them on every commit. Unit tests catch regressions early and document expected behavior. After ensuring individual components work, you integrate them into larger flows.

10.7.2 Integration Tests (React Testing Library, Vue Test Utils)

Integration tests verify interactions between components, hooks, and context. **React Testing Library** encourages testing based on user behavior:

```
import { fireEvent, screen } from '@testing-library/react';
import { App } from 'ui/App';
test('search filters products', async () => {
 render(<App />);
 fireEvent.change(screen.getByPlaceholderText('Search'), { target: { value: 'Item' } });
 expect(await screen.findByText('Item 1')).toBeInTheDocument();
});
```

Vue Test Utils mounts components with Vuex stores and Vue Router:

```
const wrapper = mount(ProductList, { global: { plugins: [store, router] } });
await router.push('/products');
expect(wrapper.text()).toContain('Product A');
```

Integration tests exercise data fetching (mocked HTTP), routing (memory router), and state management. They run slower than unit tests but catch mismatches between modules. Use msw (Mock Service Worker) to simulate HTTP responses in-browser. Structure integration tests under __tests__/integration and run them in CI as part of a "test:ci" command. Having validated interactions, you proceed to full end-to-end flows.

10.7.3 End-to-End Tests (Cypress, Playwright)

End-to-end (E2E) tests run against deployed or locally served applications in real browsers. **Cypress** provides an all-in-one test runner:

```
describe('Login Flow', () => {
 it('allows a user to log in', () => {
  cy.visit('/');
  cy.get('input[name=username]').type('user1');
  cy.get('input[name=password]').type('password');
  cy.get('button[type=submit]').click();
  cy.url().should('include', '/dashboard');
  cy.contains('Welcome, user1');
 });
});
```

Playwright supports multiple browsers:

```
const { chromium } = require('playwright');
(async () => {
 const browser = await chromium.launch();
 const page = await browser.newPage();
 await page.goto('http://localhost:3000');
 await page.fill('input#search', 'test');
 await page.click('button#go');
 await page.waitForSelector('.result');
 await browser.close();
})();
```

E2E tests validate full-stack behavior—frontend, API, database—and catch integration issues. They run slower and more brittlely, so focus on critical user journeys. Use CI parallelization and containerized test environments to keep runtimes reasonable. With E2E confidence established, you guard UI regressions and accessibility.

10.7.4 Visual Regression & Accessibility Audits

Visual regression tests catch unintended style changes by comparing screenshots pixel-by-pixel. Tools like **Percy** or **Chromatic** integrate with Storybook:

```
jobs:
 visual:
  steps:
   - run: npx chromatic --project-token $CHROMATIC_TOKEN
```

Screenshots of components or pages are compared against baselines; diffs must be approved or the build fails. This prevents CSS drift when refactoring or theming.

Accessibility audits use **axe-core** to detect common issues—missing alt attributes, poor contrast:

```
import { mount } from '@cypress/vue';
import { Button } from 'ui/atoms/Button';
import 'cypress-axe';


it('is accessible', () => {
 mount(Button, { props: { children: 'Click' } });
 cy.injectAxe();
 cy.checkA11y();
});
```

Integrating audits in unit or integration tests ensures accessibility remains first-class. Reports highlight violations, severity, and remediation guidance. By combining visual and accessibility testing, you maintain a high-quality UI that remains both functional and inclusive. After ensuring quality, we optimize performance for real-world usage.

10.8 Performance Optimization

10.8.1 Code-Splitting & Lazy-Loading

While code-splitting by route (10.5.4) reduces initial load, you can further split at component or library boundaries. In Webpack, use dynamic imports:

```
const Chart = React.lazy(() => import('react-chartjs-2'));
```

Bundle analyzers (webpack-bundle-analyzer) visualize chunk sizes:

```
npx webpack --profile --json | npx webpack-bundle-analyzer
```

You can split large vendor libraries:

```
optimization: {
 splitChunks: { chunks: 'all', name: 'vendors', test: /[\\/]node_modules[\\/]/ },
}
```

Prefetch non-critical chunks:

```
import(/* webpackPrefetch: true */ './HelpWidget');
```

This signals the browser to download in idle time. Proper chunking balances network overhead with user-perceived responsiveness. With bundles optimized, next memoize expensive computations.

10.8.2 Memoization & Pure Components

Prevent unnecessary re-renders by memoizing components and values. In React:

```
const ExpensiveList = React.memo(({ items }) => {
 // complex rendering
});


const processed = useMemo(() => heavyCompute(data), [data]);
```

React.memo shallowly compares props; provide custom comparators for deep props. In Vue, use computed properties to cache derived data. Avoid anonymous functions or object literals in props, as they break memoization. Profiling with React DevTools "why did this render?" helps identify wasted renders.

Memoization reduces CPU work and improves frame rates, especially in mobile browsers. With pure computations cached, we handle large lists smoothly.

10.8.3 Virtualization of Large Lists

Rendering thousands of rows can crash the DOM. **Windowing** libraries like react-window or react-virtualized render only visible items:

```
import { FixedSizeList as List } from 'react-window';
<List height={600} itemCount={10000} itemSize={35}>
 {({ index, style }) => <div style={style}>{items[index]}</div>}
</List>
```

Only ~20–30 rows mount at once, keeping memory and layout calculation low. In Angular, use CDK's virtualFor. Virtualization demands fixed item heights or measuring logic. For grids, use VariableSizeGrid. Scrolling remains smooth even with tens of thousands of items. Combine virtualization with infinite scrolling to load data on demand:

```
onScrollEnd={() => fetchMoreItems()}
```

Virtualization ensures performance at scale, completing our DOM-level optimizations. Finally, we guide the browser to load critical resources efficiently.

10.8.4 Resource Hints, Prefetching & CDN Caching

Resource hints (<link rel="preload">, prefetch, dns-prefetch) instruct the browser to warm up resources:

```
<link rel="preload" href="/static/main.js" as="script">
<link rel="dns-prefetch" href="//fonts.googleapis.com">
```

preload fetches critical assets early; prefetch fetches for idle time. Service workers provide fine-grained caching:

```
self.addEventListener('install', () => {
 caches.open('v1').then(cache => cache.addAll(['/','/main.js']));
});
```

Set HTTP cache headers on CDN:

```
Cache-Control: public, max-age=31536000, immutable
```

For assets with content hashes, clients can cache long-term without risk of staleness. Use Surrogate-Control for edge caching.

Measure performance with Lighthouse and Real User Monitoring (RUM) to validate improvements. By combining hints, prefetching, and CDN caching, you achieve fast, resilient front-end delivery that completes our discussion of performance optimization in a clean front-end architecture.

10.9 Accessibility & Internationalization

10.9.1 WCAG Guidelines & ARIA Roles

The Web Content Accessibility Guidelines (WCAG) define a set of success criteria organized under four principles: Perceivable, Operable, Understandable, and Robust (POUR). To satisfy these criteria, developers must ensure that all non-text content has text alternatives, that content is adaptable and distinguishable, that users can navigate and operate controls via keyboard, that text is readable and predictable, and that code remains compatible with current and future user agents, including assistive technologies. ARIA (Accessible Rich Internet Applications) roles, states, and properties provide a standardized way to communicate widget semantics to screen readers when native HTML elements are insufficient.

For example, a custom dropdown component can expose the appropriate role and state:

```
<div role="combobox" aria-haspopup="listbox" aria-expanded="false" id="country-combobox">
 <input aria-autocomplete="list" aria-controls="country-list" />
</div>
<ul role="listbox" id="country-list" hidden>
 <li role="option" aria-selected="false">Canada</li>
 <li role="option" aria-selected="false">United States</li>
</ul>
```

In this snippet, role="combobox" informs assistive technologies that the element behaves like a native combo box. aria-expanded toggles as the list is shown or hidden, and aria-selected marks the currently highlighted option.

A simple flow diagram of ARIA interactions:

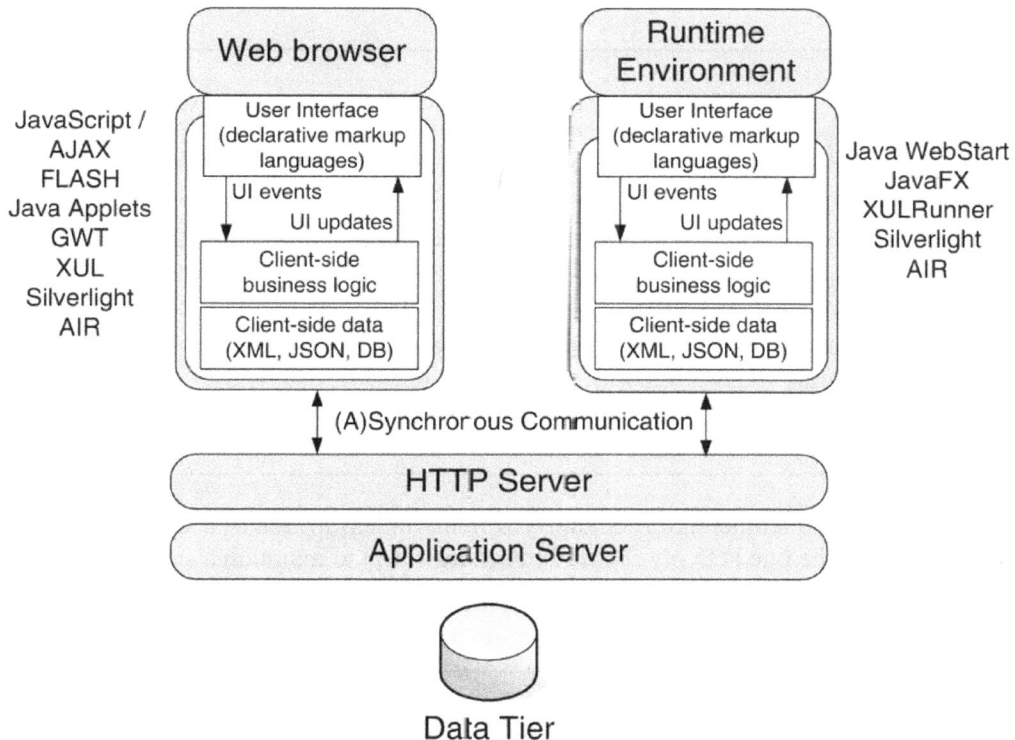

Data Tier

Ensuring all interactive components emit the correct roles and manage state changes dynamically is essential to pass WCAG Level AA. Moreover, developers should use built-in HTML elements such as <button>, <a>, and <select> wherever possible, since they carry implicit accessibility semantics without extra ARIA. When custom controls are unavoidable—like drag-and-drop lists or virtualized grids—ARIA becomes indispensable to replicate expected behaviors.

Regularly run automated accessibility checks (e.g., axe-core) alongside manual audits with screen readers like NVDA or VoiceOver to catch missing ARIA attributes. Document patterns and enforce them via code review checklists. By internalizing WCAG and ARIA best practices, your team lays a solid foundation before addressing keyboard navigation and focus management in the next section.

10.9.2 Keyboard Navigation & Focus Management

A truly accessible application allows full operation via keyboard alone. Focus order must follow visual order, interactive elements need discernible focus indicators, and custom widgets must implement keyboard event handling equivalent to native controls. For example, in a modal dialog:

```
useEffect(() => {
  const previous = document.activeElement as HTMLElement;
  const firstFocusable = dialogRef.current.querySelector('button, [href], input') as HTMLElement;
  firstFocusable.focus();
  return () => previous?.focus();
}, []);
```

This React hook snippet traps focus inside the dialog on open and restores it on close.

Implementing keyboard support for a list component involves handling keydown events and moving focus programmatically:

```
function onKeyDown(e: KeyboardEvent) {
  if (e.key === 'ArrowDown') moveFocus(currentIndex + 1);
  else if (e.key === 'ArrowUp') moveFocus(currentIndex - 1);
  else if (e.key === 'Home') moveFocus(0);
  else if (e.key === 'End') moveFocus(items.length - 1);
}
```

Here, moveFocus sets document.getElementById(items[index].id).focus(). Ensure each item has tabIndex={-1} except the one actively focused (tabIndex={0}) to maintain a single tab stop.

Use CSS to style focus rings:

```
:focus { outline: 2px solid Highlight; outline-offset: 2px; }
```

Be mindful of tabindex="0" and tabindex="-1" semantics to prevent creating "focus traps" or skipping elements. Run focus-order testing with tools like Chrome's Accessibility Inspector or keyboard-only navigation to confirm that users can reach every control in a logical sequence. By mastering keyboard navigation, you prepare the UI for localized content, which we address in the following subsection.

10.9.3 Localization of Text, Dates & Numbers

Localizing a front-end means translating user-facing text and formatting locale-sensitive data correctly. Store all strings in resource files keyed by message identifiers:

```
// en.json
{ "welcome": "Welcome, {name}!", "date.format": "MM/DD/YYYY" }
// de.json
{ "welcome": "Willkommen, {name}!", "date.format": "DD.MM.YYYY" }
```

In React with react-intl:

```
import {FormattedMessage, FormattedDate} from 'react-intl';


<FormattedMessage id="welcome" values={{name: user.name}} />
<FormattedDate value={new Date(user.birthday)} year="numeric" month="long" day="2-digit"
/>
```

The date format adapts to the locale automatically, but you can override using your resource's pattern:

```
import {IntlProvider, createIntl, createIntlCache} from 'react-intl';


const cache = createIntlCache();
const intl = createIntl({ locale, messages }, cache);
const formatted = intl.formatDate(date, { format: 'date.format' });
```

Number formatting uses Intl.NumberFormat:

```
new Intl.NumberFormat(locale, { style: 'currency', currency: currencyCode }).format(amount);
```

Storing formatting patterns in resource files allows translators to adjust formats per locale. For dynamic content in templates, ensure interpolation escapes malicious input to prevent injection.

Set up CI checks to detect missing translations or fallback to default locale. By decoupling code from text, you streamline the translation process and prepare for right-to-left locales, discussed next.

10.9.4 Right-to-Left & Bidirectional Layout Support

Supporting right-to-left (RTL) languages like Arabic requires mirroring layout and text direction. Use the dir attribute on the <html> or root <div>:

```
<html lang="ar" dir="rtl">
```

In CSS-in-JS:

```
const Container = styled.div`
 direction: rtl;
 text-align: right;
`;
```

For margins and paddings, use logical properties instead of physical ones:

```
/* instead of margin-left: 16px; */
margin-inline-start: 16px;
```

This automatically flips in RTL contexts. In frameworks like Bootstrap, include the RTL CSS build. Components that render icons or arrows need their assets mirrored—use SVGs that can be flipped via transform: scaleX(-1):

```
.icon-arrow { transform: scaleX(var(--rtl-factor, 1)); }
[dir="rtl"] { --rtl-factor: -1; }
```

Bidirectional text mixing LTR and RTL content requires Unicode BiDi control characters or explicit dir spans:

```
<p dir="auto">English كلمة English</p>
```

Test RTL layouts thoroughly: interact with forms, navigation, and complex components (date pickers, tree views). Visual regression tests should include RTL snapshots to catch unflipped styles. By accommodating RTL and bidi text, your application truly reaches global users. Having addressed accessibility and internationalization, we now move into the final chapter on front-end build pipelines and deployment.

10.10 Build Pipelines & Deployment

10.10.1 Module Bundlers & Tree-Shaking (Webpack, Rollup)

Module bundlers like Webpack and Rollup analyze your import graph to produce optimized bundles. **Tree-shaking** removes unused exports by leveraging ES module static analysis. In Webpack:

```
module.exports = {
 mode: 'production',
 entry: './src/index.tsx',
 output: { filename: 'bundle.[contenthash].js', path: path.resolve(__dirname,'dist') },
 optimization: { usedExports: true, splitChunks: { chunks: 'all' } },
 module: { rules: [ /* ts-loader, babel-loader */ ] }
};
```

mode:'production' enables minification (Terser) which also eliminates dead code. Rollup's config:

```
import resolve from '@rollup/plugin-node-resolve';
import commonjs from '@rollup/plugin-commonjs';
import { terser } from 'rollup-plugin-terser';


export default {
 input: 'src/index.js',
 output: { file: 'dist/bundle.js', format: 'iife', sourcemap: true },
 plugins: [ resolve(), commonjs(), terser() ]
};
```

Rollup excels at publishing libraries due to its flat output. Analyze bundle composition with tools:

```
npx webpack-bundle-analyzer dist/stats.json
npx rollup --config --silent --duration --summary
```

Visualize module sizes and find large dependencies to replace or lazy-load. A bundling diagram:

```
src/
 ├─ ui/
 ├─ app/
 └─ domain/
import graph → bundler → output chunks + vendor
```

Configuring aliasing, polyfills, and loaders (images, CSS) tailors bundling to project needs. With bundling optimized, we enforce code quality before deployment.

10.10.2 Linting, Formatting & Static Analysis

Automated checks maintain consistency and catch potential errors early. **ESLint** enforces coding standards:

```
// .eslintrc.json
{
 "extends":    ["eslint:recommended",    "plugin:react/recommended",    "plugin:@typescript-
eslint/recommended"],
 "rules": { "no-console": "warn", "react-hooks/exhaustive-deps": "error" }
}
```

Use **Prettier** for consistent formatting:

```
// .prettierrc
{ "singleQuote": true, "trailingComma": "all", "printWidth": 80 }
```

Integrate both:

```
npx eslint --fix src/**/*.ts{,x}
npx prettier --write .
```

Static type checking with TypeScript catches mismatches before runtime. Add additional checks:

- **SonarQube** for code smells and coverage
- **Dependency-Cruiser** to enforce module boundaries (e.g., UI → app → domain only)
- **Stylelint** for CSS conventions

Configure Git pre-commit hooks with **Husky**:

```
npx husky add .husky/pre-commit "npm run lint && npm test"
```

This pipeline prevents bad code from entering your repository. With code quality assured, we set up continuous integration and delivery pipelines.

10.10.3 CI/CD for Front-End: Testing, Building, Publishing

A robust CI/CD pipeline automates testing, building, and publishing snapshots or releases. Example GitHub Actions workflow:

```
name: CI
on: [push, pull_request]
```

```
jobs:
 build:
  runs-on: ubuntu-latest
  steps:
   - uses: actions/checkout@v3
   - name: Setup Node
    uses: actions/setup-node@v3
    with: { node-version: '18', cache: 'npm' }
   - run: npm ci
   - name: Lint & Test
    run: npm run lint && npm test
   - name: Build
    run: npm run build
   - name: Publish
    if: github.event_name == 'push' && startsWith(github.ref, 'refs/tags/')
    run: npm publish --access public
```

On merges to main, CI runs checks and builds production bundles, then deploys artifacts to storage or a content distribution network. Use **Semantic Release** to automate versioning and changelog generation based on commit messages:

```
npx semantic-release
```

For staging and production, deploy to services like Vercel, Netlify, or AWS S3 with invalidation:

```
- name: Deploy to S3
 run: aws s3 sync dist/ s3://my-app --delete
```

CI/CD ensures that every code change passes quality gates before reaching users. Once published, we manage CDN caches to propagate updates reliably.

10.10.4 CDN Invalidation & Cache-Busting Strategies

When deploying new front-end assets, CDNs cache static files globally. To ensure clients fetch updated bundles, use content hashes in filenames (bundle.[contenthash].js) so each build produces unique URLs. In HTML:

```
<script src="/static/js/bundle.abc123.js"></script>
```

Legacy caches automatically drop old files. For files without hashes—like /index.html—issue CDN invalidation:

```
aws cloudfront create-invalidation --distribution-id D123ABC --paths "/index.html"
```

Alternatively, leverage short TTL for /index.html:

```
Cache-Control: max-age=0, s-maxage=60, must-revalidate
```

This instructs CDNs to refresh the page entry every minute. Automate invalidations in your CI/CD pipeline:

```
- name: Invalidate CloudFront
  uses: jakejarvis/cloudfront-invalidate-action@v1
  with:
   distribution: ${{ secrets.CLOUDFRONT_ID }}
   paths: '["/index.html"]'
```

For asset rollouts, use **blue/green** or **canary** deployments on the CDN, gradually shifting traffic to new versions. Monitor cache hit ratios and HTTP response headers to verify that cache-busting works as intended. A CDN cache diagram:

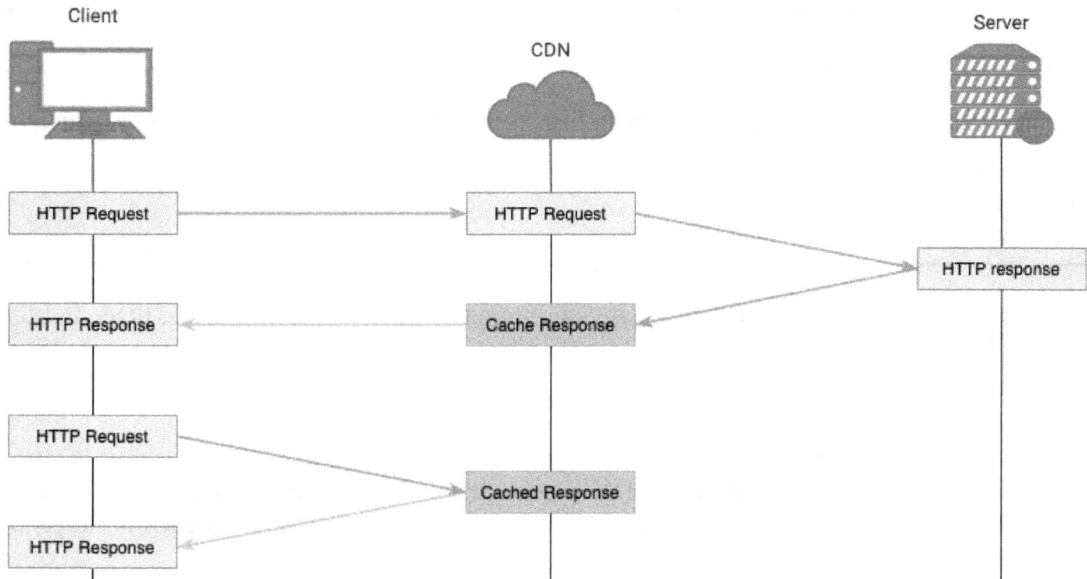

By combining hashed filenames, appropriate headers, and automated invalidation, you deliver fresh content without cache poisoning or stale asset errors, completing your front-end's clean architecture pipeline.

Conclusion

Adopting a clean architecture on the front end transforms your codebase from a brittle collection of components into a cohesive, layered ecosystem where each module has a distinct responsibility. Presentation layers focus solely on rendering, application layers orchestrate workflows and data flow, and domain layers encapsulate core business rules—each communicating through well-defined interfaces. This structure fosters reusability, simplifies testing at every level, and accelerates on-boarding of new team members by making architectural intent explicit. Moreover, clear boundaries enable independent evolution of UI frameworks, state-management libraries, and network protocols, future-proofing your application against shifting technology trends. Ultimately, Front-End Clean Architecture empowers teams to deliver engaging, high-quality user experiences with confidence and agility, even as complexity inevitably grows.

Chapter 11. Performance & Scalability Engineering

In modern software systems, delivering consistently fast and reliable experiences under variable load is as critical as functional correctness. Performance and scalability engineering transforms non-functional requirements into measurable targets, ensuring systems remain responsive even as user demands grow or traffic patterns shift. This involves not only benchmarking and tuning code paths but also understanding real-world workloads, capacity constraints, and cost implications across every layer—from in-memory caches and thread pools to database sharding and network topologies. By treating performance as a first-class citizen—building observability, profiling, and automated tests into your development process—you can uncover hidden bottlenecks early, make informed trade-offs, and avoid surprise outages when scaling to hundreds or thousands of concurrent users.

11.1 Defining Performance Objectives

11.1.1 Service-Level Indicators (SLI) & Error Budgets

A Service-Level Indicator (SLI) is a carefully chosen metric that quantifies how well a service is performing from the user's perspective—common examples include request success rate, median response time, or cache hit ratio. By selecting the right SLIs, you focus on measuring what truly matters: that users can complete their tasks. For instance, "fraction of HTTP requests returning 2xx or 3xx status codes over a rolling 5-minute window" is a classic availability SLI. Once SLIs are in place, you define Service-Level Objectives (SLOs)—target values for those SLIs (e.g., 99.9 % success rate). The difference between 100 % and the SLO is the **error budget** (0.1 % in this example), giving your team a quantified tolerance for failure.

Error budgets drive risk-aware decisions: if your service has consumed only 10 % of its error budget this week, you may safely roll out new features; if you've burned through 80 %, you should prioritize reliability work. An error-budget policy table might look like:

Error Budget Burn	Action
< 20 %	Full feature rollout permitted
20–50 %	Merge guardrails; reduced risk tests
> 50 %	Feature freeze; reliability focus

A Prometheus recording rule to track availability SLI could be:

```
groups:
- name: slis
 rules:
 - record: service:availability_percentage:ratio
 expr: |
  (sum(rate(http_requests_total{code=~"2..|3.."}[5m]))
  /
  sum(rate(http_requests_total[5m]))
  ) * 100
```

Instituting SLIs and error budgets early embeds reliability into sprint planning, preventing last-minute firefighting. With objectives grounded in real metrics, you can next tackle the nuances of latency, throughput, and tail-percentile behavior.

11.1.2 Latency, Throughput & Tail Percentiles

Latency and throughput are the twin pillars of performance measurement. **Latency** measures how long individual operations take—commonly tracked as distribution percentiles (p50, p95, p99, p99.9)—while **throughput** quantifies how many operations occur per unit time (requests per second, messages per minute). Whereas average latency can hide long-tail spikes, p95 and p99 highlight that 5 % or 1 % of requests may be significantly slower, severely impacting user experience. For example, an API with p50 = 100 ms but p99 = 2 s signals occasional outliers that must be investigated.

In Prometheus, you record request duration as a histogram:

```
- name: http_request_duration_seconds
 help: "HTTP request latency in seconds"
 type: histogram
 buckets: [0.005,0.01,0.025,0.05,0.1,0.25,0.5,1,2.5,5,10]
```

Then compute percentiles:

```
histogram_quantile(0.99, sum(rate(http_request_duration_seconds_bucket[5m])) by (le))
```

Throughput is measured simply as:

```
sum(rate(http_requests_total[1m]))
```

Plotting latency percentiles alongside throughput over time reveals whether spikes coincide with load surges. Capturing both latency distribution and throughput empowers you to differentiate between saturation (throughput caps) and latency stalls (queueing, GC pauses). With a clear picture of response-time and volume characteristics, you can now explore how cost factors influence these metrics.

11.1.3 Cost-versus-Performance Trade-offs

Every performance improvement has a cost—more CPU cores, higher-tier instances, deeper caches, or additional replicas all increase operational expenses. Quantifying cost per unit performance gain helps teams make rational trade-offs rather than chasing diminishing returns. For example, reducing median latency from 50 ms to 30 ms might require doubling instance count from 5 to 10, incurring an extra $0.50 per hour. If your service handles 10 000 requests per hour, that equates to $0.00005 per request of latency improvement, which may or may not justify the expense.

A simple Python snippet to calculate cost per request improvement:

```
cost_per_hour_old = 5 * 0.10 # $0.50
cost_per_hour_new = 10 * 0.10 # $1.00
delta_cost = cost_per_hour_new - cost_per_hour_old # $0.50
requests_per_hour = 10000
cost_per_request = delta_cost / requests_per_hour  # $0.00005
print(f"${cost_per_request:.6f} per request")
```

Coupling error-budget considerations with cost analysis ensures that reliability work stays within budget. Teams can establish **Cost-Performance SLOs**, such as "Maintain p95 < 200 ms at no more than $0.01 per 1 000 requests." By explicitly tying financial metrics to performance targets, you align technical optimizations with business reality. With cost-aware objectives defined, you're ready to model actual workloads in the next section.

11.2 Workload Characterization & Traffic Modeling

11.2.1 Synthetic vs. Production Traffic Profiles

Synthetic load tests—using tools like k6, JMeter, or Gatling—generate controlled traffic patterns (constant concurrency, ramp-up, step changes) to validate capacity under well-defined conditions. You script scenarios that mimic key user actions: login, browse catalog, checkout. A sample k6 script:

```
import http from 'k6/http';
import { sleep } from 'k6';
export let options = { stages: [
  { duration: '2m', target: 100 },
  { duration: '5m', target: 200 },
  { duration: '2m', target: 0 },
]};
export default function() {
 http.get('https://api.example.com/products');
 sleep(1);
 http.post('https://api.example.com/cart', JSON.stringify({ sku:'A1', qty:1 }));
}
```

Synthetic tests excel at reproducibility but often omit real-world variability: network jitter, session stickiness, or bursty behavior. By contrast, **production traffic profiles** are derived from live request logs or server metrics. You analyze actual request timestamps, response sizes, user geography, and client types to build statistical models. For example, ingesting request logs into a time-series database and running K-means clustering on inter-arrival times reveals hotspots.

Combining synthetic and real-traffic models ensures load tests cover both idealized and realistic conditions. With workload profiles in hand, you can capture temporal patterns—diurnal cycles and seasonal trends—in the next subsection.

11.2.2 Diurnal & Seasonal Patterns

User traffic often follows predictable **diurnal** patterns—peaks during business hours and troughs at night—as well as **seasonal** trends like end-of-month billing spikes or holiday surges. To model diurnal variation, fit a sine wave or Fourier series to historical data. For seasonal patterns, incorporate trend components or use forecasting libraries like Facebook Prophet:

```
from fbprophet import Prophet
df = pd.read_csv('request_counts.csv') # columns: ds, y
model = Prophet(yearly_seasonality=True, weekly_seasonality=True, daily_seasonality=True)
model.fit(df)
future = model.make_future_dataframe(periods=30)
forecast = model.predict(future)
```

Graphing the forecast alongside actuals highlights where your autoscaler must adapt. Incorporating these patterns into capacity planning prevents over- or under-provisioning—scaling up before expected peaks and down in off-hours. With temporal dynamics understood, you can hone in on which user activities drive the load, addressed in the next subsection.

11.2.3 User-Journey Heatmaps & Hotspots

Beyond aggregate traffic, it's crucial to map which user journeys—sequences of actions—consume the most resources. By instrumenting your application to log page views or API calls with a **journey ID** (session cookie or correlation ID), you can reconstruct paths and identify hotspots. For example:

```
{ "timestamp":"2025-05-20T12:00:00Z", "session":"abc123",
"event":"AddToCart", "sku":"XYZ", "duration_ms":120 }
```

A sequence flow diagram:

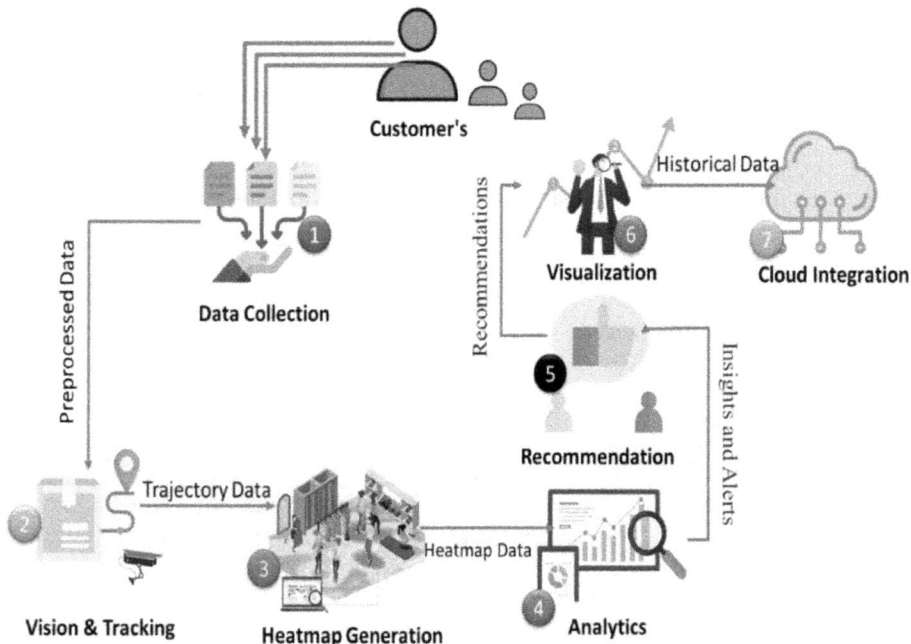

Tools like Elastic APM or DataDog can visualize such journey flows. Identifying that 60 % of requests hit /products and only 10 % reach /checkout informs where to focus performance optimizations—caching, query tuning, or frontend code-splitting.

With hotspots pinpointed, you have the insights needed to instrument observability at fine granularity, which is the focus of the next section.

11.3 Observability for Performance

11.3.1 High-Cardinality Metrics & Histograms

Basic metrics (CPU, request count) are helpful, but **high-cardinality** metrics—tagged by user, endpoint, or region—offer deeper insight into performance patterns. For instance, tracking http_request_duration_seconds by endpoint, status, and region lets you spot that p99 latency spikes only occur in the EU region for the /search endpoint. In Micrometer:

```
Timer.builder("http.requests")
 .publishPercentiles(0.5, 0.95, 0.99)
 .tags("region", region, "endpoint", endpoint)
 .register(meterRegistry)
 .record(duration);
```

Histograms capture the full distribution, from which percentiles are computed in real-time. Visualizing histograms avoids the inaccuracies of estimating percentiles from summaries. However, excessively high cardinality risks overwhelming your metrics backend, so strike a balance by only tagging on dimensions that matter for drill-downs.

By combining high-cardinality tags with histograms, you build a rich observability fabric that surfaces nuanced performance anomalies. With metrics in place, the next step is tracing individual requests across services.

11.3.2 Distributed Traces for Bottleneck Isolation

Distributed tracing stitches together span timelines across service boundaries, showing where time is spent in end-to-end requests. Using OpenTelemetry, you instrument HTTP clients and servers:

```
Span span = tracer.spanBuilder("queryProducts").startSpan();
try (Scope scope = span.makeCurrent()) {
// perform database query
List<Product> results = productRepo.find(...);
span.setAttribute("db.row_count", results.size());
```

```
} finally {
 span.end();
}
```

By examining the critical path, you may discover that a single slow RPC contributes 80 % of end-to-end latency, focusing your optimization efforts precisely. Tracing also reveals unexpected dependencies—calls to auth or logging services you didn't realize were in the hot path. Having pinpointed bottlenecks with tracing, you then correlate these insights with logs and metrics.

11.3.3 Correlating Logs, Metrics & Traces

True observability emerges when logs, metrics, and traces converge around a common context—typically a **trace ID** or **correlation ID**. In your logging framework (SLF4J, Winston), include the trace ID in every log entry:

```
MDC.put("traceId", Span.current().getSpanContext().getTraceId());
log.info("Fetched {} products", products.size());
```

Metrics can also be tagged with the trace ID or aggregated separately. In your APM, you link logs and metrics to trace spans, allowing queries such as "show logs and metrics for trace ID abcd1234."

Correlating these data sources surfaces root causes rapidly—if you see an error log in a span where metrics indicate a timeout, you know the two are linked. Tools like Elastic Observability or Grafana Tempo integrate these layers seamlessly. With a cohesive observability stack, you're ready to dig deeper into code-level performance via profiling in the next section.

11.4 Profiling & Micro-Benchmarking

11.4.1 CPU & Memory Flame Graphs

Flame graphs visualize CPU or memory stacks over time, highlighting "hot" code paths consuming the most resources. Using Linux perf and Brendan Gregg's FlameGraph scripts, capture a profile:

```
perf record -F 99 -a -g -- sleep 60
perf script | stackcollapse-perf.pl > out.folded
flamegraph.pl out.folded > cpu.svg
```

The resulting SVG shows function call hierarchies where width corresponds to total time spent. On the memory side, use heaptrack or jemalloc's jeprof to generate memory flame graphs showing allocation hotspots. Analyzing these graphs often uncovers expensive serialization routines or inefficient loops. Flame graphs empower you to target the most impactful optimizations rather than chasing arbitrary code paths. Once you've identified hotspots, you can employ more specialized profilers.

11.4.2 Application-Level Profilers (JFR, perf, eBPF)

Application-level profilers offer deeper insights into running processes. **Java Flight Recorder (JFR)**, built into the JVM, records CPU usage, lock contention, and allocation profiles with minimal overhead. Launch your service with:

```
-XX:StartFlightRecording=duration=60s,filename=recording.jfr,settings=profile
```

Analyze the .jfr file in **Java Mission Control** to see recorded hotspots, GC pauses, and thread states.

For native or polyglot applications, Linux perf provides system-wide profiling, while **eBPF** tools like bpftrace or **BCC** can trace kernel and application events dynamically:

```
bpftrace -e 'tracepoint:syscalls:sys_enter_read { @[comm] = count(); }'
```

eBPF scripts can measure network latency, file I/O, or custom tracepoints with high resolution. **perf**, **JFR**, and **eBPF** each fill different resolution and overhead trade-offs: JFR offers rich Java-specific insight at low cost, perf gives OS-level visibility, and eBPF allows custom probes without kernel modules. Combining these profilers surfaces issues—from code inefficiencies to system-level influences—so you can optimize holistic performance. Having profiled your service, you can validate improvements with micro-benchmarks.

11.4.3 Micro-Benchmark Harnesses & Pitfalls

Micro-benchmarks measure the performance of small code fragments in isolation, but they come with pitfalls. **JMH** (Java Microbenchmark Harness) is the gold standard for Java, handling warm-up iterations, JVM optimizations, and statistical analysis:

```
@BenchmarkMode(Mode.AverageTime)
@OutputTimeUnit(TimeUnit.NANOSECONDS)
public class StringConcatBenchmark {
 @Benchmark
 public String concatWithPlus() { return "a" + "b"; }
}
```

Run with:

```
java -jar benchmarks.jar -wi 5 -i 10
```

Pitfalls include dead-code elimination (the compiler removes unused results), constant folding, and measurement noise due to GC or CPU frequency scaling. Always consume benchmark results (e.g., return values) to prevent elimination, use sufficient iterations, and isolate benchmarks on unloaded machines. For JavaScript, libraries like **Benchmark.js** require careful use of defer and async to measure asynchronous code.

A code snippet using Benchmark.js:

```
const suite = new Benchmark.Suite();
suite.add('plus', function() { 'a' + 'b'; })
  .on('complete', function() {
  console.log(this[0].toString());
})
  .run({ async: true });
```

Micro-benchmarks excel at comparing two implementations (e.g., JSON vs. Kryo serialization) but don't capture system-level effects like network latency or database wiring. Always complement micro-benchmarks with real-world profiling and load tests. With micro-benchmark best practices mastered, you're equipped to validate both small and large-scale performance improvements.

11.5 Load, Stress & Soak Testing

11.5.1 Test Types and Exit Criteria

Load, stress, and soak tests each serve distinct purposes in validating system behavior under varying conditions. **Load tests** apply expected production traffic levels—peak, average, and sudden spikes—to verify that your service meets performance objectives without degradation. **Stress tests** push the system beyond its known limits, intentionally triggering resource exhaustion to observe failure modes and recovery behaviors. **Soak tests** run at moderate load for extended periods (hours to days), revealing memory leaks, resource leaks, and degradation that only surface over time.

Defining clear **exit criteria** ensures tests are meaningful and actionable. Exit criteria typically include:

1. **Error rate** below a threshold (e.g., $\leq 0.1\ \%$ HTTP 5xx).
2. **Latency percentiles** (p95, p99) within SLO (e.g., p95 < 200 ms).
3. **Resource utilization** (CPU, memory, I/O) under safe limits (e.g., CPU < 70 %, memory < 80 %).
4. No **functional failures** (data corruption, timeouts that break business logic).

Without exit criteria, tests can run indefinitely or generate inconclusive results. For example, a load test script in Gatling's Scala DSL:

```
setUp(
 scn.inject(
  rampUsersPerSec(10) to 100 during (5 minutes),
  constantUsersPerSec(100) during (10 minutes)
 )
).protocols(httpProtocol)
.assertions(
 global.successfulRequests.percent.gte(99.9),
 forAll.responseTime.percentile3.lte(200)
)
```

Here, assertions declare exit criteria: ≥ 99.9 % success and p99 ≤ 200 ms. Ensuring environment parity—using staging clusters identical to production—is crucial to avoid false confidence. Incorporate test ramp-up and cool-down phases to warm caches and allow resource stabilization. Finally, automate test runs and exit-criteria checks in CI pipelines, so that thresholds are enforced automatically before code merges. With a solid foundation in test types and exit criteria, you're ready to design realistic scenarios using specialized tools.

11.5.2 Scenario Design with JMeter, k6 & Gatling

Choosing the right tool and crafting realistic scenarios are key to meaningful performance tests. **Apache JMeter** uses XML test plans with Thread Groups to simulate users:

```
<ThreadGroup>
 <num_threads>200</num_threads>
 <ramp_time>60</ramp_time>
 <HTTPSamplerProxy guiclass="HttpTestSampleGui" testclass="HTTPSamplerProxy">
  <elementProp name="HTTPsampler.Arguments" elementType="Arguments"/>
  <stringProp name="HTTPSampler.domain">api.example.com</stringProp>
  <stringProp name="HTTPSampler.path">/products</stringProp>
  <stringProp name="HTTPSampler.method">GET</stringProp>
 </HTTPSamplerProxy>
 <ResponseAssertion/>
</ThreadGroup>
```

k6 scripts in JavaScript offer programmatic flexibility:

```
import http from 'k6/http';
import { sleep } from 'k6';
```

```
export let options = {
 vus: 50,
 duration: '15m',
 thresholds: { 'http_req_duration': ['p(95)<200'] }
};
export default function () {
 http.get('https://api.example.com/products');
 sleep(Math.random() * 3);
}
```

Gatling's Scala DSL enables complex scenario logic:

```
val scn = scenario("Checkout")
 .exec(http("View Cart").get("/cart"))
 .pause(1)
 .exec(http("Submit Order").post("/checkout").body(StringBody(session =>
session("orderJson").as[String])))
 .pause(2)
setUp(scn.inject(atOnceUsers(50))).protocols(httpProtocol)
```

Design scenarios that mimic real user journeys identified in Chapter 11.2: mix read-heavy browse with write-heavy purchase flows. Parameterize test data—user credentials, search terms—to avoid cache skew. Use CSV feeders in Gatling or JMeter to supply dynamic payloads. Monitor back-end resource metrics (DB connection pool usage, GC pause times) in tandem with request metrics.

Scenarios should include think times (sleep) to model real pacing, and vary user paths to stress different components. Integrating scenario execution into CI/CD pipelines—triggered nightly or on-demand—keeps performance regressions visible. Having crafted robust scenarios, you then introduce fault injection into these tests to validate resilience under load.

11.5.3 Fault Injection & Chaos Under Load

Fault injection under performance load tests how well systems degrade and recover when failures coincide with high traffic. Combining chaos engineering with load testing exposes cascading issues hidden under stress. Tools like **LitmusChaos**, **Gremlin**, or custom scripts can inject pod terminations, network latency, or CPU stress into your test environment. A LitmusChaos YAML for pod kill during k6 load:

```
apiVersion: litmuschaos.io/v1alpha1
kind: ChaosEngine
metadata:
 name: pod-delete-chaos
```

```
spec:
 appinfo:
  appns: default
  applabel: "app=order-service"
 experiments:
 - name: pod-delete
  spec:
   components:
    env:
    - name: TOTAL_CHAOS
     value: "2"
```

While k6 is ramping to 200 RPS, trigger CPU hogs:

```
gremlin attack cpu --target tag="order-service" --length 60s --cpu 80
```

Continuously monitor request success rates and latency. Evaluate system behavior against your error budgets and exit criteria. Identify whether bulkheads isolate failures or if load shedding occurs. Record fault-injection events in tracing systems so you can correlate anomalies to specific experiments. Blend fault injection scenarios—pod kills, DB latency, DNS failures—with your synthetic traffic profiles to approximate production incidents. Document each chaos test in a **chaos playbook** with rollback steps. By stress-testing failure modes under load, you gain confidence in system resilience before real-world incidents strike. Next, we move from validation to planning capacity to meet future demands.

11.6 Capacity Planning & Forecasting

11.6.1 Utilization Curves & Knee Point Detection

Capacity planning starts with understanding how system throughput relates to resource utilization. A **utilization curve** plots request rate (RPS) on the x-axis against CPU or latency on the y-axis. At low load, CPU and latency scale linearly; beyond a certain "knee point," latency spikes and error rates increase dramatically.

Detecting the knee point programmatically can be done by measuring second derivative changes or using piecewise linear regression. A simple Python approach using NumPy:

```
import numpy as np
from scipy.signal import argrelextrema
```

```
throughputs = np.array([100,200,300,400,500,600,700,800])
latencies = np.array([50,60,80,120,200,400,800,1600])
# Compute discrete second derivative
second_deriv = np.diff(np.diff(latencies))
knee_indices = argrelextrema(second_deriv, np.greater)[0] + 1
print("Knee at throughput:", throughputs[knee_indices])
```

Identifying the knee guides right-sizing: running significantly below it wastes money, while beyond it risks instability. Documenting knee points for each service area—API layer, database, cache—helps allocate capacity effectively. With knee detection in place, you can move on to forecasting demand over time.

11.6.2 Statistical Demand Forecasting (ARIMA, Prophet)

Predicting future demand leverages historical traffic data and time-series models. **ARIMA** models handle short-term autoregressive and moving-average patterns. **Facebook Prophet** excels at capturing multiple seasonalities (daily, weekly, yearly) and holiday effects. Using Prophet in Python:

```
import pandas as pd
from prophet import Prophet


df = pd.read_csv('requests.csv') # columns: ds,timestamp and y, request_count
model = Prophet(daily_seasonality=True, weekly_seasonality=True)
model.add_seasonality(name='monthly', period=30.5, fourier_order=5)
model.fit(df)
future = model.make_future_dataframe(periods=30) # next 30 days
forecast = model.predict(future)
model.plot(forecast)
```

The forecast plot highlights expected peaks and troughs, with confidence intervals. Use these predictions to schedule scaling events or budget allocations. Continuous model retraining integrates new data to refine forecasts. Additionally, anomaly detection on residuals flags when real traffic deviates significantly, triggering investigations or autoscaler overrides. With demand predictions in hand, you can optimize resource provisioning and cost—covered next.

11.6.3 Right-Sizing: Over- vs. Under-Provisioning

Right-sizing allocates just enough capacity to meet forecasted demand and performance SLOs at minimal cost. **Over-provisioning** reduces risk of saturation but wastes budget; **under-provisioning** saves money but risks throttling and errors. Use demand forecasts and knee-point data to compute recommended instance counts:

```
forecast_peak = forecast['yhat'].max()
desired_rps_per_instance = knee_throughput * 0.8
instances = int(np.ceil(forecast_peak / desired_rps_per_instance))
```

In Kubernetes, set HPA's minReplicas to a floor and maxReplicas to a ceiling based on these calculations. Schedule periodic reviews—weekly or monthly—to adjust right-sized numbers as traffic patterns evolve. Use spot instances or burstable VM types where low-priority workloads can absorb risk. Automate rightsizing proposals via scripts and present costs savings versus risk trade-offs to stakeholders. By right-sizing on a data-driven basis, you strike the optimal balance between performance headroom and budget adherence. Having planned capacity, the next step is to implement scaling patterns that realize these plans in production.

11.7 Horizontal & Vertical Scaling Patterns

11.7.1 Autoscaling Metrics & Policies

Autoscaling dynamically adjusts resources in response to metrics, reducing manual intervention. Two main approaches exist: **horizontal scaling** (adding/removing instances) and **vertical scaling** (adjusting instance size). In Kubernetes, a HorizontalPodAutoscaler example:

```
apiVersion: autoscaling/v2beta2
kind: HorizontalPodAutoscaler
metadata:
 name: api-hpa
spec:
 scaleTargetRef: { apiVersion: apps/v1, kind: Deployment, name: api-deploy }
 minReplicas: 3
 maxReplicas: 20
 metrics:
 - type: Resource
  resource: { name: cpu, target: { type: Utilization, averageUtilization: 60 }}
 - type: Pods
  pods: { metric: { name: http_requests_per_second }. target: { averageValue: "1000" }}
```

Here, the HPA scales pods to maintain an average CPU utilization of 60 % and ~1 000 RPS per pod. In cloud services like AWS, you configure Application Auto Scaling with CloudWatch alarms on custom metrics. Vertical scaling, such as AWS EC2 instance resizing, can be automated via AWS Lambda functions triggered by cost or performance alarms, though it often requires restart.

Define **scaling policies** with cooldown periods to avoid thrashing (rapid scale-up/down). Use predictive autoscaling—leveraging demand forecasts—to pre-scale before anticipated peaks, reducing cold-start latency. A flow diagram:

349

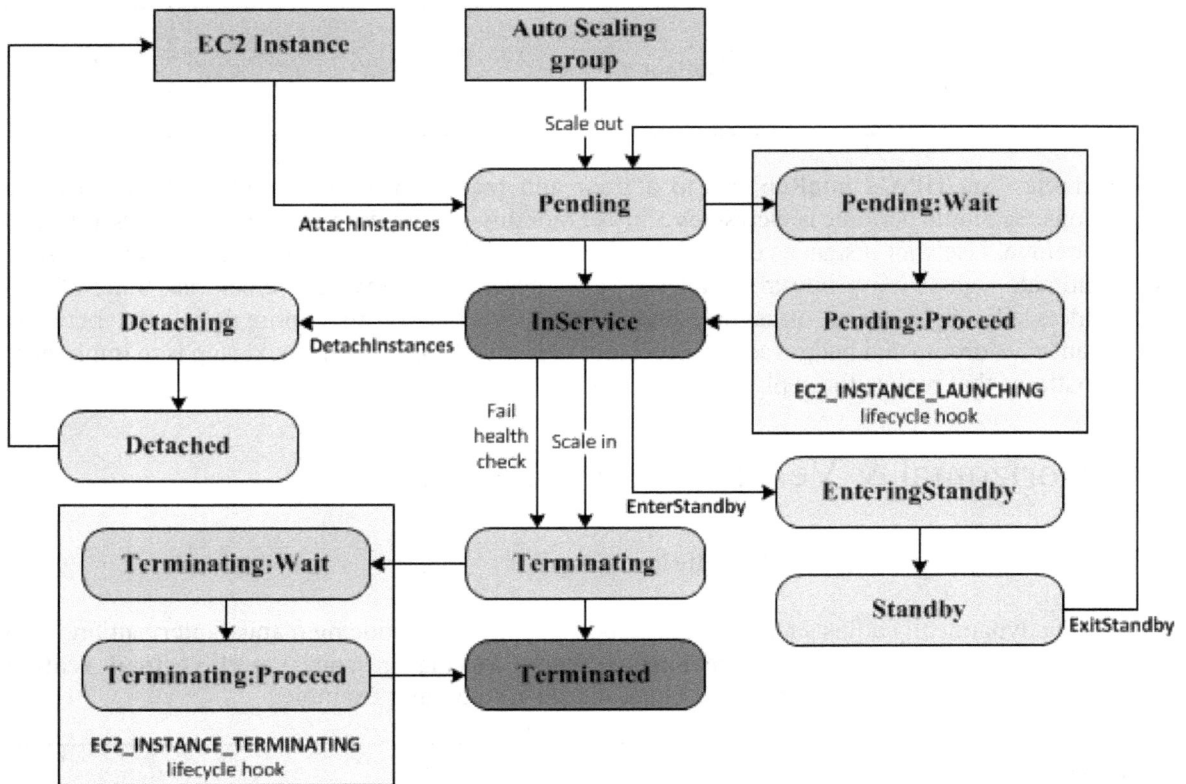

Monitor stabilization windows, and adjust thresholds iteratively based on observed behavior. With autoscaling configured, you must also partition data and workload strategically, discussed next.

11.7.2 Shard, Partition & Consistent Hashing Strategies

As data volume grows, distributing load across multiple nodes prevents single-instance bottlenecks. **Sharding** splits data by key range (e.g., user ID ranges); **partitioning** abstracts this across different back-end stores. Consistent hashing evenly distributes keys and minimizes rebalancing when nodes change. A simple Java implementation using Guava's ConsistentHash:

```
HashFunction hf = Hashing.murmur3_128();
List<Node> nodes = List.of(new Node("A"), new Node("B"), new Node("C"));
ConsistentHash<Node> ring = ConsistentHash.create(hf, nodes, 100);
Node home = ring.get("user123"); // routes to a node
```

When a node joins or leaves, only ~1/N keys move, ensuring stable routing. For databases like MongoDB or Cassandra, configure cluster buckets and token ranges accordingly. Diagram of consistent hash ring:

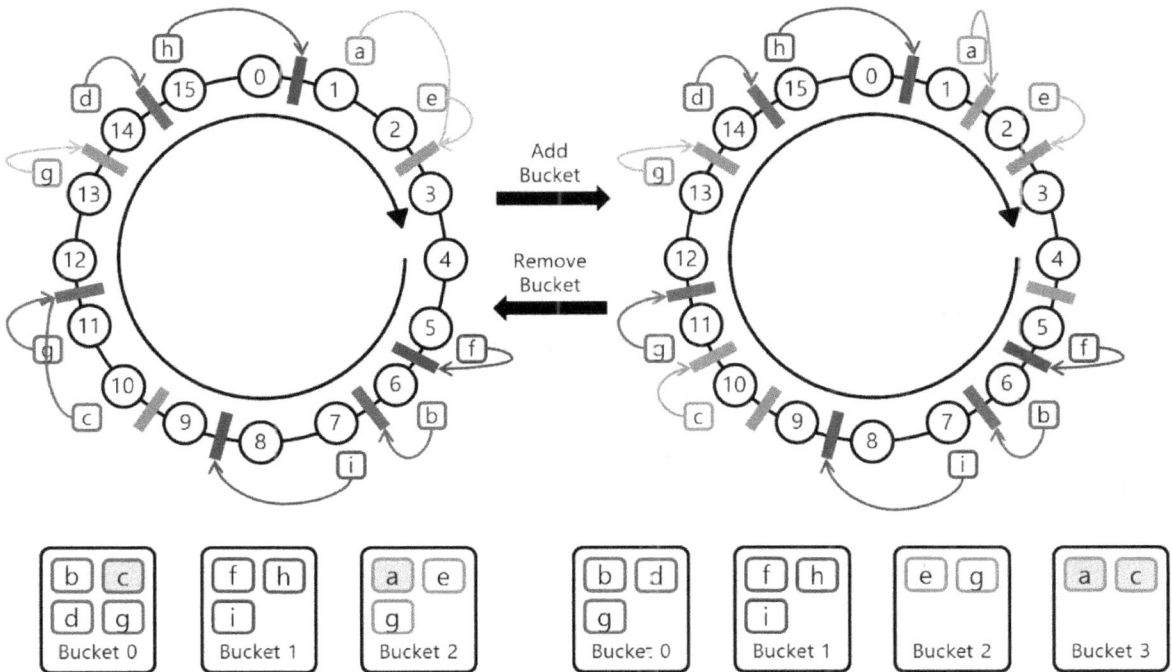

Partitioning also applies to message queues—multiple Kafka partitions allow parallel consumers. Combined with autoscaling, sharding maximizes throughput while containing failures to individual shards. After partitioning data, you must handle stateful scaling concerns like leader election and session affinity.

11.7.3 Scaling State: Leader Election, Sticky Sessions

Stateless services scale easily, but stateful components—caches, job schedulers, WebSocket servers—require special handling. **Leader election** ensures only one instance performs critical tasks. In Spring, use **LeaderInitiator** with a Zookeeper or etcd backend:

```
@Bean
public LeaderInitiator leaderInitiator(CuratorFramework client) {
 LeaderSelectorSelector selector = new LeaderSelectorSelector(client, "/leader", listener);
 return new LeaderInitiator(client, selector);
}
```

Only the elected leader runs scheduled jobs; others standby. **Sticky sessions** (session affinity) bind user sessions to specific pods to retain in-memory session state:

```
apiVersion: v1
kind: Service
metadata: { name: web }
spec:
 sessionAffinity: ClientIP
 ports: [{ port: 80 }]
 selector: { app: web }
```

Alternatively, offload sessions to a distributed store (Redis, Memcached) to eliminate affinity. For real-time connections (WebSockets), use ingress configurations or service meshes (Envoy) that support sticky routes based on cookies or headers. A leader-election diagram:

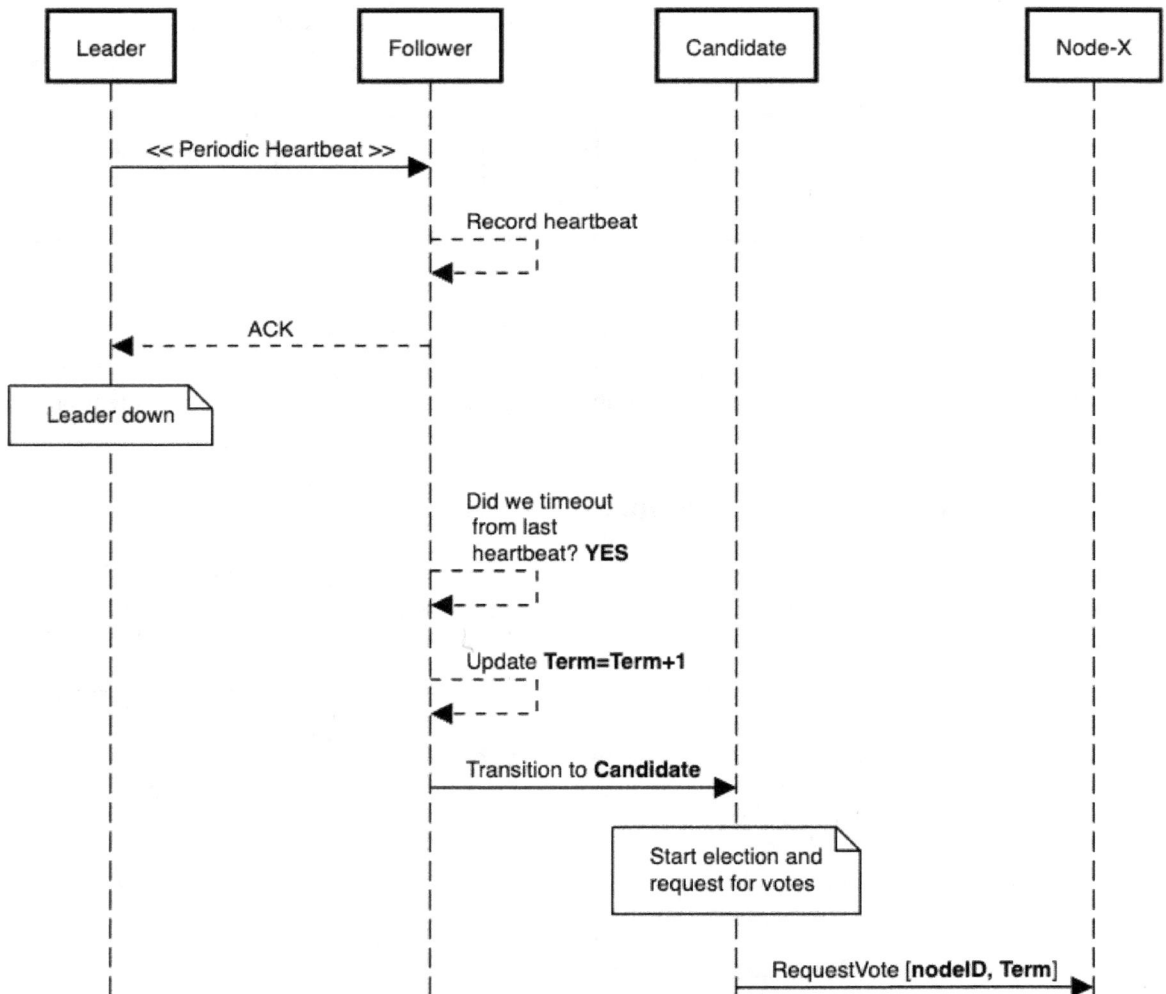

By combining sharding, autoscaling, leader election, and session strategies, you achieve both high throughput and correct stateful behavior. With scaling patterns in place, the next chapter explores concurrency and parallelism techniques to maximize resource utilization.

11.9 Caching & Data Locality

11.9.1 Hierarchical Cache-Layers (L1/L2/L3)

Implementing multiple cache layers reduces latency and alleviates load on back-end systems. An **L1 cache** lives in-process (e.g., Caffeine in Java or a local in-memory dictionary in Python), offering sub-millisecond access. An **L2 cache** sits on a co-located service (Redis or Memcached) shared by all instances in a region, with typical latencies of 1–5 ms. An **L3 cache** may be a CDN or edge cache positioned close to end users, returning data in single-digit milliseconds from global POPs.

A sample Java layering using Caffeine + Redis:

```
LoadingCache<String, Product> l1Cache = Caffeine.newBuilder()
  .maximumSize(10_000)
  .expireAfterWrite(5, TimeUnit.MINUTES)
  .build(key -> {
   // Fallback to L2 (Redis) if absent
   Product p = redisClient.get(key);
   if (p != null) return p;
   // Fallback to DB
   p = db.loadProduct(key);
   redisClient.set(key, p, Duration.ofMinutes(10));
   return p;
  });
```

Here, a cache-aside pattern populates L1 and L2 in the same loader. The L3 layer (CDN) is configured via HTTP cache headers on the API:

```
Cache-Control: public, max-age=60, s-maxage=300
```

A PlantUML diagram details request flow:

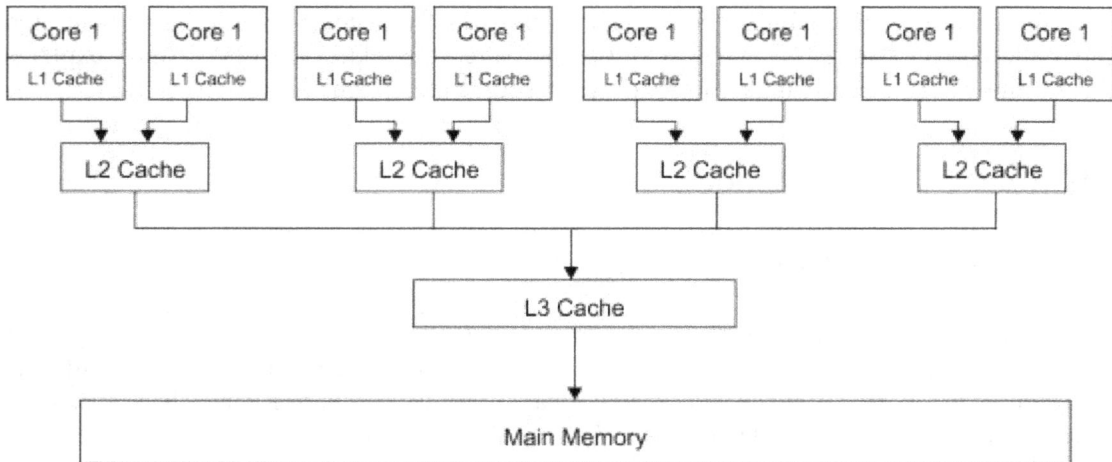

By structuring caches hierarchically, you minimize database queries, serve regional traffic from L2 caches, and offload most reads to the CDN edge. This layering also bounds cache sizes and eviction policies per layer: L1 can have small max entries and short TTL, L2 can be larger with longer TTL, and L3 relies on HTTP cache semantics. With multiple cache-levels tuned, you can next extend caching across geographies for global performance.

11.9.2 Geographically Distributed Edge Caches

Global services benefit from deploying caches at multiple regions to reduce latency and mitigate transient network failures. **CDNs** like Cloudflare or AWS CloudFront replicate static assets automatically. For dynamic API responses, consider **edge-caching** via API Gateway cache integrations or distributed key-value stores (e.g., FaunaDB, Cloudflare Workers KV).

Example AWS API Gateway stage cache:

```
CacheClusterEnabled: true
CacheClusterSize: '0.5' # GB
MethodSettings:
 - ResourcePath: '/products/*'
   HttpMethod: GET
   CachingEnabled: true
   CacheTtlInSeconds: 60
```

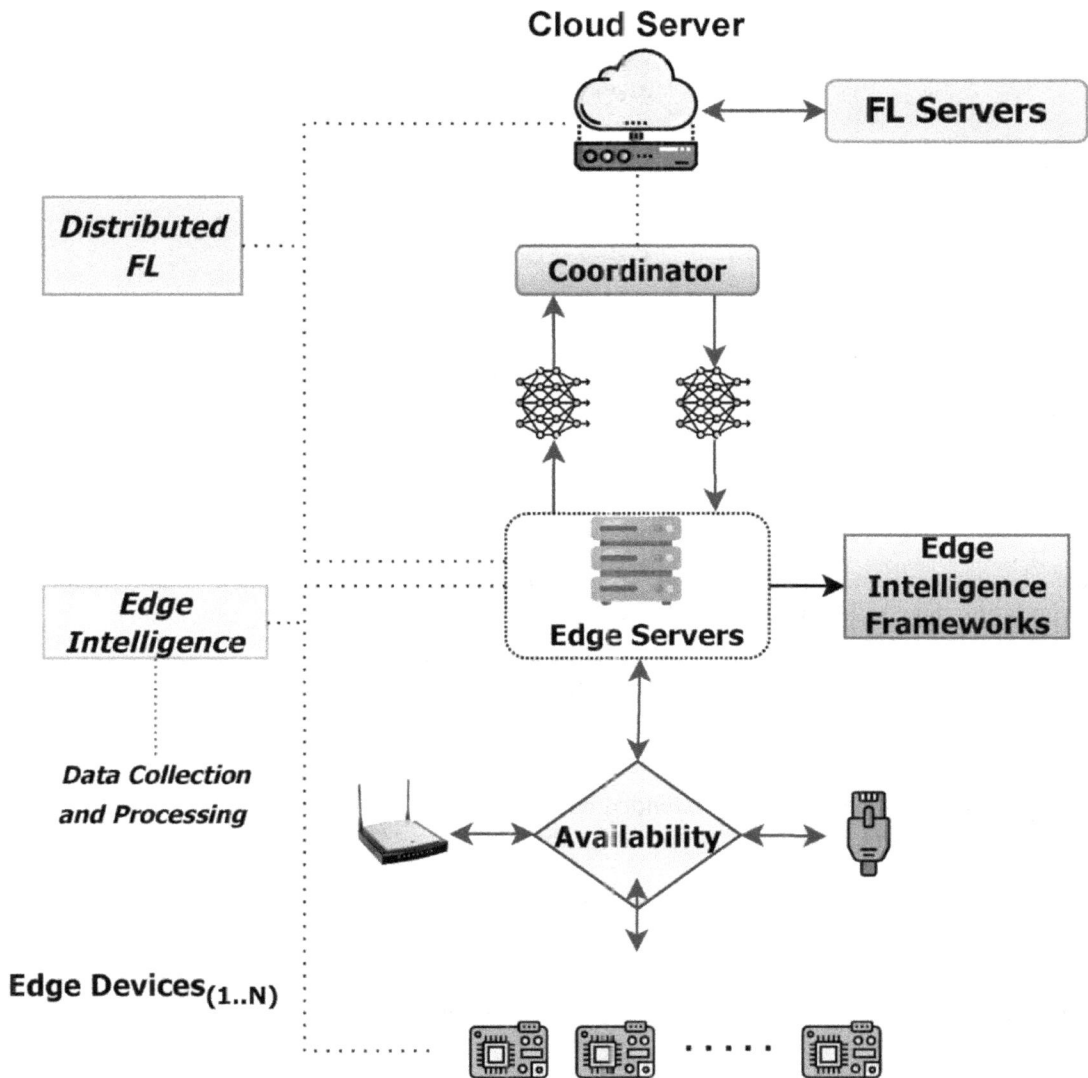

For true global edge caching of dynamic JSON, you can front your services with a service mesh sidecar that plugs into a global cache tier like **Akamai** or **Fastly**. Each edge location holds a copy of popular data, refreshed via Cache-Control or surrogate keys.

A regional cache topology:

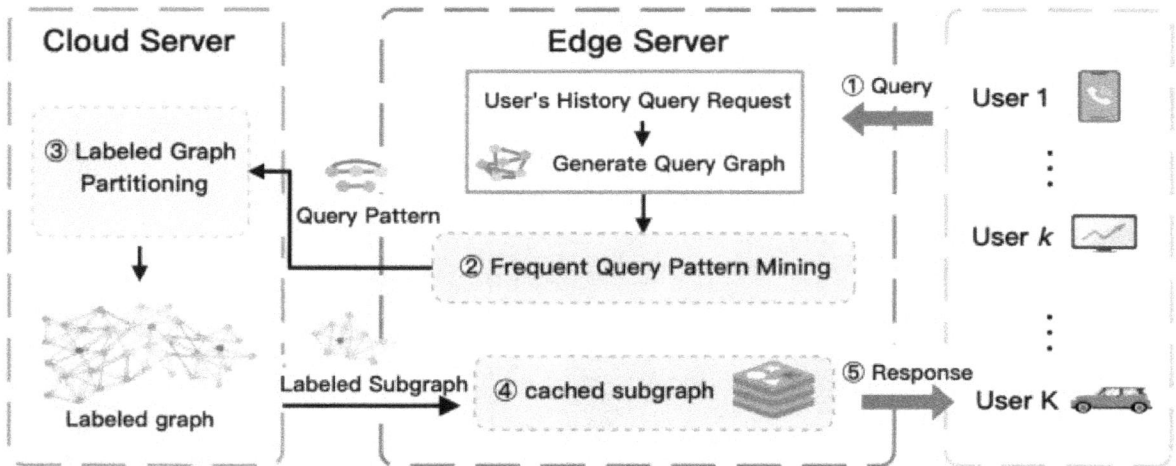

Edge caches use consistent hashing or geo-routing to direct invalidations back to the correct region. When updating data, publish a **surrogate-key** invalidation request to all edge locations:

```
curl -X POST https://api.fastly.com/service/{SERVICE_ID}/purge/{SURROGATE_KEY}
```

This global caching strategy yields single-digit-millisecond reads for most users while retaining control over data freshness. Having extended caching globally, you must ensure that caches remain consistent across layers, as detailed in the next subsection.

11.9.3 Cache Consistency: Write-Invalidate, Write-Through

Maintaining consistency across hierarchical and distributed caches demands clear invalidation or write-through strategies. In **write-through** caching, every database write also updates the cache synchronously:

```
@Transactional
public void updateProduct(Product p) {
 db.update(p);
 redisClient.set("product:"+p.getId(), p, 300);
}
```

This simplifies reads but adds latency to writes. Alternatively, **write-invalidate** evicts cache entries on updates, relying on subsequent reads to repopulate:

```
@Transactional
```

```
public void updateProduct(Product p) {
 db.update(p);
 redisClient.del("product:"+p.getId());
}
```

For multi-instance invalidations, publish cache-invalidations via a pub/sub channel:

```
redisClient.publish("cache-invalidate", "product:"+p.getId());
```

Subscribers on each instance perform local eviction. A sequence diagram:

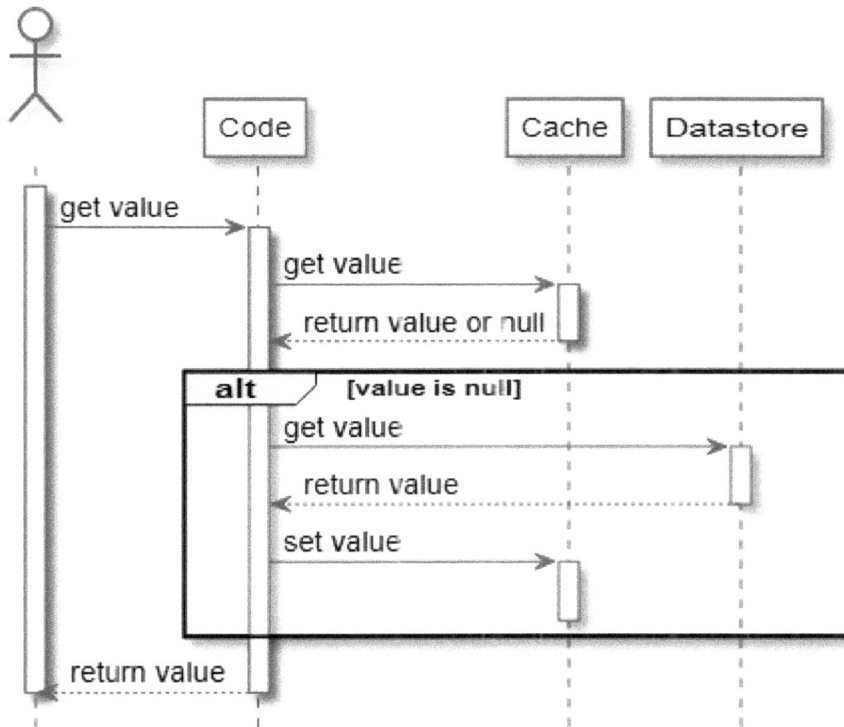

Consistency strategies must consider race conditions: if a read and write occur concurrently, stale data may slip through. Techniques like **conditional cache set** (only if version matches) or **per-entry version tags** mitigate these issues. Ensuring correctness under consistency constraints completes your caching strategy, allowing you to move on to scalable data storage architectures.

11.10 Database & Storage Scalability

11.10.1 Connection Pool Tuning & Query Plans

Database connection pools (HikariCP, c3p0) limit open connections to avoid overloading the DB. Tune pool size based on average query latency and DB capacity:

```
spring:
 datasource:
  hikari:
   maximum-pool-size: 20
   minimum-idle: 5
   connection-timeout: 30000
```

A rough formula:

```
optimal_pool_size ≈ (application_threads * db_latency_ms) / (db_latency_ms +
app_think_time_ms)
```

Monitor pool usage metrics—active vs. idle connections—and set a leakDetectionThreshold to catch unclosed connections:

```
leak-detection-threshold: 15000 # 15 seconds
```

On the query side, analyze execution plans (EXPLAIN ANALYZE in PostgreSQL) to identify missing indexes or sequential scans:

```
EXPLAIN (ANALYZE, BUFFERS)
SELECT * FROM orders WHERE created_at > now() - '1 day'::interval;
```

The plan output shows actual row counts and I/O stats. If you see Seq Scan, consider adding a btree index:

```
CREATE INDEX ON orders (created_at DESC);
```

Regularly capture slow query logs:

```
log_min_duration_statement = 500 # ms
```

Automate plan regression tests: run explain plans in CI and compare key metrics to detect plan changes. With connections and query plans optimized, you can replicate data to serve read-heavy workloads.

11.10.2 Read Replicas, Multi-Leader & CQRS Patterns

Read replicas offload SELECT traffic from a primary database. In AWS RDS:

```
engine: aurora-postgresql
replicaCount: 2
```

Applications route reads to replicas via a reader endpoint:

```
spring.datasource.read-url=jdbc:postgresql://reader.cluster-ro-xyz.us-east-
1.rds.amazonaws.com:5432/app
spring.datasource.write-url=jdbc:postgresql://cluster-xyz.us-east-1.rds.amazonaws.com:5432/app
```

Multi-leader (active-active) setups—supported by distributed databases like CockroachDB or YugabyteDB—allow writes in multiple regions with synchronous or asynchronous replication. They incur conflict-resolution complexity but reduce write latency globally.

The **CQRS** pattern separates read and write models: write operations update the **command** side (normalized schema), while read requests query a denormalized **query** side (optimized for fast LOOKUP), often populated via event streams:

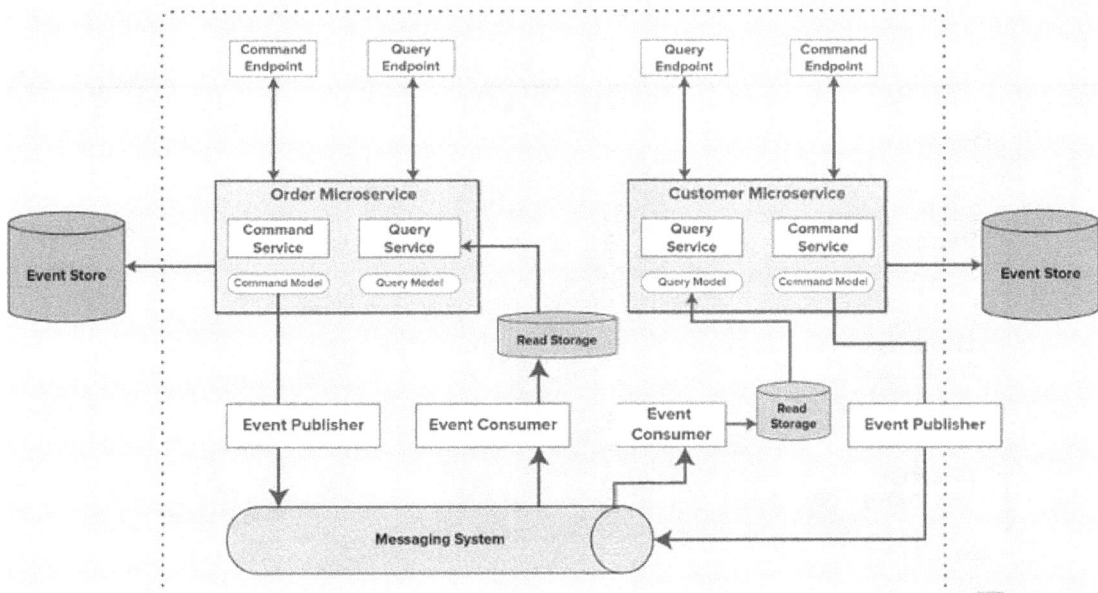

This separation lets you scale reads and writes independently, tailor schemas per workload, and support complex read queries without compromising transactional integrity. Having distributed writes and reads handled, we next manage colder, long-term storage needs.

11.10.3 Cold vs. Hot Storage Tiers & Archiving

Data hygiene and cost efficiency demand tiered storage: **hot** storage (SSD-backed, low TTL caches or transactional tables) for recent, frequently accessed data; **warm** storage (spinning disks, slower indexes) for moderately aged data; and **cold** storage (object storage like S3 Glacier) for archival compliance. Implement time-based partitions in your database:

```
CREATE TABLE events_2025_05 PARTITION OF events FOR VALUES FROM ('2025-05-01')
TO ('2025-06-01');
```

Archive old partitions to S3:

```
COPY          events_2024_01          TO          's3://archive-bucket/events/2024-01.csv'
IAM_ROLE=arn:aws:iam::123456789012:role/MyRedshiftRole;
DROP TABLE events_2024_01;
```

Use lifecycle policies on object storage:

```
{
"Rules": [
  { "Prefix":"events/2024-", "Expiration":{"Days":365} }
]
}
```

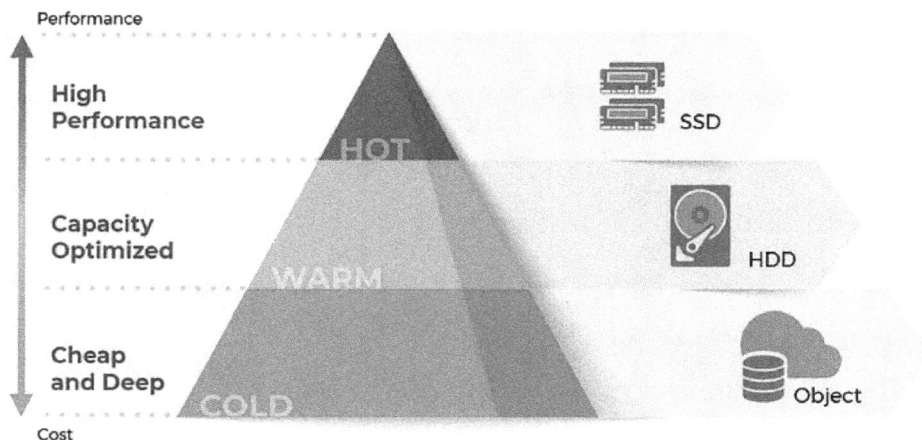

Query cold data with Athena or BigQuery to handle compliance audits without bloating primary systems. A tiered diagram:

[App] → [Hot DB (0–30 days)] → [Warm DB (30–365 days)] → [Cold Archive (>365 days)]

By tiering data, you optimize for performance where it matters and minimize costs for historical archives. With storage scalability addressed, you're prepared to identify and mitigate common performance anti-patterns.

11.11 Performance Anti-Patterns & Mitigations

11.11.1 Chatty I/O & N+1 Queries

Chatty I/O arises when services or databases exchange many small calls rather than batching work, amplifying network latency. In ORMs, the **N+1 query** problem occurs when loading a collection triggers individual queries per item:

```
List<Order> orders = orderRepo.findAll();
for (Order o : orders) {
 o.getItems().size(); // triggers SELECT * FROM items WHERE order_id=?
}
```

For N orders, this produces N+1 queries. Fix by eager-fetching with a join:

```
@Query("SELECT o FROM Order o JOIN FETCH o.items")
List<Order> findAllWithItems();
```

Or batch fetching:

```
hibernate.default_batch_fetch_size: 50
```

At the service boundary, replace chatty REST calls:

```
// Chatty: multiple HTTP calls
productService.get(productId);
inventoryService.get(productId);
pricingService.get(productId);
// Better: composite endpoint
catalogService.getProductSummary(productId);
```

Design **backend-for-frontend** (BFF) layers that aggregate multiple microservice calls into a single request, reducing round-trips. Profiling tools often highlight high RPC counts; aim to keep single user journeys under 3–5 network hops. By consolidating calls, you reduce cumulative latency and load on inter-service links. Having eliminated chatty patterns, you must also ensure your resilience mechanisms are correctly configured, detailed next.

11.11.2 Circuit-Breaker Misconfiguration

Circuit breakers protect downstream services from overload but can backfire if misconfigured. Too-low error thresholds cause premature opens; too-long open durations stall recovery. A typical Resilience4j config:

```
resilience4j.circuitbreaker:
 configs:
  default:
   failureRateThreshold: 50
   waitDurationInOpenState: 30s
   slidingWindowSize: 20
```

If the sliding window is small, transient errors open the breaker unnecessarily. If too large, the system continues to flood a failing downstream. Visualizing state transitions on a timeline helps calibrate settings:

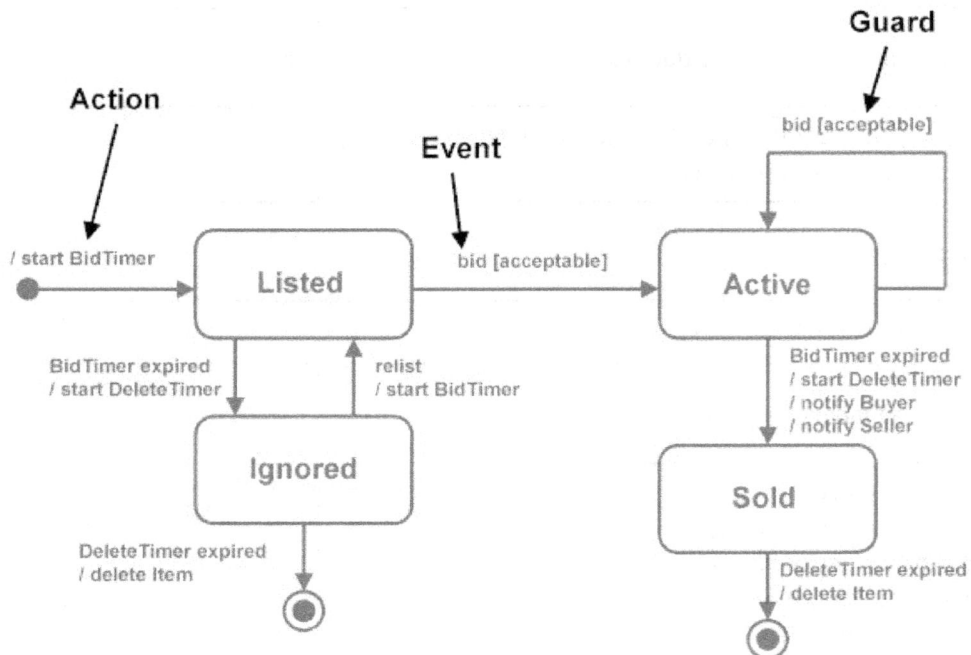

Integrate circuit-breaker events into metrics dashboards to monitor open/close rates. Combine circuit breakers with bulkheads to prevent entire service saturation. Test configurations under synthetic errors to validate correct behavior. By tuning breakers thoughtfully, you avoid "tripping" healthy services or overloading tired ones. With fault isolation behaving correctly, you can now detect and resolve memory issues.

11.11.3 Memory Leaks & GC Thrashing

Memory leaks—unbounded growth of heap usage—cause garbage collectors to run more frequently, leading to **GC thrashing** where the JVM spends most time collecting rather than executing application code. Detect leaks by monitoring heap usage over time:

```
jvm_memory_used_bytes{area="heap"}
```

If heap usage steadily increases without returning to a baseline, you likely have a leak. Use tools like **VisualVM** or **YourKit** to take heap dumps and analyze retained object graphs. In Java, fix leaks by ensuring listener registrations are removed:

```
eventBus.unregister(this);
```

And clearing thread-local variables:

```
ThreadLocal.remove();
```

Tune GC parameters to balance pause time and throughput:

```
-XX:+UseG1GC -XX:MaxGCPauseMillis=200
-XX:InitiatingHeapOccupancyPercent=70
```

G1GC's region-based collection reduces pause durations but requires adequate heap headroom.

Profiling with jstat -gc or GC logs (-Xlog:gc*) reveals pause times and frequencies. Addressing root leaks and appropriate GC tuning prevents thrashing, restoring predictable performance. Having mitigated anti-patterns, you're positioned to align performance improvements with cost goals via FinOps practices.

11.12 Cost-Aware Optimization & FinOps

11.12.1 Unit Economics Per Request

Calculating the cost to serve each request—**unit economics**—unlocks data-driven optimization. Determine total infrastructure spend per hour (compute, storage, networking) and divide by requests per hour:

```
hourly_cost = sum(instance.count * instance.rate for instance in instances)
requests_hour = metrics['http_requests_total'].rate(1h)
cost_per_request = hourly_cost / requests_hour
print(f"${cost_per_request:.6f} per request")
```

For example, $5/hour across 50 000 RPS yields $0.0001 per request. Drill down by endpoint using tagged metrics:

```
sum(rate(http_requests_total{endpoint="/checkout"}[1h])) by (instance)
```

This reveals that heavy /checkout calls cost more—in CPU, database, or third-party fees—than simple /ping endpoints. Visualize unit costs per endpoint to prioritize optimizations where they yield the greatest savings. Tying cost data to performance metrics ensures you don't optimize low-value paths at high expense. With per-unit costs clear, you can explore purchasing strategies to reduce spend in the next subsection.

11.12.2 Spot, Reserved & Savings Plans

Cloud providers offer discounted pricing for non-on-demand compute via **spot instances** (preemptible VMs), **reserved instances**, and **savings plans**. Spot instances can cost up to 90 % less but can be reclaimed at any time, ideal for stateless or batch workloads. In Terraform:

```
resource "aws_instance" "worker_spot" {
  ami       = "ami-123"
  instance_type  = "c5.large"
  spot_price    = "0.05"
  instance_interruption_behavior = "terminate"
}
```

Reserved instances or **savings plans** commit to 1- or 3-year usage in exchange for 30–60 % discounts. Evaluate purchase options by comparing **effective hourly costs** against 24/7 usage:

```
reserved_hourly = (reserved_upfront + (reserved_hourly_rate * hours_per_year)) /
hours_per_year
savings = on_demand_rate - reserved_hourly
```

Use portfolio analyses (AWS Cost Explorer) to identify under-utilized reservations and adjust. For mixed workloads, adopt a **hybrid strategy**: reserved capacity for baseline demand, spot for burst or fault-tolerant tasks, and on-demand only when necessary. This purchasing mix feeds into FinOps reports, guiding budget allocation. With discounted resources secured, automate rightsizing and scheduling to avoid waste.

11.12.3 Automated Rightsizing & Shutdown Schedulers

Even with optimal instance types, workloads ebb and flow—overnight or over weekends, many services see minimal traffic. Automate rightsizing with scripts or cloud-native tools (AWS Compute Optimizer):

```
# Pseudo-code
for instance in ec2_instances:
 utilization = cloudwatch.get_metric('CPUUtilization', instance.id)
 if utilization < 20% for 7 days:
  recommend_downsize(instance)
```

For non-critical or dev environments, implement **shutdown schedulers** via AWS Instance Scheduler or Azure Automation:

```
# AWS Instance Scheduler CRON rule
cron(0 1 * * ? *) # 1:00 AM UTC
```

At scheduled times, lambda functions stop or hibernate instances:

```
def handler(event, context):
 for inst in list_instances(tag='env:dev'):
  ec2.stop_instances(InstanceIds=[inst.id])
```

Tagging resources by environment and owner ensures policies apply only where desired. Automated rightsizing and shutdowns can cut cloud spend by 30–50 % without manual effort. Integrate recommendations into Slack or ticketing workflows for visibility. By continuously aligning performance capacity with real demand and purchase strategies, your system remains both performant and cost-efficient—completing the Performance & Scalability Engineering discipline.

Conclusion

Mastering performance and scalability is a continuous journey of measurement, analysis, and refinement. It requires a holistic approach: capturing detailed metrics and traces to pinpoint hot spots, stress-testing realistic scenarios to validate architectural assumptions, and planning capacity to meet future demand without overspending. Equally important is cultivating a performance-aware culture—

where every engineer understands the impact of design decisions on latency, throughput, and cost. With the right tools and practices in place, teams can confidently evolve their architectures, deliver delightful user experiences at scale, and maintain operational efficiency as systems and workloads inevitably grow.

Chapter 12. DevOps, CI/CD & Governance

In today's software ecosystems, the boundary between writing code and running it in production has all but disappeared. Teams must not only craft high-quality features but also automate every step of delivery—from static checks and security scans to provisioning servers and orchestrating zero-downtime rollouts. Embracing DevOps means treating your entire lifecycle as code, with fully automated pipelines that catch issues early, enforce architectural guardrails, and promote consistency across environments. At the same time, lightweight governance—through decision records, policy-as-code, and collaborative feedback loops—ensures that fast delivery does not come at the expense of maintainability, security, or compliance. This chapter shows how to weave together CI/CD practices, infrastructure automation, and governance artifacts into a unified process that empowers both developers and operators.

12.1 Automated Pipelines

12.1.1 Linting & Format Enforcement

Ensuring consistent code style and eliminating trivial issues before compilation is the first gate in any robust pipeline. Linting tools like ESLint, Pylint, or RuboCop analyze source code for stylistic violations and common bugs, catching everything from unused variables to potential security flaws. By integrating "fix" modes into pre-commit hooks, teams can automatically reformat code and apply fixes, reducing developer friction. For example, an ESLint configuration in .eslintrc.js might include:

```
module.exports = {
 env: { browser: true, es2021: true },
```

```
extends: ["eslint:recommended", "plugin:@typescript-eslint/recommended", "prettier"],
parser: "@typescript-eslint/parser",
plugins: ["@typescript-eslint"],
rules: {
 "no-unused-vars": "warn",
 "semi": ["error", "always"],
 "@typescript-eslint/no-explicit-any": "off"
 }
};
```

Coupling ESLint with Prettier via the eslint-plugin-prettier plugin ensures that formatting rules are enforced as lint rules, unifying style across the codebase. Pre-commit, a Python tool or Husky in the Node ecosystem, blocks commits until linting passes:

```
# .husky/pre-commit
npm run lint && npm run format:check
```

Because linting can be computationally intensive, it often runs on staged files locally and then on the entire codebase in CI. This two-tier approach provides rapid feedback during development while guaranteeing full coverage in the build. Visualizing linting as stage 1 in the pipeline helps stakeholders understand that no code moves forward without meeting these basic standards:

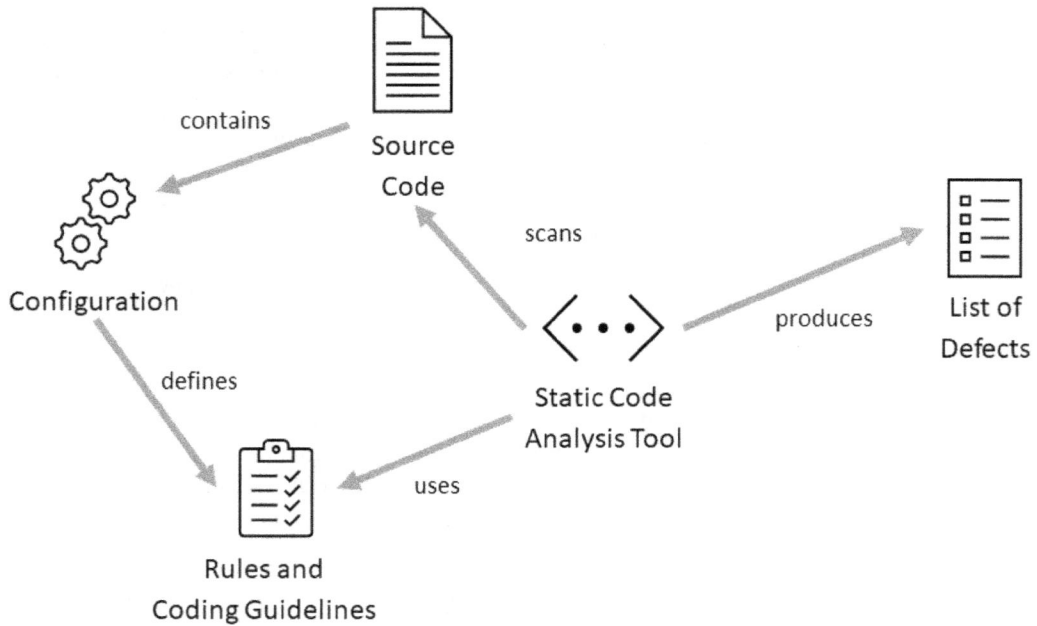

By enforcing linting early, teams prevent style debates in code reviews and reduce review friction. Consistent code style increases readability, reduces cognitive load, and improves the reliability of subsequent static analysis. With code consistently formatted and basic issues weeded out, the pipeline naturally flows into deeper static analysis and security scanning.

12.1.2 Static Analysis & Security Scanning

After stylistic checks, pipelines invoke static analysis tools that delve deeper into code semantics and potential vulnerabilities. Tools like SonarQube, CodeQL, Bandit (for Python), and FindSecBugs (for Java) scan for code smells, duplicate code, and known security hotspots—buffer overflows, SQL injections, unsanitized inputs. For instance, integrating CodeQL with GitHub Actions:

```
- name: Initialize CodeQL
 uses: github/codeql-action/init@v2
 with:
  languages: java
- name: Perform CodeQL Analysis
 uses: github/codeql-action/analyze@v2
```

Rules engines categorize findings by severity and confidence, enabling configurable thresholds to block builds only on critical issues. Security scanning also covers open-source dependencies: tools like OWASP Dependency-Check, Snyk, or npm audit traverse the dependency graph to detect CVEs. A Jenkinsfile snippet:

```
stage('Dependency Scan') {
 steps {
  sh 'mvn dependency-check:check'
  script {
   def report = readJSON file: 'target/dependency-check-report.json'
   if (report.dependencies.find { it.vulnerabilities.size() > 0 }) {
    error "Vulnerabilities detected"
   }
  }
 }
}
```

Static analysis jobs often generate HTML or dashboard reports, archived as build artifacts for audit. To prevent noise, configure baseline suppression—existing issues are tracked but don't fail builds, while new issues immediately block progress. An activity diagram:

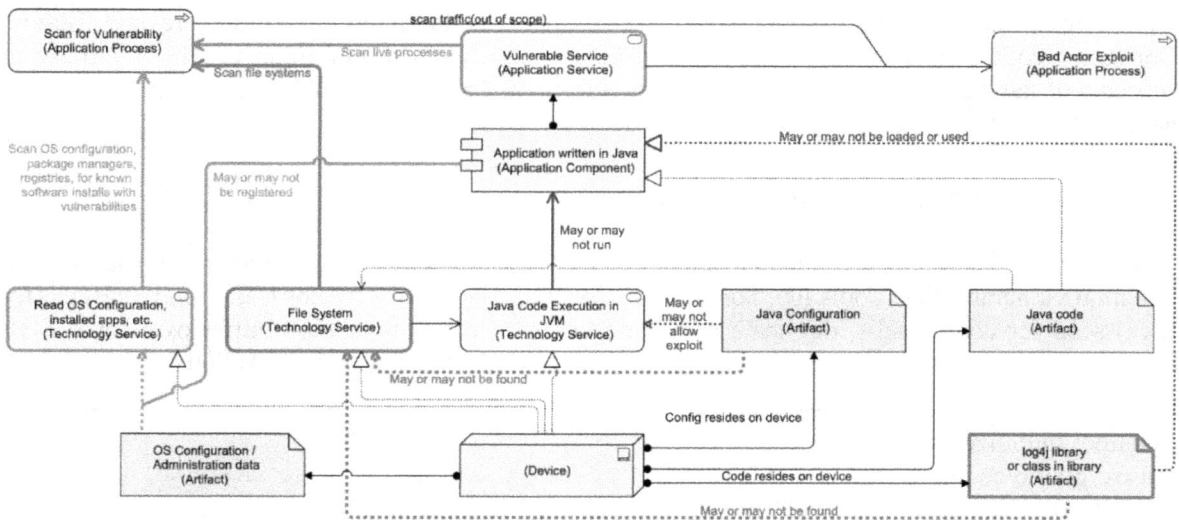

Combining style, static analysis, and dependency scanning in a single cohesive stage ensures that only high-quality, secure code advances. Once code passes these gates, the pipeline can execute architectural fitness tests to enforce structural rules.

12.1.3 Architectural Fitness Tests & Dependency Rules

Beyond syntax and security, maintaining architectural integrity requires enforcing dependency rules and module boundaries. **Fitness functions** codify architectural constraints—layering rules, banned imports, and package-dependency cycles—into automated tests. Tools like **ArchUnit** for Java, **Deptrac** for PHP, or **dependency-cruiser** for JavaScript analyze the import graph against defined policies:

```
@AnalyzeClasses(packages = "com.myapp")
public class ArchitectureTest {
 @ArchTest
 static final ArchRule no_upward_dependencies =
  slices().matching("com.myapp.(*)..").should().onlyDependOnSlices("com.myapp.$1..");
}
```

With dependency-cruiser, a JSON config defines forbidden paths:

```
{
 "forbidden": [
  { "name": "no-domain-to-ui",
   "from": { "path": "src/domain" },
   "to": { "path": "src/ui" }
```

```
    }
  ]
}
```

A build step runs these tests, and violation results are reported as build failures:

```
depcruise src --config .dependency-cruiser.json || exit 1
```

Fitness tests guard against architectural erosion—over time, teams inadvertently introduce shortcuts that violate layering. Visualizing the dependency graph as a sankey diagram highlights unexpected couplings. When a test fails, architects and developers can quickly pinpoint and remediate violations before they spread.

Embedding fitness tests in CI enforces architecture as code and keeps the system maintainable at scale. Every merge preserves intended module interactions, preventing shortcuts that lead to tangled codebases. With architecture validated, the pipeline proceeds to continuous testing and quality gates that verify functional behavior.

12.1.4 Continuous Testing & Quality Gates

Functional correctness and regression prevention hinge on a layered testing strategy—unit, integration, and end-to-end tests—automated in the pipeline. **Unit tests** run first, exercising individual functions or classes in isolation, typically completing in seconds. **Integration tests** validate interactions between modules, databases, and external services (mocked or in a test environment), often taking longer. **End-to-end (E2E) tests** spin up the full stack—frontend, backend, databases— and simulate user flows via tools like Cypress or Playwright. A GitLab CI example:

```
stages:
 - unit
 - integration
 - e2e

unit_tests:
 stage: unit
 script: npm run test:unit

integration_tests:
 stage: integration
 script:
  - docker-compose up -d test-db
```

```
  - npm run test:integration
 dependencies:
 - unit_tests


e2e_tests:
 stage: e2e
 script:
 - npm run start:staging &
 - npx cypress run
 dependencies:
 - integration_tests
```

Quality gates define thresholds—test coverage, flake rate, performance regressions—that must be met to pass. Coverage tools like **JaCoCo**, **Istanbul**, or **Coverage.py** generate reports; pipelines can fail if coverage dips below a certain percentage:

```
npm run coverage && node tools/check-coverage.js --threshold 80
```

Performance regression tests—load tests against pull-request environments—can detect degraded response times early. Combining functional and performance checks as quality gates ensures that code is both correct and performant before deployment. Results (pass/fail, coverage metrics, test durations) are displayed in merge requests for visibility. With tests passing, the pipeline can safely deploy to successive environments, orchestrated in parallel or sequence.

12.1.5 Pipeline Stages, Environments & Parallelism

Modern pipelines define multiple **stages**—build, lint, test, deploy—mapped to **environments** like dev, staging, and production. Granular stages allow fine-grained control over which jobs run where, enabling faster feedback in early stages and stricter checks later. For example, GitHub Actions separates workflows:

```
jobs:
 build:
  runs-on: ubuntu-latest
  steps: [...]
 test:
  needs: build
  runs-on: ubuntu-latest
  steps: [...]
 deploy-staging:
  needs: test
```

```
runs-on: ubuntu-latest
if: github.ref == 'refs/heads/main'
steps: [...]
```

Parallelizing independent jobs—unit tests, linting, and static analysis—reduces total pipeline time. Matrix builds can test multiple language versions or platforms concurrently:

```
strategy:
 matrix:
  node-version: [14, 16]
jobs:
 test:
  runs-on: ubuntu-latest
  strategy: ${{ matrix }}
  steps:
   - uses: actions/setup-node@v3
    with: { 'node-version': ${{ matrix.node-version }} }
   - run: npm ci
   - run: npm test
```

Environment-specific variables—API endpoints, credentials—are injected securely via secrets managers. Promotion patterns automate deployments: a successful staging deploy triggers canary or blue-green deploys to production. Viewing pipelines as directed acyclic graphs clarifies job dependencies, and visualization tools help teams optimize and debug flows. By structuring stages, leveraging parallelism, and aligning jobs to environments, automated pipelines deliver rapid feedback while upholding quality and consistency.

12.2 Infrastructure as Code

12.2.1 Declarative Definitions & Idempotence

Infrastructure as Code (IaC) treats infrastructure provisioning and configuration the same way as application code—stored in version control, reviewed in pull requests, and executed by automated tooling. Declarative IaC tools like **Terraform**, **Pulumi**, or **CloudFormation** describe desired state rather than imperative steps:

```
resource "aws_vpc" "main" {
 cidr_block = "10.0.0.0/16"
 tags = { Name = "main-vpc" }
}
```

Applying this file with terraform apply ensures that a VPC with the specified CIDR exists, creating or updating resources idempotently. Terraform's state file tracks existing infrastructure, allowing subsequent plan runs to detect drift. Declarative IaC fosters reproducibility—spinning up identical test, staging, and production environments from the same code. Parameterizing via modules and workspaces supports multi-tenant deployments and environment-specific overrides:

```
module "network" {
 source   = "./modules/network"
 cidr_block = var.vpc_cidr
}
```

By avoiding imperative scripts (bash, ansible ad-hoc modes) and trusting in declarative, idempotent definitions, teams reduce configuration drift and manual errors. With environment definitions codified, you can layer on configuration management and secrets handling to complete the provisioning picture.

12.2.2 Configuration Management & Secrets Handling

Once core infrastructure is provisioned, configuration management tools—Ansible, Chef, Puppet, or cloud-native Agents—install packages, configure services, and inject secrets. For example, Ansible playbooks can pull secrets from Vault:

```
- hosts: webservers
 tasks:
 - name: Fetch DB credentials
  hashivault_read:
   secret: secret/data/db
  register: db_creds


 - name: Configure application
  template:
   src: app.conf.j2
   dest: /etc/myapp/app.conf
  vars:
   db_user: "{{ db_creds.data.username }}"
   db_pass: "{{ db_creds.data.password }}"
```

By injecting secrets at provisioning time rather than baking them into images, you maintain confidentiality and support secret rotation without image rebuilds. For dynamic config, tools like **Consul** or **Spring Cloud Config** push updates to running services, enabling live reconfiguration. IaC pipelines typically integrate configuration management stages, ensuring that every environment emerges fully configured. Role-based access controls on secrets stores limit who can modify sensitive data, while audit logs track all read/write operations. With secrets handled securely, the next logical step is to create immutable environments via golden images or container images.

12.2.3 Immutable Environments & Golden Images

Immutable infrastructure replaces live configuration changes with new instances built from golden images, ensuring consistency and simplifying rollbacks. Tools like **Packer** build VM images with all OS packages and application dependencies baked in:

```json
{
"builders": [
  {
   "type": "amazon-ebs",
   "region": "us-east-1",
   "source_ami": "ami-0c02fb55956c7d316",
   "instance_type": "t3.medium",
   "ssh_username": "ubuntu",
   "ami_name": "myapp-{{timestamp}}"
  }
],
"provisioners": [
  { "type": "shell", "script": "scripts/install.sh" },
  { "type": "file", "source": "dist/app.jar", "destination": "/opt/app/app.jar" }
]
}
```

Packer output AMIs are then referenced in Terraform:

```
resource "aws_launch_configuration" "app" {
image_id    = data.aws_ami.myapp.id
instance_type = "t3.medium"
...
}
```

Because instances never change after launch, drift is impossible—updates always occur via new image builds. Container-based approaches (Docker) follow the same principle: build immutable images tagged by digest, push to registries, and update deployments to use the new image. This pattern eliminates configuration drift, simplifies debugging (each image is reproducible), and enables rapid rollbacks by re-deploying a previous image tag. Having established immutable artifacts, you can safely implement zero-downtime deployment strategies next.

12.2.4 Blue-Green, Canary & Rolling Upgrades

Zero-downtime deployments ensure user traffic sees only healthy versions during upgrades. **Blue-green** deployments maintain two production environments—blue (current) and green (new). A load balancer switches traffic atomically:

```
@startuml
participant LB
participant Blue
participant Green
LB -> Blue: 100% traffic
note right: Deploy new version to Green
LB -> Green: switch 100% traffic
LB --> Blue: 0% traffic
@enduml
```

A rollback is immediate: direct LB back to blue. **Canary** deployments gradually shift a percentage of traffic to the new version, monitoring error rates and latency before ramping to 100 %:

```
apiVersion: networking.istio.io/v1alpha3
kind: VirtualService
spec:
 http:
 - route:
 - destination: { host: myapp, subset: blue, weight: 90 }
 - destination: { host: myapp, subset: green, weight: 10 }
```

If green's metrics remain within thresholds, increase its weight. **Rolling upgrades** replace pods or VMs one at a time with overlap:

```
strategy:
 rollingUpdate:
  maxUnavailable: 1
  maxSurge: 1
```

Kubernetes and cloud auto-scaling groups handle rolling patterns natively. Rolling and canary approaches minimize risk and automate rollback logic. Integrating deployment strategies into IaC pipelines ensures consistency across services. With dynamic deployment patterns in place, the system can evolve continuously without service interruptions, but drift must still be detected and corrected.

12.2.5 Drift Detection & Self-Healing

Despite immutable definitions, external factors—manual changes, cloud console edits—can introduce drift. Tools like **Terraform's** plan compare actual state to declared state and report differences:

```
terraform plan -detailed-exitcode
# Exit code 2 indicates drift detected
```

Driftctl for AWS and **Config Rules** (AWS Config) or **Azure Policy** continuously evaluate resource compliance. On detection, automated remediation can occur via pipeline triggers or Lambda functions:

```
terraform apply -auto-approve
```

Or using a GitOps model with **ArgoCD** or **Flux**: drift in the cluster is synced back to the declared Git state or vice versa. Self-healing controllers (e.g., Kubernetes Operators) monitor CRDs and restore desired configurations when they diverge. A feedback loop diagram:

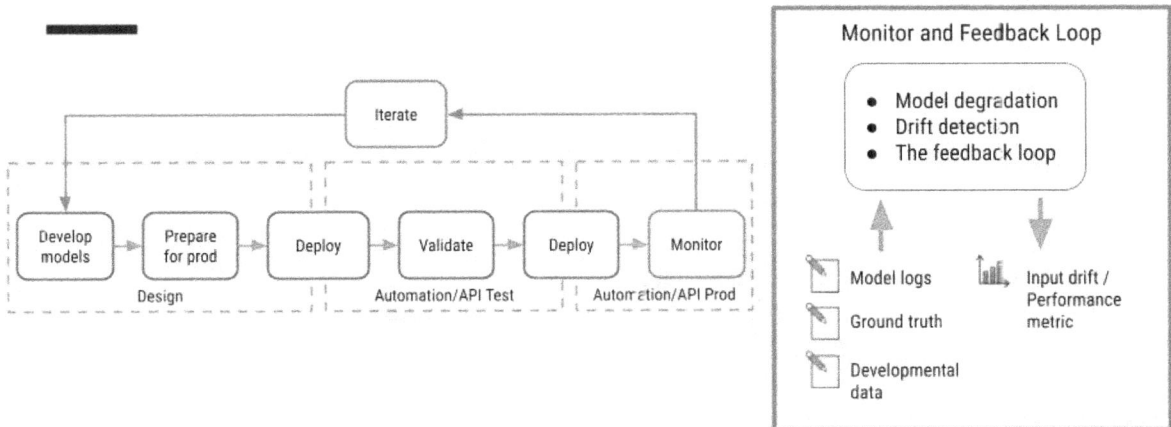

Proactive drift detection ensures environments remain trustworthy and simplifies compliance audits. With infrastructure fully automated and self-correcting, teams can focus on delivering features rather than firefighting config issues.

12.3 Architectural Decision Records (ADRs)

12.3.1 Purpose, Formats & Tooling

Architectural Decision Records (ADRs) document significant technical decisions—choice of frameworks, database engines, messaging patterns—and their rationale. ADRs serve as a lightweight governance mechanism, preserving context for future maintainers. A common ADR template (Markdown) includes:

```
# ADR 001: Choose PostgreSQL as Primary Data Store


## Context
We need a relational database for transactions, joins, and ACID guarantees.


## Decision
We will use PostgreSQL 14 on AWS RDS.


## Consequences
- Gains: robust SQL support, familiar tooling.
- Trade-offs: higher operational overhead vs. NoSQL.
```

Tools like **adr-tools**, **MkDocs ADR plugin,** or **structurizr** automate ADR creation and navigation. A typical command:

```
adr new "Use gRPC for internal RPC"
```

This generates a numbered file under docs/adr/, maintaining sequence and history. ADRs live alongside code, versioned in Git, providing traceability of when and why a decision was made. They encourage explicitness: instead of ad-hoc changes, teams review and agree on architectural shifts. With a consistent format, ADRs are searchable and linkable, forming a living architectural log that complements automated pipelines and infrastructure definitions.

12.3.2 Capturing Context, Trade-Offs & Alternatives

A high-quality ADR not only states a decision but captures the problem context, evaluated alternatives, and trade-offs. The **Context** section describes requirements and constraints—performance, scalability, team expertise. The **Alternatives** section lists options considered (e.g., MySQL, CockroachDB, DynamoDB), summarizing pros and cons:

Alternative	Pros	Cons

MySQL	Widely supported, proven performance	Lack of built-in JSON support
CockroachDB	Global distribution, PostgreSQL-compatible	Immature tooling, higher latency
DynamoDB	Serverless, auto-scaling	Requires NoSQL data modeling

The **Decision Drivers** section ranks evaluation criteria—consistency, latency, costs—often using a weighted scoring model. A small Python snippet for scoring:

```
drivers = {'consistency':0.4, 'latency':0.3, 'cost':0.3}
scores = {'mysql':(0.8,0.9,0.7), 'cockroach':(0.6,0.7,0.5)}
rankings = {k: sum(a*b for a,b in zip(drivers.values(),scores[k])) for k in scores}
```

By quantifying drivers, teams make defensible choices. The **Decision** section states the chosen option, and **Consequences** capture both expected benefits and technical debt incurred. Having thoroughly documented trade-offs, stakeholders can revisit decisions when contexts evolve, maintaining architectural agility.

12.3.3 Review Workflows & Deprecation

ADR creation should follow a lightweight review workflow—opening a pull request with the ADR document triggers automated checks (Markdown linting, link validation) and invites reviewer comments. A GitHub template like PULL_REQUEST_TEMPLATE.md prompts authors to tag architectural maintainers:

```
## Architectural Decision Record
- ADR#: 042
- Title: Use GraphQL Gateway
- Related Issues: #1234
- Reviewers: @arch-lead, @api-team
```

Each ADR PR is discussed and merged once consensus is reached. Over time, ADRs may become outdated; a **deprecation** process marks obsolete ADRs with metadata:

```
**Status:** superseded by ADR 045
```

Automated scripts can generate a summary table in README.md:

ADR	Title	Status
042	Use GraphQL Gateway	deprecated
045	Adopt gRPC for internal RPC	accepted

Deprecation ensures that new team members aren't confused by obsolete decisions. Periodic ADR reviews—announced in retrospectives—validate that architectural documentation remains relevant. With review workflows established, ADRs can be linked directly to CI/CD and release processes for full traceability.

12.3.4 Linking ADRs to CI/CD & Release Notes

To maximize ADR visibility, pipelines can surface relevant ADRs in release notes and deployment dashboards. For example, a CI job extracts ADRs merged since the last tag:

```
git log v1.2.0..HEAD --grep '^# ADR' --pretty=format:'- %s' > changelog/adr.md
```

In GitHub Actions:

```
- name: Generate ADR list
  run: git log ${{ github.event.before }}..${{ github.sha }} --grep '^# ADR' ...
  id: adr
- name: Comment ADRs on Release
  uses: actions/github-script@v6
  with:
    script: |
      github.rest.issues.createComment({
        issue_number: ${{ github.event.release.issue_number }},
        body: `### Architectural Decisions\n${{ steps.adr.outputs.adr_list }}`
      });
```

Release notes then include a section:

Architectural Decisions

- ADR 046: Migrate to Kubernetes network policies
- ADR 047: Introduce event sourcing for audit logs

Deploy dashboards (Jenkins, Spinnaker) can link to ADR files, so operators understand why certain deployment strategies were chosen. Embedding ADR references in pipeline logs—e.g., "Applying ADR 046 network policy" during deployment—closes the loop between documentation and execution. This traceability ensures that every code change aligns with the architectural narrative, fostering clarity and maintainability as the system evolves.

Conclusion

By codifying build, test, deployment, and operational workflows, organizations gain the agility to ship changes rapidly and the confidence that each release meets agreed-upon standards. Infrastructure as code and immutable environments eliminate configuration drift, while Bayesian decision records and policy enforcement embed accountability and traceability into every architectural choice. Security and compliance checks, shifted left into the pipeline, catch vulnerabilities before they reach production, and ChatOps integrations surface real-time insights and drive rapid incident response. Ultimately, this fusion of DevOps principles, continuous delivery, and lightweight governance creates a self-reinforcing engine of innovation—where every code change is safe, auditable, and instantly releasable, and where teams continuously learn and adapt based on direct feedback from their systems and users.

Chapter 13. Refactoring Legacy Systems Toward Clean Architecture

Navigating the tangled web of a mature codebase is one of the most formidable challenges software teams face. Over years of incremental feature delivery, monolithic applications accumulate technical debt, obscured business logic, and brittle dependencies that slow development and increase risk. Refactoring toward a clean, modular architecture requires a deliberate, incremental approach: carving out pieces of functionality, introducing clear boundaries, and replacing legacy components one slice at a time. This process demands more than just code changes—it requires careful coordination between teams, robust testing scaffolds to prevent regressions, and strategies for synchronizing data and behavior across old and new layers. By applying anti-corruption layers and façade patterns, teams can insulate freshly refactored services from legacy quirks, ensuring new modules communicate with the monolith without polluting their own clean design. Thoughtful sequencing of refactoring work— prioritizing high-risk hotspots and measuring each step's impact on maintainability—keeps the effort focused on areas that yield the greatest return on investment. Ultimately, refactoring a legacy system is as much a people and process exercise as it is a technical one, requiring cross-functional collaboration, clear communication of decisions, and an organizational commitment to continual evolution.

13.1 Strangling the Monolith

13.1.1 Identifying Bounded Contexts

Refactoring a monolith begins by carving it into discrete bounded contexts, each responsible for a cohesive slice of domain functionality. Bounded contexts encapsulate business capabilities—such as order processing, inventory management, and customer service—reducing coupling between unrelated features. Identifying them requires collaboration with domain experts to extract the ubiquitous language: the terms, processes, and rules that experts use daily. Event-storming workshops use colored sticky notes to map domain events, commands, and aggregates on a timeline, revealing natural boundaries. For example, events like **OrderPlaced** and **PaymentAuthorized** cluster around the order context, while **StockReserved** and **StockReplenished** remain in inventory. Visualizing these event flows helps segregate subsystems that share few interactions, guiding the decomposition of the codebase. Static analysis of the code can complement workshops: analyzing call graphs and import dependencies reveals modules with high intra-connectivity and low external coupling. Tools like Graphviz can render the module graph, highlighting tightly coupled clusters that align with business domains. In Java, you might run:

```
jdeps -recursive -dotoutput deps src/main/java
dot -Tpng deps/package-myapp.dot -o module-graph.png
```

The resulting diagram shows which packages import one another most heavily, guiding the selection of module boundaries. In addition to static structure, runtime metrics—such as frequency of cross-module calls—indicate performance-critical paths and logical interactions. Collecting telemetry on service interactions in production reveals hotspots that should be in the same context to avoid remote calls. A domain event map and a dependency graph combined form a **context map**, an essential artifact in domain-driven design. This context map can be annotated with strategic relationships: "conformist" for contexts that defer to upstream models, "anti-corruption" where translation layers are needed, and "partnership" for collaborative teams. Teams then validate the proposed contexts by reviewing real user journeys and ensuring end-to-end scenarios cross as few contexts as possible. A long user flow that touches six contexts likely indicates misplaced responsibilities and opportunities to merge contexts. After finalizing bounded contexts, establish explicit interfaces—APIs, message contracts—to mediate between them. Defining these interfaces early prevents teams from inadvertently leaking domain logic across context boundaries. Tools like OpenAPI can generate stub services for each context, enabling parallel development and incremental extraction. At this point, the monolith's decomposition blueprint is clear: each bounded context has its own codebase or module, its domain model, and its external contract, forming the foundation for strangling the monolith piece by piece.

13.1.2 Incremental Façade Patterns

Once bounded contexts are identified, the next step in strangling the monolith is to introduce incremental façade layers that intercept calls to legacy code. A façade acts as a thin wrapper around existing APIs or function calls, providing a stable interface for new modules while routing requests to the monolith underneath. This wrapper decouples new code from monolithic implementation details, allowing teams to redirect specific routes to microservices over time. For HTTP-based systems, an API gateway can implement façade patterns by proxying endpoints:

```
- path: /api/orders/**
```

```
method: GET
route:
- target: http://legacy-monolith/api/orders/{*}
  weight: 100
```

As new services come online, gateway routing weights shift (e.g., 90/10, 50/50) toward the microservice, enabling safe cutovers and quick rollbacks. In-process façade patterns use dependency injection: replace direct imports with an interface that resolves to either the legacy adapter or a new implementation:

```
public interface IOrderRepository { Order GetById(Guid id); }
public class LegacyOrderRepository : IOrderRepository { /* calls monolith */ }
public class NewOrderRepository  : IOrderRepository { /* calls microservice */ }
```

A DI container can toggle implementations based on feature flags:

```
<register          type="IOrderRepository"          use="LegacyOrderRepository"
condition="!Flag.NewOrderService"/>
<register          type="IOrderRepository"          use="NewOrderRepository"
condition="Flag.NewOrderService"/>
```

Feature flags orchestrate façade toggles at runtime without redeployment, enabling targeted canary releases. For messaging-based systems, façades wrap event producers, publishing to both the old bus and the new topic to ensure dual delivery during transition. Sequence diagrams clarify the façade flow:

```
@startuml
actor Client
participant API_Gateway
participant Façade_Service
participant Monolith
participant New_Service


Client -> API_Gateway: GET /orders/123
API_Gateway -> Façade_Service: fetchOrder(123)
alt Feature off
 Façade_Service -> Monolith: legacyFetchOrder(123)
 Monolith --> Façade_Service: OrderDTO
else Feature on
 Façade_Service -> New_Service: fetchOrder(123)
```

```
 New_Service --> Façade_Service: OrderDTO
end
Façade_Service --> API_Gateway: OrderDTO
API_Gateway --> Client: 200 OK
@enduml
```

Facade pattern – Diagram of sequence

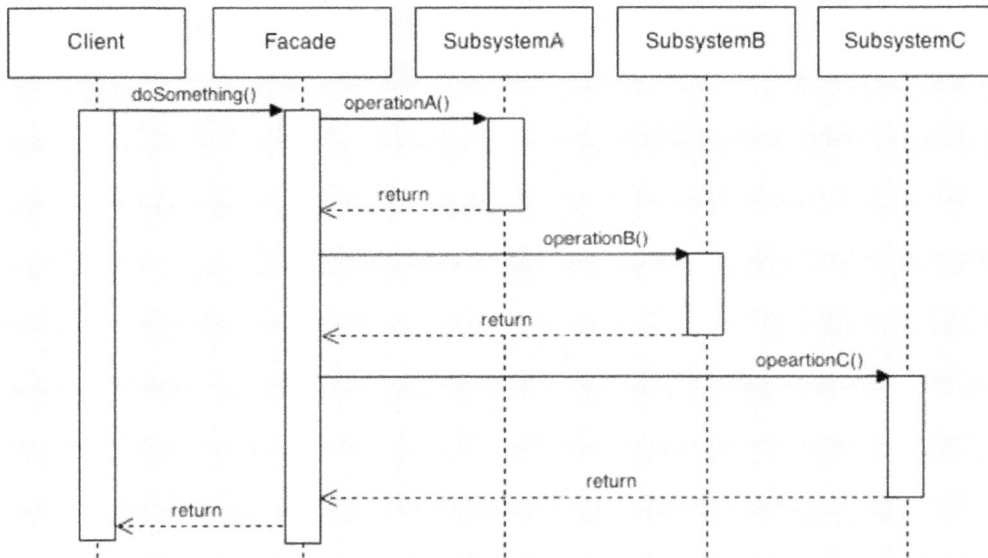

Incremental façades preserve end-user experience while enabling backend evolution at arbitrary pace. Careful instrumentation of both old and new paths—logging, metrics, and distributed tracing—ensures performance and correctness can be monitored continuously. Automated smoke tests exercise façades under both configurations, detecting deviations early. Over time, as new services prove reliable, façade code becomes the primary path and legacy adapters can be removed. Removing the old code simplifies the façade into a direct pass-through, completing the strangling process for that functionality. This approach reduces risk by localizing refactoring to small, testable slices rather than migrating entire domains at once. By incrementally shifting load, teams maintain high availability and gradual regression detection. The façade pattern thus serves as both a technical and organizational enabler, allowing backend teams to deliver new implementations independently of consumer teams. With façades in place, the next step is to insulate new modules via anti-corruption layers.

13.1.3 Designing Anti-Corruption Layers

Anti-Corruption Layers (ACLs) protect new domain models from being polluted by legacy models and translation quirks inherent in the monolith's design. An ACL acts as a boundary converter, translating data structures, exceptions, and business invariants from the legacy system's language into the clean model's language. In domain-driven design, the ACL implements interfaces in the target context, relying on adapter patterns to map entities and value objects. For example, a legacy OrderEntity with fields cust_id and order_total_cents must translate into the new domain's CustomerId and Money types:

```
public class LegacyOrderAdapter implements OrderRepository {
 private final LegacyOrderEntityRepository repo;
 public Order load(OrderId id) {
 LegacyOrderEntity e = repo.findById(id.value);
 return new Order(
 new OrderId(e.getId()),
 new CustomerId(e.getCustId()),
 Money.ofCents(e.getOrderTotalCents())
 );
 }
}
```

ACLs also handle command translations:

```
class OrderServiceACL {
 async placeOrder(cmd: PlaceOrderCommand): Promise<Order> {
 const legacyReq = {
 custId: cmd.customerId,
 items : cmd.items.map(i => i.toLegacy())
 };
 const legacyResp = await axios.post('/legacy/orders', legacyReq);
 return this.mapToDomain(legacyResp.data);
 }
}
```

Furthermore, ACLs normalize error handling, mapping legacy HTTP codes or numeric error identifiers into domain-specific exceptions:

```
try { legacyClient.CreateOrder(...); }
catch (LegacyClientException ex) when (ex.Code == 42) {
 throw new InsufficientInventoryException();
}
```

By centralizing translation logic, ACLs make the domain layer agnostic of legacy idiosyncrasies such as field name conventions or nullability rules. Testing ACLs requires both unit tests for mapping logic and integration tests against the legacy system to validate real-data transformations. A component diagram illustrates the ACL's role:

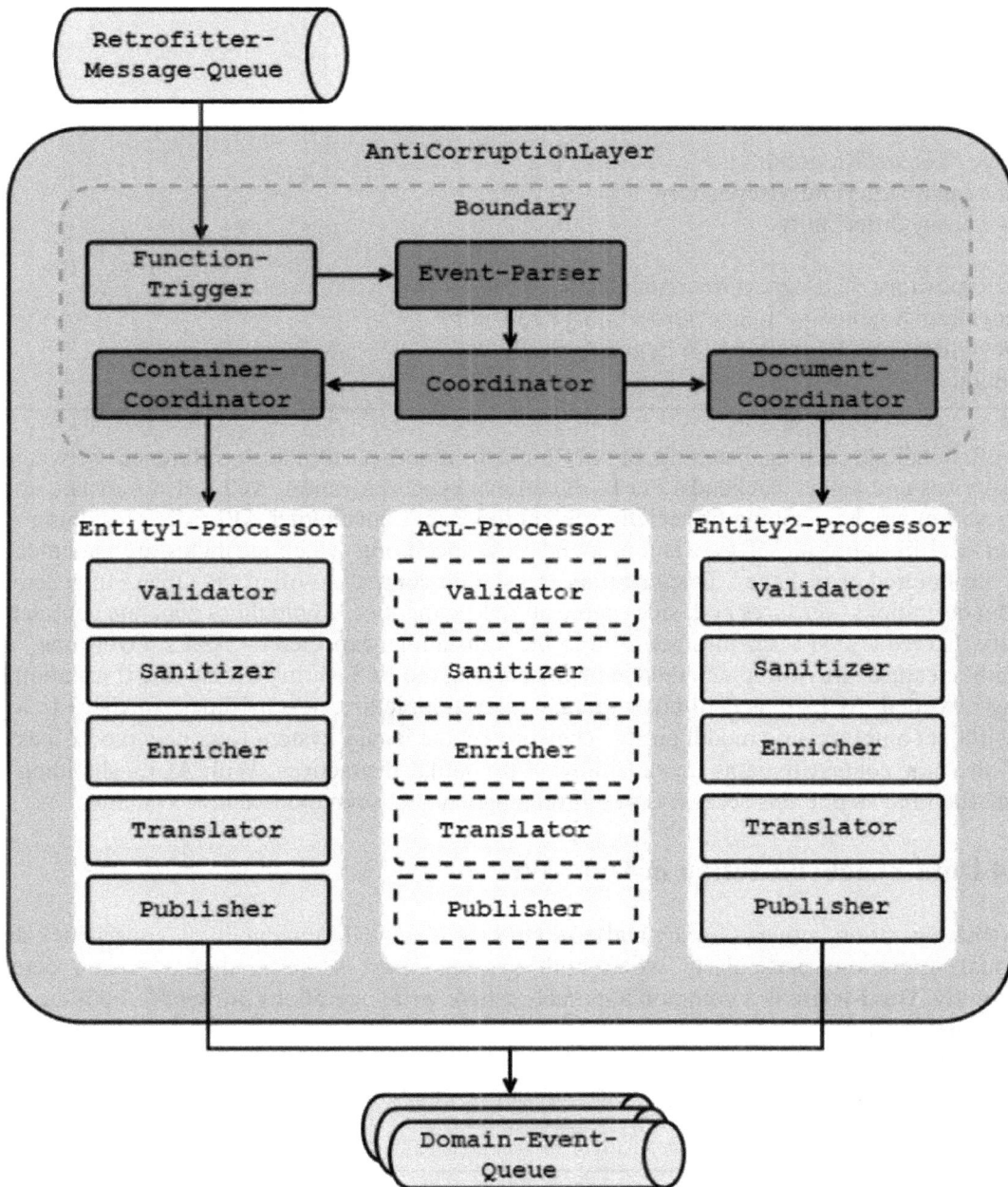

```
@startuml
package "New Domain" {
 interface OrderRepository
```

```
class Order
}
package "ACL" {
 class LegacyOrderAdapter
}
package "Legacy Monolith" {
 class LegacyOrderEntityRepository
 class LegacyOrderEntity
}
OrderRepository <|.. LegacyOrderAdapter
LegacyOrderAdapter --> LegacyOrderEntityRepository
LegacyOrderEntityRepository --> LegacyOrderEntity
@enduml
```

ACLs often include caching, batching, or retry logic to smooth performance differences between new microservices and legacy backends. For bi-directional synchronization, ACLs also translate updates to legacy commands: mapping CancelOrderEvent to legacyCancelOrder API calls. Designing ACLs requires careful definition of translation boundaries: specifying which attributes are canonical and which are ignored or reshaped. Documenting translation contracts—often via OpenAPI schemas or Protobuf definitions—ensures both sides agree on field semantics. CI pipelines generate contract tests to verify that legacy API schemas conform to the translations expected by ACLs. Over time, as the monolith's features are re-implemented in microservices, the ACL shrinks, removing translation code no longer needed. ACLs thus facilitate a gradual migration, letting new modules coexist with legacy code without compromising model purity. They protect the legacy system from new model leaks and ensure the new context remains uncontaminated by outdated practices. With ACLs shielding your domain, the final step in this section is synchronizing data between old and new systems.

13.1.4 Data Synchronization & Dual-Writes

Data synchronization between legacy and new systems is critical to maintaining consistency during a gradual migration, particularly when both systems must serve read and write operations concurrently. **Dual-write** is a common approach, where write operations are sent to both the legacy database and the new microservice, ensuring both data stores remain in sync. Implementing dual-write requires transactional guarantees to avoid partial updates: ideally, you wrap writes in a transactional outbox or saga to coordinate multiple endpoints. For example, in a Spring Boot application:

```
@Transactional
public void placeOrder(Order o) {
 legacyRepository.save(o.toLegacyEntity());
 outboxRepository.save(
  new OutboxEvent("OrderPlaced", o.toJson())
 );
```

```
}
```

A background poller reads the outbox table and publishes to a message bus, allowing new services to subscribe and update their own data store:

```
while (true) {
 List<OutboxEvent> events = outboxRepo.findUnpublished();
 events.forEach(e -> kafka.send(e.getType(), e.getPayload()));
 outboxRepo.markPublished(events);
}
```

This ensures **eventual consistency** without two-phase commits directly against the databases. Alternatively, **change data capture** (CDC) tools like Debezium stream binlog events from the legacy database into Kafka, from which downstream services materialize views in the new schema. A CDC flow:

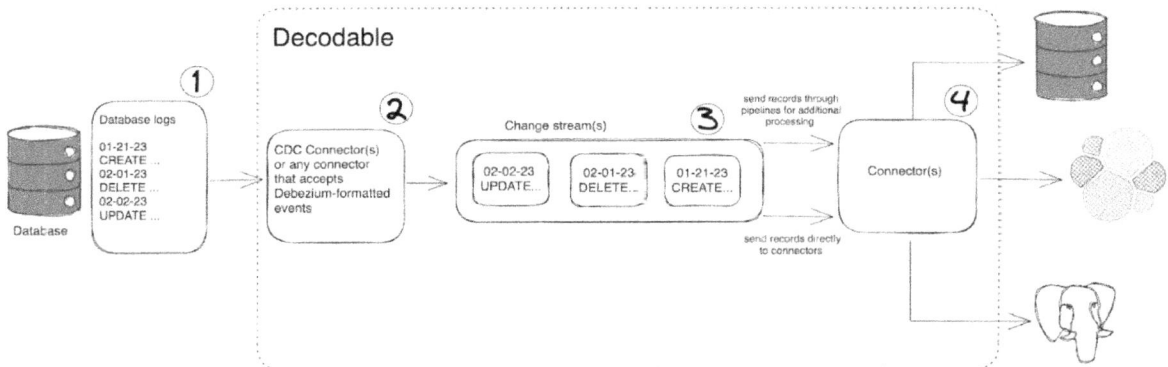

```
@startuml
database "Legacy DB" as LDB
queue  "Debezium Connector" as CDC
processor "Kafka Streams"  as KS
db   "New DB"    as NDB
LDB --> CDC: binlog events
CDC --> KS: change events
KS --> NDB: transformed writes
@enduml
```

With CDC, you avoid coupling between the legacy application code and new services, but must manage schema evolution in both systems. Hybrid dual-write + CDC architectures use outbox dual-writes to guarantee changes originating in code and CDC to capture any external operations. Conflict resolution strategies—last-write wins, source-of-truth overrides, or manual merge—must be defined for concurrent writes. Monitoring tools track lag between legacy writes and new system consumption, alerting when synchronization delays exceed thresholds. Data validation checks compare entity counts and checksums periodically to detect missing or inconsistent records. Tools like **Great Expectations** validate data in both systems against predefined expectations, catching schema drift or data anomalies. Synchronization code must handle partial failures: if the new system is down, writes to the outbox still record business events for later replay; if the legacy system is down, queue buffering can defer legacy updates. Over-provisioning outbox capacity and ensuring idempotent consumers prevents data duplication and loss. As more functionality migrates to new services, the monolith's outbox shrinks and the legacy data store can ultimately be retired. A clear migration plan defines cut-over points where new services fully own specific contexts, allowing final data backfill and removal of dual-write mechanisms.

13.2 Risk-Driven Refactor Sequencing

13.2.1 Finding High-Churn Hotspots

Risk-driven refactoring begins by pinpointing high-churn hotspots—areas of the codebase that undergo frequent changes, bug fixes, or feature additions. These hotspots often harbor both functional importance and accumulated technical debt, making them ideal candidates for early refactoring to reduce risk and cost. To identify hotspots, teams analyze version control history, computing metrics such as churn rate (lines added/removed per file) and commit frequency. A simple git command to compute churn per file:

```
git log --numstat --pretty="%H" | \
awk 'NF==3 {added[$3]+=$1; deleted[$3]+=$2} END{ \
 for (f in added) printf "%s %d\n", f, added[f]+deleted[f] }' \
| sort -nr -k2 | head -n 20
```

Files with the highest aggregate changes indicate complexity or unclear requirements causing repeated fixes. Complementing churn data with **defect density**—the number of bug reports per module—reveals files where errors concentrate. Integrating Jira or GitHub issues data via APIs can correlate commit messages with issue tags, showing which files are most often tweaked to resolve defects. Tools like **CodeScene** visualize hotspots in the IDE, overlaying code complexity metrics (cyclomatic complexity, coupling) onto churn maps.

Modules with both high churn and high complexity are particularly risky—refactoring here yields the greatest maintainability improvements. Once hotspots are identified, teams propose bounded contexts from Section 13.1 to maximize the impact of modularization. Combining hotspot analysis with architectural maps ensures cut slices cross minimal context boundaries, reducing coupling. Business criticality overlays show which hotspots correspond to high-revenue or high-risk features, guiding resource allocation. For example, if the checkout process exhibits 40% of all churn and processes 60% of transactions, it becomes the highest-priority target. Hotspot data should be reviewed in cross-functional meetings, involving developers, QA, and product owners to align technical and business priorities. Automated scripts can refresh hotspot metrics weekly, generating dashboards accessible to the team via Grafana. Tracking hotspot evolution over time reveals whether refactoring efforts are effective: hotspots should shrink as new code takes over. Establishing thresholds—e.g., files with churn >1 000 changes per year or complexity >10—flags candidates for refactoring. Dedicated "refactoring sprints" can focus on these hotspots, ensuring resources are allocated where they deliver the greatest ROI. With hotspots mapped, the next step is to estimate business and technical risk for each candidate area.

13.2.2 Estimating Business & Technical Risk

Estimating risk for refactoring efforts requires evaluating both **technical risk**—the likelihood of introducing regressions or causing outages—and **business risk**—the impact on revenue, user satisfaction, or compliance. Technical risk factors include code complexity, test coverage, number of dependencies, and historical defect rates in a module. Business risk factors consider transaction volume, SLAs, regulatory requirements, and the criticality of a feature to core workflows. Teams can use a **risk matrix** plotting technical risk on the x-axis and business impact on the y-axis, classifying modules into quadrants—high-tech-high-business modules demand caution. For example, a payments processor has high business impact (handles revenue) and potentially high technical risk (complex domain logic), placing it in the "Red Zone" requiring heavy testing and gradual rollout. Conversely, an infrequently used reporting module might score low on both axes and be refactored later. Quantitative scoring uses a 1–5 scale for each dimension and averages factors to compute composite risk scores:

Module	Churn (1–5)	Complexity (1–5)	Coverage Inv (1–5)	Impact (1–5)	Risk (Avg)
OrderService	5	4	2	5	4.0
UserController	3	3	4	3	3.25

Coverage inverted means low coverage yields higher risk, encouraging test-first refactor planning. Visualizing these scores on a bubble chart—bubble size representing defect density—surfaces modules with both high risk and high ROI. For regulatory modules (e.g., GDPR data handling), additional compliance risk multipliers raise business impact scores. Risk estimation workshops involve domain experts, QA leads, and security teams to validate factors and weightings. Documenting risk assessments in ADRs ensures transparency. As refactoring progresses, revisit risk scores: modules become safer as coverage improves and complexity decays. Automate risk re-evaluation by integrating code-metrics tools—SonarQube, CodeScene—that feed updated complexity and coverage data to risk dashboards. In an agile setting, risk-based stories include acceptance criteria covering both functional and non-functional safeguards: test coverage thresholds, performance benchmarks, and rollback plans. For high-risk modules, include extra safety nets: feature flags, canary deployments, and enhanced monitoring. Combining risk estimates with capacity and timelines forms a **refactor roadmap** mapping each module to a release cycle. With risk quantified, the next challenge is to prioritize refactoring tasks by expected return on investment and strategic impact.

13.2.3 Prioritizing by ROI & Impact

Prioritizing refactoring tasks by return on investment (ROI) aligns technical improvements with business outcomes, ensuring limited resources deliver maximum value. ROI estimation combines anticipated benefits—reduced defect resolution time, faster feature delivery, lower operational costs—with estimated refactoring effort. A formula:

$$ROI = (Benefit - Cost) / Cost$$

Benefits can be quantified in developer hours saved per week, reduced outages per quarter, or percentage improvement in cycle time. For example, a module causing two incidents monthly—each taking eight hours to resolve—costs 16 hours per month. Refactoring it reduces incidents by 75%, saving 12 hours monthly. If the refactor takes 80 hours, six-month ROI is $(72-80)/80 = -10\%$, suggesting the effort may not pay off quickly. Conversely, a module slowing features delivery by 40 hours monthly, at a 160 hour refactor cost, yields a six-month benefit of 240 hours and ROI of 50%. WSJF (Weighted Shortest Job First) refines ROI by dividing business value plus risk reduction by job size:

$$WSJF = (BusinessValue + RiskReduction) / JobSize$$

Ranking by WSJF surfaces high-impact, small-effort tasks first. A WSJF table:

Task	Value	RiskReduct	Size	WSJF
Refactor payment adapter	9	8	5	3.4
Add tests to reporting module	4	5	2	4.5
Extract user service	8	6	9	1.6

Here, adding tests scores highest, guiding immediate focus. Visualizing WSJF in a Kanban board helps teams commit to prioritized items. ROI and WSJF calculations benefit from integration with project tools: Python scripts fetch Jira estimates, assign business values, and compute scores. Prioritization sessions involve product owners validating business value, architects assessing technical debt reduction, and engineers estimating effort. Once tasks are prioritized, define acceptance criteria: coverage targets, performance metrics, and rollback plans. Refactoring spikes—timeboxed investigations—reduce uncertainty around effort before full refactors. Tracking actual versus estimated effort calibrates future ROI calculations, improving prioritization accuracy. Backlog grooming with updated churn and risk data keeps prioritization aligned to evolving needs. By ranking refactoring work by ROI and impact, teams deliver the highest business value first, preparing to measure maintainability gains.

13.2.4 Measuring Maintainability Gains

After refactoring high-priority modules, it's essential to measure maintainability gains to validate the investment and guide subsequent work. Maintainability metrics include static code-quality indicators—cyclomatic complexity, cognitive complexity, lines of code, and duplication percentages. Tools like SonarQube compute a **Maintainability Rating** (A–E) and a **Technical Debt Ratio**— estimated time to fix issues relative to code baseline. A pre-refactor report might show:

```
Technical Debt Ratio: 12.5% (25d / 200d)
Maintainability Rating: D
```

After refactoring, rerunning analysis may yield:

```
Technical Debt Ratio: 7.0% (14d / 200d)
Maintainability Rating: B
```

Cognitive complexity shrinks as large functions break into smaller, descriptive methods—reducing per-function complexity from 30 to under 10. CodeScene hotspot maps reflect decreased risk zones. Tracking **change lead time**—the median time from commit to production—for refactored versus non-refactored modules quantifies delivery acceleration. Refactored modules may see a 30% reduction in lead time, from four days to 2.8 days. Defect rates per 1 000 lines of code drop after refactoring, e.g., from 5 to 2 defects per KLOC. Developer satisfaction surveys add qualitative feedback on perceived ease of change. Integrate metrics into dashboards—Grafana, Sonar, CodeScene—for continuous visibility and feedback. Enforce maintainability improvements as acceptance criteria in pull requests, requiring that new code raises the maintainability index. For each refactoring story, include KPI targets: reduce complexity by 20%, achieve 80% test coverage, and lower coupling metrics by 30%. A Python snippet computing module coupling:

```
import networkx as nx
G = nx.DiGraph()
# add edges: module imports
```

```
coupling = {n: G.degree(n) for n in G.nodes()}
```

Plotting coupling distributions before and after refactoring shows reduced global coupling. Continual measurement prevents regression: if a refactored module's debt ratio increases, alerts trigger revisits. Ultimately, data-driven maintainability metrics ensure refactoring delivers sustained architectural quality, justifying further investment.

13.3 Cultural & Organizational Shifts

13.3.1 Skills Enablement & Training Programs

Refactoring legacy systems successfully demands more than technical blueprints—it requires equipping teams with the skills and mindsets to embrace clean-architecture principles. Skills enablement starts with targeted training programs covering domain-driven design, modularization, test-driven development, and microservices fundamentals. Workshops led by internal or external experts—Domain-Driven Design sessions, monolith-to-microservices workshops—accelerate knowledge transfer across the organization. Interactive code katas focusing on legacy-to-clean transformations allow developers to practice incremental refactoring techniques in a safe environment. For instance, a kata might present a simplified OrderService monolith and ask participants to extract a façade and anti-corruption layer in three steps. Regular brown-bag sessions showcase real-world refactor stories, demonstrating pitfalls and best practices, reinforcing code-health values. Mentoring programs pair senior architects with newer engineers, offering on-the-job guidance during actual refactoring tasks. Establishing internal certification—where developers demonstrate mastery by leading a small bounded-context extraction—encourages accountability and continuous growth. Online platforms (Pluralsight, Coursera) supplement classroom training with self-paced courses on SOLID principles, test automation, and cloud-native patterns. Embedding refactoring exercises into onboarding for new hires sets expectations that code health and architecture are core responsibilities, not optional extras. Budgeting for conference attendance enables teams to learn from industry practitioners who have tackled similar migrations at scale. Post-training assessments—quizzes, peer reviews, coding challenges—validate that learning objectives translate into practiced skills. Pair programming sessions during early refactoring sprints promote shared understanding of the legacy code and transfer knowledge to multiple team members. Documenting proven refactoring patterns and making them discoverable via an internal wiki or blog creates a living knowledge base. Champions or "clean architecture evangelists" within each team advocate best practices, review designs, and guide code reviews toward architectural compliance. Over time, teams shift from reactive problem-solving to proactive architecture reviews, preventing new technical debt. Allocating dedicated "refactoring Fridays" gives teams focused time to apply techniques without feature pressure. Tracking training attendance and refactoring impact—reduced defect rates, improved cycle time—justifies continued investment in enablement. With a workforce empowered by training and mentorship, teams can confidently tackle the organizational shifts necessary for evolutionary architecture adoption.

13.3.2 Creating Cross-Functional Refactoring Squads

Legacy refactoring is inherently cross-disciplinary—requiring collaboration among developers, QA, DevOps, product owners, and domain experts. Creating dedicated cross-functional squads ensures each team possesses the necessary skills and perspectives to decompose, rebuild, and deploy refactored modules. A typical squad includes backend and frontend developers, a QA specialist, a DevOps engineer, and a product owner representing business needs. Embedding a domain expert in the squad facilitates rapid clarification of domain rules and prevents misinterpretation during model extraction. Squad size should follow the "two-pizza team" rule—no more than 8-10 members—to maintain agility and clear communication. Each squad is empowered with end-to-end ownership: from planning a bounded-context extraction to deploying the first microservice variant. Defining clear mission statements—"Squad Hydra will extract product catalog to an independent service by Q2"—aligns squad objectives with organizational goals. Squads practice DevOps, owning CI/CD pipelines for their modules, enabling rapid iteration without waiting on centralized teams. Regular squad stand-ups and integration demos to other teams foster transparency and catch integration issues early. Avoiding resource contention requires scheduling: squads include members with available bandwidth, avoiding overloading core feature teams. Rotating members across squads prevents knowledge silos and diffuses clean-architecture practices throughout the organization. Agile ceremonies—backlog refinement, sprint planning, retrospectives—tailored to refactoring objectives ensure disciplined progress tracking. Engineering leads set up virtual war rooms for critical integration points, bringing relevant squads together to sync interfaces and contracts. Visual dashboards display metrics—classes extracted, tests added, debt ratios reduced, microservices deployed—so everyone can see progress. Celebrating each squad's successes—"Team Hydra reduced the catalog module's complexity from E to B in SonarQube"—motivates and builds momentum. Conflict resolution protocols—escalating interface contract disagreements—prevent squad standstills and drive timely decisions. Empowering squads to make architectural decisions autonomously accelerates progress and fosters ownership. Periodic knowledge-sharing forums allow squads to present lessons learned, common pitfalls, and reusable artifacts like ACL libraries. As squads complete assignments, they transition to maintenance of the new microservices, handing off legacy code for final decommissioning. Through cross-functional squads, organizations break down monolithic migration into manageable, focused efforts, balancing autonomy with alignment to a unified architecture vision.

13.3.3 Instilling an Evolutionary Architecture Mindset

An evolutionary architecture mindset emphasizes continuous, incremental change rather than large, disruptive rewrites, embracing modular growth over time. Teams adopt practices like fitness functions and automated architectural tests to ensure that the system's structure evolves safely with each code change. Fitness functions codify architectural properties—enforcing no forbidden cyclic dependencies, preserving service boundary isolation—and run in CI to catch regressions:

```
@ArchTest
static final ArchRule no_cycles =
```

```
slices().matching("com.myapp.(*)..").should().beFreeOfCycles();
```

This automation prevents architectural drift by blocking commits that violate design constraints, keeping the architecture healthy without manual review. Establishing an API contract-first approach ensures that service interfaces remain stable or are properly versioned. Continuous refactoring becomes part of the "Definition of Done": every feature branch is an opportunity to improve structure and remove duplicate code. Teams measure coupling and cohesion metrics each sprint—using SonarQube or CodeScene—to guide small structure improvements, like moving classes to more appropriate modules. Emphasizing small, reversible changes reduces risk and supports rapid feedback loops: if an extraction goes wrong, feature flags can disable the new path instantly. Organizations invest in platform-level abstractions—shared DSLs, framework libraries, and golden paths—to streamline repeated refactoring patterns like ACL generation. Feature toggles serve as architectural tools: teams merge incomplete refactors behind flags, decoupling code deployment from release schedules. Employing trunk-based development, where developers integrate to mainline frequently, ensures refactoring changes are small and conflict resolution is easy. Timing architectural work alongside feature delivery—refactoring one class per story—distributes effort and prevents large refactor sprints. Leadership reinforces the evolutionary mindset by celebrating refactoring as equal to feature work, including it in performance metrics and roadmaps. Investment in platform teams supporting architecture evolution—maintaining CI templates, governance tooling, and training—frees feature teams to focus on domain logic. Documenting patterns and best practices in a central pattern repository ensures consistency and accelerates onboarding. The evolutionary architecture transforms the culture: teams think in terms of small, reversible improvements rather than grand rewrites. Over time, the codebase organically converges toward cleaner layers and explicit boundaries, guided by continuous, automated checks and shared ownership. This mindset shift—favoring continual improvement—enables sustainable, long-term system health and adaptability.

13.3.4 Leadership Sponsorship & Change Management

For legacy refactoring initiatives to succeed, visible leadership sponsorship is essential—executive and managerial support provides the mandate and resources needed. Leaders must articulate the business value of clean architecture: reduced time-to-market, lower maintenance costs, and improved system reliability, translating technical goals into business outcomes. Regular communication from leadership—town halls, newsletters, OKR updates—reinforces the importance of refactoring as a strategic initiative, not a developer side project. Change-management frameworks like ADKAR (Awareness, Desire, Knowledge, Ability, Reinforcement) guide the human aspects of migration, ensuring people transitions accompany technical changes. **Awareness**: Leaders present the vision for a modular architecture and the risks of maintaining the status quo, using data from hotspot analyses and incident reports. **Desire**: Incentives—recognition, career growth opportunities, or dedicated refactoring days—encourage active participation. **Knowledge**: Training programs, documentation, and mentorship provide the required know-how. **Ability**: Access to tooling, environments, and protected time ensures teams can apply new skills without conflicting priorities. **Reinforcement**: Celebrating refactoring milestones, publishing metrics on debt reduction, and including architecture-related KPIs in performance reviews cement new behaviors. Governance boards or lightweight architecture committees offer guidance on complex decisions, ensuring alignment with long-term strategy without stifling agility. Establishing an architecture guild—senior engineers across teams—disseminates principles and mediates cross-team dependencies. Leaders allocate budget for specialized roles—platform engineers, DevOps champions—that underpin the migration with infrastructure and automation. Clear charters for refactoring squads define scope, authority, and success criteria aligned to organizational objectives. Risk-management plans—identifying potential disruptions, dependencies on legacy teams—are approved at leadership level to secure contingency resources. Transparent progress reporting—dashboards showing refactored modules, test-coverage improvements, performance gains—keeps stakeholders informed and engaged. Addressing organizational resistance requires active listening: feedback loops through retrospectives surface concerns that leadership can act upon. Leaders may need to adjust processes—allowing feature teams to temporarily reduce feature velocity in exchange for long-term maintainability gains. Documenting change-management decisions in ADRs and project charters provides a record for future audits and onboarding. Ongoing executive alignment—tying migration progress to business metrics like revenue growth—ensures sustained priority across fiscal cycles. With robust sponsorship and structured change-management, the organizational foundation for refactoring remains strong, positioning teams to tackle the technical challenges ahead.

13.4 Assessing Legacy Code Quality

13.4.1 Cataloging Code Smells & Technical Debt

Before refactoring, perform a comprehensive code-quality assessment, cataloging code smells and technical debt across the monolith. Code smells—symptoms of deeper design issues—include long methods, God classes, duplicated code, and excessive coupling. Automated tools like **SonarQube** or **CodeClimate** detect many smells: "Long Method" warnings for functions exceeding thresholds, "Duplicated Blocks" for cloned code, and "Complex Conditionals" for nested branches. A SonarQube violation report might list:

```
- src/main/java/com/myapp/service/OrderService.java: Long Method (200 lines, threshold: 100)
- src/main/java/com/myapp/controller/UserController.java: God Class (700 methods)
- src/main/java/com/myapp/repository/*.java: High Cognitive Complexity (>15)
```

Complement automated findings with manual audits, where senior architects inspect critical modules for nuanced smells like "feature envy" or "shotgun surgery." Record each identified smell in a **technical debt register**, capturing location, type, remediation effort estimate, and associated risk. A backlog spreadsheet might include:

ID	File	Smell Type	Risk	Effort (hrs)	Priority
SM-1	OrderService.java	God Class	High	80	1

SM-2	UserController.java	Long Method	Medium	12	3

Technical debt items also cover missing or inadequate tests, outdated libraries, and manual configuration steps. Tools like **DebtBrake** or Sonar's technical-debt view estimate remediation time and track debt ratio over time. Manual audits on build scripts, deployment configurations, and infrastructure code uncover "infra-as-code smells"—unused modules or hardcoded secrets. Cataloging across all layers—backend, frontend, infrastructure—yields a holistic debt inventory. Teams then conduct debt-prioritization workshops, grouping similar smells into refactoring stories. CI pipelines import debt data (via SonarQube's REST API) to track trends and prevent regression. Establishing **technical debt budgets**—allocating a fixed percentage of sprint capacity to debt repayment—ensures ongoing attention. By making technical debt visible and actionable, organizations avoid the "debt mortgage" scenario where accrued debt stifles innovation. Update the register as refactoring progresses to maintain an accurate debt ledger. Celebrating debt retirement—reducing debt ratio from D to B—is as important as feature delivery, reinforcing craftsmanship. With a clear inventory of code smells, you can plan targeted assessments for test coverage and architectural violations.

13.4.2 Test-Coverage Gap Analysis

A pivotal aspect of legacy code quality is test coverage—measuring how much of the codebase is verified by automated tests. Test-coverage gap analysis identifies untested or under-tested areas, guiding teams to where tests will yield the greatest regression protection.

Coverage tools—JaCoCo for Java, Istanbul/nyc for JavaScript, Coverage.py for Python—generate detailed line, branch, and method coverage reports. Running JaCoCo in Maven:

```
<plugin>
 <groupId>org.jacoco</groupId>
 <artifactId>jacoco-maven-plugin</artifactId>
 <version>0.8.8</version>
 <executions>
 <execution>
  <goals><goal>prepare-agent</goal></goals>
 </execution>
 <execution>
  <id>report</id>
  <phase>test</phase>
  <goals><goal>report</goal></goals>
 </execution>
 </executions>
</plugin>
```

...

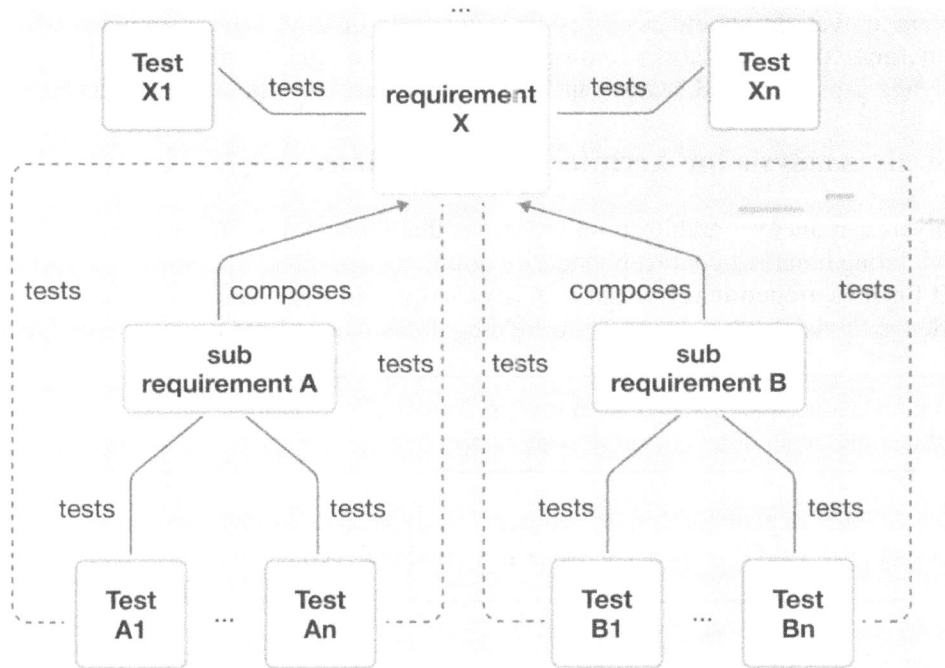

The HTML report highlights unexecuted lines in red, showing which branches and exceptions are untested. Teams define coverage thresholds—e.g., 80% line coverage and 70% branch coverage—failing builds if metrics dip below these targets:

```
npm run coverage && node tools/check-coverage.js --threshold 80
```

Mapping coverage to bounded contexts and modules reveals disparities: OrderContext at 60% versus InventoryContext at 90%. Coverage heatmaps overlay percentages on a dependency graph:

```
[OrderModule]  60%
[CustomerModule]85%
[PaymentModule] 40%
```

However, coverage alone can be misleading—100% coverage of trivial code offers little protection, whereas complex logic remains dangerous. Teams employ mutation testing frameworks—PIT for Java or Stryker for JavaScript—to inject faults and ensure tests detect failures, improving suite effectiveness. A mutation score below 80% indicates inadequate test specifications. Coverage gap analysis also examines legacy data-parsing code, configuration loaders, and error-handling branches, often untested. Prioritize writing smoke tests around critical user flows—authentication, checkout—to build confidence in core scenarios. Incremental test addition follows "if you touch it, you cover it": every bug fix or refactoring includes a corresponding test. Pair programming with QA engineers ensures new tests capture real-world edge cases. Test-coverage dashboards in CI provide trendlines:

rising coverage over sprints indicates sustained focus on quality. When combined with code-smell and debt metrics, coverage analysis forms a powerful triad of quality, maintainability, and reliability. With coverage gaps addressed, teams can detect architectural violations in the next step.

13.4.3 Static Analysis for Architectural Violations

Static analysis can uncover architectural violations that threaten long-term maintainability—such as modules violating bounded-context boundaries or unintended direct imports across layers. Tools like **ArchUnit** for Java, **dependency-cruiser** for JavaScript, and **Pyreverse** for Python automate checks of forbidden patterns. An ArchUnit rule forbidding domain code from depending on UI:

```
classes().that().resideInAPackage("com.myapp.domain..")
    .should().onlyDependOnPackages("com.myapp.domain..", "java..", "org.slf4j..");
```

This enforces the dependency rule: domain remains independent of presentation concerns. dependency-cruiser's JSON config can declare forbidden dependencies:

```
{
"forbidden": [
 {
  "name": "no-domain-to-ui",
  "from": {"path": "^src/domain"},
  "to": {"path": "^src/ui"}
 }
]
}
```

Running depcruise src --config .dependency-cruiser.json --validate in CI catches new violations early. Static analysis also verifies package cycles, which indicate monolithic entanglements:

```
slices().matching("com.myapp.(*)..").should().beFreeOfCycles();
```

Architectural rules extend to service boundaries: microservices should not depend directly on other services' data layers but use API clients or messaging interfaces. Open Policy Agent (OPA) Rego policies can enforce deployment-time checks on Terraform or Kubernetes manifests, preventing unauthorized cross-namespace communication:

```
package kubernetes.admission

deny[msg] {
```

```
input.kind.kind == "Deployment"
container := input.request.object.spec.template.spec.containers[_]
not startswith(container.image, "registry.company.com/")
msg := sprintf("Container image '%v' is not from approved registry", [container.image])
}
```

OPA integration into pipelines blocks non-compliant manifests. Dependency graphs loaded into Neo4j enable custom queries, such as "find all paths from OrderService to PaymentDB skipping the ACL." Visualization in Gephi highlights unintended shortcuts. IDE plugins offer inline feedback: GitHub code scanning alerts on PRs that introduce forbidden imports. Over time, scanning results feed into architectural gradecards, monitoring violation counts per sprint. When violations grow, a "stop-the-line" event triggers immediate remediation. Documenting rules in ADRs clarifies prohibited dependencies and guides developers during refactoring. As

13.5 Modularization & Packaging

13.5.1 Defining Clean Module Boundaries

Establishing clear module boundaries starts by grouping related functionality—domain entities, services, and repositories—into cohesive units. A good rule of thumb is that each module should have one primary responsibility and a well-defined API surface. In a Java monorepo, you might convert packages com.myapp.order and com.myapp.inventory into standalone Maven subprojects:

```
// settings.gradle
include 'order-service', 'inventory-service', 'common'
// order-service/build.gradle
dependencies {
 implementation project(':common')
}
```

Tools like **SonarQube** or **Dependency Cruiser** can visualize module coupling. For example, a Graphviz diagram (modules.dot):

```
digraph Modules {
 common -> order_service;
 common -> inventory_service;
 order_service -> inventory_service [style=dotted];
}
```

Running dot -Tpng modules.dot -o modules.png highlights unwanted dependencies (dotted lines). Modules should depend only on common utilities, not on each other, preserving independence. High cohesion means that classes within order-service share many interactions (calls, data types) while low coupling implies few cross-module references. Refactoring toward these boundaries often reveals tangled code: utility classes that reside in the wrong module or domain logic scattered across service code. By iteratively extracting classes into the correct module and updating imports, you gradually realign the code with your bounded contexts. Defining boundaries up front guides packaging and informs your build and release process, ensuring each module can be versioned, tested, and deployed independently.

13.5.2 Refactoring Toward Explicit Interfaces

Once modules are separated, you must define clear interfaces for each module's public contract. In Java, place service interfaces in the module's api subpackage:

```
// order-service/api/OrderService.java
package com.myapp.order.api;
import com.myapp.common.Order;
public interface OrderService {
 Order placeOrder(OrderRequest req);
}
```

Implementations reside in impl:

```
// order-service/impl/OrderServiceImpl.java
package com.myapp.order.impl;
import com.myapp.order.api.OrderService;
public class OrderServiceImpl implements OrderService { ... }
```

Consumers depend only on the api package, not on impl. In build files, you expose only the API artifact:

```
// order-service/build.gradle
jar { from sourceSets.main.output }
publishing { publications { mavenJava(MavenPublication) { artifactId 'order-api'; artifact tasks.jar } } }
```

This enforces the **Dependency Inversion Principle**: higher-level modules rely on abstractions, not concrete classes. Refactoring toward explicit interfaces often requires bulk moves: converting static helper calls to instance methods, introducing DTOs instead of domain objects leaking across modules, and adding adapter classes to translate between internal and external representations. Automated refactorings in IDEs (IntelliJ "Move Class") can update imports and package declarations across tens of files in seconds, preserving history and minimizing merge conflicts. Over time, the module API surface shrinks to a small, well-tested set of interfaces, reducing the cognitive load for consumers and simplifying version upgrades. With interfaces in place, you can manage versions and dependencies reliably.

13.5.3 Versioning & Dependency Management

Modules evolve at different paces, so versioning each independently is crucial. Semantic Versioning (SemVer) dictates versions as MAJOR.MINOR.PATCH, where breaking changes bump the MAJOR, backward-compatible features bump the MINOR, and bug fixes bump the PATCH. In Maven, define versions in each pom.xml:

```
<project>
 <groupId>com.myapp</groupId>
 <artifactId>order-api</artifactId>
 <version>2.1.0</version>
</project>
```

To manage inter-module dependencies without hard-coding versions everywhere, use a **Bill of Materials** (BOM):

```
<dependencyManagement>
 <dependencies>
  <dependency>
   <groupId>com.myapp</groupId>
   <artifactId>bom</artifactId>
   <version>2.1.0</version>
   <type>pom</type>
   <scope>import</scope>
  </dependency>
 </dependencies>
</dependencyManagement>
```

Modules then declare dependencies without versions:

```
<dependency>
 <groupId>com.myapp</groupId>
 <artifactId>order-api</artifactId>
</dependency>
```

npm projects use a similar approach with package.json:

```
"workspaces": ["order-service", "inventory-service"],
```

```
"dependencies": {
 "order-api": "workspace:*"
}
```

Automate releases with tools like **semantic-release** or Maven Release Plugin to ensure consistent version increments and changelog generation. CI pipelines should fail if modules declare invalid version ranges or if dependencies are not resolvable, preventing mismatched versions from creeping in. Proper versioning and dependency management allow multiple modules to coexist at different versions during a staggered migration, easing overall upgrade efforts.

13.5.4 Deploying Modules Independently

Independent deployment requires packaging each module into its own deployable artifact—JAR, Docker image, or serverless function—complete with configuration and health checks. For Docker, a Dockerfile per module:

```
# inventory-service/Dockerfile
FROM adoptopenjdk:11-jre
COPY build/libs/inventory-service.jar /app/inventory-service.jar
ENTRYPOINT ["java","-jar","/app/inventory-service.jar"]
```

Build and push:

```
docker build -t registry.example.com/inventory-service:3.0.0 .
docker push registry.example.com/inventory-service:3.0.0
```

Kubernetes Deployments reference image tags:

```
apiVersion: apps/v1
kind: Deployment
metadata: { name: inventory-service }
spec:
 replicas: 3
 template:
  spec:
   containers:
   - name: inventory-service
     image: registry.example.com/inventory-service:3.0.0
     readinessProbe:
      httpGet: { path: /health, port: 8080 }
```

Helm charts parameterize image tags and resource limits, enabling separate release cycles:

```
image:
 repository: registry.example.com/order-service
tag: 2.1.0
```

CI/CD pipelines for each module trigger on changes to its code, building artifacts and updating the staging environment automatically. Feature flags or versioned API gateways route traffic to new versions, ensuring backward compatibility. Independent deployment reduces blast radius: a faulty change in order-service doesn't require redeploying inventory-service, accelerating delivery and rollback.

13.6 Integrating New & Old Components

13.6.1 Adapter & Bridge Patterns

During migration, new modules must interact seamlessly with legacy code. The **Adapter** pattern wraps legacy interfaces in a shape the new module expects:

```
// New interface
public interface CustomerRepository { Customer find(String id); }


// Legacy class
public class LegacyCustomerDao {
 public LegacyCustomer getCustomerById(String id) { ... }
}


// Adapter
public class CustomerDaoAdapter implements CustomerRepository {
 private final LegacyCustomerDao dao;
 public CustomerDaoAdapter(LegacyCustomerDao dao) { this.dao = dao; }
 public Customer find(String id) {
  LegacyCustomer lc = dao.getCustomerById(id);
  return new Customer(lc.getId(), lc.getName());
 }
}
```

The **Bridge** pattern decouples an abstraction from its implementation, allowing either to vary independently. In a messaging context, define:

```
public interface MessageSender { void send(Message msg); }
public class EmailSender implements MessageSender { … }
public class SmsSender implements MessageSender { … }
public abstract class Notification {
 protected final MessageSender sender;
 protected Notification(MessageSender s) { this.sender = s; }
 public abstract void notify(User u);
}
```

Adapters and bridges hide legacy complexities, ensuring new modules remain focused on clean domain logic.

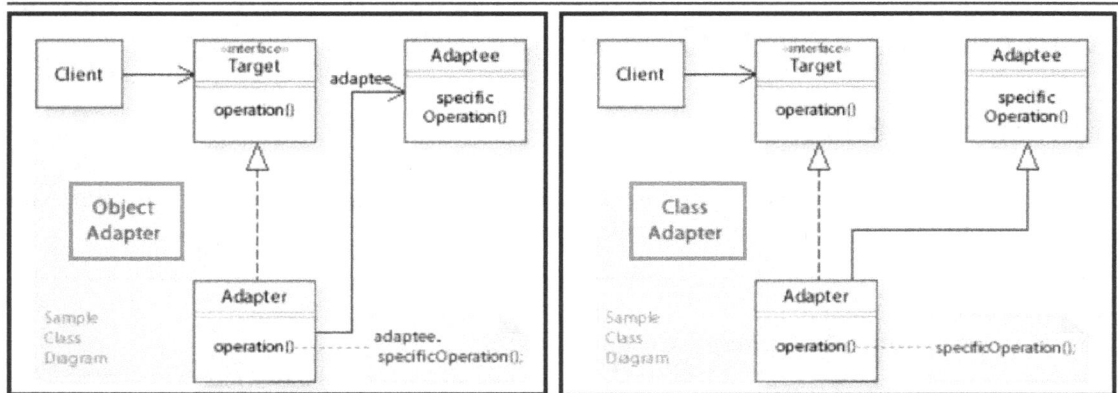

```
@startuml
interface CustomerRepository
class CustomerDaoAdapter
class LegacyCustomerDao
CustomerRepository <|.. CustomerDaoAdapter
CustomerDaoAdapter ..> LegacyCustomerDao
@enduml
```

This approach minimizes direct dependencies, reduces regression risk, and provides clear seams where legacy code can be eventually replaced completely.

13.6.2 Event-Driven Integration & Sagas

Event-driven integration decouples modules through asynchronous messaging. Legacy systems publish domain events (e.g., OrderPlaced) to a message broker (Kafka, RabbitMQ), and new services subscribe. In a Spring Boot app:

```
@Service
public class OrderPlacedListener {
 @KafkaListener(topics="order-events", groupId="inventory")
 public void onOrderPlaced(String eventJson) {
  OrderPlacedEvent ev = objectMapper.readValue(eventJson, OrderPlacedEvent.class);
  inventoryService.reserve(ev.getOrderId(), ev.getItems());
 }
}
```

Sagas coordinate distributed transactions via chained events and compensating actions. A simple saga flow:

1. **OrderService** publishes OrderCreated.
2. **PaymentService** attempts chargeCard, on success publishes PaymentSucceeded, else PaymentFailed.
3. **InventoryService** reserves stock on PaymentSucceeded, else **OrderService** rolls back on PaymentFailed.

```
@startuml
participant OrderSvc
participant PaymentSvc
participant InventorySvc
OrderSvc -> Kafka: OrderCreated
Kafka -> PaymentSvc: OrderCreated
PaymentSvc -> Kafka: PaymentSucceeded
Kafka -> InventorySvc: PaymentSucceeded
InventorySvc -> Kafka: StockReserved
@enduml
```

Event-driven sagas maintain data consistency without two-phase commit, allow eventual consistency, and enable graceful handling of partial failures during refactoring. This pattern lets legacy and new components coexist on the same message bus.

13.6.3 Strangler Gateways & BFF Layers

The **Strangler Gateway** places a routing layer in front of the monolith, directing requests for new functionality to microservices while letting the monolith handle the rest. In NGINX:

```
location /api/orders/ {
 proxy_pass http://order-service/;
}
```

```
location /api/ {
 proxy_pass http://monolith/;
}
```

As order-service grows to cover more endpoints, NGINX routes more traffic away from the monolith. A **Backend-For-Frontend (BFF)** layer tailors APIs per client (web, mobile), aggregating calls to multiple services and hiding complexity:

```
// Express.js BFF
app.get('/web/orders', async (req, res) => {
 const { userId } = req.query;
 const orders = await orderApi.fetch(userId);
 const inventory = await inventoryApi.fetchStatus(orders.map(o=>o.id));
 res.json(orders.map(o=>({ ...o, inStock: inventory[o.id] })));
});
```

Strangler gateways and BFFs simplify client migration, allowing developers to test new modules in isolation before full cutover. Gradually, the monolith's routing table shrinks, and eventually the monolith can be decommissioned.

13.6.4 Managing Backwards Compatibility

During migration, new modules must honor existing clients' expectations. Strategies include **versioned APIs**—expose /v1/orders and /v2/orders, with the latter backed by new services. Use middleware to redirect based on Accept headers or URL prefixes. A Spring example:

```
@RequestMapping("/v1/orders")
public class OrderControllerV1 { ... }


@RequestMapping("/v2/orders")
public class OrderControllerV2 { ... }
```

Deprecate old versions with clear timelines and documentation. For data schema changes, employ **expand-contract-shrink**: first expand the schema to support both old and new fields, then contract clients to use new fields, and finally remove the old schema. In Kafka, use a **schema registry** (Avro) with backward compatibility settings:

```
{ "compatibility": "BACKWARD" }
```

This ensures new producers add fields with defaults, and old consumers ignore unknown fields. Comprehensive integration testing against both old and new API versions prevents regressions. By safeguarding clients during transition, you minimize downtime and maintain trust while migrating to clean architecture.

13.7 Tooling & Automation

13.7.1 Automated Refactoring Tools (IDE-Based & CLI)

Large-scale refactoring benefits from automated tools that can apply consistent edits across thousands of files. Modern IDEs like IntelliJ IDEA and Visual Studio offer **structural refactorings**—rename symbol, move class, extract interface—that update references project-wide. For command-line automation, tools like **ts-morph** (TypeScript) or **jEnvoy** (Java) parse ASTs to apply transformations:

```
import { Project } from "ts-morph";
const proj = new Project();
proj.addSourceFilesAtPaths("src/**/*.ts");
proj.getSourceFiles().forEach(sf => {
 sf.getClasses().forEach(cls => {
  if (cls.getName() === "OldService") {
   cls.rename("NewService");
  }
 });
});
proj.saveSync();
```

CI jobs can run these scripts on dedicated refactoring branches, generating pull requests with automated changes. Linters configured with custom codemods (e.g., eslint-codemod) can enforce API migrations:

```
npx eslint --fix --rule='myorg/migrate-old-api:2' src/
```

Combined with comprehensive test suites, automated refactorings safely transform legacy code at scale, freeing developers from error-prone manual edits Logging changes and diff reviews help teams understand and accept bulk refactor pull requests.

13.7.2 CI/CD Pipelines for Legacy Releases

Legacy systems often require specialized pipelines that support both "brownfield" builds and new module releases. A Jenkins pipeline for a monolith might use:

```
pipeline {
 agent any
 stages {
 stage('Checkout') { steps { checkout scm } }
 stage('Build') { steps { sh 'mvn clean package -DskipTests' } }
 stage('Test') { steps { sh 'mvn test' } }
 stage('Deploy') {
  steps {
   sh './deploy-monolith.sh ${env.BUILD_NUMBER}'
  }
 }
 }
 }
}
```

As you extract modules, the pipeline evolves into a **multi-pipeline** architecture: one pipeline per module, with upstream/downstream triggers. For example, pushing to order-service repo triggers its own build and a deployment to staging, independent of the monolith. Feature flags coordinate releases across pipelines:

```
post {
 success {
  sh "feature-toggle enable order-service-v2"
 }
}
```

Artifact repositories like Nexus or Artifactory host both monolith WARs and microservice images, enabling rollback by selecting older artifact versions. Ensuring that legacy and new pipelines coexist smoothly is key to uninterrupted delivery as you migrate.

13.7.3 Feature Toggles & Canary Releases

Feature toggles decouple code deploys from feature launches, allowing new functionality to be merged behind flags that default to off. Libraries like **LaunchDarkly**, **FF4J**, or home-grown toggle services manage flag states:

```
if (featureManager.isEnabled("order-service-v2", userContext)) {
 orderServiceV2.placeOrder(req);
} else {
 legacyOrderService.placeOrder(req);
}
```

Canary releases combine toggles with traffic-splitting route a small percentage of real users to the new module:

```
apiVersion: split.smi-spec.io/v1alpha1
kind: TrafficSplit
metadata: { name: order-service-split }
spec:
 service: order-service
 backends:
 - service: order-service-v1
  weight: 90
 - service: order-service-v2
  weight: 10
```

Monitor error rates, latency, and business metrics specifically for the canary cohort. If metrics remain within acceptable thresholds, gradually increase the weight to 100 %. Toggle-driven canaries mitigate risk, enabling quick rollback by redirecting all traffic away from the new service. Automated pipelines can adjust weights based on predefined criteria—error budget exhaustion or manual approvals—providing a safe path through incremental migration.

13.7.4 Observability & Health Checks During Migration

Observability tools must span both legacy and new components to provide end-to-end visibility. Instrument newly extracted modules with the same metrics (Prometheus counters, histograms) and tracing headers (W3C Trace Context) used across the monolith. For health checks, implement /health endpoints:

```
@RestController
public class HealthController {
 @GetMapping("/health")
 public Health health() {
  return Health.up()
   .withDetail("database", dbService.isConnected())
   .withDetail("cache", cacheService.isHealthy())
   .build();
 }
}
```

Load balancers and orchestrators (Kubernetes readinessProbe/livenessProbe) rely on these endpoints to route traffic only to healthy instances. During migration, side-by-side deployments may expose discrepancies: the new module might have a different thread-pool configuration causing thread exhaustion under load. Dashboards should display comparative metrics: p95 latency of v1 vs. v2, error rates, resource utilization. Alerting rules target regressions in either version:

```
alert: OrderServiceErrorSpike
expr: rate(order_service_errors_total[5m]) > 0.01
for: 2m
```

Correlate logs and traces via a common correlation ID to track requests that traverse both legacy and new modules. This unified observability ensures that migration progress never degrades user experience and that issues in new code are identified and remediated swiftly.

13.8 Measuring Progress & Feedback Loops

13.8.1 Refactoring Velocity & Throughput Metrics

Measuring how quickly teams convert legacy code to the new architecture is critical for tracking momentum and predicting completion. **Refactoring velocity** can be quantified in several ways: number of files or classes migrated per sprint, lines of legacy code removed, or percentage of traffic served by new modules. For example, track legacy lines via a simple script:

```
find src/legacy -name '*.java' | xargs wc -l > legacy_loc.txt
```

Plot legacy_loc.txt over time to visualize a downward trend. **Throughput metrics** gauge how many refactoring tasks (tickets, pull requests) move from "In Progress" to "Done" each week. Integrate with Jira or GitHub via their APIs:

```
import requests
resp = requests.get('https://api.github.com/repos/myorg/monolith/pulls?state=closed')
merged = [pr for pr in resp.json() if pr['merged_at']]
print(f"Merged PRs this week: {len(merged)}")
```

Dashboards in Grafana or Power BI display these metrics alongside code-quality metrics (coverage, cyclomatic complexity), revealing if faster refactoring correlates with improved quality or vice versa. Sharing velocity transparently in retrospectives motivates teams and informs stakeholders of realistic timelines. With velocity measured, you next establish quality gates to ensure progress doesn't compromise code health.

13.8.2 Quality-Gate Dashboards & Alerts

Quality-gate dashboards combine static analysis, test coverage, and performance regression data to warn if refactoring introduces regressions. Tools like **SonarQube** enforce gates:

Metric	Condition	Status
New Code Coverage	$\geq 80\%$	OK
Bugs in New Code	0 Critical, ≤ 1 Major	OK
Duplication in Legacy Code	$\leq 5\%$	Warning

SonarQube's Quality Gate can block merges when thresholds aren't met. In Jenkins:

```
stage('Quality Gate') {
 steps {
  timeout(time: 2, unit: 'MINUTES') {
   waitForQualityGate abortPipeline: true
  }
 }
}
```

Alerts notify teams via email or ChatOps when gates fail. Custom dashboards in Kibana aggregate logs to surface frequent warning or error patterns in newly written modules. Early detection prevents technical debt from accumulating in the freshly refactored code. Quality gates, combined with velocity metrics, provide a balanced view of how fast teams are moving and how well they're maintaining standards.

13.8.3 Stakeholder Feedback & User Telemetry

Refactoring should not only improve code structure but also maintain or enhance user experience. Instrument features with user telemetry—page load times, API error rates, feature usage—to gather real feedback. In a JavaScript front end:

```
window.analytics.track('OrderPageLoaded', {
 timestamp: Date.now(),
 userId: currentUser.id
});
```

Backend services log per-request metadata—response times, payload sizes, user segments—to a monitoring backend (InfluxDB, Datadog). Feature flags enable comparing user cohorts: one using the legacy flow, another on the new module. A/B testing frameworks yield statistical significance on performance and error rates:

```
experiment:
 name: OrderFlowRefactor
 variants:
 - control: 90%
 - treatment: 10%
```

Stakeholder feedback—UX surveys, support tickets—should be mapped to specific code versions or feature flags, closing the loop between engineering and business impact. Regular demos of refactored modules soliciting stakeholder input ensure that technical progress aligns with user needs and prevents surprises at release time.

13.8.4 Continuous Improvement & Retrospectives

At the end of each refactoring sprint, conduct focused retrospectives to reflect on what went well and what didn't. Use techniques like Start-Stop-Continue to capture actionable insights:

- **Start** automated migration scripts for common patterns.
- **Stop** over-engineering small modules; focus on high-impact areas.
- **Continue** pairing legacy and new-code experts on extraction tasks.

Document outcomes in a shared space (Confluence, Git repo) linked to ADRs when necessary. Track **action items** with clear owners and deadlines:

Action Item	Owner	Due
Automate package moves via codemod	Alice	2025-07-01
Update architecture diagram with new modules	Bob	2025-06-15

Review progress on these items weekly, adjusting sprint goals accordingly. Celebrate milestones— "Monolith lines reduced by 25 %"—to recognize team efforts. Continuous improvement isn't just about code; it's about refining processes, tooling, and communication as the migration progresses. Over time, these feedback loops engrain a culture of adaptability, ensuring the clean architecture you build remains healthy and evolves gracefully.

Conclusion

Refactoring a legacy system into a clean architecture is a marathon rather than a sprint—each small, well-tested increment builds confidence and chipping away at the monolith's complexity. By embracing an evolutionary mindset, teams can balance feature delivery with systematic cleanup, using anti-corruption layers to buffer new code from old, and carefully sequencing efforts around areas of greatest churn and risk. Cultural shifts—training engineers in modular design, establishing lightweight governance through decision records, and celebrating refactoring successes—create momentum and ensure long-term sustainability. As modules emerge with explicit interfaces and independent deployability, the organization gains agility: features can be developed, tested, and released by small, focused teams without fear of unintended side effects. Continuous measurement—tracking code-quality metrics, test coverage improvements, and feedback from real users—guides the journey, validating that each refactoring step delivers tangible benefits. With persistence, clear priorities, and the right blend of technical and organizational practices, even the most entrenched monolith can be transformed into a resilient, maintainable ecosystem that supports innovation for years to come.

Chapter 14. Patterns, Anti-Patterns & Real-World Case Studies

Real-world software architectures emerge from a blend of proven design patterns and the hard-earned lessons of past mistakes. In this chapter, we explore how leading organizations harness tactical patterns—such as rich domain models, event-driven flows, and decay-resistant layering—to tackle challenges at scale, maintain high velocity, and adapt to changing requirements. We'll also shine a light on the anti-patterns that secretly undermine code quality and team productivity, from over-zealous use of reflection to bleeding framework APIs into the core business logic. Through concrete case studies spanning startups, global enterprises, and heavily regulated domains, you'll see how these concepts play out in practice: the strategic decisions, the incremental migrations, and the cultural investments that determine success or failure. By understanding both the "right" and "wrong" ways to build software, you'll gain a balanced toolkit for guiding your own architecture toward long-term resilience and maintainability.

14.1 Success Stories

14.1.1 Start-up Scale-Up: Netflix's Evolution

Netflix's journey from a monolithic DVD-rental application to a globally distributed streaming platform exemplifies how clean architectural principles can underpin hyper-growth. Initially, Netflix operated a single Java WAR file deployed in a data center, with tightly coupled services and shared databases. As traffic surged—especially after shifting to streaming—the monolith became a bottleneck: deployments risked downtime, performance under peak load degraded, and teams struggled to innovate independently. To address this, Netflix adopted the **Strangler Fig** pattern, incrementally extracting functionality into microservices behind a façade. For example, the legacy user-profile service was wrapped by a new **Eureka**-enabled microservice:

```java
@RestController
@RequestMapping("/profiles")
public class ProfileController {
 private final LegacyProfileAdapter adapter;
 @GetMapping("/{id}")
 public ProfileDTO getProfile(@PathVariable String id) {
  return adapter.fetchProfile(id);
 }
}
```

Under the hood, the adapter used Hystrix to wrap calls to the monolith, providing circuit-breaker semantics and graceful fallback:

```java
@HystrixCommand(fallbackMethod = "defaultProfile")
public ProfileDTO fetchProfile(String id) { ... }
```

This allowed Netflix to route only a percentage of traffic to the new service before cutting over entirely. To support real-time personalization and analytics, they built a **Kafka**-based event streaming platform, ingesting billions of events per day and feeding back into the recommendation engine. The chaos-engineering practice—exemplified by Chaos Monkey—intentionally terminates instances in production to validate system resilience.

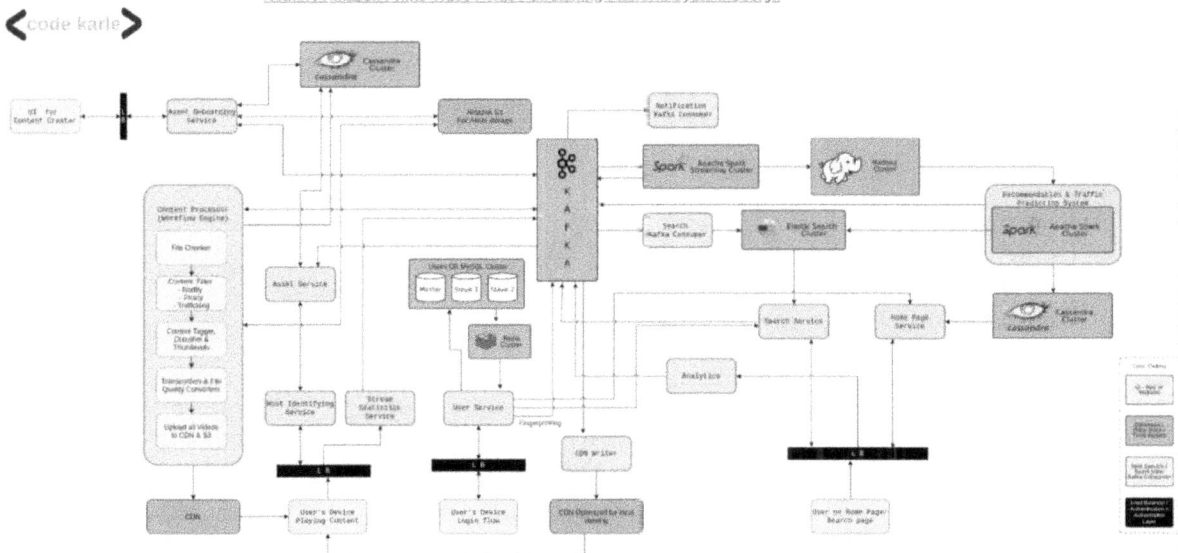

Netflix / Amazon Prime Video / Video Streaming Platform System Design

```
@startuml
rectangle Monolith
rectangle ProfileService
rectangle RecommendationService
Monolith --> ProfileService : extract profile logic
ProfileService -> Eureka : register instance
ProfileService -> Monolith : fallback via adapter
@enduml
```

Key takeaways include: start small with one service, automate failover with circuit breakers, invest early in observability, and cultivate a culture that views failures as learning opportunities. Netflix's engineering culture—"Freedom and Responsibility"—empowered teams to own services end-to-end, accelerating innovation. With this proven path, even large enterprises could emulate Netflix's incremental approach, as we explore next.

14.1.2 Enterprise Modernization: Walmart's Retail Platform

Walmart faced the mammoth challenge of modernizing its legacy Java monolith that powered inventory, pricing, and checkout across thousands of stores and a global e-commerce site. The initial system suffered from slow deployments—often monthly—and tightly coupled modules that hampered velocity. Walmart adopted Domain-Driven Design (DDD) to define bounded contexts: **Catalog**, **Order**, **Inventory**, and **Pricing**. Each context became a distinct microservice, developed by small, autonomous teams. For instance, the **InventoryService** exposed a RESTful API:

```
# OpenAPI spec excerpt
paths:
 /inventory/{sku}:
  get:
   summary: Get stock level
   parameters:
   - name: sku
    in: path
    required: true
   responses:
   '200':
    description: Stock level returned
    content: application/json
```

They standardized on Spring Boot and Docker, with Kubernetes orchestrating pods across AWS and their private data centers. A portion of the Helm chart used for templating:

```
# values.yaml
```

```
replicaCount: {{ .Values.inventory.replicas }}
image:
 repository: walmart/inventory-service
 tag: {{ .Values.inventory.tag }}
```

Walmart implemented **blue-green deployments** via Kubernetes Services and spec.selector swaps, achieving zero-downtime upgrades during high-traffic events like Black Friday. They also introduced **feature flags** (using LaunchDarkly) to gradually roll out new pricing algorithms. Instrumentation—via Prometheus exporters—tracked key SLOs such as checkout latency and inventory API error rates. These metrics drove automated autoscaling policies in Kubernetes, scaling pods when p95 latency exceeded 100 ms. Internally, cross-team Slack channels broadcast deployment notifications, turning each release into a collaborative event. Over two years, Walmart reduced lead time from code commit to production from weeks to hours, increased deployment frequency by 10×, and improved system reliability during peak loads. By mapping DDD concepts to microservice boundaries, they aligned technical teams with business domains, a theme echoed in regulated contexts next.

14.1.3 Regulated Industries: HealthCare.gov Rebuild

HealthCare.gov, the U.S. federal health insurance exchange, initially launched with a monolithic PHP/Java codebase struggling under heavy load and stringent regulatory requirements (HIPAA, FISMA). To modernize, the program office chose an API-first architecture: the legacy code remained accessible through a thin **anti-corruption layer** while new microservices—built in Java with Dropwizard—provided user authentication, enrollment, and plan selection. The anti-corruption layer translated legacy data structures into RESTful JSON:

```
@Path("/legacyUser")
public class LegacyUserAdapter {
 @GET
 @Path("/{userId}")
 @Produces(MediaType.APPLICATION_JSON)
 public UserDTO getUser(@PathParam("userId") String id) {
  LegacyUser lu = legacyClient.fetchUser(id);
  return UserDTO.fromLegacy(lu);
 }
}
```

Each new service underwent rigorous **security scanning** in the CI pipeline: static analysis with SonarQube, DAST with OWASP ZAP, and third-party dependency checks with OWASP Dependency-Check. Infrastructure as Code—via Terraform—defined AWS GovCloud resources in version-controlled modules:

```
module "rds" {
```

```
source = "terraform-aws-modules/rds/aws"
name  = "hcgov-rds"
engine = "postgres"
...
kms_key_id = var.kms_key_id
}
```

Continuous compliance was enforced with Chef InSpec tests against AWS Config rules:

```
describe aws_rds_db_instance(db_instance_identifier: 'hcgov-rds') do
 it { should_not be_publicly_accessible }
end
```

Traffic was phased to the new services via API Gateway stage variables, enabling canary rollouts under strict change-approval processes. Detailed audit logs—stored in immutable S3 buckets—tracked every API call, satisfying regulatory audit requirements. As a result, HealthCare.gov improved uptime to 99.9 %, slashed page-load times by 40 %, and passed FISMA audits with fewer findings. These outcomes highlight that even heavily regulated systems can embrace clean architecture without compromising compliance. The common themes across these success stories inform our next section on key success factors.

14.1.4 Key Success Factors & Common Themes

Across Netflix, Walmart, and HealthCare.gov, several recurring elements underpin successful architectural transformation:

1. **Executive Sponsorship**: All three had strong backing from leadership, securing budget and organizational commitment to multi-year refactoring projects.
2. **Dedicated Teams**: "Strangler" or "modularization" squads focused solely on carving out monolithic functionality, insulated from day-to-day feature work.
3. **Domain Alignment**: Using Domain-Driven Design to define bounded contexts ensured that technical modules mirrored business domains, simplifying team ownership and reducing cross-domain coupling.
4. **Incremental Rollout**: Phased migrations—via Strangler Fig, blue-green, or canary deployments—minimized risk and allowed validation in production with real user traffic.
5. **Observability & Automation**: Early investment in logging, metrics, and tracing, alongside CI/CD with quality and security gates, ensured safe, measurable change.
6. **Resilience Engineering**: Circuit breakers, bulkheads, and chaos experiments hardened systems against failure.
7. **Cultural Practices**: Frequent retrospectives, cross-team demos, and learning sessions fostered a shared engineering mindset.
8. **Feature Flags & Toggles**: Decoupling code releases from feature activation provided a safety net for rapid rollback and experimentation.

A simplified Sankey diagram illustrates the flow from monolith to microservices:

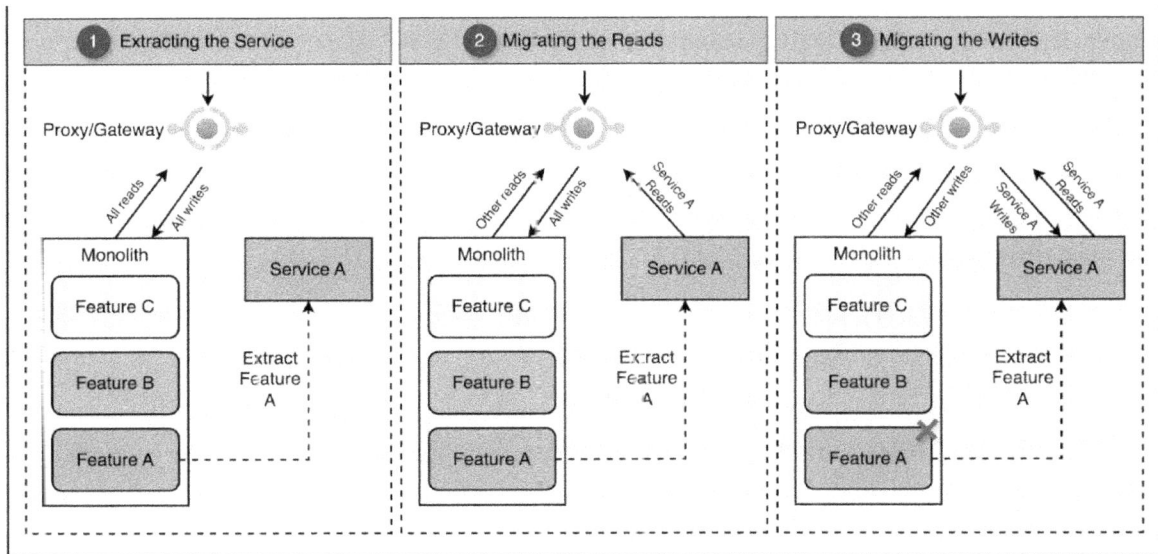

These factors combine to create a virtuous cycle: small, safe increments build confidence, enabling bolder architectural moves. Having learned from these successes, we now turn to the pitfalls teams often face when patterns are misused or ignored.

14.2 Common Pitfalls & Anti-Patterns

14.2.1 Anemic Domain Models

An **anemic domain model** arises when entities are mere data holders—DTOs—with business logic scattered in service layers or procedural scripts. This anti-pattern violates the **Encapsulation** principle: data and behavior that operate on that data should reside together. For instance, consider an Order entity devoid of behavior:

```
public class Order {
 private String id;
 private List<OrderItem> items;
 private BigDecimal total;
 // getters/setters only
}
// Elsewhere
public class OrderService {
 public void calculateTotal(Order order) {
```

```
BigDecimal sum = order.getItems().stream()
 .map(i -> i.getPrice().multiply(new BigDecimal(i.getQty())))
 .reduce(BigDecimal.ZERO, BigDecimal::add);
order.setTotal(sum);
 }
}
```

Here, calculateTotal() lives outside Order, leading to scattered business rules. This scattering results in several drawbacks:

1. **Low Cohesion**: Domain logic is spread across classes, making it hard to locate and maintain.
2. **Poor Discoverability**: Developers must search service layers for business rules, increasing onboarding time.
3. **Test Fragility**: Tests must instantiate entities and services separately, complicating setup.
4. **Invariants Violation**: With no centralized guard, invalid states can slip through (e.g., negative quantities).

In contrast, a **rich domain model** embeds behavior:

```
public class Order {
 private final String id;
 private final List<OrderItem> items = new ArrayList<>();
 private BigDecimal total = BigDecimal.ZERO;


 public void addItem(OrderItem item) {
  if (item.getQty() <= 0) throw new DomainException("Qty must be > 0");
  items.add(item);
  total = total.add(item.getPrice().multiply(BigDecimal.valueOf(item.getQty())));
 }
 public BigDecimal getTotal() { return total; }
}
```

This change localizes invariants, ensures total is always consistent, and allows simple unit tests on Order. Identifying anemia can be automated: static analysis tools can flag classes with only fields and getters/setters but no methods. The diagram before and after:

Domain Model

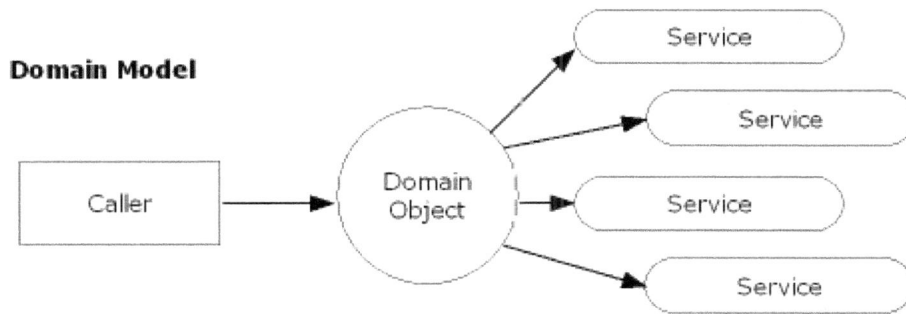

Anemic Domain Model/Transaction Script

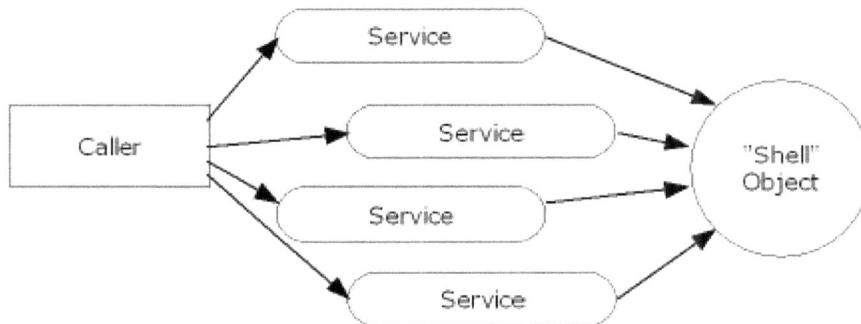

```
@startuml
class Order { -id, -items, -total }
class OrderService { -calculateTotal(o:Order) }
@enduml


@startuml
class Order { +addItem(), +getTotal() }
@enduml
```

Refactoring toward rich models not only improves maintainability but shifts code toward a more expressive, intention-revealing style. With domain logic no longer anemic, teams avoid the next pitfall: over-dependence on framework APIs.

14.2.2 Framework-Driven Design

Framework-driven design occurs when the application's architecture is dictated by the capabilities and conventions of a chosen framework rather than by domain requirements. Common symptoms include domain classes importing framework packages—Spring's @Entity or JPA's EntityManager—blurring the lines between business logic and infrastructure. For example:

```
@Entity
public class Customer {
@Id
private String id;
@OneToMany(mappedBy="customer")
private List<Order> orders;
// business methods omitted
}
```

Here, Customer is coupled to JPA, making it hard to test without spinning up an ORM context. Worse, services may rely on framework-specific APIs:

```
@Service
public class CustomerService {
@Autowired private EntityManager em;
public Customer getById(String id) { return em.find(Customer.class, id); }
}
```

This tight coupling yields multiple issues:

1. **Test Difficulty**: Unit tests require complex wiring or heavy mocking of framework components.
2. **Upgrade Friction**: Framework upgrades can break domain code unexpectedly.
3. **Poor Portability**: Switching to a different persistence technology or exposing domain logic in a non-Java context becomes arduous.
4. **Boundary Violations**: Domain logic inadvertently invades service and infrastructure layers.

The remedy lies in enforcing **ports and adapters**: domain code should depend on interfaces, with framework code confined to the outermost layer. For instance:

```
// domain
public interface CustomerRepository { Optional<Customer> findById(String id); }
// infra
@Repository
public class JpaCustomerRepository implements CustomerRepository {
@PersistenceContext private EntityManager em;
public Optional<Customer> findById(String id) {
 return Optional.ofNullable(em.find(Customer.class, id));
}
```

```
}
```

The domain layer remains framework-agnostic, facilitating pure unit tests. Package-boundary rules—enforced via ArchUnit—can prevent imports from ..domain.. into ..spring....

By isolating framework code, architecture remains resilient to framework churn. Having addressed framework-driven design, we next examine the pitfalls of over-reliance on reflection and meta-programming.

14.3 Patterns for Sustainable Architecture

14.3.1 Rich Domain Models & DDD Tactical Patterns

Moving from anemic data structures to rich domain models ensures business rules live alongside the data they govern. A **rich domain model** encapsulates both state and behavior in the same class, preserving invariants and preventing invalid states. For example, an Order aggregate root enforces order validity:

```java
public class Order {
 private final String id;
 private final List<OrderItem> items = new ArrayList<>();
 private OrderStatus status = OrderStatus.CREATED;


 public Order(String id) {
  this.id = Objects.requireNonNull(id);
 }


 public void addItem(Product p, int qty) {
  if (status != OrderStatus.CREATED) {
   throw new DomainException("Cannot add items once order is finalized");
  }
  if (qty <= 0) throw new DomainException("Quantity must be positive");
  items.add(new OrderItem(p, qty));
 }


 public Money total() {
  return items.stream()
   .map(i -> i.getProduct().getPrice().multiply(i.getQuantity()))
   .reduce(Money.zero(), Money::add);
```

```
}

public void finalizeOrder() {
 if (items.isEmpty()) throw new DomainException("Order must contain at least one item");
 status = OrderStatus.FINALIZED;
 }
}
```

In this example, Order prevents adding items after finalization and enforces a non-empty order before finalizing. By embedding these rules within the aggregate, you eliminate "leaky abstractions" and ensure that every Order instance adheres to its lifecycle. **Value Objects**—immutable types like Money or Address—represent concepts rather than mere primitives, enabling equality by value and self-validation:

```
public final class Money {
 private final BigDecimal amount;
 private final Currency currency;
 public Money(BigDecimal amt, Currency cur) { ... }
 public Money add(Money other) { ... }
 // equals/hashCode by amount+currency
}
```

DDD tactical patterns further refine models: **Entities** have identity; **Value Objects** are identified by their properties; **Factories** encapsulate complex creation logic; **Repositories** abstract persistence; and **Domain Events** record state changes:

```
public interface OrderRepository {
 Order find(OrderId id);
 void save(Order order);
}


public class OrderPlacedEvent {
 private final OrderId orderId;
 private final Instant occurredOn;
 // getters...
}
```

Using **Domain Services** for operations that don't naturally fit within a single entity—like calculating shipping costs—keeps entities focused. A ShippingService might implement:

```
public class ShippingService {
 public Money calculate(Order order, Address destination) { ... }
}
```

Finally, **Aggregates** group entities and value objects with a clear root, ensuring all access goes through the root to maintain invariants.

Transitioning to layered and hexagonal architectures provides the structural scaffolding to house these rich models, isolating them from infrastructure concerns—a topic we explore next.

14.3.2 Layered, Hexagonal & Clean Architecture

While rich domain models organize business logic internally, structuring the overall codebase into clear layers prevents coupling and maximizes maintainability. The **Layered Architecture** pattern separates concerns into Presentation, Application, Domain, and Infrastructure layers. Dependencies flow inward: Presentation → Application → Domain → Infrastructure. However, layered designs can still entangle infrastructure in domain code. **Hexagonal Architecture** (Ports & Adapters) refines layering by encapsulating external systems—databases, web frameworks, message buses—behind interface boundaries known as ports. Adapters implement ports and reside at the perimeter:

```
@startuml
package "Domain" {
 interface OrderRepository
 class Order
}
package "Application" {
 class OrderService
}
package "Adapters" {
 class RestController
 class JdbcOrderRepository
}
RestController --> OrderService
OrderService --> OrderRepository
JdbcOrderRepository ..|> OrderRepository
OrderService --> Order
@enduml
```

Clean Architecture generalizes hexagonal architecture, adding a distinction between use cases (Application layer) and enterprise-wide policies (Domain layer), and grouping all frameworks and drivers at the outermost layer.

Implementing Clean Architecture in code involves:

1. Defining domain entities and interfaces in a domain module with no external dependencies.
2. Placing application logic—use case implementations—in an application module, depending only on domain interfaces.
3. Housing adapters—REST controllers, database repositories—in an infrastructure module that depends on application and domain.
4. Keeping frameworks (Spring, JPA) in the infrastructure layer, injecting dependencies via constructor injection:

```
@Configuration
public class AppConfig {
 @Bean
 public OrderService orderService(OrderRepository repo) {
  return new OrderServiceImpl(repo);
 }
 @Bean
 public OrderRepository orderRepo(EntityManager em) {
  return new JpaOrderRepository(em);
 }
}
```

Benefits of this approach include high testability—domain and application modules can be tested without starting any framework—and clear conceptual separation, reducing cognitive load when reasoning about code. With infrastructure isolated, you can build event-driven systems and CQRS on this solid foundation, described in the next section.

14.3.3 Event-Driven & CQRS Patterns

As system complexity grows, tightly coupling reads and writes to the same model can hamper performance and scalability. **Command Query Responsibility Segregation (CQRS)** separates write operations (commands) from read operations (queries), allowing each side to be optimized independently. Writes mutate the domain via commands handled by a **command handler**, which publishes domain events:

```
public class CreateOrderCommandHandler {
 private final OrderRepository repo;
 private final EventBus bus;


 public CreateOrderCommandHandler(OrderRepository r, EventBus b) { ... }


 public OrderId handle(CreateOrder cmd) {
  Order order = new Order(cmd.getId());
```

```
cmd.getItems().forEach(i -> order.addItem(i.getProduct(), i.getQty()));
repo.save(order);
bus.publish(new OrderCreatedEvent(order.getId(), order.total()));
return order.getId();
}
}
```

Read models subscribe to these events and update denormalized representations stored in fast, query-optimized stores (e.g., Elasticsearch, Redis). For instance:

```
public class OrderCreatedListener {
 @EventListener
 public void on(OrderCreatedEvent e) {
  readRepository.save(new OrderView(e.getOrderId(), e.getTotal()));
 }
}
```

An **event-sourcing** variant persists each domain event as the source of truth. The aggregate state is reconstructed by replaying events:

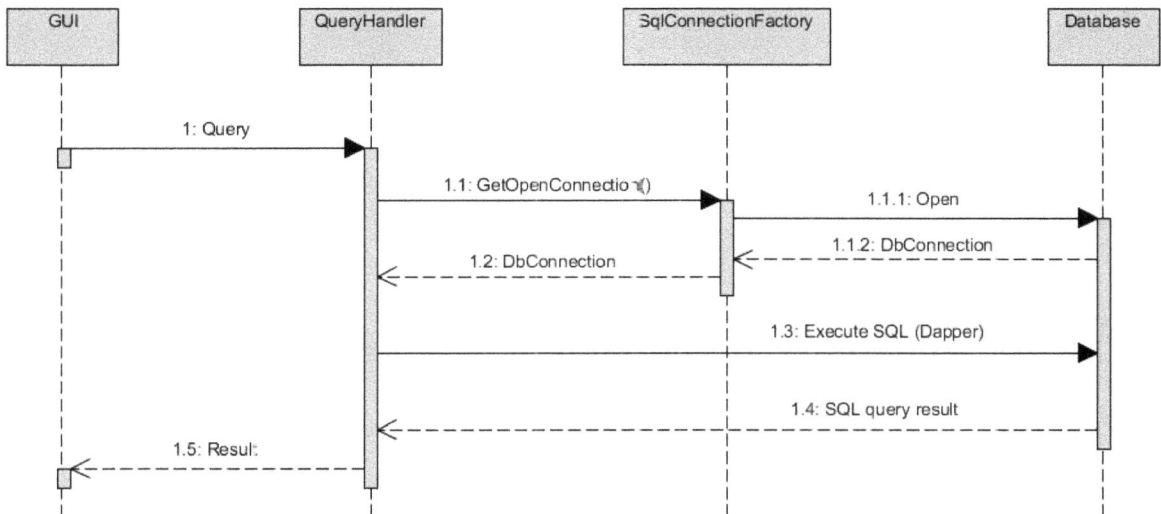

```
public Order rehydrate(OrderId id, List<DomainEvent> history) {
 Order ord = new Order(id);
 history.forEach(ord::apply);
 return ord;
```

```
}
```

A tUML sequence diagram for CQRS flow:

Decoupling reads and writes improves scalability—multiple read replicas can serve queries while the write path remains protected—and enables complex read patterns without bloating write schemas. The asynchronous nature demands careful handling of data consistency and versioning, but the performance and flexibility gains often justify the complexity. Having laid out event-driven and CQRS strategies, we can next consider how to migrate incrementally with strangler and façade patterns.

14.3.4 Strangler Fig & Façade Patterns

Incremental migration of a monolith into microservices requires routing logic that gradually shifts functionality without downtime. The **Strangler Fig** pattern uses a gateway or façade to route requests either to the legacy system or to a new microservice based on path, headers, or feature flags. For example, an NGINX configuration:

```
http {
 map $request_uri $upstream {
  ~^/orders/.*$ order_service;
  default monolith;
 }
 upstream order_service { server order-service:8080; }
 upstream monolith { server monolith:8080; }


 server {
  listen 80;
  location / {
   proxy_pass http://$upstream;
  }
 }
}
```

As the new order-service matures, more routes under /orders shift to it until the legacy order code can be removed. A **Façade** in code hides the migration details:

```
public class OrderFacade {
 private final LegacyOrderClient legacy;
 private final OrderService newService;
```

```
public OrderFacade(LegacyOrderClient l, CrderService n) { ... }


public OrderDTO getOrder(String id) {
 return featureFlag.isEnabled("use-new-order")
  ? newService.fetch(id)
  : legacy.fetch(id);
 }
}
```

This approach minimizes risk by keeping legacy and new code running side by side under tight control. Over time, you decommission the cld paths entirely, completing the strangulation. With routing patterns established, we round out sustainable architecture with resilience patterns.

14.3.5 Resilience Patterns: Bulkhead, Circuit Breaker, Retry

In distributed systems, failures are inevitable, so building resilient services is paramount. The **Bulkhead** pattern isolates resources—thread pools, connections—per client or service to prevent cascading failures. In Resilience4j:

```
resilience4j.bulkhead:
 instances:
  orderServiceBulkhead:
   maxConcurrentCalls: 20
   maxWaitDuration: 100ms
```

Annotate service methods:

```
@Bulkhead(name = "orderServiceBulkhead' )
public Order getOrder(String id) { ... }
```

The **Circuit Breaker** pattern prevents repeated calls to a failing service, allowing time for recovery. Configuration:

```
resilience4j.circuitbreaker:
 instances:
  paymentCB:
   failureRateThreshold: 50
   slidingWindowSize: 100
```

```
    waitDurationInOpenState: 30s
```

Applied via annotation:

```
@CircuitBreaker(name = "paymentCB", fallbackMethod = "fallbackPayment")
public PaymentStatus process(Payment p) { ... }
```

Fallback method:

```
public PaymentStatus fallbackPayment(Payment p, Throwable t) {
 return PaymentStatus.PENDING;
}
```

The **Retry** pattern attempts failed calls with backoff:

```
resilience4j.retry:
 instances:
  inventoryRetry:
   maxAttempts: 3
   waitDuration: 200ms
```

Annotate:

```
@Retry(name = "inventoryRetry")
public Stock reserve(StockRequest req) { ... }
```

By applying these patterns uniformly and monitoring their metrics—bulkhead queue lengths, circuit-breaker state transitions, retry counts—teams build systems that degrade gracefully under load and recover autonomously. These resilience patterns complete the sustainable architecture toolkit, leading naturally into runtime metrics and governance checklists.

14.4 Checklist for Sustainable Architecture

14.4.1 Key Metrics to Watch

Maintaining a healthy architecture requires constant vigilance of both code-level and runtime metrics. **Code-level metrics** include **cyclomatic complexity**—average branches per method—tracked by tools like SonarQube to spot overly complex functions. **Coupling** metrics measure the number of dependencies each module has; high coupling suggests modules are entangled, making changes risky.

Duplication percentage highlights copied-and-pasted logic that should be refactored. **Test coverage**—lines, branches, and mutation coverage—ensures that critical code paths remain tested; coverage on new code is especially vital to prevent regressions during refactoring. **Technical debt ratio**, computed as estimated remediation time divided by total development time, signals unsustainable growth in debt.

On the **runtime** side, **Service-Level Indicators (SLIs)** such as **p95/p99 latency**, **error rate**, and **throughput** align directly with user experience. **Resource utilization**—CPU, memory, thread usage—reveals saturation points. **Queue depths** for messaging systems (Kafka lag, RabbitMQ queue length) indicate backpressure and processing delays. **Circuit-breaker** metrics (failure rate, state transitions) and **bulkhead** queue counts show resilience health. **Deployment frequency** and **lead time** metrics gauge velocity; if they decline, architecture may be deteriorating. **Change failure rate**—percentage of deployments causing incidents—flags instability. Plotting these metrics over time on dashboards (Grafana, Kibana) with alert thresholds ensures anomalies trigger immediate investigation.

A sample Prometheus scrape and alert rule:

```
scrape_configs:
 - job_name: 'app-metrics'
  static_configs:
   - targets: ['app1:9100','app2:9100']


alerting:
 alert_rules:
 - alert: HighP99Latency
  expr: histogram_quantile(0.99, sum(rate(http_request_duration_seconds_bucket[5m])) by (le)) > 0.5
  for: 2m
  labels: { severity: 'page' }
  annotations:
   summary: "P99 latency > 500ms"
```

By continuously tracking and responding to these metrics, teams ensure their architecture remains both performant and maintainable. Regular metric reviews feed into sprint retrospectives, guiding refactoring priorities and preventing unnoticed decay. With a clear picture of system health, teams can ask the right architectural questions at every sprint, as described next.

14.4.2 Questions for Every Sprint Review

Embedding architecture review into sprint ceremonies prevents erosion and keeps technical quality aligned with business goals. At the end of each sprint, teams should explicitly ask:

1. **Dependency Check**: "Has any code in the domain layer imported infrastructure or framework packages this sprint?" Violations indicate layering rules have been broken.
2. **Test Coverage**: "Did test coverage on new or modified modules meet our minimum threshold (e.g., 80%)?" Low coverage on riskier areas warrants additional tests.
3. **Complexity**: "Have we introduced any methods or classes with cyclomatic complexity above the agreed limit (e.g., 10)?" High complexity may hide business logic that should be refactored into domain models.
4. **Performance Impact**: "Do performance benchmarks for newly added features maintain p95 latency under 200ms?" Any degradation should trigger profiling.
5. **Security Checks**: "Have all new dependencies passed our vulnerability scans?" Unvetted libraries risk introducing CVEs.
6. **API Compatibility**: "Did any breaking changes occur in public APIs? Were they documented and versioned?" Backwards compatibility must be maintained for client integrations.
7. **Documentation Updates**: "Did we update ADRs and README files to reflect architectural changes?" Missing documentation delays onboard and creates knowledge gaps.
8. **Feature Flags**: "Are feature toggles for new modules appropriately scoped and scheduled for removal?" Orphaned flags clutter code.
9. **Observability**: "Did we instrument new code with appropriate metrics, logs, and traces?" Without observability, diagnosing issues becomes guesswork.
10. **Technical Debt**: "What technical debt have we incurred and how will we pay it down?" Identifying debt items prevents unchecked accumulation.

Recording answers in a **Sprint Architecture Review** document ensures accountability. A typical review template:

```
# Sprint 42 Architecture Review


## Dependency Violations
- None / [List of files]


## Test Coverage
- Module X: 78% (below target)
- Module Y: 95% (OK)


## Complexity Alerts
- OrderService.calculateTax(): complexity=15


## Performance
- Checkout flow p95 increased from 180ms to 225ms
```

```
…etc.
```

This ritual makes architecture an ongoing concern rather than a one-off event, reinforcing sustainable practices. Having structured sprint reviews, teams can also codify automated fitness functions to enforce these same checks programmatically.

14.4.3 Architecture Fitness Functions

Automating architectural governance reduces human overhead and catch violations early in CI. **Fitness functions** encode rules—dependency boundaries, API stability, performance budgets—as executable tests. For Java, **ArchUnit** tests enforce package dependencies:

```
@AnalyzeClasses(packages = "com.myapp")
public class LayerDependencyTest {
 @ArchTest
 static final ArchRule domainNotDependOnInfra =
  noClasses()
   .that().resideInAPackage("..domain..")
   .should().dependOnClassesThat().resideInAPackage("..infrastructure..");
}
```

For JavaScript, **dependency-cruiser** uses a config:

```
{
"forbidden": [
  { "name": "no-domain-to-ui",
  "from": { "path": "src/domain" },
  "to": { "path": "src/ui" }
  }
 ]
}
```

Performance budgets can be automated with **Lighthouse CI** for front-end, enforcing fastest-metric thresholds:

```
{
"ci": {
"collect": { "url": ["http://localhost:8080"] },
 "assert": {
```

```
"assertions": {
 "first-contentful-paint": ["error", { "maxNumericValue": 2000 }],
 "interactive": ["warn", { "maxNumericValue": 3000 }]
 }
 }
 }
 }
}
```

API stability checks use **Swagger Diff** to compare OpenAPI specs, failing builds on breaking changes:

```
swagger-diff v1.yaml v2.yaml --fail-on breaking
```

Each fitness function runs in CI, blocking merges if thresholds are violated. Dashboards aggregate failures across branches, guiding teams toward corrective action. Automating these checks prevents drift between intended and actual architecture—complementing manual sprint-review questions. With governance codified, we finalize our checklist with practices around debt and documentation.

14.4.4 Technical Debt & Documentation

Technical debt comprises shortcuts or aged code that will require future work. Left unmanaged, debt compounds and degrades velocity. To track it effectively, teams should:

1. **Catalog Debt Items**: Create backlog tickets annotated with labels like tech-debt or refactoring. Each ticket should include a **description**, **estimated remediation effort**, and **business impact**.
2. **Prioritize** debt with a simple ROI formula:

$$\text{ROI} = \frac{\text{Reduction in maintenance effort}}{\text{Remediation effort}}$$ Higher ROI items get scheduled earlier.

3. **Estimate** using T-shirt sizing (S/M/L) or story points, providing visibility into planned work.
4. **Allocate** a fixed percentage of each sprint (e.g., 10–20%) for debt remediation to prevent debt from overwhelming feature work.
5. **Review** debt backlog items during release planning and retrospectives, adjusting priorities as new debt emerges.

Documentation combats "knowledge debt." Key artifacts include:

- **Architectural Decision Records (ADRs)**: Each ADR captures the **context**, **decision**, **alternatives**, and **consequences**. Storing ADRs in a dedicated folder (e.g., docs/adr/) ensures they version alongside code.

- **Module README files**: Each module should include a README.md explaining its purpose, dependencies, public API, and deployment instructions.
- **API documentation**: Generated OpenAPI specs or gRPC .proto files must be published to a central portal, keeping consumer teams aligned.
- **Runbooks** for operational procedures: Stored in code repos or wikis, providing step-by-step guides for common tasks.
- **Diagrams**: High-level architecture, sequence flows for major features, and data-flow diagrams should be updated whenever ADRs introduce changes.

Regular sweeps—every quarter—ensure stale documentation is pruned, and ADRs are marked as "superseded" when decisions evolve. This disciplined approach to debt and documentation ensures the architecture remains transparent and maintainable over the long term. Next, we outline governance and team practices that sustain these efforts.

14.4.5 Governance & Team Practices

Sustainable architecture requires not only technical checks but also organizational practices that foster collective ownership. Key governance activities include:

1. **Architecture Review Board (ARB)**: A lightweight, rotating committee of senior engineers convenes bi-weekly to review significant changes—new ADRs, major module dependencies, or high-risk migrations.
2. **Architecture Champions**: Appoint one "champion" per team each sprint who advocates for clean architecture practices, mentors peers on domain modeling, and enforces fitness functions. Rotate this role to spread knowledge.
3. **Communities of Practice**: Establish cross-team guilds—Domain Modeling Guild, DevOps Guild, Testing Guild—where practitioners share patterns, anti-patterns, and lessons learned through brown-bag sessions and internal blogs.

4.   **Pull Request Templates**: Standardize PR descriptions to include sections for **Architecture Impact**, **Testing**, **Observability**, and **Documentation**, ensuring each merge addresses these facets:

```
## Description
<!-- What does this change do? -->


## Architecture Impact
<!-- Which module boundaries are affected? -->


## Testing
<!-- Unit/Integration/E2E tests added? -->
```

```
## Observability
<!-- Metrics/Traces/Logs changes? -->


## Documentation
<!-- ADRs updated? README updated? -->
```

5.   **Guild-Led Code Reviews**: Encourage at least one reviewer from outside the immediate team, ideally a guild member, to ensure cross-pollination of architectural knowledge and prevent siloed design decisions.

6.   **Weekly KPI Review**: Include a short segment in the sprint review to glance at architecture health metrics (complexity, debt backlog, fitness-function passes/fails), keeping the team aware of architectural trends.

7.   **Blameless Postmortems**: After incidents or major refactoring hurdles, hold blameless postmortems documenting root causes, celebrate successes, and generate improvement items.

8.   **Continuous Education**: Provide quarterly training—book clubs on "Domain-Driven Design," workshops on Clean Architecture, pair-programming sessions to onboard new members.

By embedding these practices into the team's rhythm, architecture remains a living concern, not a relic of initial design. Empowered teams, robust processes, and shared responsibility form the backbone of sustainable architecture—culminating the strategies and safeguards laid out in this chapter.

14.5 Patterns vs Anti-Patterns Comparison Matrix

14.5.1 Domain Modeling

Rich domain models place data and behavior together, enabling entities and value objects to enforce their own invariants rather than relying on external services or scripts. In a rich model, an Order entity might encapsulate methods like addItem(), applyDiscount(), and calculateTotal(), throwing domain-specific exceptions when constraints are violated. This approach ensures that invalid states—such as negative quantities or missing customer details—cannot occur, since the domain object itself guards against them. By contrast, the anemic model anti-pattern reduces domain objects to mere data carriers, with service classes littered across the codebase containing procedural logic that manipulates those DTOs. This scattering of logic leads to low cohesion: developers must hunt through multiple services to understand how an Order truly behaves.

A concrete example of a rich entity:

```
public class Order {
 private final String id;
```

```
private final List<OrderItem> items = new ArrayList<>();
private Status status = Status.NEW;


public void addItem(Product p, int quantity) {
 if (quantity <= 0) throw new DomainException("Quantity must be positive");
 items.add(new OrderItem(p, quantity));
}


public Money calculateTotal() {
 return items.stream()
  .map(item -> item.getProduct().getPrice().multiply(item.getQuantity()))
  .reduce(Money.zero(), Money::add);
}


public void complete() {
 if (items.isEmpty()) throw new DomainException("Cannot complete empty order");
 status = Status.COMPLETED;
 }
}
```

Contrast this with an anemic DTO:

```
public class OrderDTO {
 public String id;
 public List<OrderItemDTO> items;
 public BigDecimal total;
}
public class OrderService {
 public BigDecimal calculateTotal(OrderDTO dto) {
 // logic here, far from the data
 }
}
```

To migrate toward a rich model, teams can iteratively extract logic from service methods into domain entities, writing unit tests that verify behavior at the entity boundary. Static analysis tools—such as SonarQube rules or custom scripts—can detect classes lacking any domain methods, flagging candidates for enrichment.

By embedding behavior in the domain layer, you gain discoverability—developers can simply read an entity's interface to understand valid operations—and guarantee that business rules are enforced regardless of where entities are used. This increased coherence reduces bug rates and simplifies refactoring. As domain models become richer, services shrink in scope: they orchestrate use cases rather than house core logic. Having solidified your domain layer, you can next apply structural patterns that protect it from infrastructure churn.

14.5.2 Layering

A well-layered architecture divides code into concentric rings, each with distinct responsibilities and strict dependency rules. The core **Domain Layer** contains entities, value objects, and interfaces (ports) but no knowledge of external frameworks. Surrounding it, the **Application Layer** implements use cases in terms of domain interfaces, orchestrating workflows without direct data access. The outer **Infrastructure Layer** provides concrete implementations—repositories, message brokers, and web frameworks—adhering to port interfaces. By enforcing dependencies inward only, you prevent domain code from inadvertently depending on database schemas or web frameworks, thus safeguarding business rules from infrastructural fluctuations.

An example directory structure reflecting these layers:

```
src/
  ├── domain/      # Entities, value objects, repository interfaces
  ├── application/   # Use-case services, DTOs, application exceptions
  └── infrastructure/  # JPA repositories, REST controllers, RabbitMQ clients
```

In Java with Spring Boot, adapter configuration isolates framework dependencies:

```
@Configuration
public class InfrastructureConfig {
 @Bean
 public OrderRepository orderRepo(EntityManager em) {
  return new JpaOrderRepository(em);
 }
}
```

The **Clean Architecture** anti-pattern—framework-driven monolith—occurs when domain classes import javax.persistence annotations or when Spring stereotypes (@Service, @Controller) litter core packages. This pattern couples core logic to a specific framework, hindering testing and portability. Tools like **ArchUnit** can enforce layering:

```
@ArchTest
static final ArchRule noDomainDependsOnInfra =
```

```
slices().matching("..domain..").should().notDependOnClassesThat().resideInAPackage("..infrastr
ucture..");
```

Maintaining this structure allows you to swap out frameworks—migrating from JPA to MongoDB, for instance—without touching the domain or application layers. When layering boundaries are honored, each layer can be tested in isolation: domain logic via plain unit tests, application services via mocks of domain ports, and infrastructure via integration tests. This separation accelerates development, reduces regressions, and makes the system resilient to changes in external libraries. With a robust layering strategy, you can now coordinate interactions between modules using integration patterns that further decouple services.

14.5.3 Integration

Decoupling modules requires integration patterns that avoid tight coupling through shared libraries or direct references. The **Event Bus** pattern publishes domain events to a message broker (e.g., Kafka, RabbitMQ), allowing subscribers to react asynchronously. This approach fosters eventual consistency and loose coupling: producers know nothing of their consumers. For example, an OrderService might publish an OrderCreatedEvent:

```
public class OrderCreatedEvent {
 private final String orderId;
 private final BigDecimal total;
 // constructors, getters...
}


public class OrderService {
 private final ApplicationEventPublisher publisher;
 public void createOrder(Order o) {
  repo.save(o);
  publisher.publishEvent(new OrderCreatedEvent(o.getId(), o.calculateTotal()));
 }
}
```

Subscribers, perhaps in the **ShippingService**, listen and act:

```
@Component
public class ShippingListener {
 @EventListener
 public void handle(OrderCreatedEvent evt) {
  shippingService.scheduleDelivery(evt.getOrderId());
```

```
    }
  }
```

This decoupling contrasts with the anti-pattern of tight coupling via shared libraries, where two modules share a common jar containing both domain and service code, inadvertently coupling their release cycles. Shared libraries often lead to version conflicts and prevent independent deployment.

For long-running processes or distributed transactions, the **Saga** pattern sequences a series of local transactions orchestrated by events or a central coordinator. A **choreography-based saga** might look like:

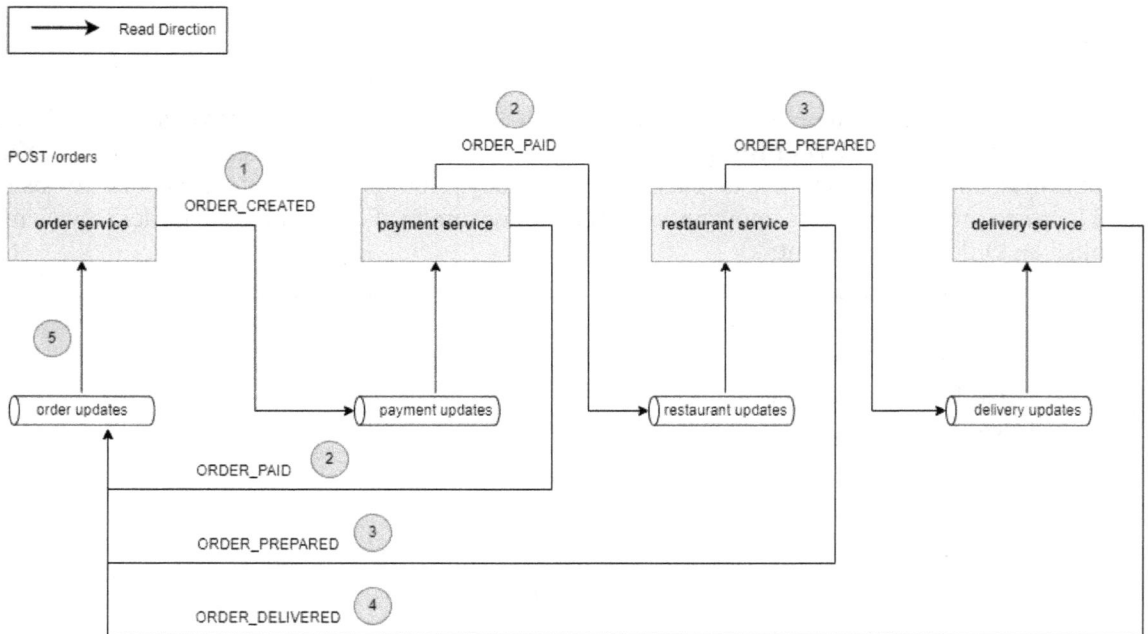

Alternatively, an **orchestration-based saga** uses a central SagaCoordinator to invoke each step.

The **Façade Gateway** pattern adds a unifying API layer in front of microservices, translating client requests into calls to multiple downstream services, smoothing over API heterogeneity. In Node.js:

```
app.get('/api/orders/:id', async (req, res) => {
 const order = await orderService.fetch(req.params.id);
 const shipments = await shippingService.fetchByOrder(req.params.id);
 res.json({ order, shipments });
});
```

By isolating integration logic in a façade or BFF, client apps avoid coupling to numerous microservices. This pattern transitions naturally into resilience concerns: asynchronous integration introduces new failure modes, addressed by fault-tolerance patterns next.

14.5.4 Fault Tolerance

Distributed integrations necessitate robust fault-tolerance patterns to handle service failures, network issues, and resource exhaustion. The **Circuit Breaker** prevents cascading failures by opening when downstream error rates exceed a threshold, and closing only after a cooldown period. Using Resilience4j:

```
resilience4j.circuitbreaker:
 instances:
  paymentCB:
   slidingWindowSize: 50
   failureRateThreshold: 50
   waitDurationInOpenState: 30s
```

Annotated in code:

```
@CircuitBreaker(name = "paymentCB", fallbackMethod = "paymentFallback")
public PaymentStatus charge(Payment p) { ... }
public PaymentStatus paymentFallback(Payment p, Throwable ex) {
 log.warn("Payment service unavailable, deferring charge", ex);
 return PaymentStatus.PENDING;
}
```

The **Bulkhead** pattern isolates threads or connections per service to prevent resource exhaustion in one area from impacting others. In Resilience4j:

```
resilience4j.bulkhead:
 instances:
  inventoryBulkhead:
   maxConcurrentCalls: 20
   maxWaitDuration: 100ms
```

Annotated:

```
@Bulkhead(name = "inventoryBulkhead")
public Stock checkStock(String sku) { ... }
```

Retries with **Exponential Backoff** help transient network errors:

```
resilience4j.retry:
 instances:
  retryPolicy:
   maxAttempts: 3
   waitDuration: 200ms
   retryExceptions:
   - java.io.IOException
```

Annotated:

```
@Retry(name = "retryPolicy")
public Data fetchData() { ... }
```

These patterns guard against the anti-pattern of global locks and shared mutable state, which serialize requests and introduce contention hotspots. Instead of synchronizing on a global object—a common source of deadlocks and throughput degradation—use localized bulkheads. A sequence diagram illustrating retry with backoff:

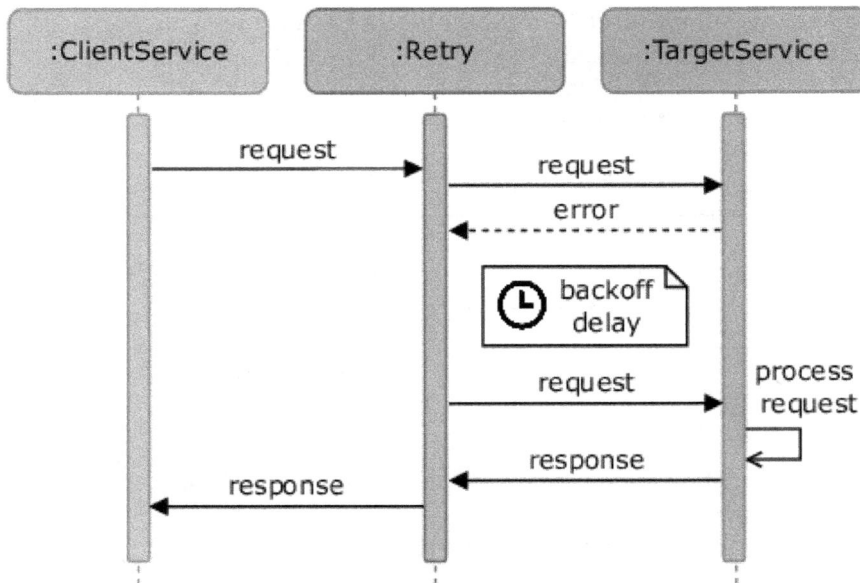

By composing retries, bulkheads, and circuit breakers, systems degrade gracefully, isolating failures and recovering without manual intervention. As fault-tolerance patterns mature, you can scale systems horizontally—our next focus.

14.5.5 Scalability

To handle growing workloads, systems must scale both reads and writes without bottlenecks. **CQRS** (Command Query Responsibility Segregation) partitions write and read models, enabling each to scale independently. Write operations update a normalized data store, publishing events to update denormalized read stores optimized for queries.

Read replicas in relational databases offload read traffic. In PostgreSQL:

```
primary_conninfo: 'host=primary-db port=5432'
host replication replicator replica-db/32 md5
```

Clients route reads to replica endpoints:

```
SET transaction_read_only = TRUE;
SELECT * FROM orders WHERE id = '123';
```

Sharding distributes data across multiple nodes based on a shard key (e.g., customer ID). A consistent-hash ring ensures minimal data movement when nodes are added or removed:

```
ConsistentHash<Node> ring = ConsistentHash.create(hashFunc, nodes, 100);
Node shard = ring.get(customerId);
```

This prevents the single-database bottleneck anti-pattern where one database instance becomes the system's throughput limiter. Microservices deployed across multiple regions further scale horizontally; each region hosts its own database shards and read replicas, synchronized via asynchronous replication:

```
# AWS RDS global cluster
GlobalClusterIdentifier: my-global-cluster
```

Load balancers use **client IP affinity** or **DNS-based routing** to direct users to their nearest regional cluster, reducing latency and distributing load. A global overview diagram:

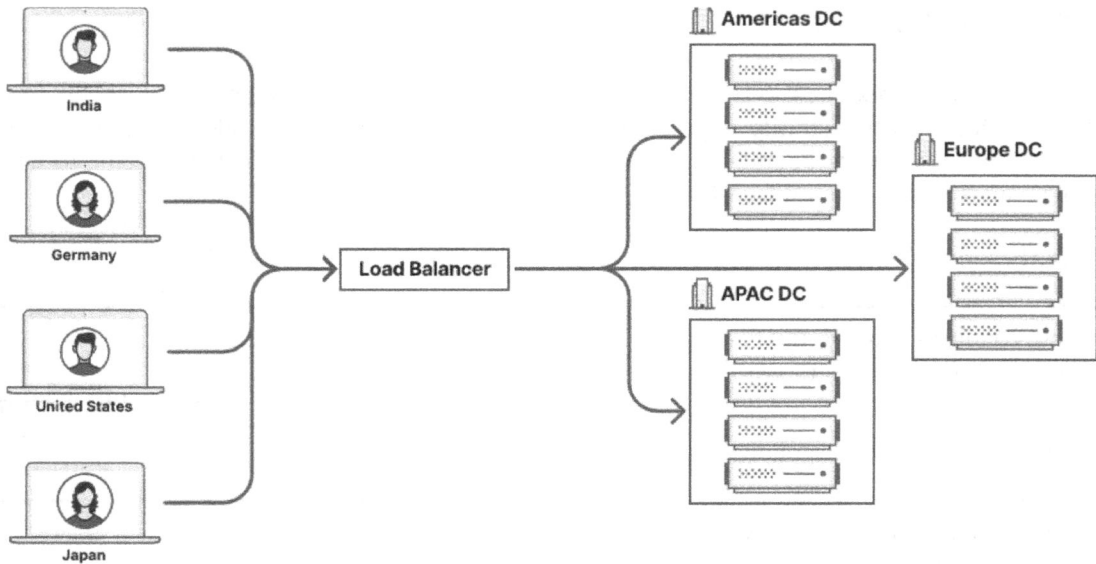

By combining CQRS, read replicas, and sharding, systems can scale both read-heavy and write-heavy workloads gracefully. As data volumes and request rates grow, independent scalability of components ensures that no single bottleneck chokes overall throughput. With scalability strategies in place, the final frontier is deployment patterns that safely deliver code at scale.

14.5.6 Deployment

Zero-downtime deployments and safe rollouts are essential in systems serving millions of users. The **Strangler Fig** pattern transitions routing from monolith to microservices incrementally via gateway configurations:

```
map $uri $target {
 ~^/orders/.*$ order-service;
 default legacy-service;
}
server {
 listen 80;
 location / { proxy_pass http://$target; }
}
```

This avoids big-bang cutovers, which unleash untested changes in one fell swoop and create high rollback risk. Instead, **Blue-Green Deployments** maintain two identical production environments (blue and green). Deploy the new version to the idle environment, execute smoke tests, then switch the router.

In Kubernetes, use two Services with labels to effect the switch:

```
kind: Service
spec:
 selector:
  app: my-service
  version: blue  # switch to green when ready
```

Canary Releases route a fraction of traffic to the new version, monitoring error and latency metrics before ramping up. An Istio VirtualService snippet:

```
apiVersion: networking.istio.io/v1alpha3
kind: VirtualService
spec:
 http:
 - route:
  - destination: { host: my-service, subset: stable, weight: 90 }
  - destination: { host: my-service, subset: canary, weight: 10 }
```

Automated pipelines adjust weights based on SLO compliance, enabling safe incremental rollouts. Feature flags coordinate client-side changes, ensuring that UI components only surface new functionality when the back end is fully deployed. A deployment pipeline in GitLab CI:

```
stages:
 - build
 - test
 - deploy


deploy_canary:
 stage: deploy
 script:
  - kubectl apply -f canary-deployment.yaml
  - kubectl apply -f canary-virtualservice.yaml
```

Manual fall-back anti-patterns—where rollbacks require hand-typed commands or redeploying entire clusters—are replaced by automated rollback logic triggered when canary metrics exceed thresholds. Combining blue-green, canary, and feature-flag strategies ensures high confidence deployments with minimal user impact. By mastering deployment patterns, teams close the loop on sustainable architecture—delivering robust systems that evolve continuously and safely.

Conclusion

Patterns and anti-patterns are two sides of the same coin: one offers a path forward, the other warns of hidden pitfalls. As we've seen through detailed examples and real-world stories, the true measure of architectural success lies not in adherence to any single doctrine, but in the team's ability to choose fitting patterns, recognize when they no longer serve, and course-correct in the face of new constraints. Sustainable architecture demands ongoing vigilance—tracking metrics that surface degrading dependencies, asking critical questions at each sprint boundary, and fostering an environment where every developer feels empowered to propose and document improvements. Armed with these insights and checklists, your organization is well-equipped to navigate complexity, avoid common traps, and continuously evolve its systems to meet both present demands and future challenges.

www.ingramcontent.com/pod-product-compliance
Lightning Source LLC
Chambersburg PA
CBHW061740210326
41599CB00034B/6744